The Complete Guide to

WILD FLOWERS

The Complete Guide to

WILD FLOWERS

DAVID SUTTON

Illustrated by
Peter Chesterton, John Davis & Colin Emberson

WHSMITH
EXCLUSIVE
· BOOKS ·

The publishers would like to thank the following for kindly supplying photographs for this book.

Page 1 Swift Picture Library; 9 Heather Angel; 10 Heather Angel; 11 Heather Angel; 12 S & O Mathews; 13 S & O Mathews; 14 Heather Angel; 26 Swift Picture Library; 28 Swift Picture Library; 31 J & M Bain/NHPA; 34 H. Reinhard/Bruce Coleman; 40 J. Sauvanet/NHPA; 41 D. A. Sutton; 48 R. Tidman/NHPA; 57 A–Z Collection; 60 J. Shaw/NHPA; 63 Gillian Beckett; 64 L. Campbell/NHPA; 67 S & O Mathews; 72 Wildlife Matters; 80 K. Wothe/Bruce Coleman; 81 Swift Picture Library; 86 M. Leach/NHPA; 89 A–Z Collection; 91 Swift Picture Library; 93 E. A. Janes/NHPA; 97 Swift Picture Library; 106 E. A. Janes/NHPA; 112 M. I. Garwood/NHPA; 116 E. A. Janes/NHPA; 117 Heather Angel; 120 G. Cambridge/NHPA; 130 Swift Picture Library; 135 E. A. Janes/NHPA; 140 H. Reinhard/Bruce Coleman; 143 O. Mobbs/Bruce Coleman; 144 S & O Mathews; 148 Swift Picture Library; 167 Swift Picture Library; 170 S & O Mathews; 177 Swift Picture Library.

Grisewood & Dempsey Ltd, Elsley House
24–30 Great Titchfield Street
London W1P 7AD

First published in 1989 by Grisewood & Dempsey Ltd.
Some of the material in this book is taken from
Kingfisher Guide to the Wild Flowers of Britain and Europe (1988).

ISBN 0-906279-61-5

Printed in Italy

Editor: Janice Lacock
Design: Terry Woodley
Picture Research: Sarah Donald
Hand lettering: Jack Potter

Front cover: Chalk stream, Common Poppy,
Back: Burnet rose
Half-title: Deciduous woodland with Bluebells,
           Greater Stitchwort, Wood Spurge
           and Yellow Archangel
Title page: Indian Balsam

CONTENTS

Introduction

This Field Guide is designed to be taken with you when you take a walk in the countryside or through parts of towns where plants are left to grow wild. Wherever possible, take the book to the plant and not *vice versa*. It is illegal to dig up wild plants in several countries, and the picking of wild flowers by 'flower lovers' has led to the virtual extinction of many attractive species.

In an illustrated Field Guide to plants, it is not possible to include all species for the area: a standard set of European floras and illustrations would take up one or two library shelves and would be far too costly and heavy to take into the countryside. A selection must be made. The main categories for exclusion are non-flowering plants, such as conifers, ferns and mosses; trees and shrubs, with the exception of plants such as Heathers and Roses which are usually thought of as 'flowers'; and grass-like plants including sedges and rushes – for all of these are identified using more technical detail and require specialist treatment. Preference has been given to the common and widespread plants. Many of the foreign species that have become naturalized are included; they are now often more common that the native plants.

The final selection of more than 800 species gives a reasonable coverage of at least the common plants of the United Kingdom, Ireland, northern France, Belgium, Luxembourg, Holland, West Germany and Denmark, and includes many plants of Norway and Sweden. Some plants have been included because they are highly distinctive and well-known despite their rarity (for example, Lady's-slipper: page 183).

Equipment
Finding and identifying wild flowers is an immensely satisfying hobby requiring a minimum of expense. A hand-lens with a magnification of about ten times is a useful purchase for examining the structure of flowers. It is possible to buy one with a small scale attached for making accurate measurements. A notebook is useful for recording details of the plant, particularly the colouring, number, relative size and extent of fusion of the petals; the arrangement and division of the leaves; and the sort of fruit, including any method by which it opens and the number produced by a single flower.

You may wish to record your 'find' with a photograph. A single-lens reflex camera is the most useful sort of camera for general photography of flowers. In order to see any detail of small flowers it is necessary to buy some sort of close-up lens, preferably giving about 1:1 reproduction. When taking a picture, bear in mind that the flower is usually much brighter than its background. It may be necessary to under-expose the film by one or even two f.-stops, to avoid losing detail in the petals. Using electronic flash can make it easier to obtain a good depth of focus, sharpness and reliable exposures, but gives a less 'natural' result. Try to identify your plant in the field wherever possible, because identification from photographs can prove difficult.

Plant names
Common names vary greatly and some species have over a hundred local names in a single country. As a simplification, English-language names have been standardized to the list published by the Botanical Society of the British Isles (Dony, Jury and Perring, 1986). Plants lacking a common name are usually recently naturalized, or grow only in certain countries covered by the book.

Scientific names are more stable and international in usage. Most are consistent with the standard European flora (Tutin *et al.* (Editors), 1964–1980) but some are updated using more recent British floras. Each scientific name is made up of a genus (plural: genera) name, with an initial capital letter, and a species name starting with a small letter. A third, subspecies (abbreviated subsp.) name is used to distinguish geographical variation within a species. A multiplication symbol (×) between the first two names indicates a hybrid between two species. An example is Hybrid Avens (*Geum × intermedium*). Abnormal methods of seed production in some plants result in large numbers of populations, each behaving as a species, known as species aggregates (abbreviated agg., as in the Brambles, *Rubus fruticosus* agg.) and generally differing in very minor characters. Such aggregates are largely outside the scope of this book.

How to Use this Book

If you find a plant and have no idea of what it is, use the key starting on page 18 – which should limit your search to a specific group of pages. If you have a rough idea of the identity, turn to the relevant part of the book (using the colour codes explained right) and you will find similar species grouped on adjacent pages. Match the species against the illustrations, but always check through the description for confirmation. The description of the plant is mostly summarized in a facts panel, which contains the same elements for every species. This layout departs from the practice in most field guides and floras, where the descriptions are often very brief and inconsistent.

The arrangement of species on a page is for a main species (of which several different elements are illustrated) and up to four further similar species. For the similar species, only the parts of the plant used for identification are shown, rather than a whole plant or flowering shoot. These similar species are often as common as the first.

Order of plants

The plants in this book are arranged more or less in systematic order. Those genera with similar construction of flowers and fruit are placed together in a family and given a single name in the list below. The families are grouped into 24 sections for convenience. At the start of each section, there is a summary of the important characteristics of each family, information on where most of the species occur in the world and details of any commercially important species in medicine, agriculture or horticulture.

Each family or group of families is given a colour reference marker. Use this coloured square at the corner of the pages to help you find the different groups of plants as you flick through the book.

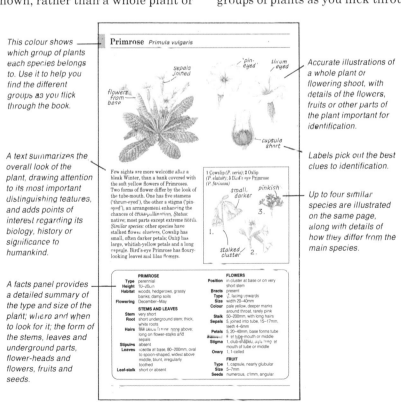

This colour shows which group of plants each species belongs to. Use it to help you find the different groups as you flick through the book.

A text summarizes the overall look of the plant, drawing attention to its most important distinguishing features, and adds points of interest regarding its biology, history or significance to humankind.

A facts panel provides a detailed summary of the type and size of the plant; where and when to look for it; the form of the stems, leaves and underground parts, flower-heads and flowers, fruits and seeds.

Accurate illustrations of a whole plant or flowering shoot, with details of the flowers, fruits or other parts of the plant important for identification.

Labels pick out the best clues to identification.

Up to four similar species are illustrated on the same page, along with details of how they differ from the main species.

Asarabacca and Mistletoe

Docks, Goosefoots, Hop and Nettles

Pinks and Purslanes

Buttercups and Water-lilies

Cabbages, Poppies, Fumitories and Mignonettes

Stonecrops, Saxifrages and Sundews

Roses and Grass-of-Parnassus

Peas

Crane's-bills, Spurges, Wood-sorrels and Flaxes

St John's-worts, Milkworts and Balsams

Violets, Mallows, Rock-roses and Cucumbers

Willowherbs, Loosestrifes and Water-milfoils

Carrots and Ivy

Primroses, Heathers, Wintergreens and Thrift

Bedstraws, Gentians and Periwinkles

Bindweeds, Jacob's-ladder and Water-starworts

Mints, Vervains and Forgot-me-nots

Figworts, Nightshades and Broomrapes

Butterworts and Plantains

Valerians, Teasels, Honeysuckles and Moschatel

Daisies and Bellflowers

Arrowhead, Frogbit, Flowering-rush and Pondweeds

Lilies, Daffodils and Irises

Orchids, Lords-and-Ladies and Duckweeds

The History of Wild Flowers

In order to understand why wild flowers grow where they do today, it is necessary to have a basic understanding of the events that have shaped the flora of the region. Before about 15,000 years ago, much of the northern part of Europe was covered by a continuous sheet of ice, for the world was still in the grip of the last glaciation. Then the ice began to retreat, and bare ground left behind became available for colonization. Immediately south of the ice, tundra-like conditions had prevailed but in the warmer refuges of southern Europe, many familiar trees, shrubs and herbs still survived. Although plants are generally perceived as static, lacking the faculty of movement common to animals, seeds of plants travel great distances by varied means. When the ice first started to retreat, such colossal volumes of water were still frozen solid that the sea-level was about 30 metres lower than it is today. What are now France, Britain and Ireland were connected by land, so that the earliest colonist plants had no difficulty spreading through the area.

Quick-growing herbaceous plants were the first to flower and set seed in the new surroundings, but trees and bushes with wind-dispersed seeds soon arrived. Slow-growing, heavy-seeded trees were among the last to arrive. As the sea-level rose to its present level, land connections between many parts of the area were severed, making further immigration of species much more difficult. This has resulted in the less species-rich floras of Britain, Ireland and many of the smaller European islands. Gradually, the herbs and bushes gave way to a succession of trees and most of northern Europe disappeared under an almost continuous forest. The main exceptions were mountain-tops, cliffs, screes, coastlines, rivers and the extreme north.

Then about 5,000 years ago, a dramatic change took place. People, with a more settled life-style than the early hunter-gatherers that had preceded them, arrived in the area and started cutting and burning trees to create farmland. As implements of stone and flint were replaced by bronze and iron, more and more of the ancient forests fell. Successive waves of human colonists, coming from the south and east, brought their own crops and with them the weeds of crops.

As forests dwindled so trees became more valuable, for they were still in demand as timber for building, or as charcoal for smelting iron. Complete eradication of the forests was only avoided in the populated areas by the designation of protected areas in which game could still be hunted by the wealthy.

There have been limited gains to offset some of the destruction of the forests. Hedgerows planted to delimit property offer small but vital oases in agricultural land that has become virtually sterile from the point of view of native plants and animals. In addition, the increased costs of importing timber has led to a gradual process of reafforestation. Unfortunately, most of these forests are essentially monocultures of exotic trees and resemble field crops more than natural vegetation. Woodland and other undeveloped land set aside for recreational use also offer a haven for wild flowers.

Recent history of the vegetation is dominated by humans. Large numbers of foreign species have been introduced from all over the world, either deliberately as garden plants and crops, or inadvertently with crop seed and imported products such as sheep's fleeces. Many of these species have become 'naturalized' and are now commoner than native species. Thus, it becomes more and more difficult to find any natural vegetation – and great care must be taken to protect what little remains.

Where to Find Wild Flowers

Where a plant will grow is determined by a combination of many factors, including temperature, exposure to sun and wind, rainfall, type of soil (especially the presence of certain minerals and drainage), plus the influence of the surrounding plants and animals. A combination of latitude and altitude gives a rough correlation to the mean temperature of a locality, though the proximity of the sea, and particularly warm sea currents, have a significant effect of the local climate. Plants such as Field Eryngo (p.99), which are rare and restricted to the south of the area covered by the book, are often more common towards the Mediterranean region. Mountain plants of the south, such as Mountain Avens (p.69), can often be found at much lower altitudes in the extreme north.

Alkaline and acidic soils

Soils formed over chalk or limestone rocks are alkaline and lime-rich. Plants tolerating such soils, including many Orchids, are usually not found elsewhere. These rocks are porous and rain-water quickly drains away, leaving the surface relatively dry and creating additional problems for plants. In hilly areas, the soil is often very shallow and supports a distinctive form of grassland. Beech woodland is also typical of chalk and limestone hill country, the fine roots of the Beech spreading very widely in the shallow soil. Rock ledges on limestone cliffs have shallow pockets of soil which dry rapidly, but the relatively harsh conditions are home to a distinctive range of species, including the rare Cheddar Pink (p.40). On steep slopes, fragments of rock broken away by frost action form screes, where plants such as Jacob's-ladder (p.117) can be found.

Similar alkaline or base-rich soils are formed above certain other rocks and on coastal dunes containing large amounts of sea-shells. Grassy areas on the stabilized parts of such dunes are home to the curious Lizard Orchid (p.182). Heathers (p.107) and Bilberry (p.108) require a soil that is lime-free. They are found on the acid soils which occur above granite, sandstone, gravel or sand, and dominate the vegetation forming heathland in lowland areas. Relatives of Heather are also very important elements of the vegetation on the upland acid, peaty soils of moorland and the drier areas of bogs.

Saline soils

Plants which survive on the salty soils around the coast usually do not grow elsewhere. On the drier parts of salt-marshes, Common Sea-lavender (p.111) and Sea Aster (p.150) are found, while Sea-purslane (p.33) clings to the edges of channels and Glasswort (p.33) is found on the mud. Ledges of sea-cliffs are home to Rock Samphire (p.101) and Rock Sea-spurrey

Formed in estuaries where waves are prevented from scouring the mud and silt, salt-marshes are home to a distinctive range of wild flowers. Sea-lavender favours the drier parts, with Sea-purslane fringing the channels, and Glasswort running right down into the waterlogged mud.

Where to Find Wild Flowers

Yellow-eyed, pale lilac flowers of Water Violet smother a reed-fringed, fen waterway. This and many other aquatic plants have become much rarer in recent years because of the wholesale drainage of such wetlands.

(p.38), whereas exposed short turf at the top of sea-cliffs provides a habitat for Sea Carrot (p.105) and Sea Campion (p.39). Sea Bindweed (p.118) and Sea Pea (p.76) are found on sand-dunes or sometimes on the upper margin of beaches. Salting of roads in winter produces saline road-verges, which sometimes contain coastal species.

Rainfall and water-table
The level of water in soil is determined by a balance between rainfall, the ability of the soil to retain moisture, the local water-table and other factors. In general, the western parts of northern Europe receive a higher annual rainfall than the east, owing to the presence of the Atlantic and predominantly westerly winds. Some plants, such as the Large-flowered Butterwort (p.141), are found only in regions of high rainfall towards the south-west of the area covered by the book. Other plants needing wetter soils are found in marshes, bogs and fens, or close to streams, rivers and lakes.

Bogs and fens
Where soil remains waterlogged, the dead growth of each year commonly does not rot but turns into peat. Such an area is usually acidic and known as a bog but, where it overlies chalk or limestone, it can be quite alkaline and the area is known as a fen. Bogs and fens support quite different species. The acid soils of bogs are usually very low in nutrients that are essential for plant growth. Some plants, such as Round-leaved Sundew (p.61), have managed to rectify this deficiency by catching their own nutrients in the form of insects. Bogs are commonly found in natural depressions but, in areas of high rainfall, the bog can cover level ground, or even hillsides, forming what is termed a blanket bog. Fens formerly occupied great expanses of low-lying land, overlying lime-rich boulder clay, but many were drained to provide rich agricultural land. Wild flowers restricted to fens, such as the Fen Orchid (p.182), are consequently much rarer today. Wet, but not peaty, soils can occur in low-lying areas and are called marshes; they usually have more or less neutral soils.

Water-meadows
Where meadows lying in river-valleys are seasonally flooded, rather than continually waterlogged, a rich assemblage of grasses and tall herbaceous plants are formed; species such as Fritillary (p.172) are found here. In the past much more than the present, controlled flooding was deliberately maintained during the winter months as a means of keeping the ground free of frost and encouraging early growth for

grazing. Such pastures are termed water-meadows. Marginal plants grow in the wet soils close to bodies of water such as rivers and streams; they include Butterbur (p.158) and Nodding Bur-marigold (p.154). Some plants are rooted at the margins of streams or ponds, and grow out over the water, with buoyant stems holding the leaves and flowers above the surface. Water-cress (p.51) and Brooklime (p.137) fall into this category.

Ponds and lakes

True aquatic plants need to grow in the water and often have submerged or floating leaves. The depth of water is an important factor in determining which species grow where. Many species, such as the Common Water-crowfoot (p.42) and Common Water-starwort (p.119), are rooted in the substrate and are restricted to relatively shallow water. Fluctuations in the depth of water mean that these plants are sometimes left exposed, and both species have rather different-looking land-forms. The White Water-lily (p.42) and Yellow Water-lily (p.42) are also rooted aquatics but can grow in deeper water, for they have very long stalks to the leaves and flowers. Plants such as Greater Bladderwort (p.141) float just beneath the surface of the water and are not rooted in the substrate. Because of this they can grow in the deep water of lakes or artificially created bodies of water, such as flooded brick-pits.

Free-floating plants, growing on the surface of the water, do not need long roots to reach the substrate, nor do they need long flowering stems to reach up into the air. By utilizing the surface film of water to disperse pollen, some have dispensed with showy flowers. The smallest flowering plants in the area are the free-floating Duckweeds (p.178). Acidity or alkalinity of the water is also important. Water-soldier (p.168) is found in alkaline conditions, but Water Lobelia (p.142) is only found in acidic waters, such as upland tarns and lakes.

Dry habitats

At the other end of the spectrum, some plants prefer to grow on free-draining, dry soils, such as those formed in crevices amongst rocks, scree or shingle. Stonecrops (p.62) are specially adapted to such arid conditions as they have thick, succulent leaves. Stone walls provide a similar habitat to rock-crevices and many similar species are found here. As brickwork ages and the mortar starts to crumble, it too provides an artificial substitute for the natural habitat of these plants.

Another artificial rocky, well-drained habitat is provided by railway embankments. The type of stone may determine many of the species which grow here

Some wild flowers have benefited from human intervention. Rosebay Willowherb is commonly found in an urban environment, where it favours abandoned demolition sites. Parachute-like seeds carry it to new sites, where its roots spread underground to form large clumps.

In limestone hill country, an old hay meadow abounds with herbaceous wild flowers, including Meadow Buttercup, Red Clover & Yellow-rattle. Without an annual cycle of mowing and grazing, trees would reclaim the land and this pastoral landscape would revert to forest.

but some, such as the Rosebay Willowherb (p.95), are less particular. Where there are remains of cinders from the days of steam trains, characteristic species such as Small Toadflax (p.134) abound. Along the upper edge of shingle banks on sea-shores, a distinct assemblage of species can be found, including Sea-holly (p.99) and Yellow Horned-poppy (p.49). Relatively dry, sandy soils, such as those of heaths, favour species including Harebell (p.149), Hare's-foot Clover (p.77) and Common Stork's-bill (p.84).

Cultivated land

Some plants require the ground to be completely cleared or disturbed before seeds will germinate: these are the 'weeds' of cornfields or other cultivated ground. They include Common Chickweed (p.36), Common Poppy (p.49) and Cornflower (p.162). Such plants are mostly annuals; that is, the seeds germinate

and the plants grow to produce flowers and fruits in the space of a single year. Seeds are usually small, and large numbers are produced, enabling the species to colonize large areas rapidly. If the ground gradually becomes covered by grasses or other plants, then the seeds of annuals may remain in a resting state in the soil for many years, eventually germinating when the ground is cleared again. Sadly, many of the cornfield species have become rare in recent years due to the widespread use of selective weedkillers and more stringent seed-cleaning techniques.

Grassland

The majority of plants thrive in competition with other species, and sometimes have a positive need for them to provide support or even sustenance. Plants such as Field Scabious (p.147) and Meadow Buttercup (p.43) coexist with grasses and other herbaceous plants in

Thrift thrives on exposed cliff-tops and ledges, where it is frequently buffeted by salt-laden, gale-force winds. Other plants favouring this habitat include Sea Campion and Sea Carrot.

sunny meadows. The nature of the soil, especially the acidity or alkalinity and moisture content, influence which species are found in particular grasslands. Chalk grassland contains many characteristic species such as Clustered Bellflower (p.149) and Carline Thistle (p.161). Grazing pressures or the mowing regime of artificially maintained grasslands can have either beneficial or detrimental effects on which species survive.

Woodland

Relatively few wild flowers can grow in the deep shade of mature woodland; most woodland flowers are found in clearings and on the lighter margins. Those that do grow on the woodland floor, such as Bluebell (p.171) and Ramsons (p.173), complete much of their early growth and flowering before the trees fully open their leaves. They are able to start into growth rapidly as

they have underground food-storing structures such as bulbs or swollen, subterranean stems.

Large climbers, such as Ivy (p.98) and Traveller's-joy (p.46), use the trees as support and grow through the foliage, seeking the light. Yellow Bird's-nest (p.139) and Bird's-nest Orchid (p.183) can survive in deep shade as they do not require sunlight to produce their own sustenance, unlike most other wild flowers. Instead, with the aid of a fungus, they feed off the deep layer of leaf litter that covers the floor of Beech woodlands. Plantations of coniferous trees have very little ground flora, as the needle-like fallen leaves are toxic and very slow to decay. Natural Pine woodland is less dense and supports a limited range of species. Woodlands on lime-rich soils support a different flora to those on acidic soils. Herb-Paris (p.174) and Dog's Mercury (p.85) have a preference for lime-rich soils, where they can carpet the woodland floor.

Hedgerows

These provide an extension to woodland. They allow many species of the woodland margin, such as Red Campion (p.38), to survive in areas where they would otherwise have been eradicated. Some of the oldest hedgerows are actually narrow strips of woodland left between the properties of different owners. Climbing plants, such as Black Bryony (p.92), White Bryony (p.92) and Honeysuckle (p.145), grow particularly well in these conditions. Hedgerows with their banks or ditches are rich in species, since they combine several habitats. Species mingle that would otherwise remain distant and hybrids may form, such as between Cowslip and Primrose.

Human intervention

Within the area covered by the book and throughout virtually all of these combinations of latitude, altitude, underlying rock, rainfall and drainage, a major factor which determines where plants now grow is the influence of man. Some plants, such as Common Nettle (p.29) and Soapwort (p.40), benefit from present or past interaction. Many weeds are able to colonize land that man has disturbed for his crops or transportation systems. Most forms of grassland represent an unstable form of vegetation; if left, they would gradually revert to scrub, then something approaching the forests that once covered most of the region. In any particular area, the expected species may not be there. There may be hidden reasons for this, especially if there is a history of drainage, deep ploughing, use of herbicides, or replacement of the former diversity of species by resowing pasture. Except for the most remote areas and much of the coastal or aquatic habitats, man has had a most profound effect on the vegetation of the whole of northern Europe.

In light shade, Bluebells, Greater Stitchwort, Wood Spurge and Yellow Archangel carpet the floor of deciduous woodland. Most of these plants will complete their flowering before the tree leaves open fully.

How to Identify Wild Flowers

Identifying wild flowers becomes easier with experience. Half the battle is knowing what to look for. The main distinguishing features are summarized in the following section, with an explanation of some terms used in the book.

Sometimes it is easy to identify a plant to a family or a group of species but difficult to go beyond this stage (for example, in the Carrot and Daisy Families). Technical details for distinguishing these species are given as labels on the main illustrations.

Type

Plants which grow from seed, flower and fruit within a single year are called annuals. Biennials start into leafy growth (often forming a rosette of leaves) in one year but flower in the next. Perennials flower and fruit over successive years. Aquatic plants live floating or submerged in water. Parasitic wild flowers obtain nourishment from other plants, and saprophytes from decaying leaves; neither has green pigment.

aquatic plant

Stems

Stems may be upright, angled upwards or low-growing. Some plants have distinct lines, angles, or wing-like sides to the stems. The long, rooting stems produced by Wild Strawberry are called runners. Climbing plants often have twining stems, twisting clockwise or anticlockwise; others climb by means of twining leaf-stalks or tendrils. All

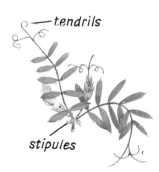

tendrils

stipules

heights are expressed in centimetres to make them comparable. Heights vary from Rootless Duckweed, at less than one tenth of a centimetre, to climbers like Traveller's-joy with stems several thousand times taller, becoming thick and woody, and reaching the tops of trees.

Roots

Included under this heading are all below-ground parts. Most annuals have finely divided, fibrous roots. A long, tapered tap-root is found in many biennials; perennials often die back to a woody stock. Some plants have creeping, rooting underground stems, which can form new plants. A bulb is a short stem with fleshy leaf-bases; the corm of Cyclamen is a short, swollen, upright underground stem; tubers of Hemlock Water-dropwort are swollen parts of the roots. Parasitic plants have specialized roots that invade the tissues of other plants.

swollen stem

Leaves and stipules

Note the arrangement of the leaves, whether paired or otherwise arranged on the stem or all at the base (often as a rosette); the shape of the blade (expanded part), whether it is divided into leaflets, and whether the edge is unbroken, toothed, spiny or lobed. Plants which grow both in water and on land can

have two sorts of leaf. Leaves usually have a stalk at the base, and beneath this there may be a pair of stipules. Those of Large Bird's-foot-trefoil resemble an extra pair of leaflets.

stipules

Hairs

The presence or absence of hairs, and size, shape, density or position can help identify a species. Hairs may be gland-tipped and sticky or make the plant look woolly. Gland-tipped hairs surrounding the leaf of Round-leaved Sundew are capable of movement and act like tentacles, entrapping the insects that this plant preys on. Hairs can be stiff and bristle-like; those of Dog-rose are modified to form sharp prickles.

sticky hairs

Flowers

Although size and colour are usually the most obvious features of flowers, there are many other useful characteristics for identification. But first it is important to understand the structure of a flower.

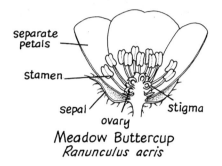

Meadow Buttercup
Ranunculus acris

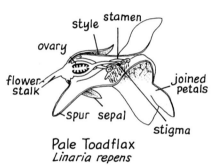

Pale Toadflax
Linaria repens

Sepals

The outermost parts of the flower are the sepals. Although the number, shape, size or even colour of sepals may vary between species, most are green and rather leaf-like. Note whether the sepals differ in size or are joined at the base. Thrift has joined sepals

sepals joined

which form a papery, funnel-shaped structure. In Dandelion, the sepals of the individual flowers form a ring of bristles and become the 'parachute' of the fruits.

Petals

The number of petals is important, and whether they are equal or unequal. There are two common ways that inequality may be expressed: an outer ring of petals can differ in size from an inner ring of petals, or upper petals differ from lower petals. Look to see whether the petals are joined together towards the base, instead of being separate. There is not always an obvious tube-like part, but if petals are joined then they usually fall together, as in the Forget-me-nots.

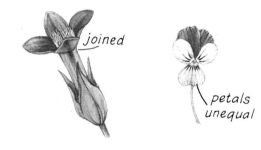

joined

petals unequal

Perianth

If the petals and sepals are not readily distinguishable, then the term perianth applies to both. The parts of the perianth can be green and sepal-like, as in Sea-purslane, or petal-like, as in Fritillary.

perianth

Type

The male () parts of a flower are the stamens, whereas the female (♀) parts are the stigma, usually with a stalk-like part (style), attaching it to the ovary. Most flowers have both male and female parts and are termed hermaphrodite (☿). Male and female parts can be on separate types of flower – both on the same plant, as in Sea-purslane, or on different plants, as in Common Nettle.

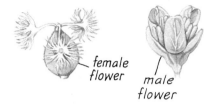

female flower

male flower

Stamens

The number of stamens, and whether they are hidden by the base of the petals or protruding, can help distinguish plants. Native species of the Pea family have the bases of the stamens (filaments) joined to form a tube. In flowers of the Daisy family and Bellflowers, the stamens join above to form a tube with the pollen-bearing parts (anthers) opening inwards.

joined stamens

Stigmas and ovary

A flower can have a single ovary or multiple ovaries, as in the Buttercups. The ovary can have a single stigma or many, and a stigma may have two or more lobes. Inside, there may be a single cavity containing the developing seeds, or the ovary can be few- or many-celled through division by internal walls. An ovary has one or more ovules and may be above the base of the petals or beneath, as in Willowherbs and Orchids.

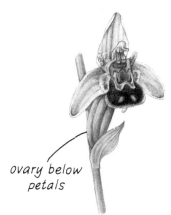

ovary below petals

Flower-stalk
This can vary from being upright to turning downwards, so that the flower is nodding or pendulous. The stalk may be much longer than the flower, or shorter, or sometimes absent.

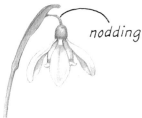

nodding

Flower-head
Flowers can arise singly from the base of a leaf or tip of a stem, but often are clustered to form a flower-head. This may be elongated, unbranched and spike-like, or branched in some way. A branched, umbrella-shaped head, with flowers mostly at the same level, is typical of the Carrot family. The flowers may be so tightly clustered that the whole flower-head appears as a single flower, as in the Daisies. The tiny flowers in the head are called florets. The florets in the centre are often smaller and of a different shape to the outer, strap-shaped florets. Surrounding the florets is a ring of green structures called bracts and the whole flower-head has a stem resembling a flower-stalk.

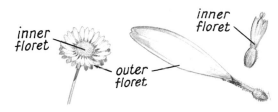

inner floret

outer floret

inner floret

Bracts
These occur mostly at the base of a flower-stalk or at the base of a flower-head. They are generally like small leaves but can be papery or scale-like. Bracts are often larger towards the base of a flower-head and become indistinguishable from normal leaves. The slender bracts of the Bluebell are coloured like the flowers. Some species of the Daisy family, such as Corn Chamomile, have tiny bracts between the florets of the flower-head. The spike-like flower-head of Lords-and-Ladies is enclosed by a large, hood-like bract.

bluish bract

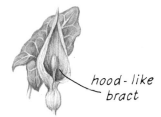

hood-like bract

Fruits and seeds
Once fertilized, the ovules develop into seeds and the ovary forms a fruit. Important things to note about fruits are the number of them produced by a single flower, whether they are fleshy or dry, and whether they open to release the seeds. A typical fleshy sort of fruit is the berry of a Bilberry. Wild Strawberry appears to have a berry-like fruit but this is the swollen base of the flower, the actual fruits being the pips on the surface. By far the majority of fruits have outer layers which become dry as the fruit ripens. The fruit of the Poppy (a capsule) opens by a ring of pores around the top. Pods are elongated fruits that split open, and are found in relatives of the Peas. Plants related to the Cabbages have pod-like fruits, that differ in having an internal dividing wall. Dry fruits that do not open are usually nut-like, containing a single seed. Some have hooks or parachutes that help them disperse. Number, size, shape, surface features and colours of seeds can all be useful for distinguishing species.

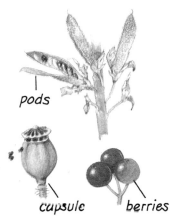

pods

capsule   berries

Key to Species

This key provides an illustrated guide to groups of species and their page numbers. At each stage, read the first numbered statement and see if it describes your plant. If not, then the second statement with the same number includes all other plants left at that stage of the key. Move on to the next statement below and repeat the process. Some of the distinctive groups of wild flowers fall within the first few categories but many wild flowers need closer examination.

1 water plants; leaves mostly floating or submerged
2 flowers green or brown, usually without distinct petals
3 tiny plants (less than 2cm) without distinct stems and leaves
Duckweeds 178

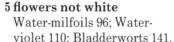

3 plants larger than 2cm, stems and leaves distinct
Water-milfoils 96; Water-starwort 119; Shoreweed 142; Pondweeds 169.

2 flowers with distinct petals, not green or brown
4 leaves with edge toothed, lobed or with separate leaflets
5 flowers white
6 flowers in umbrella-shaped heads
Fool's Water-cress, Lesser Marshwort, Lesser Water-parsnip, Water-dropworts 102.

6 flowers not in umbrella-shaped heads
Water-crowfoots 42; Water-cresses 51; Water-soldier 168.

5 flowers not white
Water-milfoils 96; Water-violet 110; Bladderworts 141.

4 leaves with edge unbroken
7 leaves in small tuft at base of plant
Shoreweed, Mudwort, Awlwort, Water Lobelia 142.

7 leaves not in small tuft at base of plant
8 flowers with three petals
Arrowhead, Frogbit 168.

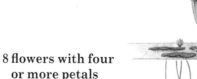

8 flowers with four or more petals
Amphibious Bistort 30; Water-lilies 42.

1 not water plants or all leaves normally out of water
9 leaves and stems without green pigment
Dodder 119; Broomrapes 139; Bird's-nest Orchid 183. (Also see Colt's-foot 158; Meadow Saffron 172.)

9 leaves and stems with green pigment
10 flowers green or brown, usually without distinct petals
11 plants climbing
12 leaves paired, on opposite sides of stem
Hop 29; Traveller's-joy 46.

12 leaves spirally arranged or on alternate sides of stem
Black-bindweed 30; Bryonies 92; Ivy 98.

11 plants not climbing
13 flowers are a stalked ovary and jointed stamens in cup-like base ringed by glands
Spurges 85.

13 flowers not in cup-like base
14 leaves on stems, in pairs or clusters at same level
15 leaves with edge unbroken
16 stem with just one pair or cluster of leaves
Herb-Paris 174; Twayblades 182.

16 stems with many pairs or clusters of leaves
Mistletoe 27; Nettles 29; Sea-purslane, Glassworts 33; Pearlworts 37; Branched Plantain 143.

15 leaves with edge toothed, lobed or with separate leaflets
17 flowers with both petals and sepals
Wood Sage 125; Figworts 132; Moschatel 145.

17 flowers with no distinction between petals and sepals
Nettles 29; Golden-saxifrages 63; Mercuries 85.

14 leaves all at base of plant or scattered around stem
18 leaves all in tuft at base of plant
Mountain Sorrel 31; Plantains 142–143; Lords-and-Ladies 178; Orchids 182.

18 leaves not in tuft at base of plant; stems leafy
19 leaves toothed, lobed or divided into leaflets
20 leaves toothed or shallowly lobed
Docks 31; Goosefoots 32–33; Golden-saxifrages 63; Lady's-mantle 71; Carrots 98.

20 most leaves divided nearly to base or with separate leaflets
Hellebores 45; Meadow-rues 47; Swine-cress 54; Burnets 69; Lady's-mantle 71; Carrots 100–101; Mugwort 155.

19 leaves with edge unbroken
21 stem surrounded by papery tube at base of leaves
Docks 30–32.

21 stem without papery tube at base of leaves
22 flowers with one petal larger than others
Orchids 179, 182.

22 flowers with equal petals or petals absent
Asarabacca 27;
Pellitory-of-the-wall 29; Goosefoots 32–33;
Cudweeds 153.

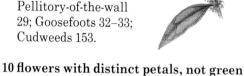

10 flowers with distinct petals, not green or brown
23 flowers in compact, rounded heads
24 leaves spiny
Sea-holly 99; Thistles 160–161.

24 leaves not spiny (or absent on flower)
25 individual flowers of head like pea-flowers (lowest 2 petals joined, boat-shaped, overlapped by 2 side petals, upper petal largest)
Clovers 77–78.

25 individual flowers of head not like pea-flowers
26 stamens separate
Astrantia 99; Thrift 111; Teasels 147; Sheep's-bit 150.

26 stamens joined into tube
27 florets all strap-shaped (head dandelion-like)
Dandelions 163–166.

27 at least inner florets tubular
28 leaves mostly paired
Daisies 152, 154.

28 leaves on alternating sides of stem or all at base
29 fruits with a parachute of hairs or bristles
Daisies 150–154, 158–159, 162.

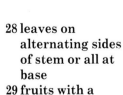

29 fruits without a parachute
Daisies 152, 155–157.

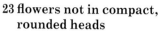
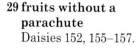

23 flowers not in compact, rounded heads
30 flowers in broad, flat-topped or umbrella-shaped clusters
31 flat-topped cluster composed of daisy-like flower-heads
Hemp-agrimony 151; Yarrow 155; Tansy 157.

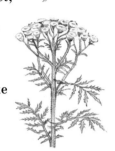

31 flat-topped cluster composed of individual flowers
32 flowers with several ovaries (forming several fruits)
Stonecrops 61–62; Meadowsweet 65.

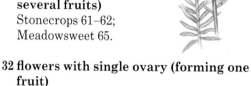

32 flowers with single ovary (forming one fruit)
Carrots 98–105.

30 flowers not in broad, flat-topped clusters
33 petals of different sizes
34 petals separate at the base
35 ovary (and developing fruit) beneath base of petals and sepals
Daffodils, Irises 175–176; Orchids 179–183.

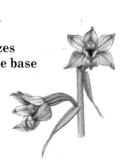

35 ovary (and developing fruit) above base of petals and sepals or absent
36 plant with pea-flowers (lowest 2 petals joined, boat-shaped, overlapped by 2 side petals, upper petal largest)
Peas 73–80.

36 plant not with pea-flowers
37 leaves (or leaf-like branches) with edge unbroken
Weld 59; Milkworts 87; Butcher's-broom 174.

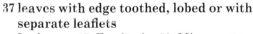

37 leaves with edge toothed, lobed or with separate leaflets
Larkspurs 47; Fumitories 50; Mignonettes 59; Balsams 87; Violets 90.

34 petals joined above base
38 fruit deeply divided into four nut-like parts
Vervain, Mints 124–129.

38 fruit not divided into four nut-like parts
39 flowers with spur at base
Toadflaxes 133–134; Butterworts 141.

39 flowers without spur at base
40 climber or small shrub
Honeysuckles 145.

40 not climber or small shrub
41 upper part of flower hood-like
Figworts 138–139.

41 upper part of flower not hood-like
42 flowers with 4 petal-lobes
Figworts 136–137.

42 flowers with 5 petal-lobes
Figworts 132–133, 135–136, 138.

33 petals all the same size
43 petals fewer than 4 or more than 5
44 flowers with 3 or fewer petals
45 flowers with 2–3 petals

Enchanter's-nightshades 95; Arrowhead 168; Flowering-rush 169.

45 flowers with single petal-like hood or lobe to petal-tube
Birthwort 27; Lords-and-Ladies 178.

44 flowers with 6 or more petals
46 leaves with edge toothed, lobed or with separate leaflets
Buttercups 44–46.

46 leaves with edge unbroken or absent when flowering
47 stems leafless, leaves all at base of plant or absent when flowering
48 ovary above base of petals or hidden at base of plant
Lilies 171–173.

48 ovary beneath base of petals
Daffodils 175–176.

47 stems leafy
Black Bryony 92;
Loosestrifes 94;
Chickweed Wintergreen
111; Lilies 172–175.

43 flowers with 4–5 petals
49 petals separate to the base
50 flowers with 4 petals
51 flowers with 10 or more stamens
52 flowers with more than 1 ovary, forming more than 1 fruit
Traveller's-joy 46;
Meadow-rues 47;
Tormentil 70.

52 flowers with 1 ovary, forming 1 fruit
Baneberry 47; Poppies 49–50.

51 flowers with 2–6 stamens
53 leaves with edge toothed, lobed or with separate leaflets

54 fruits elongated (usually much longer than wide)
Cabbages 51, 53, 58.

54 fruits about as long as wide
Cabbages 51, 53–56, 58.

53 leaves with edge unbroken
Pearlworts 37;
Allseed 82;
Cabbages 53–56.

50 flowers with 5 petals
55 leaves on stems, in pairs or clusters at same level
56 leaves with edge toothed, lobed or with separate leaflets
Crane's-bills 83–84.

56 leaves with edge unbroken
57 stamens 10 or less
Pinks, Purslanes 35–40;
Fairy Flax 82.

57 stamens numerous (more than 10)
St John's-worts 88;
Rock-roses 92.

55 leaves all at base of plant or scattered around stem
58 flowers with more than 1 ovary
59 leaves thick and succulent
Stonecrops 61–62.

59 leaves not thick and succulent
60 stipules present at base of leaves
Buttercups 42, 47; Roses 65–66, 68, 69–71.

60 stipules absent from base of leaves
Buttercups 43–47.

58 flowers with 1 ovary
61 leaves with edge unbroken
   Bistorts 30;
   Sundews 61; Grass-of-Parnassus 65;
   Flaxes 82.

61 leaves with edge toothed, lobed or with separate leaflets
62 leaves with separate leaflets
   Roses 67–68; Wood-sorrels 82.

62 leaves toothed or lobed
   Saxifrages 62–63;
   Mallows 91.

49 petals joined above base
63 flowers with 4 petals
64 leaves in rings around stem
   Heathers 107; Bedstraws 114–115.

64 leaves paired or scattered around stem
   Willowherbs 94–96;
   Heathers 107–108.

63 flowers with 5 petals
65 leaves on stems, in pairs or clusters at same level
   Pimpernels 109–110;
   Gentians 113; Periwinkles 114; Valerians 146.

65 leaves all at base of plant or scattered around stem
66 plants climbing or trailing
   White Bryony 92; Bindweeds 118;
   Nightshades 131.

66 plants not climbing or trailing
67 fruit splits into four small, nut-like parts (ovary 4-lobed)
   Forget-me-nots 121–123.

67 fruit does not split into four small, nut-like parts (ovary not 4-lobed)
68 leaves with separate leaflets
   Bogbean 110; Jacob's-ladder 117.

68 leaves without separate leaflets
69 flowers with 8–10 stamens
   Wintergreens 107; Bilberry 108.

69 flowers with 5 stamens
70 flowers white
   Brookweed 111;
   Nightshades 131.

70 flowers not white
71 ovary (and developing fruit) beneath base of sepals
   Bellflowers 149–150.

71 ovary (and developing fruit) above base of sepals
   Primroses 108–109; Thrift 111; Nightshades 131;
   Mullein 132.

Plants and People

The association between plants and people goes back much further than recorded history. Native plants formed the staple diet of the first hunter-gatherer inhabitants of the region, long before plants were imported from other areas. Evidence provided from remains of Stone Age people and their encampments shows that they ate seeds of Fat-hen and other species of the Goosefoot family, plants which today are regarded as weeds. Plants played a major role in the lives of early Europeans; in addition to human food, they provided building materials, food and enclosures for livestock, clothing, weapons, medicines and dyes.

Food plants
As people became farmers, they carried seeds and roots of useful plants with them as they moved from area to area. Thus diets gradually incorporated different plants from outside northern Europe. With the development of various methods of transport, it became possible to import plant materials from other areas and many local plants were abandoned. However, some of the garden vegetables used today were derived from native species. Descendants of those wild progenitors still survive, such as the Wild Parsnip plants which occur on waste ground through much of the area. Some of the other edible wild plants were deliberately introduced as cultivated plants in the past, yet are ignored today; Alexanders and Ground-elder fall into this category. There are only a few exceptions to this almost wholesale abandonment of native food-plants, the most familiar being such fruits as blackberries and wild strawberries.

Medicinal plants
Herbal remedies were formerly the only ones available to people, but most have long since been abandoned. However, a few species are still used today and are very much a part of modern medicine. There is increasing interest in natural plant products, for they are less alien to biological systems than synthetic drugs produced in factories, and possibly have fewer deleterious side-effects. Already research into native plant products has yielded drugs of value against certain types of cancer.

Plants have also provided natural insecticides. They were used as strewing herbs, not only to keep the air smelling fresh, but to repel or destroy insect parasites such as fleas. Plants such as the Common Fleabane were put to this use, as is commemorated in the common name.

Plant products
Plants have been exploited for many purposes other than as foods and medicines. Common Nettle and Flax, for example, provide fibres which can be woven into a fine cloth. Flax also yields the useful linseed oil. Another oil-yielding plant of increasing importance in northern Europe is Rape. Petals and fruit (or sometimes other parts of plants) were used to provide dyes and cosmetics. Weld and Woad were both important dye-plants. Soapwort provided soap before the artificial substance that bears that name today.

Mystical plants
Plants have also played an important role in religions and superstitions and some still survive in country folklore. Sometimes the significance has been lost in antiquity. For example, in different countries of northern Europe, a range of species including Common Poppy and Greater Stitchwort were thought to bring on thunder and lightning. Interestingly, some plants have had a history of changing associations: Mistletoe was important in Druid ceremonies but now is associated with the Christian religious festival of Christmas.

Plants for pleasure
In recent years, there appears to be a growing appreciation for the natural charm and beauty of wild flowers. This may be a reaction to the artificial environments we live and work in, and to the plant-breeders art, where size and intensity of colour in flowers have often been sought at the expense of intricacy of marking, scent or subtlety of form. For some it is a slowly dawning realization that much of what we had has been lost, and that unless we take conservation seriously, then many wild flowers will disappear forever.

Glasswort is an edible native plant with a crisp, succulent flavour. It is now only eaten in a few coastal areas.

Though potentially lethal if used incorrectly, Foxglove, like Deadly Nightshade, yields a number of medicines of paramount importance.

Wild Flower Gardening

During recent years interest in the creation of wild flower gardens has grown, partly arising out of a greater concern for conservation. In the past, the gardener was no ally of wild flowers – many species have been brought to the very edge of extinction by avid gardeners who sought their bulbs and roots in the wild. Today it is illegal to uproot wild plants in many countries and, for the rarest species, even taking seeds from wild plants can be against the law. Fortunately it is unnecessary, for an increasing number of specialist nurseries are producing plants and seeds of native species, which are widely distributed through garden centres and supermarkets.

A wild flower meadow

There are many different sorts of wild flower garden that can be created. The simplest is the wild flower meadow, created initially by leaving an area of lawn uncut. This allows many broad-leaved plants, such as Cat's-ear and Selfheal, to grow through the grass and flower. However, wild gardens are not just an excuse for the lazy gardener. Careful thought is required to make the most of a plot of land and exploit its potential fully. The aim is to select only those plants which would normally grow in similar conditions and to try and recreate a natural plant community. In order to increase the range of species in the meadow, seed can be sown directly in autumn or spring, or plants can be grown in pots and transferred to the meadow. Oxeye Daisy and Yarrow can be attractive additions and are tolerant of a wide range of soils. The inclusion of Wild Thyme, Marjoram and Common Sorrel will produce a continuous supply of fresh herbs. With alkaline soils over chalk or limestone, plants such as Common Milkwort, Maiden Pink and Clustered Bellflower are desirable. If the soil is naturally damp then try Ragged-Robin, or the curious Fritillary, which can be purchased readily as bulbs. Wild flower meadows do require some mowing but, to encourage the natural spread of particular wild flowers, only cut after their seeds have ripened.

In general, the desirable wild flowers do rather better on poor soils than rich soils: soils rich in nitrates favour plants like Common Nettle and many weeds. If the soil is too rich to grow meadow flowers successfully, a solution is to skim off the top few centimetres of soil and grass and resow with a mixture of selected meadow grasses and wild flowers.

Other wild flower gardens

The main exception to the rule concerning richer soils is if you wish to grow plants of cornfields. Common Poppy, Cornflower, Corn Marigold and Corncockle are easy to grow from seed and will soon provide a colourful display. They are annual plants so die at the end of the season and will need to be replaced to give a similar display the following year. It is best to save some seed for sowing next season, as much of that dispersed naturally will rot or be eaten before it can grow. Such plants also need cleared ground as they are easily swamped by perennial grasses and other plants. A completely different sort of wild garden can be created with the benefit of a few established trees. A woodland garden will cater for many attractive species including Bluebell, Foxglove, Lords-and-Ladies, Primroses and Solomon's-seal. Alternatively, grow mountain plants on simulated cliff-ledges or scree. With the provision of even a small pond, a range of aquatic and marginal plants can be added. Flowering-rush and Arrowhead are attractive plants for the edge of the pond, while Water Violet, Frogbit and Curled Pondweed could be planted in the water.

Once a community of native plants has become established in the garden, a range of animals associated with the plants will gradually follow. It is well worth including a clump of the Common Nettle for the larvae of many species of butterfly feed almost exclusively on the young shoots. A well-planted pond will bring many animals into the garden, and encourage the brilliantly coloured dragonflies and damselflies. Frogs and Toads will help keep the slugs off your vegetable patch. If you want to attract the larger animals to your garden, start with the plants and smaller animals that they feed on. There is no point using weedkillers or poisoning slugs and snails if you want to see hedgehogs, thrushes or kestrels. Free of herbicides and pesticides, the wild flower garden can provide a real contribution to conservation.

Chicory produces a magnificent display of sky-blue flowers and later provides finches with a supply of seed. Young leaves can be used in salads, and roasted chicory roots make a coffee substitute or extender.

Asarabacca and Mistletoe

In the past Asarabacca and Birthwort provided powerful, herbal remedies and were widely cultivated, but such usage has long since been abandoned because of the toxicity of the plants. However, both are still cultivated for the unusual foliage and curiosity value. Mistletoe is also familiar because of its use in Christmas decorations.

Most species of the family to which Asarabacca belongs are found in tropical or warm-temperate forests. They include many lianes, which climb high into the forest canopy. Some have much larger flowers, such as the curious Dutchman's Pipe (*Aristolochia macrophylla*), which is often cultivated in greenhouses.

Mistletoe is the only northern European species of a mainly tropical family, and is not closely related to any other native plant. It is a parasite on trees and can be found on a range of broad-leaved, and even some coniferous, trees. It attaches itself to its host by sucker-like roots which invade the conducting tissues of the host's branch or trunk. The fruit of the Mistletoe is a white berry with sticky flesh surrounding the seeds. This enables the seeds to stick to a branch while the seedling germinates.

On a leafless branch in the depth of winter, a clump of Mistletoe remains in green leaf. Such an unexpected sight led superstitious people to confer magical properties on the plant.

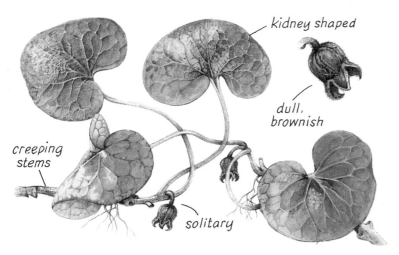

kidney shaped

dull, brownish

creeping stems

solitary

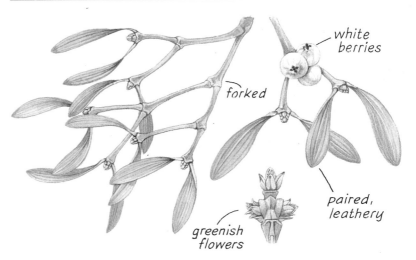

white berries

forked

paired, leathery

greenish flowers

The lustrous, kidney-shaped leaves of this species are more noticeable than the curious 3-lobed flowers which are held close to the ground. Both the native Asarabacca and exotic relatives are popular as garden plants for their cyclamen-like foliage. Asarabacca was once used for respiratory ailments and complaints of the liver; it is used no longer because of harmful side effects. *Status:* native or escaped from cultivation; widespread but rare in Britain, absent from Ireland. *Similar species:* Birthwort has more upright stems and clusters of tubular, yellow flowers.

Birthwort (*Aristolochia clematitis*)

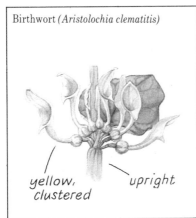

yellow, clustered

upright

Bright, yellowish-green foliage springing from the branch of an otherwise bare tree in winter distinguishes the Mistletoe from a distance. Its special roots invade the tissues of the host tree and take nourishment, although the plant makes some of its own food using sunlight. Mistletoe grows on a large range of deciduous trees; it is especially common on Apple, although uncommon on Oak and found only rarely on conifers. Birds eating the berries wipe off sticky seeds from their beaks on to a branch, where the seeds grow into new plants. Mistletoe is familiar through the

Christmas tradition of kissing under a sprig of the plant – magical properties have been attributed to the plant throughout the ages. In particular, the plants that grew on Oak featured much in ancient ceremonies of the Druids. Mistletoe has been used medicinally to treat heart disease and many different nervous disorders. *Status:* native; most of area except for some northern parts and Ireland. (There are no similar species.)

ASARABACCA		**FLOWERS**	
Type	perennial	**Position**	single, from tip of stem
Height	low-growing	**Bracts**	absent
Habitat	woods	**Type**	♂ inconspicuous
Flowering	May–August	**Size**	11–15mm
		Colour	dull purplish brown
STEMS AND LEAVES		**Stalk**	longer than flower
Stem	5–10cm long, creeping, rooting	**Perianth**	3, triangular, equal, pointed, joined at base into short tube
Root	branched, creeping stock	**Stamens**	12
Hairs	short hairs on stems and flowers	**Stigmas**	usually 6
		Ovary	1, usually 6-celled
Stipules	absent		
Leaves	on alternate sides of stem, 25–100mm, kidney-shaped, glossy dark green, tip rounded, edge smooth, base heart-shaped	**FRUIT**	
		Type	capsule, opening irregularly, globular, the perianth attached
		Size	7–9mm
Leaf-stalk	longer than blade	**Seeds**	numerous, 2–3mm, flattened

MISTLETOE		**FLOWERS**	
Type	perennial	**Position**	3–5 clustered at tip of stem, on ♂ or ♀ plants
Height	20–100cm	**Bracts**	joined to flower-stalks
Habitat	parasite mainly on deciduous trees	**Type 1**	♂ without sepals
Flowering	February–April	**Type 2**	♀ with 4 sepals, 2–4mm
		Size	4–6mm
STEMS AND LEAVES		**Colour**	greenish yellow
Stem	woody at base, repeatedly forking, green	**Stalk**	short
Root	specially modified to invade wood of tree	**Perianth**	4, sepal-like, broadest at base, blunt
		Stamens	4, joined to petals
Hairs	absent	**Stigma**	1
Stipules	absent	**Ovary**	1, 1-celled
Leaves	paired on opposite sides of stem, 50–80mm, narrow, sometimes curved, leathery, tip blunt, edge unbroken, base narrowed	**FRUIT**	
		Type	1, berry, white, mostly globe-shaped
		Size	6–10mm
Leaf-stalk	short	**Seeds**	1, sticky

Docks, Goosefoots, Hop and Nettles

This group includes some well-known plants, especially the infamous Nettle and its antidote, the Docks. Most of the plants have small flowers lacking showy petals, since they are pollinated by the wind. There is no distinction between petals and sepals. Hop and Nettle plants have all-female or all-male flowers. In the Goosefoots, plants may have both male and female flowers or some species have hermaphrodite flowers. Docks include all three variations, and species of Bistort, belonging to the same family, have showy, insect-pollinated flowers.

Goosefoots are able to tolerate unusually high concentrations of inorganic salts in the soil and are consequently important components of the vegetation of salt-marshes. Many species have special adaptations to withstand arid conditions and some, such as the Glassworts, have cactus-like, leafless stems. Economically important plants of the family include the Beetroot, Sugar Beet and Spinach.

The Hop is often included in the same family as the Figs, a family of mainly tropical or subtropical trees and shrubs. The main differences from the tropical plants, apart from growth habit, are the floral parts in fives instead of fours, and the lack of milky sap. Nettles and Hop are sometimes included in the same family but Nettles differ in having a single style and stigma.

Draped over a hedgerow, a female Hop plant carries a heavy crop of cone-like fruiting-heads. The aromatic fruits from cultivated plants provide dried hops for beer-making.

Humulus lupulus **Hop**

A rather coarse, tough vine climbing by tendril-like tips to the twining stems. The backward-pointing, stiff hairs provide extra anchorage but can give a painful scratch. Cultivated plants are trained up strings supported by tall poles in fields. Tough fibres from the stems have been used in the manufacture of cloth and a form of paper has also been made from the stems. Tips of young shoots are edible and can be used fresh in salads or cooked like Asparagus, the latter method being favoured by the Romans. Hops produce the characteristic bitter taste of beer, a use extending at least back to the Middle Ages, and belong to the same family as the drug plant that yields marijuana. Extracts from the female flowers have a mild sedative action and have been used for insomnia and nervous ailments. *Status:* native or often naturalized; common, most of area. (There are no similar species.)

twining / female flower / female / male / lobed leaves / papery scales / male flower / cone-like fruit

Urtica dioica **Common Nettle**

A species notorious on account of stinging hairs which cover most of the plant. Brushed lightly, the brittle tip of the stiff hair breaks off depositing a small drop of formic acid which causes the stinging sensation. Young shoots, rich in Vitamin C, can be eaten: the stinging action is destroyed by cooking. Some populations of the Common Nettle do not sting, but the reputation of the species ensures that those are rarely detected. Nettles provide the main food plant for many familiar butterflies. *Status:* native; common in most of area. *Similar species:* Small Nettle is an annual favouring lighter soils. Pellitory-of-the-wall has red stems and leaves with softer, stingless hairs.

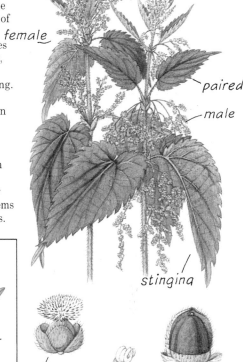

female / paired / male / stinging / female flower / male flower / nut-like fruit

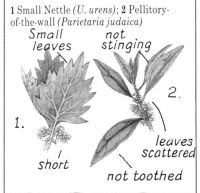

1 Small Nettle (*U. urens*); **2** Pellitory-of-the-wall (*Parietaria judaica*)

Small leaves / not stinging / 1. / short / 2. / leaves scattered / not toothed

---

	HOP			Bracts	♀ up to 10mm, oval, becoming papery
Type	perennial		**Type 1**	♂ in loose, branched cluster
Height	300–600cm		**Type 2**	♀ in cone-like head, 15–20mm, yellowish green
Habitat	hedges and bushes			
Flowering	July–August		**Size**	c5mm
			Colour	green
	STEMS AND LEAVES		**Stalk**	present only in ♂
Stem	climbing, twisting clockwise		**Perianth**	♂ 5-parted, ♀ undivided
Root	fibrous		**Stamens**	♂ with 5
Hairs	stiff, backward-pointing		**Stigmas**	♀ with 2
Stipules	present		**Ovary**	1, 1-celled
Leaves	paired on opposite sides of stem, mostly 100–150mm, 3–5 lobed, pointed, edge toothed, base heart-shaped		**FRUIT**	
Leaf-stalk	about equal to blade		**Type**	cone of papery scales enclosing nut-like fruits
	FLOWERS		**Size**	cone 30–50mm
Position	numerous, in pendulous clusters, ♂ and ♀ flowers on different plants		**Seeds**	not released

	COMMON NETTLE			and ♀ flowers on different plants
Type	perennial			
Height	30–150cm		**Bracts**	absent
Habitat	hedgerows, woods, waste places; mainly rich soils		**Type 1**	♂ with equal perianth-lobes
Flowering	June–August		**Type 2**	♀ with unequal perianth-lobes, c1mm
			Size	1.5–2mm
	STEMS AND LEAVES		**Colour**	yellowish green
Stem	creeping or upright		**Stalk**	absent
Root	tough, yellow, fibrous		**Perianth**	4-parted
Hairs	stiff, mostly stinging		**Stamens**	4, springing open when ripe
Stipules	present		**Stigma**	1, feathery
Leaves	paired on opposite sides of stem, 40–80mm, oval, tip pointed, edge sharply toothed, base heart-shaped		**Ovary**	1, 1-celled
Leaf-stalk	shorter than blade		**FRUIT**	
	FLOWERS		**Type**	single, nut-like, oval, enclosed by withered flower
Position	numerous, in branched, spike-like clusters from leaf-base; ♂		**Size**	1–1.5mm
			Seeds	not released

Amphibious Bistort *Polygonum amphibium*

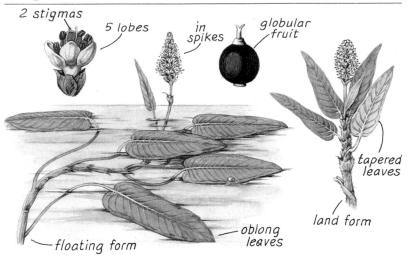

2 stigmas
5 lobes
in spikes
globular fruit
tapered leaves
land form
oblong leaves
floating form

An attractive plant with spikes of pink or red flowers, usually rising from the surface of a lake. There is a land form with more upright stems and tapered, hairy leaves. The common name refers to this amphibious nature, but 'bistort', meaning 'twice twisted', refers to the convoluted roots of Common Bistort. *Status:* native, in suitable places through most of region. *Similar species:* Common Bistort has slender, upright stems, smaller upper leaves and three stigmas. The nearly hairless Redshank and hairy Pale Persicaria are two weed species with smaller flowers.

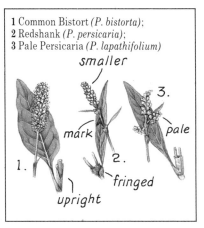

1 Common Bistort *(P. bistorta)*;
2 Redshank *(P. persicaria)*;
3 Pale Persicaria *(P. lapathifolium)*

smaller
mark
pale
1.
2.
3.
fringed
upright

	AMPHIBIOUS BISTORT
Type	perennial
Height	floating form 30–75cm long; land form to 50cm
Habitat	lakes, canals, slow-moving rivers or by water
Flowering	July–September
	STEMS AND LEAVES
Stem	floating, rooting, sometimes upright
Root	creeping rhizome
Hairs	hairless or with short hairs
Stipules	joined forming tube
Leaves	spirally arranged on stem
Leaves 1	floating form 50–150mm, oblong, blunt, edge unbroken, base square or heart-shaped
Leaf-stalk	20–60mm
Leaves 2	land form pointed, base broader, rounded

Leaf-stalk	mostly short
	FLOWERS
Position	numerous, in blunt spike at tip of stem
Bracts	scale-like
Type	♀
Size	5–7mm
Colour	pink or red
Stalk	shorter than flower
Perianth	5-lobed, 3–5mm, lobes petal-like, equal
Stamens	5
Stigmas	2
Ovary	1, 1-celled
	FRUIT
Type	single, nut-like, enclosed by dried flower, globular, brown
Size	2–3mm
Seeds	not separate

Knotgrass *Polygonum aviculare*

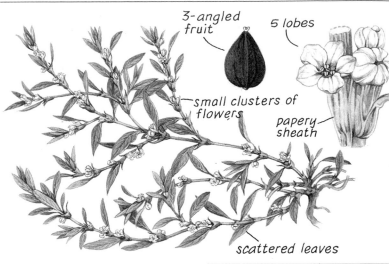

3-angled fruit
5 lobes
small clusters of flowers
papery sheath
scattered leaves

Although very common, Knotgrass is often overlooked because of its rather insignificant flowers. The common name refers to the swelling where the leaf joins the stem in many species of Knotgrass. *Status:* native; common through most of region. *Similar species:* Water-pepper, from damp places, has longer flower-heads, brown stipules. Black-bindweed is a climbing plant of cultivated and waste ground. Much larger at up to 2m tall, Japanese Knotweed was introduced to gardens but is now widely naturalized.

1 Water-pepper *(P. hydropiper)*;
2 Black-bindweed *(Fallopia convolvulus)*; 3 Japanese Knotweed *(Reynoutria japonica)*

long head
2.
3.
1.
climbing
much larger

	KNOTGRASS
Type	annual
Height	5–100cm
Habitat	cultivated land, waste places, often near sea
Flowering	July–October
	STEMS AND LEAVES
Stem	upright or low-growing
Root	fibrous
Hairs	absent
Stipules	silvery, joined forming tube round stem
Leaves	spirally arranged around stem, 20–50mm, spear-shaped, tip pointed, edge unbroken, base narrowing into stalk
Leaf-stalk	about equal to stipules

	FLOWERS
Position	single or in loose clusters of 2–6 from base of leaf
Bracts	insignificant
Type	♀
Size	3–4.5mm
Colour	greenish with pink or white edges
Stalk	absent
Perianth	5-lobed, 2–3mm, joined at base into short tube
Stamens	5–8
Stigmas	2
Ovary	1, 1-celled
	FRUIT
Type	1, nut-like, 3-angled, enclosed by dried flower
Size	2.5–3.5mm
Seeds	not separate

Rumex acetosella Sheep's Sorrel

Perhaps the most distinctive feature of this plant is the foliage, which acquires a brilliant crimson hue late in the season and on poor soils. Pollen is carried by the wind from the male plants to the feathery stigmas of the female plants. *Status:* native; common, most of area. *Similar species:* Common Sorrel has leaves with backward-pointing lobes, the upper clasping the stem. Formerly prized as a vegetable, the acid-tasting leaves were used much as lemons are today. Mountain Sorrel has kidney-shaped leaves mostly arising near the root.

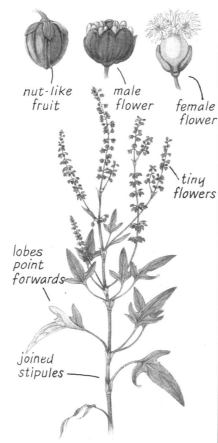

nut-like fruit

male flower

female flower

tiny flowers

lobes point forwards

joined stipules

1 Common Sorrel (*R. acetosa*);
2 Mountain Sorrel (*Oxyria digyna*)

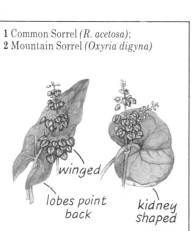

winged

lobes point back

kidney shaped

SHEEP'S SORREL
Type	perennial
Height	up to 30cm
Habitat	heaths, grassland, waste ground; acid soils
Flowering	May–August

STEMS AND LEAVES
Stem	upright or turning upright
Root	creeping, budding to make new stems
Hairs	absent
Stipules	joined forming tube
Leaves	on alternate sides of stem, up to 40mm, narrowly oval, often red-tinged, pointed, base usually with 2 forward-curving lobes
Leaf-stalk	longer than blade or absent above

FLOWERS
Position	numerous, in branched clusters, ♂ and ♀ flowers on different plants
Bracts	absent
Type 1	♂ with stamens
Type 2	♀ 1.5–2mm, with ovary
Size	c2mm
Colour	green, becoming crimson
Stalk	nearly equal to flower
Perianth	6-lobed, 3 small, 3 larger
Stamens	6
Stigmas	3, feathery
Ovary	1, 1-celled

FRUIT
Type	single, nut-like, 3-angled, enclosed by withered flower
Size	1.3–1.5mm
Seeds	not released

Pollen from the tiny male flowers of Sheep's Sorrel is borne by the wind.

Broad-leaved Dock *Rumex obtusifolius*

A large-leaved plant, familiar to gardeners as a difficult weed to pull and to children as an antidote for the nettle's sting. The lobes of the perianth change in shape in fruit and differ between species, forming wings, inflated bladders or wart-like bumps. *Status:* native; generally common although rarer in north. *Similar species:* three Docks lack the long teeth on the perianth-lobes. Curled Dock has broad, rounded lobes; Clustered Dock has lobes only half as large; and the aquatic Water Dock has triangular lobes with an elongated outgrowth.

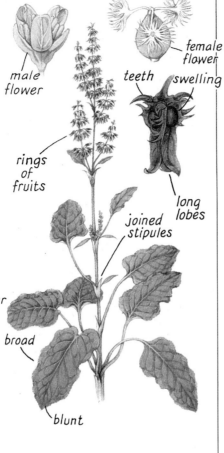

male flower

female flower

teeth   swelling

rings of fruits

joined stipules

long lobes

broad

blunt

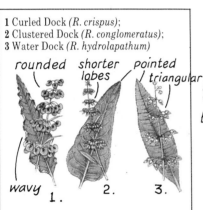

1 Curled Dock *(R. crispus)*;
2 Clustered Dock *(R. conglomeratus)*;
3 Water Dock *(R. hydrolapathum)*

rounded   shorter lobes   pointed triangular

wavy   1.   2.   3.

BROAD-LEAVED DOCK		FLOWERS	
Type	perennial	**Position**	numerous, in rings
Height	60–120cm	**Bracts**	absent
Habitat	field margins, hedgerows, cultivated, waste ground	**Type**	mostly ☿
		Size	c3mm
Flowering	June–October	**Colour**	green and white, turning crimson
STEMS AND LEAVES		**Stalk**	usually longer than flower
Stem	upright, branched	**Perianth**	6-lobed, 1–2mm, the 3 large inner triangular with long teeth and corky outgrowth
Root	stout tap-root		
Hairs	underside of leaves slightly hairy	**Stamens**	6
Stipules	joined forming tube	**Stigmas**	3, feathery
Leaves	on alternate sides of stem, to 250mm, oblong or upper tapered, blunt, edge fine-toothed, base square or heart-shaped	**Ovary**	1, 1-celled
		FRUIT	
		Type	1, nut-like, surrounded by flower
		Size	5–6mm
Leaf-stalk	longer than blade on lower leaves, shorter above	**Seeds**	not released

Fat-hen *Chenopodium album*

Perhaps the most common of a group of similar weed species with rather fleshy stems, Fat-hen is often striped with white or pink, and has angular leaves. It has been used as a vegetable and grain since the Stone Age, although largely abandoned in recent times. *Status:* native; common throughout area. *Similar species:* Good-King-Henry is perennial with triangular leaves, often lobed at the base. Orache species have separate male and female flowers, the latter enclosed by two bracts. Spear-leaved Orache has leaves squarer-based than Common Orache.

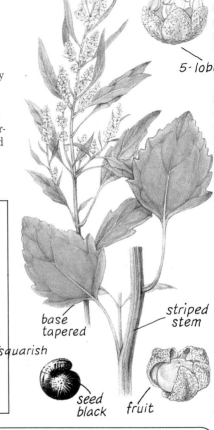

tiny flowers

5-lobe

base tapered

striped stem

seed black

fruit

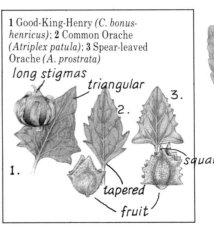

1 Good-King-Henry *(C. bonus-henricus)*; 2 Common Orache *(Atriplex patula)*; 3 Spear-leaved Orache *(A. prostrata)*

long stigmas   triangular   3.

2.

1.

squarish

tapered   fruit

FAT-HEN		FLOWERS	
Type	annual	**Position**	numerous, in small clusters grouped in spikes
Height	10–150cm		
Habitat	cultivated and waste ground; mostly rich soils	**Bracts**	present
		Type	☿
Flowering	July–October	**Size**	c1.5mm
		Colour	pale green
STEMS AND LEAVES		**Stalk**	more or less stalkless
Stem	upright, often striped with pink, slightly ridged	**Perianth**	5-lobed, each c1mm, oval, sepal-like
Root	fibrous	**Stamens**	5
Hairs	small, swollen, giving a floury look	**Stigmas**	2 on forked style
		Ovary	1, 1-celled
Stipules	absent		
Leaves	spirally arranged, 12–82mm, diamond- to spear-shaped, tip pointed, edge unbroken or shallowly toothed, base wedge-shaped	**FRUIT**	
		Type	1, not opening, forming thin layer, enclosed by withered flower
		Size	1.3–2mm
Leaf-stalk	shorter than blade	**Seeds**	1, 1.25–1.85mm, black, faintly grooved

Halimione portulacoides Sea-purslane

Found in salt-marshes, forming shrubby mounds with silvery leaves and tight clusters of tiny flowers, Sea-purslane tolerates flooding but prefers upper parts of the marsh, fringing the edges of channels. *Status:* native; coasts, except for parts of north. *Similar species:* glossy-leaved Sea Beet, its fruits loosely clustered together, is the same species as cultivated Beetroot and Sugar Beet. Frosted Orache, from sandy shores, has diamond-shaped, toothed leaves and thick bracts, while Grass-leaved or Shore Orache has narrow, scarcely toothed leaves and thin bracts.

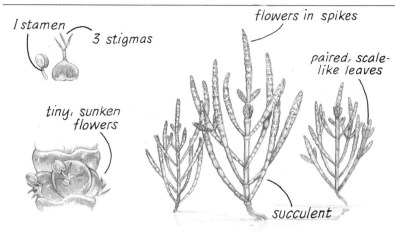

male flower

female flower

fruit

tiny flowers

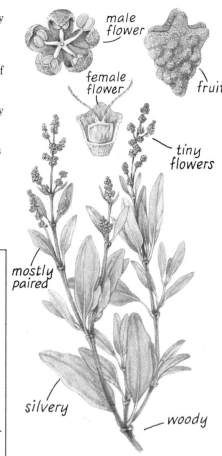

mostly paired

silvery

woody

1 Sea Beet (*Beta vulgaris* subsp. *maritima*); 2 Grass-leaved Orache (*Atriplex littoralis*); 3 Frosted Orache (*A. laciniata*)

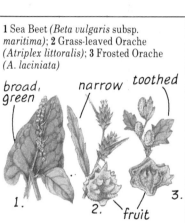

broad, green

narrow

toothed

1.

2.

fruit

3.

SEA-PURSLANE			FLOWERS	
Type	perennial		**Position**	numerous, spikes at stem-tip or leaf-base, ♂ and ♀ flowers on same plant
Height	45–150cm			
Habitat	salt-marshes, usually on top edges of gulleys		**Bracts**	2 3-lobed, bract-like parts cover ♀ flower
Flowering	July–September		**Type 1**	♂ with perianth
			Size	c2mm
STEMS AND LEAVES			**Colour**	mostly brownish yellow
Stem	woody below, turning upwards, often rooting		**Stalk**	absent
			Perianth	5-lobed
Root	short, creeping rhizome		**Stamens**	5
Hairs	swollen, floury-looking		**Type 2**	♀ without perianth, c1.5mm
Stipules	absent		**Stigmas**	2
Leaves	paired on opposite sides of stem or alternate above, 10–40mm, elliptical, slightly fleshy, blunt, edge unbroken		**Ovary**	1, 1-celled
			FRUIT	
			Type	1, not opening, thin, hidden by 3-lobed bracts
Leaf-stalk	3–10mm		**Size**	3–5mm
			Seeds	1, c3mm, not released

Salicornia europaea Glasswort

I stamen

3 stigmas

flowers in spikes

paired, scale-like leaves

tiny, sunken flowers

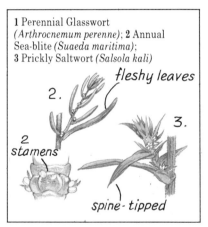

succulent

A seemingly leafless succulent plant, at times so plentiful that acres of salt-marsh are covered by nothing else. The anomaly of an apparent desert-plant immersed in water is explained by the sea-water's salinity, which draws water from the plant. *Status:* native; common around coasts except for parts of north. *Similar species:* Perennial Glasswort has woody, rooting stems and flowers with two stamens. Related salt-marsh plants with more normal leaves include Annual Sea-blite with bluntish leaves, and Prickly Saltwort with spine-tipped leaves.

1 Perennial Glasswort (*Arthrocnemum perenne*); 2 Annual Sea-blite (*Suaeda maritima*); 3 Prickly Saltwort (*Salsola kali*)

fleshy leaves

2.

2 stamens

3.

spine-tipped

GLASSWORT			FLOWERS	
Type	annual		**Position**	clusters of 3 on stem-segments towards stem-tip, forming tapered spike
Height	10–40cm			
Habitat	salt-marshes; sandy mud		**Bracts**	present
Flowering	August		**Type**	♀, partly sunken into stem-segment
STEMS AND LEAVES			**Size**	c2.5mm
Stem	upright, often yellowish green, translucent		**Colour**	green
			Stalk	absent
Root	fibrous		**Perianth**	indistinctly 3-lobed, roundish, succulent
Hairs	absent			
Stipules	absent		**Stamen**	1, shortly stalked, scarcely projecting
Leaves	paired on opposite sides of stem, joined except for tips into tube forming stem-segments, succulent, tip blunt, edge unbroken		**Stigmas**	3
			Ovary	1, 1-celled
			FRUIT	
			Type	single, papery-walled
Leaf-stalk	absent		**Size**	c2mm
			Seeds	1.2–1.8mm, covered with hairs

Pinks and Purslanes

Plants of the Pink family are mostly herbaceous, sharing characteristics such as paired, undivided leaves and hermaphrodite flowers with five separate, equal petals. The four or five sepals are either separate, as in the Chickweeds, or joined into a tube, as in the Campions. Sometimes there are small bracts around the base of the sepals, as in the Maiden Pink. The petals usually have a distinct stalk-like base and an expanded, often notched or bilobed, upper part. The family of the Pinks is large and, of the many familiar horticultural species, the Carnation probably has the greatest commercial value as a crop. Native species include plants with moderately large flowers, such as the Campions or Soapworts, and ones with very much smaller flowers, such as the Chickweeds and Mouse-ears.

Purslanes have very similar flowers and fruits but differ in having only two sepals. Most species of the family are more or less succulent, but this characteristic is not particularly marked in the European species. These include the Springbeauty, an introduced plant from North America, with its distinctive cup formed by a pair of fused leaves beneath the flowers, and the tiny-flowered, aquatic Blinks. The family includes several garden plants with brightly coloured flowers.

Like bright jewels, the spotted flowers of Maiden Pink spring from dry, sunny grassland. An uncommon sight, this relative of garden Pinks and Carnations is said to derive its common name from its similarity in colour to that of a blushing maiden.

Montia perfoliata **Springbeauty**

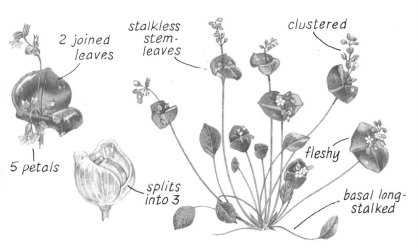

2 joined leaves

stalkless stem-leaves

clustered

5 petals

splits into 3

fleshy

basal long-stalked

Rather a succulent-looking plant with a pair of rounded leaves joined near the top of the stem, forming a green, cup-like foil for the white flowers. *Status:* introduced from western North America; scattered in south and west of area. *Similar species:* Pink Purslane differs in the larger, pink flowers and the stem leaves are not joined by their bases. Although related, Blinks looks quite different, with branched, rooting stems, narrow leaves and tiny flowers. It is usually found in water or on damp, seasonally flooded ground.

1 Pink Purslane (*M. sibirica*);
2 Blinks (*M. fontana*)

pink

tiny flowers

1.

not joined

narrow

2.

		FLOWERS	
SPRINGBEAUTY		**Position**	few, in unbranched cluster
Type	annual	**Bracts**	absent
Height	10–30cm	**Type**	⚥
Habitat	cultivated and waste ground; mainly sandy soils	**Size**	5–8mm
		Colour	white
Flowering	May–July	**Stalk**	twice as long as sepals
		Sepals	2, 1.5–3mm, oval
STEMS AND LEAVES		**Petals**	5, 2–3mm, all similar, sometimes notched at tip
Stem	more or less upright		
Root	fibrous	**Stamens**	5, joined to petals
Hairs	absent	**Stigmas**	3
Stipules	absent	**Ovary**	1, 1-celled
Leaves	at base or paired on opposite sides of stem		
		FRUIT	
Leaves 1	basal 10–25mm, elliptical to diamond-shaped, pointed to bluntish, edge unbroken	**Type**	single capsule, splitting into 3 parts, nearly globular
Leaf-stalk	longer than blade	**Size**	c2.5mm
Leaves 2	2 stem-leaves joined, more or less blunt	**Seeds**	1–3, c2mm, black, glossy
Leaf-stalk	absent		

Stellaria holostea **Greater Stitchwort**

The thread-like lower part of Stitchwort's stem looks impossibly thin and supports the plant only with the aid of its neighbours. Mixed with powdered acorns, the plant was used to treat a stitch or similar pains in the side. *Status:* native, common throughout area. *Similar species:* three other Stitchworts have whitish, papery bracts. Marsh Stitchwort has flowers 12–18mm across and bluish leaves; Lesser Stitchwort has flowers 5–12mm long and green leaves; Bog Stitchwort has smaller flowers, with petals shorter than the sepals.

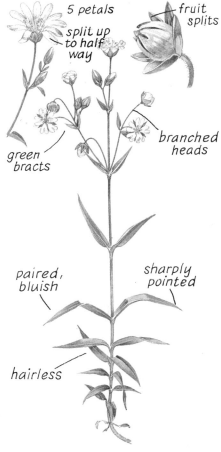

5 petals

split up to half way

fruit splits

branched heads

green bracts

paired, bluish

sharply pointed

hairless

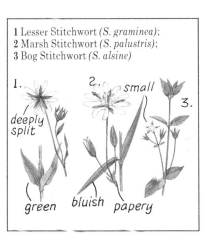

1 Lesser Stitchwort (*S. graminea*);
2 Marsh Stitchwort (*S. palustris*);
3 Bog Stitchwort (*S. alsine*)

1.

deeply split

2.

small

3.

green

bluish

papery

		FLOWERS	
GREATER STITCHWORT		**Position**	few, in loose heads
Type	perennial	**Bracts**	leaf-like
Height	15–60cm	**Type**	⚥
Habitat	woods or hedgerows	**Size**	20–30mm
Flowering	April–June	**Colour**	white
		Stalk	longer than flower
STEMS AND LEAVES		**Sepals**	5, 6–9mm, spear-shaped, with narrow, papery edge
Stem	turning upwards, slender at base, sharply 4-angled	**Petals**	5, 8–12mm, equal, split to about half-way
Root	slender, creeping stock		
Hairs	hairless or hairy above	**Stamens**	10
Stipules	absent	**Stigmas**	3
Leaves	paired on opposite sides of stem, 40–80mm, narrowly spear-shaped, bluish, finely pointed, edge rough, base rather broad	**Ovary**	1, 1-celled
		FRUIT	
		Type	globular capsule, splitting into 6
Leaf-stalk	absent	**Size**	6–8mm
		Seeds	numerous, 1.5–2mm, kidney-shaped, reddish-brown, rough with tiny outgrowths

Common Chickweed *Stellaria media*

This ubiquitous weed flowers at almost any time of the year, as weather permits, with insignificant petals shorter than the sepals. The stems are rather fleshy but weak, so that the Chickweed flops over the ground or other plants. Poultry and cage birds are fond of the seed. *Status:* native; very common throughout area. *Similar species:* two related species differ in having stalked leaves and ten stamens. Greater Chickweed has petals little longer than the sepals; and Wood Stitchwort has petals about twice as long as the sepals. Water Chickweed has large petals and five stigmas.

1 Greater Chickweed *(S. neglecta)*;
2 Wood Stitchwort *(S. nemorum)*;
3 Water Chickweed *(Myosoton aquaticum)*

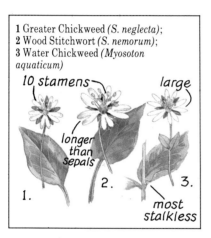

COMMON CHICKWEED		FLOWERS	
Type	annual	Position	many, loose head at stem-tip
Height	5–40cm	Bracts	present
Habitat	cultivated and waste ground; mostly rich soils	Type	☿
		Size	6–10mm
Flowering	January–December	Colour	white
		Stalk	lengthening in fruit
STEMS AND LEAVES		Sepals	5, narrow papery edge
Stem	much-branched, low-growing, turning upwards	Petals	5, mostly shorter than sepals, deeply 2-lobed
Root	slender tap-root	Stamens	usually 5, rarely up to 8
Hairs	2 lines along stem, sepals stickily hairy	Stigmas	3
		Ovary	1, 1-celled
Stipules	absent		
Leaves	paired on opposite sides of stem, 3–25mm, oval or elliptical, pointed, edge unbroken	**FRUIT**	
		Type	single capsule, narrowly egg-shaped, splits into 6
Leaf-stalk	stalked or upper stalkless	Size	5–6mm
		Seeds	many, 0.9–1.3mm, kidney-shaped, rough

Common Mouse-ear *Cerastium fontanum* subsp. *glabrescer*

Trailing through short grass or over open ground, the softly hairy shoots of the Common Mouse-ear often cover extensive areas bearing small clusters of starry, white flowers. *Status:* native; widespread throughout area. *Similar species:* Field Mouse-ear has larger petals, about twice as long as the sepals. Two annuals with petals no longer than the sepals are distinguished by the fruit-stalk. Sticky Mouse-ear is short-stalked, so there are tight clusters of fruits; and Little Mouse-ear has longer stalks and loose heads in fruit.

1 Sticky Mouse-ear *(C. glomeratum)*;
2 Little Mouse-ear *(C. semidecandrum)*; 3 Field Mouse-ear *(C. arvense)*

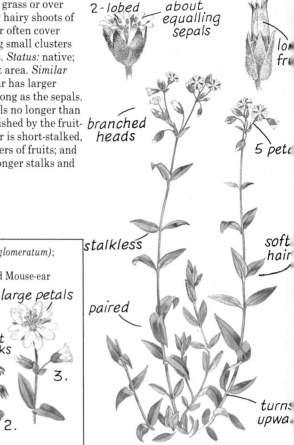

COMMON MOUSE-EAR		FLOWERS	
Type	perennial	Position	widely branched heads
Height	5–50cm	Bracts	upper papery-edged
Habitat	grassland, shingle, dunes	Type	☿
Flowering	April–September	Size	7–10mm
		Colour	white
STEMS AND LEAVES		Stalk	longer than flowers, hairy
Stem	low-growing, turning upright	Sepals	5–7, 3–5mm, oval, papery-edged, hairy except at tip
Root	slender, creeping stock		
Hairs	dense, white, flowers rarely stickily hairy	Petals	5, about equalling sepals, all similar, 2-lobed
Stipules	absent	Stamens	10, rarely 5
Leaves	paired on opposite sides of stem, 10–25mm, lower spear-shaped, blunt, base slender, upper oblong or elliptical, broad-based	Stigmas	5
		Ovary	1, 1-celled
		FRUIT	
Leaf-stalk	absent	Type	single, capsule, opening by 10 teeth, cylindrical, slightly curved
		Size	9–12mm
		Seeds	many, 0.4–0.8mm, kidney-shaped, reddish-brown, rough

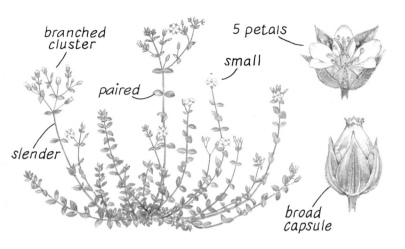

Arenaria serpyllifolia Thyme-leaved Sandwort

branched cluster

5 petals

small

paired

slender

broad capsule

A low-growing and easily overlooked plant, with sprawling, untidy stems and small, white flowers. This colonizer of bare ground is apparently distasteful to browsing rabbits. *Status:* native; common throughout area. *Similar species:* the more delicate Slender Sandwort has smaller flowers and a narrower, straight-sided capsule. Three-nerved Sandwort has larger leaves and flowers with much longer stalks. Sea Sandwort, from the strand-line of sandy beaches, has fleshy leaves and almost petalless female flowers on different plants from the male.

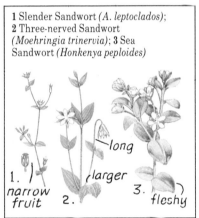

1 Slender Sandwort (*A. leptoclados*); **2** Three-nerved Sandwort (*Moehringia trinervia*); **3** Sea Sandwort (*Honkenya peploides*)

1. narrow fruit

long

2. larger

3. fleshy

	THYME-LEAVED SANDWORT		**FLOWERS**	
Type	annual or biennial	**Position**	numerous, in branched heads
Height	2.5–25cm	**Bracts**	present
Habitat	arable fields, downs, cliffs, walls; sandy or chalky soil	**Type**	☿
		Size	5–8mm
Flowering	June–August	**Colour**	white
		Stalk	most longer than flowers
	STEMS AND LEAVES	**Sepals**	5, 3–4.5mm, broadly spear-shaped, pointed
Stem	slender, turning upwards	**Petals**	5, equal, oval, undivided, shorter than sepals
Root	fibrous		
Hairs	roughly hairy throughout	**Stamens**	10 or fewer
Stipules	absent	**Stigmas**	3
Leaves	paired on opposite sides of stem, 2.5–8mm, oval, broadest below middle, grey-green, pointed, edge unbroken, broad-based	**Ovary**	1, 1-celled
		FRUIT	
		Type	single, capsule, opening by 6 teeth, oval, the sides curved
Leaf-stalk	mostly stalkless	**Size**	c4mm
		Seeds	many, 0.5–0.7mm, kidney-shaped, blackish, rough

Spergula arvensis Corn Spurrey

sepals nearly equal petals

fruit splits open

tiny seeds

5 petals

white

widely branched heads

Leaves of this plant are paired but each bears such a conspicuous basal tuft of leaves that the plant seemingly has rings of leaves. Corn Spurrey can be a serious weed in farmland, although its seeds were once used for meal or animal-feed. *Status:* native; weed, common, most of area. *Similar species:* the smaller Pearlworts lack stipules. Procumbent Pearlwort has four petals shorter than the sepals, or lacks petals. Knotted Pearlwort has five petals about twice as long as its sepals. Annual Knawel has only the five sepals, with the ovary half sunken in the flower-base.

clustered leaves

stipules

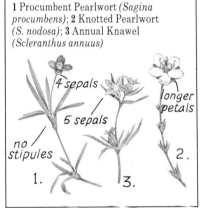

1 Procumbent Pearlwort (*Sagina procumbens*); **2** Knotted Pearlwort (*S. nodosa*); **3** Annual Knawel (*Scleranthus annuus*)

4 sepals

5 sepals

longer petals

no stipules

1.

3.

2.

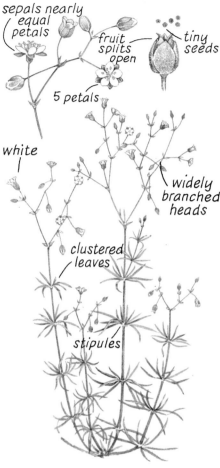

	CORN SPURREY		**Type**	☿
Type	annual	**Size**	4–7mm
Height	7.5–40cm	**Colour**	white
Habitat	arable fields, waste land; mainly lime-free soil	**Stalk**	10–25mm, base bent back, turning upright in fruit
Flowering	June–August	**Sepals**	5, 3–5mm, oval, edge narrowly papery
	STEMS AND LEAVES	**Petals**	5, equal, oval, undivided, just longer than sepals
Stem	turning upwards, bent at leaf-joints		
Root	fibrous	**Stamens**	10 or fewer
Hairs	stickily hairy throughout	**Stigmas**	5, short
Stipules	papery, soon falling	**Ovary**	1, 1-celled
Leaves	paired, each with basal tuft of leaves, 10–80mm, straight-sided, blunt, fleshy, edge unbroken	**FRUIT**	
		Type	single, capsule, opening by 5 teeth, egg-shaped
Leaf-stalk	absent	**Size**	5–6mm
	FLOWERS	**Seeds**	many, 1.2–1.5mm, round, often encircled by a wing, black, smooth or rough
Position	in widely branched heads		
Bracts	small, papery		

Greater Sea-spurrey *Spergularia media*

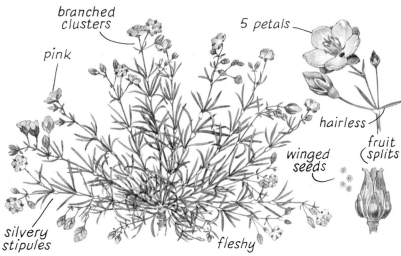

branched clusters

pink

5 petals

hairless

fruit splits

winged seeds

fleshy

silvery stipules

The fleshy shoots and attractive pink flowers of Sea-spurreys may be found on the drier parts of a salt-marsh, where flooding is restricted to exceptional high tides. *Status:* native; coasts throughout area. *Similar species:* no other species has all the seeds winged. Rock Sea-spurrey has dense, sticky hairs and grows on cliffs or among rocks. Lesser Sea-spurrey has smaller, deeper flowers and prefers drier parts of salt-marshes or salty places inland. Sand Spurrey has much smaller flowers and is often found on sandy soils inland.

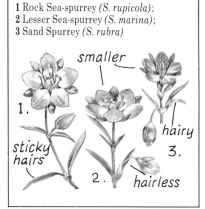

1 Rock Sea-spurrey *(S. rupicola)*;
2 Lesser Sea-spurrey *(S. marina)*;
3 Sand Spurrey *(S. rubra)*

smaller

sticky hairs

hairy

1.

2.

3.

hairless

GREATER SEA-SPURREY		
Type	perennial	
Height	10–35cm	
Habitat	salt-marshes; mud or sand	
Flowering	June–September	
STEMS AND LEAVES		
Stem	many, low-growing, turning or angled upwards	
Root	stout, branched stock	
Hairs	hairless or sepals sometimes stickily hairy	
Stipules	triangular, papery, silvery	
Leaves	paired on opposite sides of stem, 10–25mm, straight-sided, fleshy, tip hard, blunt to sharp, edge unbroken	
Leaf-stalk	absent	

FLOWERS	
Position	in widely branched head
Bracts	mostly small
Type	♂
Size	7.5–12mm
Colour	pink to whitish
Stalk	present
Sepals	5, 4–5mm, separate, blunt
Petals	5, 4.5–5.5mm, oval, blunt, edge not lobed
Stamens	usually 10
Stigmas	3
Ovary	1, 1-celled
FRUIT	
Type	single, capsule, splits into 3, withered sepals attached
Size	7–11mm
Seeds	c1.5mm, round, encircled by a pale wing

Red Campion *Silene dioica*

Typically a plant of the woodland margin, Red Campion is easily recognized by its rose-pink flowers and softly hairy leaves. This day-flowering Campion is usually pollinated by bees or hover-flies. *Status:* native, common except for parts of south. *Similar species:* Moss Campion is much smaller, with hairless leaves and grows on mountains. A plant of wet places, Ragged-Robin has deeply divided petals and hairless leaves. Sticky Catchfly has sticky stems just beneath each leaf and, like the previous species, capsules with five teeth.

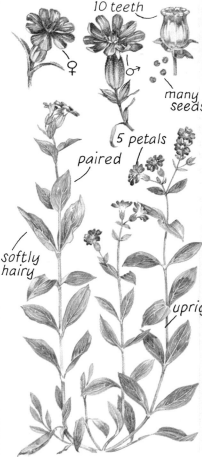

10 teeth

♀

♂

many seeds

5 petals

paired

softly hairy

uprig

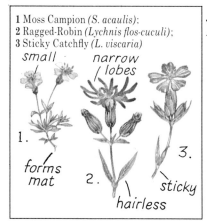

1 Moss Campion *(S. acaulis)*:
2 Ragged-Robin *(Lychnis flos-cuculi)*;
3 Sticky Catchfly *(L. viscaria)*

small

narrow lobes

1.

forms mat

2.

3.

sticky

hairless

RED CAMPION		
Type	perennial	
Height	20–90cm	
Habitat	woods, hedgerows, cliffs or limestone screes; mostly lime-rich soil	
Flowering	May–June	
STEMS AND LEAVES		
Stem	turning upright	
Root	slender, creeping stock	
Hairs	soft, may be sticky above	
Stipules	absent	
Leaves	paired on opposite sides of stem, 4–10mm, oval or oblong, pointed, edge unbroken	
Leaf-stalk	winged or upper stalkless	
FLOWERS		
Position	numerous, branched head at stem-tip, ♂ and ♀ flowers on different plants	

Bracts	present
Type	open during day, scentless
Size	18–25mm
Colour	rose-pink, rarely white
Stalk	5–15mm
Sepals	5, 12–17.5mm, joined into tube with pointed teeth
Petals	5, deeply 2-lobed with stalk-like base
Stamens	♂ with 10
Stigmas	♀ with 5
Ovary	1, 1-celled
FRUIT	
Type	1, capsule, opening by 10 curled back teeth, oval
Size	10–15mm
Seeds	many, black, kidney-shaped, rough with tiny outgrowths

Silene alba White Campion

Large, creamy-white flowers that open in the evening make the White Campion seem to glow in the dusk. Moths, drawn by the scent, pollinate the flowers. White Campion forms pink-flowered hybrids where it grows with Red Campion. *Status:* native or introduced to parts of west; common in most of the area. *Similar species:* several white-flowered Campions have only three stigmas. Bladder Campion and Sea Campion have swollen, bladder-like sepal-tubes, the latter species with cushion-like growth and few-flowered stems. Nottingham Catchfly has drooping flowers and smaller petals.

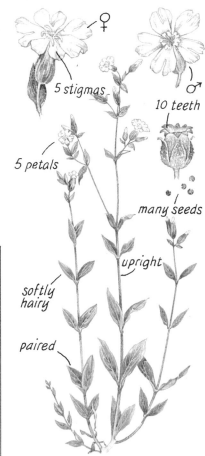

1 Bladder Campion *(S. vulgaris* subsp. *vulgaris)*; 2 Sea Campion *(S. vulgaris* subsp. *maritima)*; 3 Nottingham Catchfly *(S. nutans)*

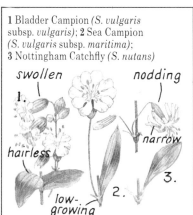

	WHITE CAMPION
Type	perennial
Height	30 -100cm
Habitat	cultivated and waste ground, hedgerows
Flowering	May–September
	STEMS AND LEAVES
Stem	upright, mostly branched
Root	thick, almost woody stock
Hairs	soft, stickily hairy above
Stipules	absent
Leaves	paired on opposite sides of stem, 30–100mm, elliptical or spear-shaped, pointed, edge unbroken, base narrowed
Leaf-stalk	only on lower leaves
	FLOWERS
Position	few, in branched heads, ♂ and ♀ on different plants
Bracts	present
Type	day-flowering, slight scent
Size	25–30mm
Colour	white
Stalk	elongating in fruit
Sepals	5, 23–30mm, joined into tube with narrow teeth
Petals	5, deeply 2-lobed
Stamens	♂ with 10
Stigmas	♀ with 5
Ovary	1, 1-celled
	FRUIT
Type	single, capsule, opens by 10 teeth, egg-shaped
Size	o15mm
Seeds	numerous, 1.3–1.5mm, kidney shaped, grey, rough

White Campion has deeply notched petals, each with scales at the base.

Soapwort *Saponaria officinalis*

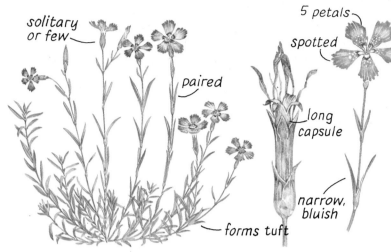

Clumps of bluish foliage and large pink flowers enable Soapwort to be identified readily. Once an invaluable commodity, the plant was used for washing with long before soap, a usage that still persists in parts of the world. *Status:* native or naturalized in north. *Similar species:* plants with similar pinkish flowers include Cowherb, which has an inflated sepal-tube. Night-flowering Catchfly opens by night but the yellow-backed petals roll up in the morning. Corncockle, which has long sepals, was once abundant in cornfields but is now rare.

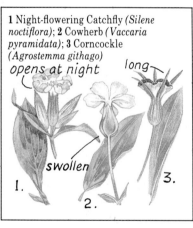

1 Night-flowering Catchfly (*Silene noctiflora*); 2 Cowherb (*Vaccaria pyramidata*); 3 Corncockle (*Agrostemma githago*)

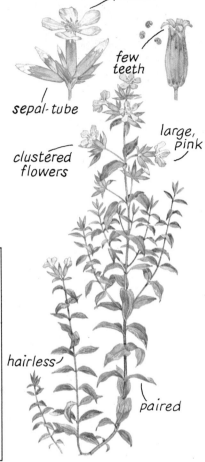

SOAPWORT		FLOWERS	
Type	perennial	**Position**	few, in heads at stem-tips
Height	30–90cm	**Bracts**	present
Habitat	hedgerows, damp woods, grassy banks, roadsides, often near water or houses	**Type**	⚥
		Size	*c*25mm
		Colour	pink
Flowering	July–September	**Stalk**	very short
		Sepals	5, 18–20mm, joined into tube with short teeth
STEMS AND LEAVES		**Petals**	5, oval, tip rounded or notched, base stalk-like
Stem	upright or angled upwards, sometimes branched above	**Stamens**	10
		Stigmas	2, rarely 3
Root	stout rhizome and long, slender, underground stems	**Ovary**	1, 1-celled
Hairs	more or less hairless	**FRUIT**	
Stipules	absent	**Type**	single, capsule, almost oblong, opens by 4–5 teeth
Leaves	paired on opposite sides of stem, 50–100mm, oval or elliptical, pointed, edge unbroken	**Size**	2–2.5mm
		Seeds	many, *c*1.8mm, kidney-shaped, blackish, rough
Leaf-stalk	absent		

Maiden Pink *Dianthus deltoides*

Slender stems and leaves make this plant almost invisible in grassland, until the opening flowers of intense pink herald its presence. Pinks have long been cultivated, and often differ greatly from their wild progenitors. *Status:* native; scattered localities in lowland parts of area. *Similar species:* Cheddar Pink, one of the rarest native species in Britain and specially protected by law, has larger, pale flowers. Deptford Pink has clustered flowers with slender bracts. Childing Pink has small heads of flowers, opening singly, enclosed by broad, papery scales.

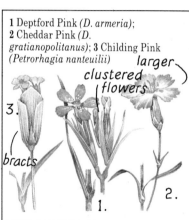

1 Deptford Pink (*D. armeria*); 2 Cheddar Pink (*D. gratianopolitanus*); 3 Childing Pink (*Petrorhagia nanteuilii*)

MAIDEN PINK		Bracts	present
Type	perennial	**Type**	⚥, scentless
Height	15–45cm	**Size**	16–20mm
Habitat	dry grassy places, fields, banks and hills	**Colour**	deep pink with pale spots or white, banded deep pink
Flowering	June–September	**Stalk**	present
		Sepals	5, 12–17mm, joined into tube, 2–4 scales at base
STEMS AND LEAVES		**Petals**	5, equal, broad, toothed, the base stalk-like
Stem	forming low tufts, turning upright to flower	**Stamens**	10
Root	slender, creeping stock	**Stigmas**	2
Hairs	rough hairs on leaf-edges	**Ovary**	1, 1-celled
Stipules	absent		
Leaves	paired, 10–25mm, narrowly spear-shaped, bluish, pointed or lowest blunt, edge unbroken	**FRUIT**	
		Type	single, capsule, opening by 4 teeth, cylindrical
Leaf-stalk	absent	**Size**	*c*15mm
		Seeds	many, 2–2.5mm, oval, flattened, black
FLOWERS			
Position	1–3, at stem-tips		

Buttercups and Water-lilies

Despite the similarity of their flowers, this group consists of two separate families, one being predominantly terrestrial and the other entirely aquatic. Both are generally regarded as having a number of primitive characteristics, and are often classified near the Magnolias. Buttercups form a large family containing many familiar garden plants, such as Aquilegias, Anemones, *Clematis*, Delphiniums and Winter Aconites. The native flowers are mostly insect-pollinated though some, notably Meadow-rues, are wind-pollinated and have insignificant flowers. There is much variation in the form of the fruit. Some have a capsule which splits open to release the seeds. In contrast, Buttercups have small, dry, almost nut-like fruits which do not open. Instead, many have hooks on the fruit and are dispersed by animals. Pasqueflowers have long, feathery plumes on the fruits that aid dispersal by wind.

Water-crowfoots belong to the Buttercup family but are aquatic plants, most of which have finely divided, submerged leaves. The Water-lilies are similar in many respects to the Buttercups, particularly the Yellow Water-lily. All species are aquatic with submerged fleshy stems and broad, commonly floating leaves. Many species are grown for ornament and the seeds or fleshy stems of some are edible.

Restricted to shallow water, the white flowers of Common Water-crowfoot form a halo around the edge of a pond.

White Water-lily *Nymphaea alba*

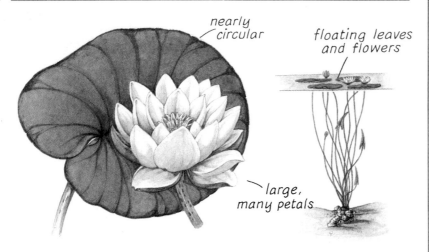

nearly circular

floating leaves and flowers

large, many petals

Large, white, cup-shaped flowers and nearly circular leaves floating on the water's surface easily identify the White Water-lily. Plants in the north-west often have much smaller flowers than elsewhere. *Status:* native; throughout area. *Similar species:* Yellow Water-lily has smaller flowers held above the water surface. The ripe fruit has an odd alcohol-like smell. Least Water-lily is even smaller and has non-overlapping petals. True to its name, Fringed Water-lily has fringed petals but also elongated stems, short leaf-stalks, and is a relative of the Gentians.

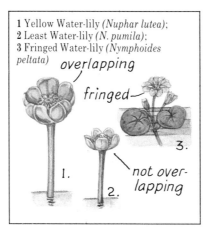

1 Yellow Water-lily *(Nuphar lutea);*
2 Least Water-lily *(N. pumila);*
3 Fringed Water-lily *(Nymphoides peltata)*

overlapping

fringed

not over-lapping

	WHITE WATER-LILY		FLOWERS	
Type	perennial	**Position**	few	
Height	underwater, up to 300cm	**Type**	⚲, floating, scented	
Habitat	lakes and ponds	**Size**	50–200mm	
Flowering	July–August	**Colour**	white	
		Stalk	up to 3m	
	STEMS AND LEAVES	**Sepals**	4, spear-shaped, whitish	
Stem	short, forming a rhizome	**Petals**	20–25, spirally arranged	
Root	fleshy from rhizome	**Stamens**	numerous	
Hairs	absent	**Stigmas**	many, forming radiating lines on top of ovary	
Stipules	present	**Ovary**	1, many-celled	
Leaves	at base of plant, 100–300mm, nearly circular, floating, dark, glossy green above, often reddish below, rounded, edge unbroken, base forming deep cleft in circular outline		FRUIT	
		Type	single, spongy capsule, opens underwater, oval to nearly globular	
Leaf-stalk	up to 3m	**Size**	16–40mm	
		Seeds	numerous, c3mm, floating	

Common Water-crowfoot *Ranunculus aquatilis*

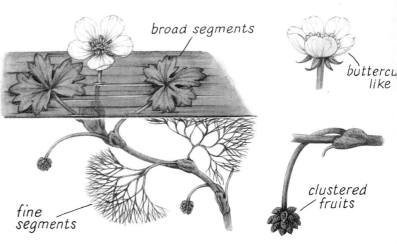

broad segments

buttercup like

fine segments

clustered fruits

Dotted over the surface of a pond sometimes in great profusion, Water-crowfoot's white and yellow-centred flowers contrast to perfection the reflected blue of a summer's sky. This is a true amphibious plant, having mastered both land and water. Out of the water the leaves are lobed like those of Buttercups, but submerged leaves are finely divided. *Status:* native; most lowland areas. *Similar species:* species in flowing waters, like River Water-crowfoot and Thread-leaved Water-crowfoot, have only the finely divided leaves; Ivy-leaved Crowfoot has only the land form of leaf.

1 River Water-crowfoot *(R. fluitans);*
2 Thread-leaved Water-crowfoot *(R. trichophyllus);* 3 Ivy-leaved Crowfoot *(R. hederaceus)*

1. all long, fine

2. all fine

all broad 3.

	COMMON WATER-CROWFOOT		FLOWERS	
Type	perennial or annual	**Position**	1, opposite upper leaf	
Height	very variable	**Bracts**	absent	
Habitat	ponds, slow streams or ditches	**Type**	⚲	
Flowering	May–June	**Size**	12–18mm	
		Colour	white with yellow base	
	STEMS AND LEAVES	**Stalk**	20–50mm	
Stem	underwater or low-growing	**Sepals**	usually 5	
Root	fibrous	**Petals**	5, 5–10mm, equal	
Hairs	sparse, mainly on stipules and stalks of upper leaves	**Stamens**	13 or more	
		Stigmas	1 per ovary	
Stipules	present	**Ovaries**	numerous, 1-celled	
Leaves	spirally arranged			
Leaves 1	underwater, 30–60(–80)mm, with hair-like segments		FRUIT	
Leaf-stalk	often shorter than blade	**Type**	numerous, nut-like, not opening, egg-shaped, short-beaked, hairy, in rounded head	
Leaves 2	floating, nearly circular, with 3–7 toothed lobes			
		Size	1.5–2mm	
Leaf-stalk	usually longer than blade	**Seeds**	1, not released	

Ranunculus acris Meadow Buttercup

One of the most familiar summer flowers, Meadow Buttercup abounds in pastures everywhere. The rich yellow of the cup-shaped flowers is associated in folklore with the yellow butter from cattle that graze the pastures. *Status:* native; common, most of area. *Similar species:* two other Buttercups have a stalked middle lobe to the leaves. Creeping Buttercup has creeping, rooting stems, and Bulbous Buttercup has a bulb-like base to the stem and sepals bent downwards. Goldilocks Buttercup has basal leaves that are less divided, and often has petals missing.

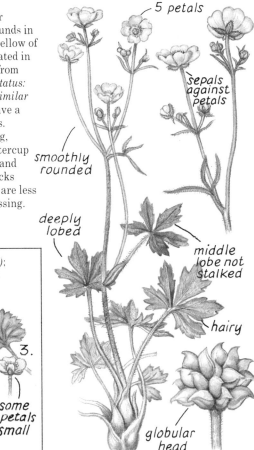

1 Bulbous Buttercup (*R. bulbosus*);
2 Creeping Buttercup (*R. repens*);
3 Goldilocks Buttercup (*R. auricomus*)

1. stalked
bent back
grooved
bulb-like
creeping
2.
3.
some petals small

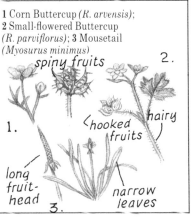

5 petals
sepals against petals
smoothly rounded
deeply lobed
middle lobe not stalked
hairy
globular head

Ranunculus sceleratus Celery-leaved Buttercup

Lobed, glossy leaves with broad, fleshy leaf-stalks give a vague resemblance to Celery, which grows in similar damp places, and provide the plant with its common name. The flowers are much smaller than those of most common buttercups, and give way to unusually long heads of tiny fruits. *Status:* native; common, most of area. *Similar species:* Corn Buttercup has few spiny fruits. The hairy Small-flowered Buttercup has few, hooked fruits. A buttercup relative with much more elongated heads, which give the plant its common name, is the Mousetail.

1 Corn Buttercup (*R. arvensis*);
2 Small-flowered Buttercup (*R. parviflorus*); 3 Mousetail (*Myosurus minimus*)

spiny fruits
2.
1.
hooked fruits
hairy
long fruit-head
3.
narrow leaves

5 petals
elongated heads
small flowers
grooved
hairless
lobed leaves
fleshy stalks

MEADOW BUTTERCUP		FLOWERS	
Type	perennial	**Position**	numerous, in branched head from upper stem
Height	15–100cm		
Habitat	damp meadows, grassy places; lime-rich or neutral soils	**Bracts**	present
		Type	mostly ♂, cup-shaped
		Size	18–25mm
Flowering	June–July	**Colour**	glossy yellow or whitish
		Stalk	longer than flower
STEMS AND LEAVES		**Sepals**	usually 5, oval, hairy, pressed against petals
Stem	upright, base hollow		
Root	fibrous from stout stock	**Petals**	usually 5, 6–11mm, rounded
Hairs	pressed close on leaves, projecting on stem	**Stamens**	numerous
		Stigmas	1 per ovary
Stipules	absent	**Ovaries**	numerous, 1-celled
Leaves	basal with 2–7 toothed lobes; stem-leaves scattered, upper narrowly lobed	**FRUIT**	
		Type	many in rounded head, nut-like, not opening, egg-shaped, hooked beak, smooth
Leaf-stalk	long or stalkless above		
		Size	2.5–3mm
		Seeds	1, not released

CELERY-LEAVED BUTTERCUP		FLOWERS	
Type	annual	**Position**	numerous, in widely branched heads
Height	20–60cm		
Habitat	ponds, ditches or streams; damp soil or mud	**Type**	♂
		Size	5–10mm
Flowering	May–September	**Colour**	pale yellow
		Stalk	furrowed
STEMS AND LEAVES		**Sepals**	usually 5, bent downwards
Stem	upright, stout, hollow	**Petals**	5, equal, narrowly oval, little longer than sepals
Root	fibrous		
Hairs	more or less hairless	**Stamens**	numerous
Stipules	absent	**Stigmas**	1 per ovary
Leaves	spirally arranged around stem; lowest kidney shaped, 3-lobed, each lobe toothed or lobed again; uppermost with narrow, unbroken lobes	**Ovaries**	numerous, 1-celled
		FRUIT	
		Type	70–250 in oblong head, nut-like, not opening, rounded, slightly beaked
Leaf-stalk	long, broad-based or absent above		
		Size	<1mm
		Seeds	1, not released

Lesser Celandine *Ranunculus ficaria* subsp. *ficaria*

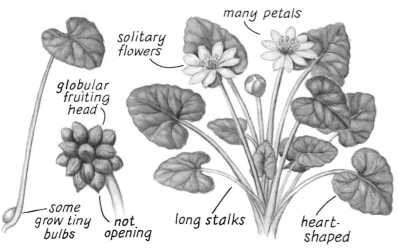

many petals

solitary flowers

globular fruiting head

some grow tiny bulbs

not opening

long stalks

heart-shaped

The rich yellow flowers open with the Spring sunshine, often in such great numbers that they carpet with gold a woodland floor or hedge-bank. Some plants have tiny swollen buds called bulbils at the base of the leaves, and all plants have small tubers through which they are able to last the Winter. *Status:* native, common throughout area. *Similar species:* Winter Aconite is similarly a Spring flower with numerous yellow petals, but differs in the collar-like bracts below the flower and the lobed leaves which grow only after flowering is finished.

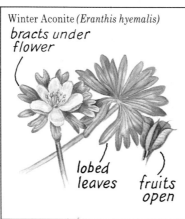

Winter Aconite (*Eranthis hyemalis*)

bracts under flower

lobed leaves

fruits open

	LESSER CELANDINE		FLOWERS	
Type	perennial	Position	single, at tip of stem	
Height	5–25cm	Bracts	absent	
Habitat	woods, hedgerows, grassy places, stream-banks	Type	⚘	
		Size	20–30mm	
Flowering	March–May	Colour	bright, glossy yellow, fading nearly white	
STEMS AND LEAVES		Stalk	much longer than flower	
Stem	angled upwards, base rooting	Sepals	3, oval	
Root	fibrous, with many small, swollen tubers	Petals	8–12, narrowly oval	
		Stamens	numerous	
Hairs	absent	Stigmas	1 per ovary	
Stipules	absent	Ovaries	numerous, 1-celled	
Leaves	from base and spirally arranged around stem, 10–40mm, heart-shaped, blunt or rounded, edge shallowly toothed, base notched	**FRUIT**		
		Type	many in rounded head, not opening, egg-shaped to globular, short-beaked	
Leaf-stalk	base broad, overlapping other stalks	Size	up to 2.5mm	
		Seeds	1, not released	

Lesser Spearwort *Ranunculus flammula*

Common by streamsides and in damp meadows, this buttercup relative can be distinguished from the more usual kinds by the narrow leaves without lobes. The plant should be treated with care for it is acrid, like other Buttercups: leaves or roots ground with salt quickly blister the skin and, in the sixteenth century, such a preparation was used to treat sores caused by bubonic plague. *Status:* native; common throughout area. *Similar species:* Greater Spearwort is generally a taller plant, often over a metre tall, differing in the larger leaves and flowers.

5 petals

branched stems

grooved

narrow leaves

globular fruiting head

not lobed

base rooting

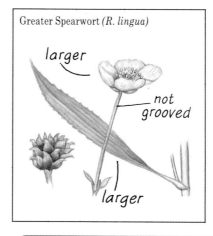

Greater Spearwort (*R. lingua*)

larger

not grooved

larger

	LESSER SPEARWORT		FLOWERS	
Type	perennial	Position	1 or few, in branched head at tip of stem	
Height	8–50cm			
Habitat	wet places	Type	⚘	
Flowering	May–September	Size	8–20mm, rarely 25mm	
		Colour	pale yellow, glossy	
STEMS AND LEAVES		Stalk	present	
Stem	angled upwards, sometimes creeping and rooting	Sepals	5, greenish yellow	
		Petals	5, equal, broadly oval to nearly circular	
Root	fibrous			
Hairs	more or less hairless	Stamens	numerous	
Stipules	absent	Stigmas	1 per ovary	
Leaves	spirally arranged on stem, 10–50mm, mostly spear-shaped or oval, rarely narrow, blunt to sharp, edge unbroken or toothed, base rounded, heart-shaped or tapered	Ovaries	numerous, 1-celled	
		FRUIT		
		Type	20–60 in rounded head, nut-like, not opening, egg-shaped, bluntly beaked tip, minutely pitted	
Leaf-stalk	long below, absent above	Size	1–2mm	
		Seeds	1 per fruit, not separate	

Helleborus viridis Green Hellebore

broad sepals

petals

green

deeply lobed

fruit

An imposing plant with large, hand-shaped leaves but, unusually for such a large-flowered species, the flowers are green and easily overlooked. The sepals are large and showy, whereas the petals are reduced to tubular structures which produce nectar. This is a close relative of the white-flowered Christmas Rose of gardens. *Status:* native or introduced in some places; scattered localities in southern half of the area. *Similar species:* Stinking Hellebore is easily distinguished by the smaller, more cup-shaped or almost globular flowers, edged with reddish purple.

Stinking Hellebore (*H. foetidus*)

reddish edge

cup-shaped

GREEN HELLEBORE		FLOWERS	
Type	perennial	Position	2–4, in widely branched head at tip of stem
Height	20–40cm	Type	☿
Habitat	woods and scrub, moist, lime-rich soils or scree	Size	30–50mm
		Colour	yellowish green
Flowering	March–April	Stalk	slightly nodding
		Sepals	5, equal, elliptical or oval, petal-like
STEMS AND LEAVES		Petals	9–12, much smaller than sepals, tubular, green
Stem	upright, little-branched		
Root	stout, blackish stock	Stamens	numerous
Hairs	absent or few above	Stigmas	1 per ovary
Stipules	absent	Ovaries	3–8, 1-celled
Leaves	from base or scattered on stem, basal leaves usually 2, with 7–13 elliptical, finger-like, pointed lobes, edge toothed	**FRUIT**	
		Type	3–8, pod-like, splits down inner edge to release seeds
Leaf-stalk	long or absent on stem-leaves	Size	c20mm
		Seeds	numerous, with fleshy white ridge on one side

Caltha palustris Marsh-marigold

One of the most imposing plants of damp meadows in late Spring, but at its most luxuriant in wet woodland. Much folklore has been associated with the large, golden, cup-shaped flowers and the plant has been given many common names, including May-blobs and Kingcups. *Status:* native; common but rarer towards south. *Similar species:* Globeflower, named after the ball-shaped buds and young flowers, is a mountain plant of similar wet places. There is a double form grown in gardens, which has petal-like stamens.

splitting open

several fruits

many stamens

cup-shaped

not lobed

base heart-shaped

broad

Globeflower (*Trollius europaeus*)

globular

deeply lobed

MARSH-MARIGOLD		FLOWERS	
Type	perennial	Position	few, wide-branched head from upper part of stem
Height	15–30mm, rarely 60mm	Type	☿
Habitat	ditches, damp woods, marshes; wet soils	Size	16–50mm
		Colour	bright golden-yellow, often tinged green beneath
Flowering	March–July	Stalk	much longer than flower
STEMS AND LEAVES		Perianth	5–8 segments, 10–25mm, equal, rounded
Stem	upright or sometimes low growing, hollow	Stamens	50 100
Root	fibrous from thick, fleshy underground stem	Stigmas	1 per ovary
		Ovaries	5–15, 1-celled
Hairs	absent		
Stipules	absent	**FRUIT**	
Leaves	mostly at base of plant, few scattered around stem, kidney-shaped or triangular, tip rounded, edge toothed, base heart-shaped	Type	5–15, pod-like, elongated, splitting along inner face, realeasing seeds
		Size	9–18mm
Leaf-stalk	long or nearly stalkless stem-leaves	Seeds	numerous, up to 2.5mm

Wood Anemone *Anemone nemorosa*

A Spring flower which often grows in such great profusion that it carpets the floor of woodland with delicate, many-petalled flowers of white, tinged and veined with purple. The main leaves arise from the ground only after flowering is completed. *Status:* native; often very common, throughout area. *Similar species:* Blue Anemone is grown for its beautiful blue flowers and often becomes naturalized. The native, summer-flowering Pasqueflower has larger, purple flowers and heads of long-plumed fruits. Pale Pasqueflower grows in mountains only in the east of the area.

usually 6 petals
many stamens
cluster of fruits
not opening
solitary
3 · stem-leaves
lower leaf long-stalked

1 Blue Anemone *(A. apennina)*;
2 Pasqueflower *(Pulsatilla vulgaris)*;
3 Pale Pasqueflower *(P. vernalis)*

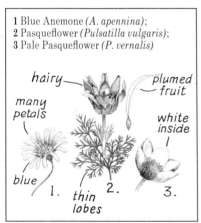

hairy
many petals
blue
plumed fruit
white inside
1.
thin lobes
2.
3.

WOOD ANEMONE			
Type	perennial	**Bracts**	absent
Height	6–30cm	**Type**	☿
Habitat	deciduous woods; all but most acid or wet soils	**Size**	20–40mm
		Colour	white, tinged and veined with purplish pink, rarely reddish purple
Flowering	March–May		
		Stalk	long, upright or nodding
STEMS AND LEAVES		**Perianth**	5–9 segments, usually 6–7, equal, oblong-elliptical
Stem	upright, unbranched		
Root	fibrous from thin, creeping underground stem	**Stamens**	50–70
		Stigmas	1 per ovary
Hairs	absent or sparse on leaves	**Ovaries**	10–30, 1-celled
Stipules	absent		
Leaves	3 around stem, 1–2 from base after flowering, 3-parted, with pointed, toothed lobes	**FRUIT**	
		Type	10–30, nut-like, not opening, in pendulous, globular clusters, egg-shaped, beaked, downy
Leaf-stalk	long or stem-leaves short		
		Size	4–4.5mm
FLOWERS		**Seeds**	1 per fruit, not released
Position	single, from tip of stem		

Traveller's-joy *Clematis vitalba*

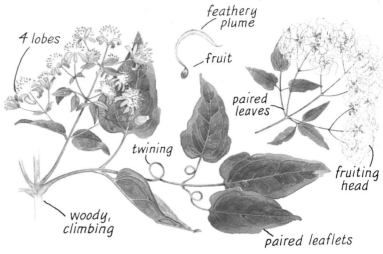

feathery plume
4 lobes
fruit
paired leaves
twining
fruiting head
woody, climbing
paired leaflets

Draped over bushes or trees, this plant is perhaps most familiar when the cloud-like masses of white-plumed fruits earn another common name, 'Old Man's Beard'. The thick, rope-like stems loop and twist their way to the tree-tops, like tropical lianas. *Status:* native, southern half of area. *Similar species:* two species are native to the south-east of the area but are cultivated and sometimes escape. Alpine Clematis is a mountain plant with blue and white flowers. *Clematis recta* has non-climbing, annual stems and large heads of tiny, white, hawthorn-scented flowers.

1 Alpine Clematis *(C. alpina)*;
2 *C. recta*

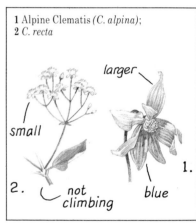

larger
small
2.
not climbing
blue
1.

TRAVELLER'S-JOY			
Type	perennial	**FLOWERS**	
Height	up to 30m	**Position**	many in broad head from tip of stem or leaf-base
Habitat	woods, scrub or hedgerows; mostly lime-rich soils		
		Bracts	present
Flowering	July–August	**Type**	☿, fragrant
		Size	c20mm
STEMS AND LEAVES		**Colour**	greenish white
Stem	woody, vine-like, becoming very stout	**Stalk**	about equalling flower
		Perianth	usually 4, hairy beneath
Root	woody stock	**Stamens**	numerous
Hairs	hairless except for flowers	**Stigmas**	1 per ovary
Stipules	absent	**Ovaries**	numerous, 1-celled
Leaves	paired, either side of stem, 1–2 pairs of oval, pointed, toothed leaflets 30–100mm long, leaflet or tendril at tip, leaflets usually toothed, base rounded to heart-shaped	**FRUIT**	
		Type	numerous, nut-like with long, whitish, feathery plume, not opening, in a rounded cluster
		Size	c25mm
Leaf-stalk	twining	**Seeds**	1, not released

Aquilegia vulgaris **Columbine**

Columbine has unusual nodding flowers: all five of the petals are horn-shaped, each tip drawn out and curved over into a hollow spur. The spur contains a drop of sweet nectar, and it is this that attracts pollinating insects to the plant. *Status:* native but cultivated and often escaping. *Similar species:* Larkspur has only one spur and one pod-like fruit. Forking Larkspur differs in the wider branching, divided lower bracts and shorter fruit. The hooded or helmet-shaped purple flowers of Monk's-hood conceal the extremely poisonous nature of the plant.

1 Forking Larkspur *(Consolida regalis);* **2** Larkspur *(C. ambigua);* **3** Monk's-hood *(Aconitum napellus)*

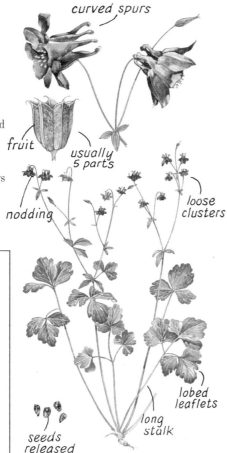

	COLUMBINE		FLOWERS
Type	perennial	**Position**	few, in loose cluster towards top of stem
Height	40–100cm		
Habitat	damp places on lime-rich soils, woods, fens	**Type**	☿
		Size	30–50mm
Flowering	May–June	**Colour**	blue, white or pink
		Stalk	nodding
	STEMS AND LEAVES	**Sepals**	5, 15–30mm, oval, pointed, coloured like petals
Stem	upright, branched above		
Root	short, thick, stock	**Petals**	5, c30mm, oblong, with curved, spur-like base
Hairs	hairless or softly hairy		
Stipules	absent	**Stamens**	c50
Leaves	basal or scattered around stem, divided into blunt, irregularly 3-lobed, toothed, leaflets, bluish green above	**Stigmas**	1 per ovary
		Ovaries	5, rarely 10, 1-celled
			FRUIT
		Type	5, rarely 10, pod-like, opening along inner edge, upright
Leaf-stalk	long, broad-based to absent on stem leaves		
		Size	15–25mm
		Seeds	numerous, 2–2.5mm, globular, black, glossy

Thalictrum flavum **Common Meadow-rue**

A stiffly upright plant of marshy places, forming clumps of rather coarse, dark leaves, cut into wedge-shaped leaflets. The most conspicuous feature of the fluffy flowers is the cluster of yellow stamens. *Status:* native, most of area except parts of north. *Similar species:* two species with smaller leaflets and nodding flowers are Lesser Meadow-rue, which has widely branched flower-heads, and Alpine Meadow-rue, which has unbranched spikes of flowers. Baneberry has a similar look in flower, though with coarse, toothed leaves, but it is easily distinguished in fruit by its black berries.

1 Lesser Meadow-rue *(T. minus);* **2** Alpine Meadow-rue *(T. alpinum);* **3** Baneberry *(Actaea spicata)*

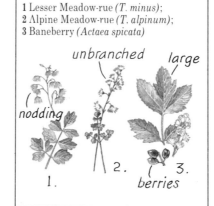

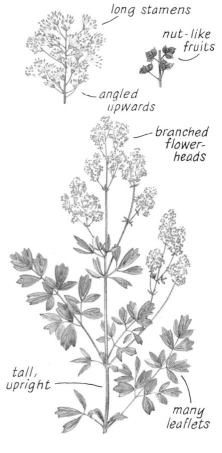

	COMMON MEADOW-RUE		FLOWERS
Type	perennial	**Position**	numerous in dense, branched heads
Height	50–100cm		
Habitat	meadows, fens, stream-banks; wet soils	**Bracts**	present
		Type	☿, fragrant, upright
Flowering	July–August	**Size**	6–10mm
		Colour	whitish yellow
	STEMS AND LEAVES	**Stalk**	about equalling flower
Stem	upright, little-branched	**Perianth**	4, 3–4mm, narrow
Root	from creeping, slender, underground stem	**Stamens**	numerous, yellow, held above flower
Hairs	more or less hairless	**Stigmas**	1 per ovary
Stipules	present	**Ovaries**	few, 1-celled
Leaves	basal or spirally arranged around stem, divided 2–3 times, with oval to wedge-shaped leaflets, dark green above, tip bluntish, 3–4 lobed towards tip		**FRUIT**
		Type	few, nut-like, not opening, egg-shaped to ellipsoid with 6 ribs
Leaf-stalk	present or upper stalkless	**Size**	1.5–2.5mm
		Seeds	1, not released

Cabbages, Poppies, Fumitories and Mignonettes

The flowers of this grouping of families characteristically have four petals, though the number in the Mignonettes is somewhat variable. The petals are more or less equal in Poppies and most Cabbages, but unequal in the Mignonettes and Fumitories. Of these families, the Cabbage family is much the largest, with many agriculturally important species such as Brussels Sprouts, Cauliflower and Oilseed Rape, as well as vegetables of minor importance, such as Cress and Horseradish, and ornamental plants like Alyssum, Stocks and Wallflower.

Poppies are now more familiar as plants of waste ground or new road verges, rather than the abundant cornfield weeds that they once were. Most species have the characteristic fruit; a capsule with pores around the top through which the seeds escape. However, the fruits of the Sea Poppy and Greater Celandine split longitudinally to release the seeds.

Fumitories generally have divided, somewhat fern-like foliage and curious flowers with unequal petals. The family includes the garden plant, Love-lies-bleeding.

Mignonettes are generally seen as roadside weeds in northern Europe, but one species is cultivated in gardens for its sweet scent. Weld was formerly widely cultivated as a dye-plant.

Arable fields with the scarlet of Common Poppy stretching to the horizon were once a familiar sight, but are now rare.

Papaver rhoeas Common Poppy

Poppies paint a new road verge or embankment a brilliant hue in their first year, but rapidly decline and after a few years exist only as seeds in the soil, waiting until the land is turned again. Once a common sight in cornfields, more effective seed cleaning and use of selective herbicides have made Poppies much rarer. *Status:* native; often very common, rare in parts of north. *Similar species:* two Poppies have elongated fruits: the Long-headed Poppy with a smooth fruit, and the Prickly Poppy with a spiny fruit. Opium Poppy has purplish flowers and much larger capsules.

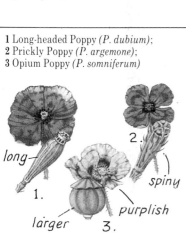

1 Long-headed Poppy (*P. dubium*);
2 Prickly Poppy (*P. argemone*);
3 Opium Poppy (*P. somniferum*)

long

1.

larger

2.

spiny

purplish

3.

4 petals

nodding buds

over-lapping

leaflets

broad capsule

	COMMON POPPY		Type	
Type	annual		**Size**	70–100mm
Height	20–60cm		**Colour**	scarlet, rarely pink or white, usually with blackish blotch at base
Habitat	newly dug and waste ground, arable fields		**Stalk**	longer than flower
Flowering	June–August		**Sepals**	2, bristly, soon falling
			Petals	4, 20–40mm, rounded, crumpled, soon falling
	STEMS AND LEAVES		**Stamens**	numerous, anthers bluish
Stem	upright, milky sap		**Stigmas**	8–12, forming radiating bands on top of ovary
Root	slender taproot		**Ovary**	1, with 8–12 cells
Hairs	stiff, outward-pointing			
Stipules	absent			**FRUIT**
Leaves	at base or spirally around stem, 30–150mm, cut into narrow lobes or leaflets, upper leaves mostly 3-lobed, pointed, toothed		**Type**	1, capsule, opens by ring of pores at top, nearly globular, smooth
Leaf-stalk	present or upper stalkless		**Size**	10–20mm
			Seeds	many, *c*1mm, blackish
	FLOWERS			
Position	single, from base of leaf			
Bracts	absent			

Glaucium flavum Yellow Horned-poppy

A striking plant of coastal dunes and shingle banks, with large yellow flowers held above blue-green foliage. Its curved, horn-like fruits, unlike those of the cornfield Poppies, split open lengthways leaving the seeds embedded in a middle wall. *Status:* native, most coasts. *Similar species:* Welsh Poppy, a plant of inland, mostly mountainous, areas, has leaves that are more divided, and much shorter fruits which open by pores like common Poppies. This species is related to the magnificent blue Himalayan Poppy, which is cultivated in gardens.

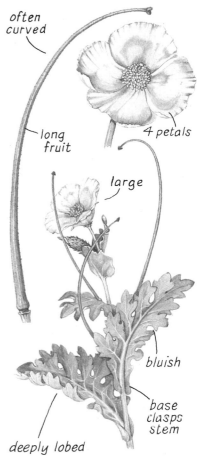

often curved

4 petals

long fruit

large

bluish

base clasps stem

deeply lobed

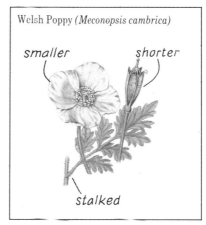

Welsh Poppy (*Meconopsis cambrica*)

smaller

shorter

stalked

	YELLOW HORNED-POPPY			FLOWERS
Type	perennial or biennial		**Position**	single, from base of leaf
Height	30–90cm		**Bracts**	absent
Habitat	mainly dunes or shingle banks by sea		**Type**	
Flowering	June–September		**Size**	60–90mm
			Colour	yellow
	STEMS AND LEAVES		**Stalk**	short
Stem	upright, branched, with yellow sap when cut		**Sepals**	2, separate, soon falling
Root	thick tap-root		**Petals**	4, almost equal, nearly circular
Hairs	rather sparse, rough		**Stamens**	numerous, yellow
Stipules	absent		**Stigmas**	2, nearly stalkless
Leaves	from base or scattered around stem, 150–350mm, bluish green, tip blunt, edge lobed and toothed, often wavy		**Ovary**	1, 2-celled
				FRUIT
Leaf-stalk	present or absent on upper leaves		**Type**	1, capsule, 2 sides splitting almost to base, long, thin, usually curved
			Size	150–300mm
			Seeds	numerous, minutely pitted

Greater Celandine *Chelidonium majus*

The flowers of Greater Celandine look like tiny yellow Poppies, but its fruits appear more like those of the Cresses and Cabbages. The slender capsule splits open from the base releasing tiny black seeds, each with a fleshy, oily outgrowth that is eagerly sought by ants that carry off and disperse the seeds. The plant was formerly widely used for the treatment of sore or cloudy eyes, although the bright orange sap is acrid and poisonous. External application of the sap was used to treat warts, corns and ringworm, although it will equally damage any skin that it touches. In Russia, the plant has been used as an anti-cancer drug. The native distribution of Greater Celandine has been obscured by innumerable escapes from cultivation; it is now found in gardens mostly as a weed. *Status:* native or introduced in some localities; common, throughout area. (There are no similar species.)

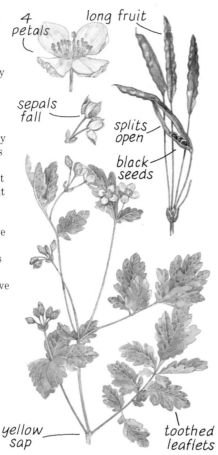

4 petals

long fruit

sepals fall

splits open

black seeds

yellow sap

toothed leaflets

GREATER CELANDINE		FLOWERS	
Type	perennial	**Position**	2–6, from tip of stem
Height	30–90cm	**Bracts**	present
Habitat	banks and walls, often near houses	**Type**	♀
		Size	20–25mm
Flowering	May–August	**Colour**	bright yellow
		Stalk	about equalling flower
STEMS AND LEAVES		**Sepals**	2, separate, soon falling, hairy
Stem	upright, branched, with orange sap	**Petals**	4, up to 10mm, oval, broadest above middle
Root	woody stock, covered with fibres from old leaf-bases	**Stamens**	numerous, yellow
Hairs	sparse	**Stigma**	1, 2 lobes on short style
Stipules	absent	**Ovary**	1, 1-celled
Leaves	at base of plant or scattered around stem, cut into 2–3 pairs of leaflets with leaflet at tip, blunt, edge with rounded teeth	**FRUIT**	
		Type	1, capsule, splitting from bottom, narrow
		Size	30–50mm
Leaf-stalk	long below, absent above	**Seeds**	many, 1.5–2mm, black with fleshy, white outgrowth

Common Fumitory *Fumaria officinalis*

This plant's name suggests a smoky nature, inspired partly by the look of finely divided, greyish leaves on widely branched stems and the tiny, dull purple flowers. Fumitory also has an acrid smell to the root and the sap makes eyes weep. *Status:* native; common throughout most of area. *Similar species:* White Ramping-fumitory has climbing stems, broader leaf-segments and larger, white flowers, tipped with purple. Corydalis species have many-seeded pods. Yellow Corydalis has bright yellow flowers, and Climbing Corydalis climbs and has small, creamy-white flowers.

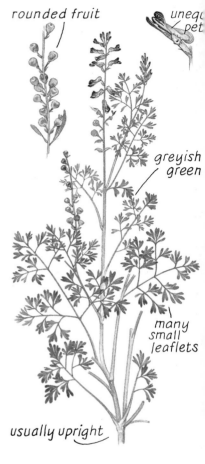

rounded fruit

unequal petal

greyish green

many small leaflets

usually upright

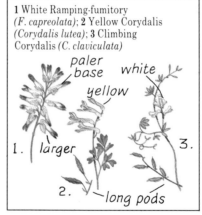

1 White Ramping-fumitory (*F. capreolata*); 2 Yellow Corydalis (*Corydalis lutea*); 3 Climbing Corydalis (*C. claviculata*)

paler base

white

yellow

1. larger

2.

3.

long pods

COMMON FUMITORY		Bracts	narrow, pointed, shorter than flower-stalk
Type	annual		
Height	12–40cm	**Type**	♀
Habitat	cultivated ground; mostly light soils	**Size**	7–9mm
		Colour	pink with blackish-purple tips to inner petals
Flowering	May–October	**Stalk**	shorter than flowers
		Sepals	2, 2–3.5mm, oval, toothed at base, soon falling
STEMS AND LEAVES		**Petals**	4, unequal, inner pair joined, hidden by larger, outer pair
Stem	nearly upright or climbing		
Root	slender tap-root	**Stamens**	2
Hairs	hairless	**Stigma**	1, 2-lobed
Stipules	absent	**Ovary**	1, 1-celled
Leaves	spirally arranged, 20–100mm, many spear-shaped or oblong, bluish lobes	**FRUIT**	
		Type	1, nut-like, not opening, globular, blunt or notched
Leaf-stalk	present, lower broad-based	**Size**	2–2.5mm
FLOWERS		**Seeds**	1, not released
Position	10–40, in crowded spike from opposite leaf-base		

Alliaria petiolata Garlic Mustard

A fresh-looking plant in late Spring, when heads of snow-white flowers and broad, pale green leaves contrast starkly with the gathering shade of the woodland or hedgerow. A garlic-like aroma advertises its presence. *Status:* native; common except in some northern parts. *Similar species:* Honesty, a common garden escapee, has larger, purplish or white flowers. Its nearly circular fruits split revealing a silvery inner wall. Perennial Honesty, with fruits more pointed, is native to the east of the area. The fragrant Dame's-violet has slender fruits and narrower leaves.

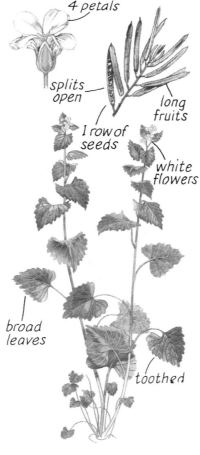

4 petals
splits open
long fruits
1 row of seeds
white flowers
broad leaves
toothed

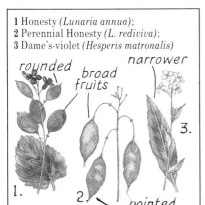

1 Honesty (*Lunaria annua*);
2 Perennial Honesty (*L. rediviva*);
3 Dame's-violet (*Hesperis matronalis*)

rounded broad fruits
narrower
1.
2.
pointed
3.

Nasturtium officinale Water-cress

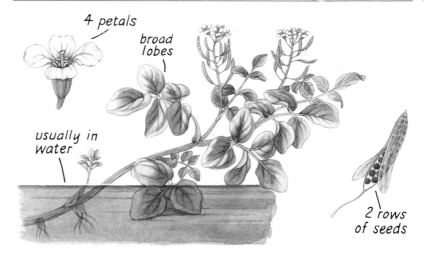

4 petals
broad lobes
usually in water
2 rows of seeds

Best known as a salad plant or garnish with hot-tasting leaves, Water-cress is a species of the Cabbage family which normally grows in shallow water. Fleshy, hollow stems bear dark green leaves, paired leaflets and spikes of white, four-petalled flowers. Plants from stagnant water or where sheep graze should not be eaten because of the parasitic liver-fluke, which also attacks humans. *Status:* native; lowland, throughout area. *Similar species.* Narrow-fruited Water-cress often has leaves tinged with purple, especially in Autumn, and narrow fruits with a single row of seeds.

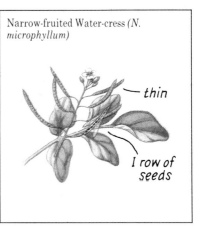

Narrow-fruited Water-cress (*N. microphyllum*)

thin
1 row of seeds

	GARLIC MUSTARD		
Type	biennial or perennial		
Height	20–120cm		
Habitat	woods, hedgerows, by walls; mostly lime-rich soils		
Flowering	April–June		
	STEMS AND LEAVES		
Stem	upright, usually branched		
Root	whitish tap-root, fibrous roots produce new shoots		
Hairs	sparse to hairless above		
Stipules	absent		
Leaves	basal or spirally around stem, 30–120mm, kidney-shaped to triangular, garlic-smelling, wavy or toothed, base heart-shaped		
Leaf-stalk	long below, short above		

	FLOWERS
Position	c30 in head at stem-tip
Bracts	absent
Type	↓
Size	5–10mm
Colour	white
Stalk	2.5–13mm
Sepals	4, 2.5–3.5mm, oval, whitish
Petals	4, 4–6mm, rounded, base stalk-like
Stamens	6
Stigma	1
Ovary	1, 2-celled
	FRUIT
Type	1, pod-like, slender, straight, sides 3-veined, splits from base to top, seeds in 1 row
Size	35–60mm
Seeds	3–18, c3mm, angular, black

	WATER-CRESS		
Type	perennial		
Height	10–60cm		
Habitat	ditches, streams, rivers; wet soil or shallow water		
Flowering	May–October		
	STEMS AND LEAVES		
Stem	low-growing, turning upright, rooting, often floating, hollow		
Root	branched, creeping stock		
Hairs	absent		
Stipules	absent		
Leaves	spirally arranged, 1–4 pairs of leaflets, leaflet at tip, each elliptical to circular, blunt, edge unbroken or partly toothed		
Leaf-stalk	present or absent above		

	FLOWERS
Position	many, in spike-like heads
Bracts	absent
Type	↓
Size	4–6mm
Colour	white
Stalk	8–12mm
Sepals	4, alternating with petals
Petals	4, equal, rounded with stalk-like base
Stamens	6
Stigma	1, sometimes 2-lobed
Ovary	1, 2-celled
	FRUIT
Type	1, pod-like, level or curving upwards, sides swollen with faint mid-vein, seeds in 2 rows
Size	13–18mm
Seeds	many, c2mm, egg-shaped shallowly pitted

Hedge Mustard *Sisymbrium officinale*

Commonly growing close to roads and tracks, plants of Hedge Mustard often have a dusty, neglected look. Almost stalkless fruits are held stiffly upright, pressed close to the stems, and give a spidery look. Hedge Mustard was formerly used in cough medicines and was also eaten in salads, soups and omelettes. *Status:* native; common, most of area. *Similar species:* Tall Rocket has more leaflets or lobes, the upper very narrow, and longer, stalked fruits. Flixweed has leaves cut into very many small lobes. Treacle Mustard has undivided leaves covered with odd short-stalked, T-shaped hairs.

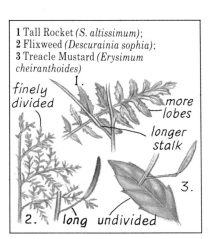

1 Tall Rocket (*S. altissimum*);
2 Flixweed (*Descurainia sophia*);
3 Treacle Mustard (*Erysimum cheiranthoides*)

finely divided

more lobes

longer stalk

3.

1.

2. long undivided

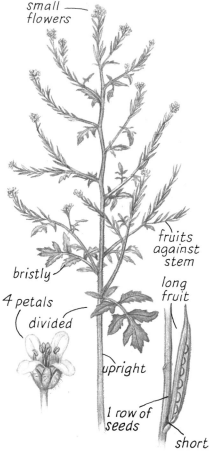

small flowers

bristly

4 petals divided

fruits against stem

long fruit

upright

1 row of seeds

short

HEDGE MUSTARD		
Type	annual	
Height	30–90cm	
Habitat	waste ground, arable fields, hedgebanks	
Flowering	June–July	
STEMS AND LEAVES		
Stem	upright, branched above	
Root	slender tap-root	
Hairs	bristly, pointing down on stems	
Stipules	absent	
Leaves	basal or scattered around stem, 50–80mm, cut into 1–5 pairs of narrow, toothed lobes, broad lobe at tip	
Leaf-stalk	present or absent above	
FLOWERS		
Position	many, in spike at stem-tip	

Bracts	absent	
Type	⚥	
Size	3–3.5mm	
Colour	pale yellow	
Stalk	1–2mm	
Sepals	4, 1.5–2mm, oblong, blunt	
Petals	4, 2–4mm, equal, oblong, rounded, base stalk-like	
Stamens	6, 4 long, 2 short	
Stigma	1	
Ovary	1, 2-celled	
FRUIT		
Type	1, pod-like, held close to stem, sides hairy, 3-veined, splits from base, slender, seeds in 1 row	
Size	10–15mm	
Seeds	10–20, *c*1mm, egg-shaped, orange-brown	

Creeping Yellow-cress *Rorippa sylvestris*

This robust, virtually hairless species of the Cabbage family grows in wet places and has broad heads of yellow, four-petalled flowers. *Status:* native, most of area except parts of north. *Similar species:* Northern Yellow-cress has much shorter fruits. Winter-cresses have a rounded lobe at the leaf-tip, fruits with a distinct middle vein on each side, and seeds in one row. Winter-cress is sometimes used like Water-cress in salads or boiled like spinach; this species has toothed upper leaves. American Winter-cress has lobed upper leaves and fruits twice as long.

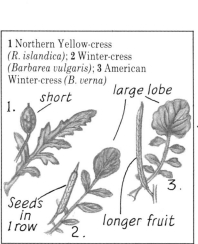

1 Northern Yellow-cress (*R. islandica*); 2 Winter-cress (*Barbarea vulgaris*); 3 American Winter-cress (*B. verna*)

1.

short

large lobe

stalked

3.

Seeds in 1 row

2.

longer fruit

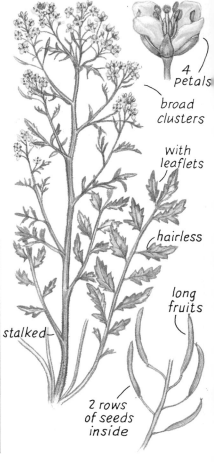

4 petals

broad clusters

with leaflets

hairless

long fruits

2 rows of seeds inside

CREEPING YELLOW-CRESS		
Type	perennial	
Height	20–50cm	
Habitat	damp ground or where water stands in winter	
Flowering	June–August	
STEMS AND LEAVES		
Stem	upright, branched, angled	
Root	fibrous, from creeping, underground stems	
Hairs	more or less hairless	
Stipules	absent	
Leaves	spirally arranged, lower leaves with oblong or spear-shaped, toothed leaflets either side, leaflet at tip, upper leaves lobed	
Leaf-stalk	present or absent above	

FLOWERS		
Position	spikes in branched head	
Bracts	absent	
Type	⚥	
Size	*c*5mm	
Colour	yellow	
Stalk	5–12mm	
Sepals	4, alternating with petals	
Petals	4, 4–5mm, equal, oval, rounded, base stalk-like	
Stamens	6	
Stigma	1, slightly 2-lobed	
Ovary	1, 2-celled	
FRUIT		
Type	1, pod-like, thin, sides swollen, scarcely veined, seeds mostly in 2 rows	
Size	9–18mm	
Seeds	many, *c*0.7mm, red-brown	

Cardamine pratensis Cuckooflower

Attractive lavender flowers, opening at a time of the year when the cuckoo starts to call, mark out the clumps of Cuckooflower in a meadow or by a stream. The seeds are effectively dispersed by the pod, which splits open suddenly, hurling the seeds from the plant. *Status:* native; throughout region. *Similar species:* Large Bitter-cress has purple anthers. Explosive fruits are also found in two small-flowered species, making them troublesome in gardens. The annual Hairy Bitter-cress mostly has four stamens, whereas Wavy Bitter-cress has six and is usually perennial.

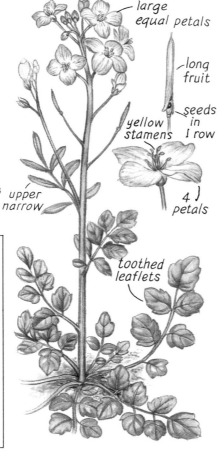

large equal petals
long fruit
seeds in 1 row
yellow stamens
4 petals
upper narrow
toothed leaflets

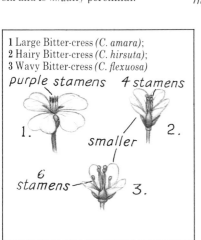

1 Large Bitter-cress (*C. amara*);
2 Hairy Bitter-cress (*C. hirsuta*);
3 Wavy Bitter-cress (*C. flexuosa*)

purple stamens   4 stamens
1.   2.
      smaller
6 stamens   3.

Erophila verna Common Whitlowgrass

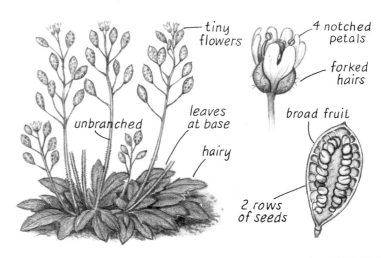

tiny flowers
unbranched
leaves at base
hairy
4 notched petals
forked hairs
broad fruit
2 rows of seeds

A diminutive plant of dry, often shallow or sandy soil, that has a rosette of leaves densely covered with odd Y-shaped or branched hairs. The short, flattened fruits quickly ripen and split open, revealing a silvery inner wall and two rows of seeds. *Status:* native, most of area except for parts of north. *Similar species:* several species from dry places lack the notch in the petals. Wall Whitlowgrass has taller, leafy stems. Much longer fruits are a feature of Thale Cress, which has cylindrical fruits, and Hairy Rock-cress, which has flattened fruits and winged seeds.

1 Wall Whitlowgrass (*Draba muralis*); 2 Thale Cress (*Arabidopsis thaliana*); 3 Hairy Rock-cress (*Arabis hirsuta*)

long fruit
1.
2.   3.
leafy stem   upright

CUCKOOFLOWER

Type	perennial		
Height	15–60cm		
Habitat	meadows or streams; damp soil or shallow water		
Flowering	April–June		

STEMS AND LEAVES

Stem	upright, usually unbranched
Root	short, nearly horizontal stock, many fibrous roots
Hairs	sparse, on leaves
Stipules	absent
Leaves	basal or spirally arranged, lower with broad, toothed leaflets, upper leaves with narrow, unbroken leaflets
Leaf-stalk	present

FLOWERS

Position	7–20, in rounded heads which elongate in fruit
Bracts	absent
Type	♀
Size	12–18mm
Colour	lilac, rarely white
Stalk	8–25mm
Sepals	4, 3–4mm, papery edges, tip violet
Petals	4, 8–13mm, equal, oval, often notched, base stalk-like
Stamens	4–6
Stigma	1, sometimes 2-lobed
Ovary	1, 2-celled

FRUIT

Type	1, pod-like, suddenly coils open, slender, seeds in 1 row
Size	25–40mm
Seeds	numerous, c2mm, oblong

COMMON WHITLOWGRASS

Type	annual		
Height	2–20cm		
Habitat	dry places, often among rocks or on walls		
Flowering	March–June		

STEMS AND LEAVES

Stem	straight or base branched
Root	fibrous
Hairs	dense, forked or star-shaped
Stipules	absent
Leaves	in rosette at base, 10–15mm, elliptical or spear-shaped, pointed, edge unbroken or 1–2 teeth
Leaf-stalk	broad

FLOWERS

Position	in a rounded head, elongating in fruit
Bracts	absent
Type	♀
Size	3–6mm
Colour	white, some tinged red
Stalk	1.5–6mm
Sepals	4, 1.5–2.5mm
Petals	4, 1.5–6mm, equal, deeply notched, base stalk-like
Stamens	6, 4 long, 2 short
Stigma	1
Ovary	1, 2-celled

FRUIT

Type	1, pod-like, oval, usually broadest above middle, flattened, sides split leaving broad inner wall, seeds in 2 rows
Size	3–9mm
Seeds	40–60, 0.3–0.4mm, flattened

Common Scurvygrass *Cochlearia officinalis*

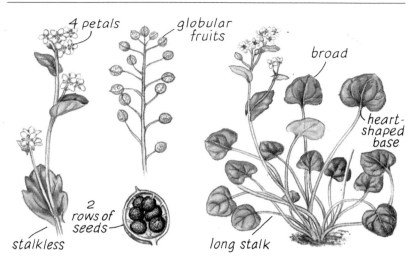

4 petals

globular fruits

broad

heart-shaped base

2 rows of seeds

stalkless

long stalk

A distinctive feature of sea-cliffs, shingle banks or the upper limits of salt-marshes, this low-growing plant has rather succulent, mostly kidney-shaped leaves and white, four-petalled flowers. Rich in Vitamin C, its leaves were used to combat scurvy, a disease once prevalent in sailors and caused by deficiency of the vitamin. *Status:* native; most coastal areas. *Similar species:* Danish Scurvygrass has smaller flowers and mostly stalked stem-leaves. English Scurvygrass has a tapered base to the lower leaves, and flattened fruits.

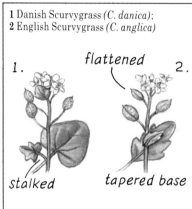

1 Danish Scurvygrass (*C. danica*); 2 English Scurvygrass (*C. anglica*)

flattened

1.

2.

stalked

tapered base

	COMMON SCURVYGRASS		FLOWERS	
Type	biennial or perennial	**Position**	in elongated head	
Height	5–50cm	**Bracts**	absent	
Habitat	sea-cliffs, drier parts of salt-	**Type**	♂, fragrant	
	marshes, mountains	**Size**	8–10mm	
Flowering	May–August	**Colour**	white, rarely tinged lilac	
		Stalk	4–7	
	STEMS AND LEAVES	**Sepals**	4	
Stem	low or angled upwards	**Petals**	4, oblong, base stalk-like	
Root	long, stout tap-root	**Stamens**	6	
Hairs	hairless	**Stigma**	1	
Stipules	absent	**Ovary**	1, 2-celled	
Leaves	basal *c*15mm, nearly circular, fleshy, blunt, edge usually unbroken, base heart-shaped; stem-leaves scattered, narrower, edge wavy or toothed, base clasps stem	**FRUIT**		
		Type	1, pod-like, globular, each side splits open, seeds in 2 rows on inner wall	
		Size	3–7mm	
Leaf-stalk	longer than blade on basal leaves, absent above	**Seeds**	2–32, 1.5–2mm, egg-shaped, reddish brown	

Swine-cress *Coronopus squamatus*

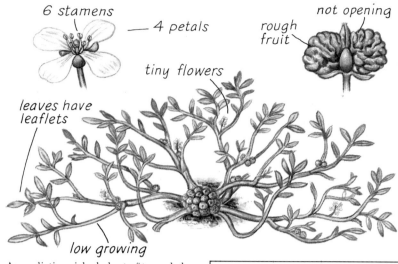

6 stamens

4 petals

not opening

rough fruit

tiny flowers

leaves have leaflets

low growing

An undistinguished plant of trampled ground, Swine-cress is common by paths and other tracks but is easily overlooked because the flowers are minute. These flowers are pollinated automatically so the plant can set a full complement of seed regardless of the weather or presence of insects. *Status:* native; common mainly in south of region. *Similar species:* Lesser Swine-cress has only two stamens and smaller, almost smooth fruits notched at the tip, and a longer stalk.

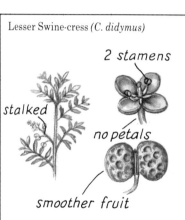

Lesser Swine-cress (*C. didymus*)

2 stamens

stalked

no petals

smoother fruit

	SWINE-CRESS		FLOWERS	
Type	annual or biennial	**Position**	crowded clusters at tip of main stem, elongated heads opposite upper leaves	
Height	5–30cm			
Habitat	waste ground, particularly where trampled	**Bracts**	absent	
		Type	♂	
Flowering	June–September	**Size**	*c*2.5mm	
		Colour	white	
	STEMS AND LEAVES	**Stalk**	1.5–3mm	
Stem	low-growing, branched, main stem short	**Sepals**	4, shorter than petals	
		Petals	4 or 0, 1–1.5mm, equal, oblong, base stalk-like	
Root	slender tap-root			
Hairs	absent	**Stamens**	6	
Stipules	absent	**Stigma**	1	
Leaves	spirally around stem, with spear-shaped or oval, pointed segments or leaflets, lower leaflets sometimes toothed or lobed	**Ovary**	1, 2-celled	
		FRUIT		
		Type	1, not opening, nearly kidney-shaped, roughly ridged	
Leaf-stalk	long below, short above	**Size**	*c*2.5 × 3–4mm	
		Seeds	2, 2–2.5mm, not released	

Camelina sativa **Gold-of-pleasure**

A slender plant with narrow, arrow-shaped leaves and branched heads of four-petalled, golden-yellow flowers. It was formerly common as a weed among many crops. The seeds are similar in size and shape to those of Flax and were probably spread when Flax was more widely cultivated. Gold-of-pleasure was also cultivated in its own right, for the seeds yield an edible oil. *Status:* introduced, occasionally naturalized; scattered through area, mainly in south-east. *Similar species:* Woad has pendulous, oblong fruits and was formerly cultivated for a blue dye extracted from its leaves.

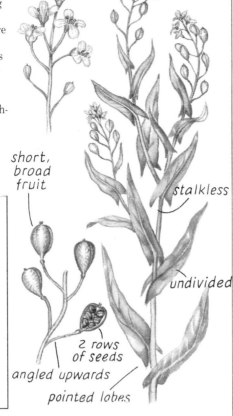

4 petals

short, broad fruit

stalkless

undivided

2 rows of seeds

angled upwards

pointed lobes

Woad (*Isatis tinctoria*)

nodding

narrow

	GOLD-OF-PLEASURE		FLOWERS	
Type	annual	**Position**	many, in branched heads	
Height	30–80cm	**Bracts**	absent	
Habitat	arable fields, especially of corn, flax and lucerne	**Type**	♂	
		Size	width c3mm	
Flowering	June–September	**Colour**	yellow	
		Stalk	up to 25mm in fruit	
	STEMS AND LEAVES	**Sepals**	4, upright	
Stem	upright, branched above	**Petals**	4, up to 5mm, equal, rounded, base stalk-like	
Root	slender, yellow tap-root			
Hairs	sometimes hairy	**Stamens**	6	
Stipules	absent	**Stigma**	1	
Leaves	spirally arranged on stem, lower oblong or spear-shaped, edge unbroken, toothed or rarely lobed, base tapered; upper with pointed basal lobes clasping stem	**Ovary**	1, 2-celled	
		FRUIT		
		Type	1, pod-like, egg-shaped, each swollen side splits away leaving 2 rows of seeds on middle wall	
Leaf-stalk	absent	**Size**	6–9mm	
		Seeds	8–24, 1–2mm, egg-shaped	

Armoracia rusticana **Horse-radish**

A robust plant with dark green, finely toothed, crinkly leaves, sometimes half a metre long. This is the same species as the cultivated plant used for making the hot and pungent horseradish sauce, commonly to accompany roast beef, prepared from peeled and grated roots. The aroma of the sauce is given off when a leaf is lightly crushed. *Status:* introduced; widely naturalized, most of region. *Similar species:* Dittander has broad, toothed leaves, although mostly smaller and not crinkled. Its hairy fruits, containing only two seeds, are produced in abundance whereas those of Horse-radish rarely develop.

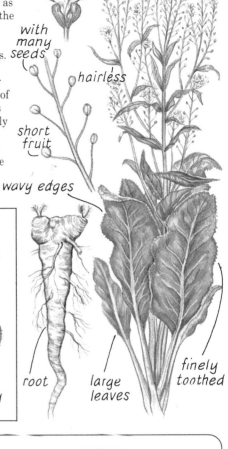

4 petals

with many seeds

hairless

short fruit

wavy edges

root

large leaves

finely toothed

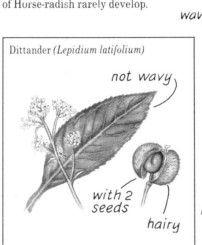

Dittander (*Lepidium latifolium*)

not wavy

with 2 seeds

hairy

	HORSE-RADISH		FLOWERS	
Type	perennial	**Position**	many, in branched head	
Height	up to 125cm	**Bracts**	absent	
Habitat	fields, stream banks, waste places	**Type**	♂	
		Size	8–9mm	
Flowering	May–June	**Colour**	white	
		Stalk	up to 200mm	
	STEMS AND LEAVES	**Sepals**	4, c3mm	
Stem	upright, leafy, branched	**Petals**	4, 5. 7mm, equal, oval, base stalk-like	
Root	thick stock, sometimes branched, long tap-root			
		Stamens	6, 4 long, 2 short	
Hairs	absent	**Stigma**	1, slightly 2-lobed	
Stipules	absent	**Ovary**	1, 2-celled	
Leaves	basal or scattered on stem, basal 300–500mm, oval or oblong, blunt, fine-toothed, crinkled, some lobed; stem-leaves elliptical or spear-shaped, pointed	**FRUIT**		
		Type	single, pod-like, rarely matures, globular, sides split, seeds in 2 rows	
Leaf-stalk	to 300mm or absent above	**Size**	4–6mm	
		Seeds	16–24, egg-shaped	

Shepherd's-purse *Capsella bursa-pastoris*

A widespread weed often found in gardens and waste places, distinguished by small, heart-shaped fruits. A preparation from the leaves has long been used against inflammation and bleeding, and is still found in some medicines. *Status:* native; common throughout area. *Similar species:* Shepherd's Cress has two petals much smaller than the other two. Species differing in having one-seeded fruits include Smith's Pepperwort, which has narrower fruits winged at the top, and Hoary Cress which has larger, flatter-topped flower-heads and fruits that do not open.

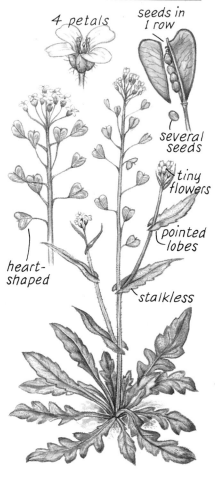

4 petals
seeds in 1 row
several seeds
tiny flowers
pointed lobes
heart-shaped
stalkless

1 Shepherd's Cress (*Teesdalia nudicaulis*); 2 Smith's Pepperwort (*Lepidium heterophyllum*); 3 Hoary Cress (*Cardaria draba*)

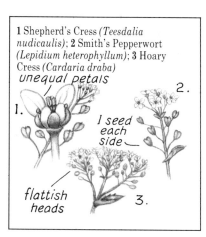

unequal petals
1 seed each side
1.
2.
flattish heads
3.

	SHEPHERD'S-PURSE		FLOWERS	
Type	annual or biennial	**Position**	in elongated heads
Height	3–40cm	**Bracts**	absent
Habitat	cultivated land, road and path-sides, waste places	**Type**	☿
		Size	width c2.5mm
Flowering	January–December	**Colour**	white
		Stalk	lengthening in fruit
	STEMS AND LEAVES	**Sepals**	4, c1.5mm, upright
Stem	upright or angled upwards	**Petals**	4, 2–3mm, oval, tip notched, base stalk-like
Root	slender tap-root	**Stamens**	6, sometimes absent
Hairs	hairless or sparsely hairy	**Stigma**	1, on short stalk
Stipules	absent	**Ovary**	1, 2-celled
Leaves	basal rosette, few on stem; lowest spear-shaped, broad near tip, lobed; stem-leaves toothed or unbroken, 2 pointed lobes clasp stem	**FRUIT**	
		Type	1, heart-shaped or triangular, tip notched, sides part leaving 1 row of seeds on thin inner wall
Leaf-stalk	only on lowest leaves	**Size**	6–9mm
		Seeds	12–24, 0.8–1mm, oblong to egg-shaped, pale brown

Field Penny-cress *Thlaspi arvense*

A weed with rounded, broadly winged fruits that have led to its common name. Although the fruits are a little like those of Honesty, when they split the middle wall is much narrower and less attractive. Field Penny-cress can grow in such great quantity on farmland that it becomes a serious pest. *Status:* native or introduced; most of area. *Similar species:* Perfoliate Penny-cress has narrowly winged, heart-shaped fruits. Alpine Penny-cress is a mountain plant with smaller, untoothed leaves and triangular fruits with a spike at the tip.

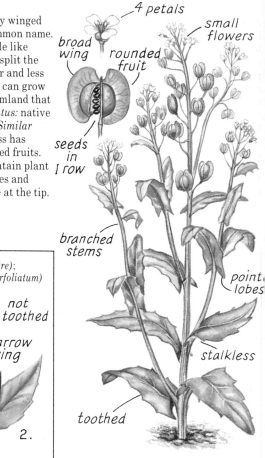

4 petals
small flowers
broad wing
rounded fruit
seeds in 1 row
branched stems
point lobes
stalkless
toothed

1 Alpine Penny-cress (*T. alpestre*); 2 Perfoliate Penny-cress (*T. perfoliatum*)

long point
not toothed
narrow wing
1.
tapered
2.

	FIELD PENNY-CRESS		FLOWERS	
Type	annual	**Position**	elongated heads
Height	10–60cm	**Bracts**	absent
Habitat	arable fields or waste places	**Type**	☿
Flowering	May–July	**Size**	4–6mm
		Colour	white
	STEMS AND LEAVES	**Stalk**	lengthening in fruit
Stem	upright, branched above	**Sepals**	4, 1.5–2mm, narrow
Root	slender tap-root	**Petals**	4, 3–4mm, equal, base stalk-like
Hairs	absent	**Stamens**	6, 4 long, 2 short
Stipules	absent	**Stigma**	1, slightly 2-lobed
Leaves	spirally arranged on stem, spear-shaped to oval, most sparsely toothed; 2 pointed lobes at base of upper leaves clasp stem	**Ovary**	1, 2-celled
		FRUIT	
		Type	1, pod-like, circular, flattened, edge wing-like, notched, sides split away leaving seeds in 1 row on narrow inner wall
Leaf-stalk	only lowest stalked	**Size**	12–22mm
		Seeds	10–16, 1.5–2mm, ridged

Brassica nigra **Black Mustard**

A tall plant with smooth, bluish upper leaves and wide-branched stems bearing heads of yellow, 4-petalled flowers. It is cultivated for mustard, made from the ground seeds. *Status:* native near coast, mostly escaped elsewhere; commonest in south. *Similar species:* the fields of yellow commonly seen are mostly a form of Rape, grown for an edible oil extracted from the seeds. Rape has stalkless upper leaves as does Wild Turnip, which has mostly bristly, green leaves, and Wild Cabbage, which has hairless, bluish leaves, and has given rise to cultivated Cabbage, Cauliflower and Broccoli.

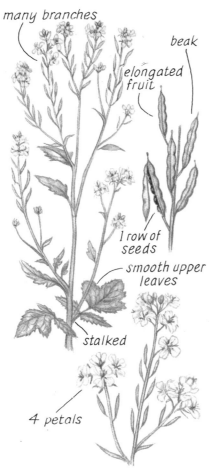

many branches

beak

elongated fruit

1 row of seeds

smooth upper leaves

stalked

4 petals

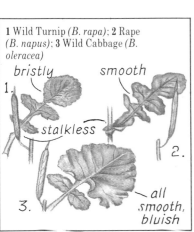

1 Wild Turnip *(B. rapa)*; **2** Rape *(B. napus)*; **3** Wild Cabbage *(B. oleracea)*

bristly

smooth

1.

stalkless

2.

3.

all smooth, bluish

	BLACK MUSTARD		FLOWERS	
Type	annual	**Position**	many, short heads elongate
Height	up to 100cm	**Bracts**	absent
Habitat	cliffs by sea, stream banks, waste places	**Type**	⚥
		Size	8–10mm
Flowering	May–August	**Colour**	bright yellow
	STEMS AND LEAVES	**Stalk**	shorter than flower
Stem	rather stout, much-branched	**Sepals**	4, 4–5mm
Root	slender tap-root	**Petals**	4, 7–9mm, base stalk-like
Hairs	bristly below, hairless above	**Stamens**	6
Stipules	absent	**Stigma**	1, slightly 2-lobed
Leaves	scattered, to 160mm, bluish, lower broad, 1–3 pairs of lobes, large lobe at tip; upper narrow, edge wavy or unbroken	**Ovary**	1, 2 celled
			FRUIT	
		Type	1, pod-like, 4-angled, upright, tip beak-like, sides split away leaving seeds in 1 row
Leaf-stalk	present	**Size**	12–20mm
		Seeds	4–10, nearly globular

Fields of golden Rape are grown as a source of edible oil.

Charlock *Sinapis arvensis*

A coarse, bristly plant with the typically cross-shaped flowers of species of the Cabbage family. The fruits are distinctive, with a long, conical beak at the tip. Young leaves and buds can be eaten, or seeds used like mustard, but this plant is a pest to farmers in that it infests fields and its seeds can survive for half a century. *Status:* probably native; throughout area. *Similar species:* White Mustard has fruits with a curved, flatter beak, up to eight seeds, and is grown for mustard and cress. Annual Wall-rocket has short-beaked fruits with many seeds in two rows.

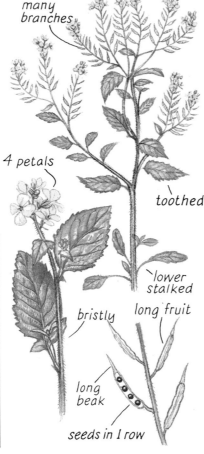

many branches

4 petals

toothed

lower stalked

long fruit

bristly

long beak

seeds in 1 row

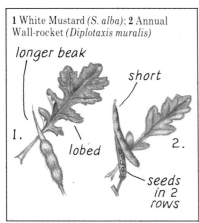

1 White Mustard *(S. alba)*; **2** Annual Wall-rocket *(Diplotaxis muralis)*

longer beak

short

1.

lobed

2.

seeds in 2 rows

CHARLOCK		FLOWERS	
Type	annual	**Position**	numerous, elongated heads
Height	30–80cm	**Bracts**	absent
Habitat	arable land; especially lime-rich and clay soils	**Type**	+
		Size	12–17mm
Flowering	May–July	**Colour**	bright yellow
		Stalk	about equalling flower
STEMS AND LEAVES		**Sepals**	4, spreading apart
Stem	upright, usually branched	**Petals**	4, 9–12mm, base stalk-like
Root	slender tap-root	**Stamens**	6, 4 long, 2 short
Hairs	stiffly hairy, sometimes hairless above	**Stigma**	1, slightly 2-lobed
		Ovary	1, 2-celled
Stipules	absent		
Leaves	scattered on stem, to 200mm; lower with few, small lobes and large, toothed lobe at tip; upper with edge coarsely toothed	**FRUIT**	
		Type	1, pod-like, usually hairless, tip long, conical, beak-like, swollen sides split away, seeds in 1 row
Leaf-stalk	on lower leaves only	**Size**	25–40mm
		Seeds	8–24, c3mm, globular, reddish brown

Sea Rocket *Cakile maritima*

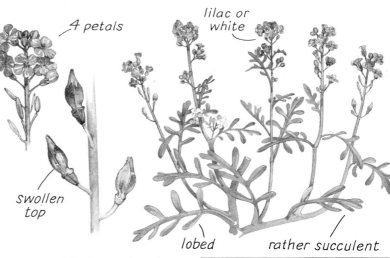

4 petals

lilac or white

swollen top

lobed

rather succulent

A common and distinctive plant of the drift-line of sandy or shingle sea-shores, usually with succulent, lobed leaves and lilac flowers. At the top of each short fruit is a corky-walled segment which breaks away with its single seed, to float in the sea while wind and tide carry it to some distant shore. *Status:* native; all round coasts. *Similar species:* several other species of the Cabbage family grow on the shore. Sea Stock has greyish, hairy, scarcely lobed leaves and slender fruits. Sea-kale has large, wavy-edged leaves and branched heads of pale flowers.

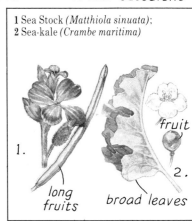

1 Sea Stock *(Matthiola sinuata)*; **2** Sea-kale *(Crambe maritima)*

1.

long fruits

fruit

2.

broad leaves

SEA ROCKET		FLOWERS	
Type	annual	**Position**	numerous, crowded in short spike at branch-tip
Height	15–45cm		
Habitat	drift-lines of sand and shingle beaches	**Bracts**	absent
		Type	+
Flowering	June–August	**Size**	8–12mm
		Colour	purple, lilac or white
STEMS AND LEAVES		**Stalk**	about equalling flower
Stem	low-growing or angled upwards, branched	**Sepals**	4, 3–5mm, upright
		Petals	4, 6–10mm, base stalk-like
Root	slender tap-root	**Stamens**	6
Hairs	absent	**Stigma**	1
Stipules	absent	**Ovary**	1, 2-celled
Leaves	spirally arranged, 30–60mm, lower mostly with oblong, rarely toothed lobes; upper with few or no lobes	**FRUIT**	
		Type	1, pod-like, not opening, upper part pointed, corky-walled, breaking off when ripe; lower part remains on plant
Leaf-stalk	only on lower leaves	**Size**	10–25mm
		Seeds	1–2, 4–5mm, smooth

Raphanus raphanistrum **Wild Radish**

bristly-leaved plant with variably oloured, cross-shaped flowers, but ommonly pale yellow veined with lilac. he slender fruits are distinctive, being trongly constricted between the seeds. *tatus:* mostly native, introduced in orth; common weed, throughout area. *imilar species:* Sea Radish is a coastal lant with more numerous, crowded eaflets and the short-beaked fruit has ven narrower sections between the eeds. The cultivated Radish is a related pecies which has the swollen, edible ap-root and fruits lacking constrictions etween the seeds.

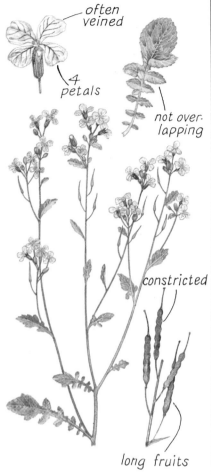

often veined

4 petals

not over-lapping

constricted

Sea Radish (*R. maritimus*)

narrower between seeds

many leaflets

overlapping

long fruits

A tall, stiffly upright plant with slender spikes of greenish-yellow flowers above narrow, wavy-edged, dark green leaves. This is the plant for centuries used by dyers to produce a bright yellow dye, and Dyer's Rocket is an alternative common name. It is a relative of the Mignonette of gardens, grown for its scented flowers. *Status:* native; throughout area, but rarer in north and west. *Similar species:* Wild Mignonette is a smaller, branched plant with deeply lobed leaves. Corn Mignonette is similar but has white flowers and ripe fruits that hang down.

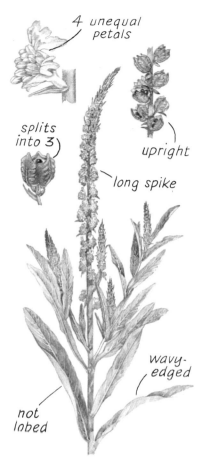

4 unequal petals

splits into 3

upright

long spike

wavy-edged

not lobed

1 Wild Mignonette (*R. lutea*); 2 Corn Mignonette (*R. phyteuma*)

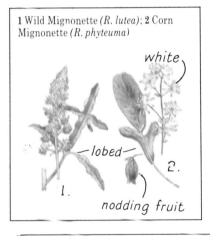

white

lobed

2.

1.

nodding fruit

WILD RADISH		**FLOWERS**	
Type	annual	Position	many, in head at stem-tip
Height	20–60cm	Bracts	absent
Habitat	arable fields, waste ground;	Type	♂
	mainly lime-free soil	Size	15–22mm
Flowering	May–September	Colour	yellow, lilac or white, most with darker veins
		Stalk	10–50mm
STEMS AND LEAVES		Sepals	4, 5–10mm, upright
Stem	upright, hardly branched	Petals	4, 12–20mm, base stalk-like
Root	slender, whitish tap-root	Stamens	6, 4 long, 2 short
Hairs	bristly throughout	Stigma	1
Stipules	absent	Ovary	1, 2-celled
Leaves	scattered on stem, lower with 1–4 pairs of wide-spaced lobes and large top lobe, edge toothed; upper smaller, lobed or toothed		
		FRUIT	
		Type	1, pod-like, narrowed between seeds, thick walls, tip narrow, seedless, beak-like, fruit breaks into 1-seeded segments
Leaf-stalk	present	Size	30–90mm
		Seeds	3–8, 1.5–3mm, rounded

WELD		**FLOWERS**	
Type	biennial	Position	many in spike-like clusters
Height	50–150cm	Bracts	present
Habitat	waste or arable ground, walls; often lime-rich soil	Type	♂
		Size	4–5mm
Flowering	June–August	Colour	yellowish-green
		Stalk	c1mm
STEMS AND LEAVES		Sepals	4, remaining in fruit
Stem	upright, ribbed, hollow, hardly branched	Petals	3–5, mostly 4, front petal slender, others cut into 3 or more lobes
Root	tap-root		
Hairs	more or less hairless	Stamens	20–25
Stipules	with sticky hairs	Stigmas	3
Leaves	forming rosette in first year, lance-shaped, 25–120mm, edge unbroken, wavy, upper oblong, spirally arranged	Ovary	1, 1-celled
		FRUIT	
		Type	1, capsule, nearly globular, tip opens by 3 teeth
Leaf-stalk	only on some upper leaves	Size	5–6mm
		Seeds	numerous, 0.0–1mm, black, smooth, glossy

Stonecrops, Saxifrages and Sundews

All these families have similar, hermaphrodite flowers. The Saxifrages are variously defined as a family and often taken to include a wide range of shrubby plants, such as the Black-currant, Gooseberry, Hydrangea and Mock-orange, in addition to the herbaceous species of Saxifrage. It is not an easy family to recognize since the plants lack any particularly distinctive features. Most have five or four petals though some, such as the Golden-saxifrages, lack petals.

Stonecrops are more or less succulent plants, many of which are grown as house-plants. The largest concentration of species in the world is found growing in desert and semi-desert regions of South Africa. In the mountains of southern Europe, there are many species of Houseleek (*Sempervivum*) and some are grown in gardens. The Stonecrop genus (*Sedum*) is more widespread and several species are native in northern Europe.

The final family, the Sundews, includes plants with a very unusual method of nutrition – they catch insects. This is probably an evolutionary adaptation to habitats poor in nitrates. The leaves are covered with specialized hairs which move to entrap their prey.

Held in a fatal embrace, a damselfly lies trapped by the tentacle-like hairs of Round-leaved Sundew. Each moveable hair bears sticky droplets and holds fast while the prey is digested.

Drosera rotundifolia **Round-leaved Sundew**

A rosette of leaves fringed with hairs, each tipped with a glistening, sticky, red droplet identifies the Sundew. The hairs are capable of movement and, tentacle-like, curve round to embrace an insect trapped by the sticky droplets. An enzyme-rich fluid is secreted and the leaf digests the hapless insect. *Status:* native; scattered throughout area. *Similar species:* two other Sundews have elongated leaves: the Great Sundew, which has a long stalk bearing the flowers well above the leaves, and the Oblong-leaved Sundew, which has a much shorter stalk about equalling the leaves.

1 Great Sundew *(D. anglica)*;
2 Oblong-leaved Sundew *(D. intermedia)*

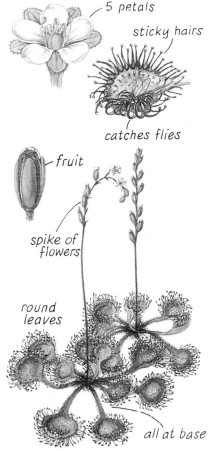

5 petals
sticky hairs
catches flies
fruit
spike of flowers
round leaves
all at base

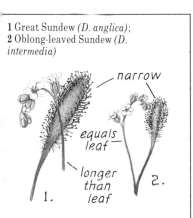

narrow
equals leaf
longer than leaf
1.
2.

	ROUND-LEAVED SUNDEW			**FLOWERS**	
Type	perenial		**Position**	6–10, in curved, spike-like head	
Height	6–25cm		**Bracts**	absent	
Habitat	bogs or by water on heaths and moors; acid soil		**Type**	☿	
			Size	c5mm	
Flowering	June–August		**Colour**	white	
			Stalk	shorter than flower	
	STEMS AND LEAVES		**Sepals**	5, blunt, toothed	
Stem	slender, mostly leafless		**Petals**	5, equal, oval, broadest above middle, tip blunt	
Root	fibrous				
Hairs	on leaf-blades, gland-tipped, longest on edges		**Stamens**	5	
Stipules	fringed		**Stigmas**	6, on 3 forked styles	
Leaves	rosette at base, blade to 10mm, circular, nearly horizontal, edge unbroken, fringed with tentacle-like hairs		**Ovary**	1, 1-celled	
			FRUIT		
			Type	1, capsule, covered by remains of flower, splits to release seeds	
Leaf-stalk	15–30mm, hairy		**Size**	6–8mm	
			Seeds	many, long, slender, winged from both sides	

Sedum telephium **Orpine**

A broad-leaved, succulent plant with rounded, dense heads of purple flowers. It is related to the 'Ice Plant' of gardens, and is similarly popular with bees. *Status:* native; scattered over much of area but rarer in the north. *Similar species:* Roseroot is a mountain plant with similar foliage but yellowish, 4-petalled flowers on male or female plants. Though with a very different shape of leaf, Navelwort has flowers and fruits of similar structure but with petals joined into a tube. It is common on walls and banks in the west.

1 Roseroot *(Rhodiola rosea)*;
2 Navelwort *(Umbilicus rupestris)*

5 petals
flattish heads
toothed
fleshy
5 narrow fruits

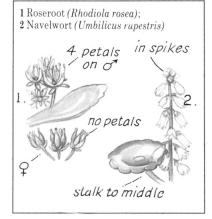

4 petals on ♂
in spikes
1.
no petals
♀
2.
stalk to middle

	ORPINE			**FLOWERS**	
Type	perennial		**Position**	many, crowded in rounded head at tips of stems	
Height	20–60cm				
Habitat	woods and hedgerows		**Bracts**	present	
Flowering	July–September		**Type**	☿	
			Size	9–12mm	
	STEMS AND LEAVES		**Colour**	reddish purple	
Stem	upright, hardly branched, usually coveral		**Stalk**	shorter than flower	
			Sepals	5 shorter than petals, spear shaped, pointed	
Root	stout, carrot-like tubers		**Petals**	5, 3–5mm, spear-shaped, pointed	
Hairs	absent				
Stipules	absent		**Stamens**	10	
Leaves	spirally placed on stem, 20–80mm, oval or oblong, bluish, often red-tinged, fleshy, blunt, toothed, base wedge-shaped or rounded		**Stigmas**	1 to each ovary	
			Ovaries	5, 1-celled	
			FRUIT		
Leaf-stalk	mostly stalkless		**Type**	5, pod-like, upright, slender, splitting to release seeds	
			Size	5–7mm	
			Seeds	numerous, small, elongated	

Biting Stonecrop *Sedum acre*

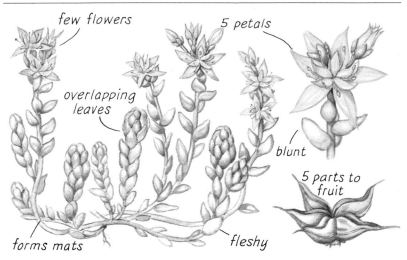

few flowers

5 petals

overlapping leaves

blunt

5 parts to fruit

forms mats

fleshy

This dwarf, succulent plant of dry, sunny places, has small, overlapping leaves and short stems forming mats. It is common on walls, rocks, cindery edges of railway tracks, or even old roofs. The leaves are hot-tasting, hence the common name. *Status:* native; most of area except parts of north. *Similar species:* Reflexed Stonecrop is larger with longer, pointed leaves and flattish heads of yellow flowers. Two white-flowered species are English Stonecrop, which has tiny leaves and few flowers, and White Stonecrop, which has oblong leaves and broad heads of tiny flowers.

1 Reflexed Stonecrop (*S. reflexum*);
2 English Stonecrop (*S. anglicum*);
3 White Stonecrop (*S. album*)

many flowers

1.

white

pointed

small

2.

longer

3.

	BITING STONECROP			FLOWERS	
Type	perennial		**Position**	2–4 per branch, few branches near stem-tip	
Height	2–10cm		**Bracts**	present	
Habitat	dunes, shingle, dry grassy places, walls		**Type**		
Flowering	June–July		**Size**	c12mm	
			Colour	bright yellow	
	STEMS AND LEAVES		**Stalk**	nearly stalkless	
Stem	creeping, numerous, forms mats, turning upwards		**Sepals**	5, oval, blunt-tipped	
Root	fibrous		**Petals**	5, 8–9mm, spear-shaped, pointed, spreading apart	
Hairs	absent		**Stamens**	10	
Stipules	absent		**Stigmas**	1 per ovary	
Leaves	spirally around stem, 3–5mm, nearly triangular, broad-based, thick, succulent, mostly overlapping, blunt, edge unbroken		**Ovaries**	5, 1-celled	
				FRUIT	
			Type	5, pod-like, pointed, spread apart, top splits	
Leaf-stalk	absent		**Size**	5–6mm	
			Seeds	many, c1mm, egg-shaped	

Meadow Saxifrage *Saxifraga granulata*

A delightful meadow plant with snow-white flowers and lobed, kidney-shaped leaves. At the base are tiny bulb-like buds, which serve to propagate the plant. A double form is sometimes grown in gardens. *Status:* native; scattered localities, mainly east of area. *Similar species:* two mountain species are Starry Saxifrage, its rosettes of leaves found especially where water seeps over rocks, and Mossy Saxifrage, which forms moss-like cushions on rocks. Rue-leaved Saxifrage is a small annual plant of dry, mainly lowland places, its leaves often tinged with red.

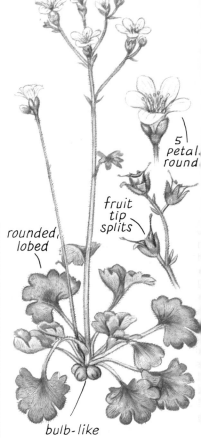

5 petal round

fruit tip splits

rounded, lobed

bulb-like

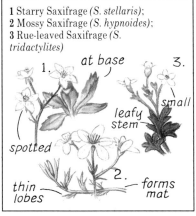

1 Starry Saxifrage (*S. stellaris*);
2 Mossy Saxifrage (*S. hypnoides*);
3 Rue-leaved Saxifrage (*S. tridactylites*)

at base

1.

3.

small

leafy stem

spotted

thin lobes

2.

forms mat

	MEADOW SAXIFRAGE			FLOWERS	
Type	perennial		**Position**	2–12, in widely branched head at tip of stem	
Height	10–50cm		**Bracts**	small, slender	
Habitat	dryish grassland; all but acid soils		**Type**		
Flowering	April–June		**Size**	10–15mm	
			Colour	white	
	STEMS AND LEAVES		**Stalk**	4–20mm, stickily hairy	
Stem	single, upright		**Sepals**	5, oval, tip blunt	
Root	fibrous, bulb-like buds from base of lowest leaves		**Petals**	5, 10–17mm, oval	
			Stamens	10	
Hairs	scattered, long, white, stickily hairy above		**Stigmas**	2, on long styles	
Stipules	absent		**Ovary**	1, 2-celled	
Leaves	rosette at base, few on stem, blade 5–30mm, most kidney-shaped, lobed; upper sharply toothed, base wedge-shaped			**FRUIT**	
			Type	1, capsule, egg-shaped, splits along upper edge	
Leaf-stalk	longer than blade or short on stem-leaves		**Size**	6–8mm	
			Seeds	many, egg-shaped, rough	

Chrysoplenium oppositifolium Opposite-leaved Golden-saxifrage

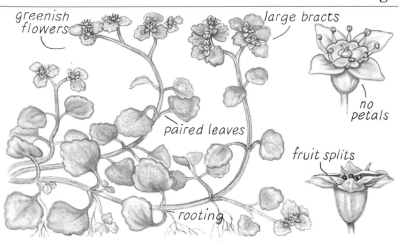

greenish flowers · large bracts · paired leaves · no petals · fruit splits · rooting

A plant of shady banks, among tree-roots or beneath boulders, brightening the gloom with a yellowish colour to the entire top of the plant. The rounded leaves are rather succulent, and are sometimes eaten in the mountains of north-eastern France. *Status:* native; common, most of area. *Similar species:* Alternate-leaved Golden-saxifrage differs in its creeping, underground, scaly stems, from which most of the kidney-shaped leaves arise. Most flowering stems have only a single leaf, but if there are more they are not paired.

Alternate-leaved Golden-saxifrage (*C. alternifolium*)

not paired · kidney shaped · long stalk

OPPOSITE-LEAVED GOLDEN-SAXIFRAGE	
Type	perennial
Height	5–15cm
Habitat	wet, shady places, often by streams or springs
Flowering	April–July
STEMS AND LEAVES	
Stem	low-growing, rooting, forming large patches, turning upwards to flower
Root	fibrous
Hairs	scattered, pressed close to lower leaves, upper leaves hairless
Stipules	absent
Leaves	paired on opposite sides of stem, 10–20mm, circular, blunt, edge unbroken or with shallow, rounded teeth, base square or broadly wedge-shaped
Leaf-stalk	about equalling blade, upper shorter
FLOWERS	
Position	few, in flattish heads
Bracts	leaf-like, greenish yellow
Type	♀
Size	3–4mm
Colour	greenish yellow
Stalk	absent
Sepals	4–5, oval to triangular
Petals	absent
Stamens	8
Stigmas	2, on separate styles
Ovary	1, 1-celled
FRUIT	
Type	1, capsule, splits down centre
Size	5–6mm
Seeds	many, blackish, rough

Biting Stonecrop forms low domes smothered with starry, yellow flowers.

Roses and Grass-of-Parnassus

The Roses represent a large family embracing such diverse species as the Roses and Brambles of hedgerows and petal-less species such as the Lady's-mantles. The family produces many familiar fruits, such as apples, cherries, peaches, pears, plums and strawberries, in addition to the horticulturally important Roses. The flowers tend to be conspicuous as most are insect-pollinated. Animal-dispersal of the fruits is common, either through the animal eating the fruits or carrying them externally. The hooked fruits of plants such as Agrimony or the Pirri-pirri-bur catch on the animal's fur or wool. Fruits are often fleshy and berry-like with a hard, stone-like centre surrounding the seed. A Bramble fruit is actually a cluster of such fruits around an enlarged base. In the Wild Strawberry, the individual fruits are dry but sunken into the fleshy base of the flower. Similarities with the Buttercup family are seen in the flowers and fruiting heads of Cinquefoils and Wood Avens, which resemble those of some species of Buttercup, while the plumed fruits of Mountain Avens parallel those of the Pasqueflower.

Grass-of-Parnassus is sometimes treated as a separate family, or at other times included within the Saxifrages. The flowers are most noticeable for the curious sterile stamens (staminodes), which are fringed and tipped with glistening glands.

The modified stamens of Grass-of-Parnassus are fringed and gland-tipped to attract insects.

Parnassia palustris **Grass-of-Parnassus**

fruit opens

5 petals

fringed

long stalk

heart-shaped

most at base

This beautiful, honey-scented, moorland flower is not at all grass-like but has long-stemmed, white, cup-shaped flowers, delicately veined with green, and a tuft of heart-shaped leaves. It was formerly found more widely on marshy ground, but its range has been restricted by drainage and 'improvement' of land. Five of the stamens have been transformed into special structures, fringed with glistening drops, which attract insects with the false promise of abundant nectar. These structures distinguish the species from those of the Saxifrage family, which otherwise have a rather similar structure to the flowers. Grass-of Parnassus has been used in the past to treat liver and nervous complaints. *Status:* native; widespread but rather scattered, rarer in south. (There are no similar species.)

GRASS-OF-PARNASSUS	
Type	perennial
Height	10–30cm
Habitat	marshes and moors; wet ground
Flowering	July–October

STEMS AND LEAVES	
Stem	upright, straight
Root	short, upright stock
Hairs	hairless
Stipules	absent
Leaves	most basal, 10–50mm, heart-shaped, bluish green, often red-spotted beneath, sharpish, edge unbroken; 1 stem-leaf near base of flowering stem
Leaf-stalk	longer than blade, absent on stem-leaf

FLOWERS	
Position	single, on long stalk from base of single stem-leaf
Bracts	absent
Type	♀
Size	15–30mm
Colour	white, grey-green veins
Stalk	much longer than flower
Sepals	5, spear-shaped
Petals	5, 7–12mm, equal, oval, tip notched
Stamens	5, with 5 modified stamens fringed with sticky drops
Stigmas	4, not stalked
Ovary	1, 1-celled except at base

FRUIT	
Type	1, capsule, egg-shaped, 4 grooves, splits into 4
Size	15–20mm
Seeds	many, 1.5–2mm, oblong

Filipendula ulmaria **Meadowsweet**

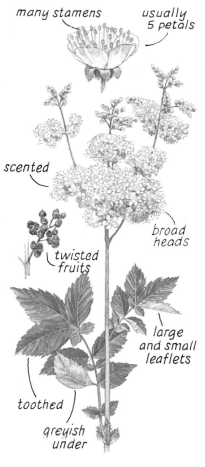

many stamens

usually 5 petals

scented

twisted fruits

broad heads

large and small leaflets

toothed

greyish under

Often forming large clumps, especially in damp meadows, with frothy heads of creamy-white, sweetly scented flowers, Meadowsweet was formerly used as a sort of air-freshener, strewn on the floor of houses. The flowers were used to flavour mead and to make herbal teas. *Status:* native; common throughout the area. *Similar species:* Meadowsweet has twisted clusters of fruits, but the related Dropwort has straight fruits. This species – which is resident in drier, lime-rich soils – has more numerous, smaller leaflets and fewer, larger flowers in each head.

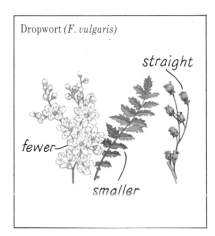

Dropwort (*F. vulgaris*)

straight

fewer

smaller

MEADOWSWEET	
Type	perennial
Height	60–120cm
Habitat	meadows, marshes, fens, by rivers, streams; wet ground
Flowering	June–September

STEMS AND LEAVES	
Stem	upright, scarcely branched
Root	fibrous from pink rhizome
Hairs	mostly hairless, dense grey hairs beneath leaves
Stipules	present
Leaves	on alternate sides of stem, 300–600mm, up to 5 pairs of main leaflets, smaller leaflets between, 3-lobed leaflet at tip, dark green above, greyish below, pointed, coarse teeth with finer teeth
Leaf-stalk	present

FLOWERS	
Position	many, in branched heads
Bracts	absent
Type	♀
Size	5–10mm
Colour	creamy white
Stalk	shorter than flower
Sepals	usually 5, triangular, bent back, downy
Petals	usually 5, 2–5mm, oval
Stamens	20–40
Stigmas	1 per ovary
Ovaries	6–10, 1-celled

FRUIT	
Type	6–10, not opening, twisted together spirally, hairless
Size	c2mm
Seeds	2 per fruit, not released

Cloudberry *Rubus chamaemorus*

smooth
male
crinkly
turns orange
lobed leaves
female
small stipules

Cloudberry is a rather surprising plant, producing its succulent, raspberry-like fruits on short, herb-like stems near ground level instead of the shrubby growth normally associated with such fruits. The leaves are also unusual in that they have radiating lobes and a rather crinkly texture. *Status:* native; common in some mountain areas, absent from much of the south. *Similar species:* Stone Bramble is a plant of rocky places, usually in woodland shade, and differs from Cloudberry in having leaves divided into three leaflets and scarlet ripe fruits.

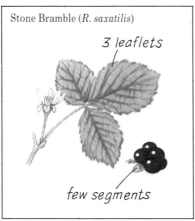

Stone Bramble (*R. saxatilis*)

3 leaflets

few segments

CLOUDBERRY		FLOWERS	
Type	perennial	**Position**	single, at stem-tip, ♂ and ♀ flowers on separate plants
Height	5–20cm		
Habitat	mountains, moors and bogs; damp ground	**Bracts**	absent
		Type 1	♂ with numerous stamens
Flowering	June–August	**Type 2**	♀ with 1 stigma per ovary
		Size	18–30mm
STEMS AND LEAVES		**Colour**	white
Stem	flowering stems upright, replaced each year	**Stalk**	present
		Sepals	5, shorter than petals, oval, pointed
Root	long, creeping rhizome		
Hairs	short	**Petals**	5, 8–15mm, oval, blunt
Stipules	oval, papery	**Ovaries**	few, 1-celled
Leaves	on alternate sides of stem, 15–80mm, few, rounded, with 5–7 triangular, blunt, toothed lobes, base heart-shaped	**FRUIT**	
		Type	few, berry-like segments in a rounded cluster with middle attached when shed, turns red, then orange
Leaf-stalk	10–70		
		Size	cluster 15–20mm
		Seeds	1 per fruit, not released

Dewberry *Rubus caesius*

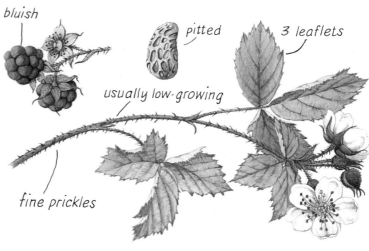

bluish
pitted
3 leaflets
usually low-growing
fine prickles

Commonly an understorey plant of woodland, it has low, arching, spiny stems, rooting at the tip, making hoop-like obstacles to trip up the unwary. This is one of the smaller Brambles, with few fruit-segments developing from each flower. *Status:* native; widespread, commonest in south. *Similar species:* Bramble is a name given to many species, differing in details of stem-angles, prickles, hairs or leaf-shape, and requiring considerable expertise for accurate identification. Raspberry differs by its paired leaflets and red fruits of which the centre usually stays on the plant.

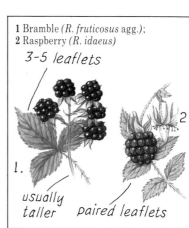

1 Bramble (*R. fruticosus* agg.);
2 Raspberry (*R. idaeus*)

3–5 leaflets

2.

1.

usually taller

paired leaflets

DEWBERRY		FLOWERS	
Type	perennial	**Position**	few, in branched head from stem-tip or leaf-base
Height	up to 45cm		
Habitat	scrub, woodland, grassland; mostly lime-rich soil	**Bracts**	absent
		Type	♀
Flowering	June–September	**Size**	20–25mm
		Colour	white or pink-tinged
STEMS AND LEAVES		**Stalk**	slender, sparsely prickly
Stem	arching, tip roots, not angled, sparsely prickly, waxy, lasts 2 years, flowers in second	**Sepals**	5, long-pointed, white-edged
		Petals	5, nearly circular, equal
		Stamens	numerous
Root	fibrous	**Stigmas**	1 per ovary
Hairs	sparse, mainly above	**Ovaries**	2–5, rarely to 20, 1-celled
Stipules	spear-shaped, on leaf-stalk		
Leaves	scattered around stem, 3 oval or diamond-shaped, toothed or lobed leaflets	**FRUIT**	
		Type	2–5, rarely to 20, berry-like parts, black, whitish, waxy covering; base stays with segments when shed
Leaf-stalk	present		
		Size	8–18mm
		Seeds	single, not released

Rosa canina Dog-rose

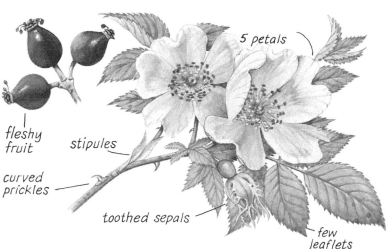

5 petals

fleshy fruit

stipules

curved prickles

toothed sepals

few leaflets

One of the most familiar of all wild flowers, abounding in hedgerows and adorning them with its delicately scented, shell-pink flowers. In the autumn, red, berry-like fruits or hips are attractive. Children are still given rose-hip syrup, which is rich in Vitamin C. *Status:* native; common through most of area but rarer in parts of north. *Similar species:* there are many forms and species of wild Rose. Harsh Downy-rose, which has hairy leaves and fruits, has straight prickles. Sweet-briar has sticky, apple-scented hairs beneath the leaves and the sepals stay on the ripening fruit.

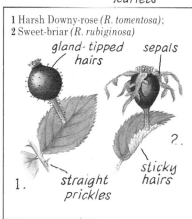

1 Harsh Downy-rose (*R. tomentosa*);
2 Sweet-briar (*R. rubiginosa*)

gland-tipped hairs

sepals

straight prickles

sticky hairs

1.

2.

	DOG-ROSE		FLOWERS	
Type	perennial	Position	1–4, at ends of stems
Height	100–300cm	Bracts	broad
Habitat	woods, scrub, hedges	Type	
Flowering	June–July	Size	15–25mm, rarely 50mm
		Colour	pink or white
	STEMS AND LEAVES	Stalk	5–20mm
Stem	arching, with strongly curved or hooked prickles	Sepals	5, lobed, bent back, falling in fruit
Root	woody stock	Petals	5, 20–25mm
Hairs	absent or sometimes short hairs beneath leaves	Stamens	numerous
		Stigmas	many in conical head
Stipules	long, broad, on leaf-stalk	Ovaries	numerous, 1-celled
Leaves	on alternate sides of stem, with 2–3 pairs of oval or elliptical, toothed leaflets, each 15–40mm		FRUIT
		Type	1, berry-like, egg-shaped or ellipsoidal, outer layer formed from flower-base, contains nut-like fruits, scarlet, smooth
Leaf-stalk	present	Size	10–20mm
		Seeds	1 to each nut-like fruit, not released

Delicately scented flowers make Dog-rose a favourite hedgerow flower.

Burnet Rose *Rosa pimpinellifolia*

many leaflets

white petals

sepals attached

blackish

fine, straight prickles

This dainty little Rose is most common near the sea, spreading by suckers to cover large areas on old dunes and heaths. The plant is easily recognized: the fruits are almost black, instead of the red of other species. The leaves have small, toothed leaflets and resemble those of Salad Burnet or Burnet Saxifrage. *Status:* native; absent from extreme north, most common by coast. *Similar species:* Field-rose is a more robust white-flowered species, and has larger, broader leaflets up to 20mm across and styles joined forming a beak-like tip to the fruit.

Field-rose (*R. arvensis*)

beak-like tip

few leaflets

BURNET ROSE		FLOWERS	
Type	shrub	**Position**	single, at tip of stem
Height	10–40mm, rarely 100mm	**Bracts**	absent
Habitat	mainly coastal, dunes, heaths, or on limestone	**Type**	♀
		Size	20–40mm
Flowering	May–July	**Colour**	creamy white, rarely pink
		Stalk	15–25mm
STEMS AND LEAVES		**Sepals**	5, 10–18mm, narrow, not toothed
Stem	upright, with many straight prickles or bristles	**Petals**	5, 10–20mm, rarely 25mm, broad, notched
Root	from creeping underground stems	**Stamens**	numerous
Hairs	more or less absent	**Stigmas**	1 per ovary, forming rounded head
Stipules	narrow, lobed at tip	**Ovaries**	numerous, 1-celled
Leaves	on alternate sides of stem, 3–5 pairs of leaflets, leaflet at tip, each 5–20mm, oval to circular, blunt, edge toothed	**FRUIT**	
		Type	single, globular, blackish, leathery or scarcely fleshy
Leaf-stalk	absent	**Size**	10–15mm
		Seeds	not released

Agrimony *Agrimonia eupatoria*

A stiffly upright plant, with slender spikes of yellow flowers and rather coarse leaves with leaflets of varying size. The nodding fruits have a ring of hooked spines, which may catch in an animal's fur, thus effecting dispersal. Agrimony once had many uses, including as an antidote for snake-bite and to give relief from colds, in the form of a wine with oranges, lemons, and ginger. *Status:* native; most of area except parts of north. *Similar species:* Fragrant Agrimony is rarer, more robust, and has sweetly scented flowers; the lowest spines of the fruit are bent backwards.

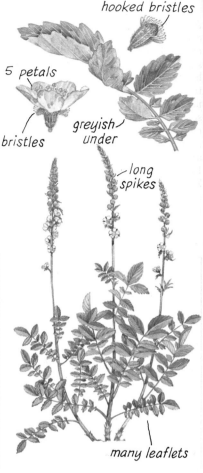

hooked bristles

5 petals

bristles

greyish under

long spikes

many leaflets

Fragrant Agrimony (*A. procera*)

fragrant

green under

bristles bent back

AGRIMONY		FLOWERS	
Type	perennial	**Position**	many, in spike at stem-tip
Height	30–60cm	**Bracts**	present, lower 3-lobed
Habitat	grassy places, hedgebanks, fields and road-verges	**Type**	♀
		Size	5–8mm
Flowering	June–August	**Colour**	golden yellow
		Stalk	1–3mm, shorter than flower
STEMS AND LEAVES		**Sepals**	5, oval, pointed
Stem	upright, mostly unbranched	**Petals**	5, oval
Root	rhizome	**Stamens**	10–20
Hairs	gland-tipped on stems, grey-woolly beneath leaves	**Stigmas**	1 per ovary
		Ovaries	1–2, 1-celled
Stipules	leaf-like		
Leaves	on alternate sides of stem, most near base, 3–6 main pairs of elliptical, coarse-toothed leaflets, 20–60mm long, small leaflets between, leaflet at tip; upper leaves with few leaflets	**FRUIT**	
		Type	single, conical, hard wall encloses 1–2 nut-like fruits, grooved, ring of hooked spines near top
Leaf-stalk	short	**Size**	6–7mm
		Seeds	not released

Sanguisorba officinalis Great Burnet

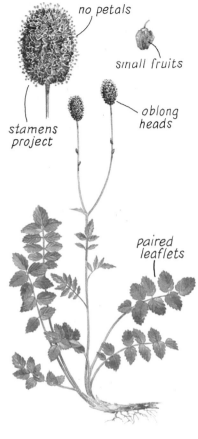

A tall plant with long, bare stalks ending in mahogany-red, oblong heads of petal-less flowers with tassel-like stamens. Its leaves were used to staunch bleeding. *Status:* native; common, throughout area except for parts of north. *Similar species:* Salad Burnet is smaller, with rounder heads. Its cucumber-flavoured leaves were used in salads or cooling drinks. Pirri-pirri-bur and related plants, naturalized in Britain and Ireland, arrived from New Zealand and Australia in wool waste or as garden plants. Barbed spines on the fruit stick to fur or wool.

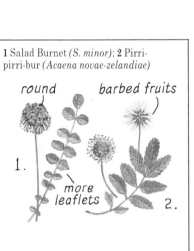

1 Salad Burnet (*S. minor*); **2** Pirri-pirri-bur (*Acaena novae-zelandiae*)

	GREAT BURNET		FLOWERS	
Type	perennial	**Position**	10–20 in oblong head, 10–30mm long, from stem-tip	
Height	30–100cm			
Habitat	grassy places; damp soils	**Bracts**	2–3 beneath each flower	
Flowering	June–September	**Type**	⚥	
		Size	4–5mm	
	STEMS AND LEAVES	**Colour**	dull purplish red	
Stem	upright, branched above	**Stalk**	absent	
Root	thick rootstock	**Sepals**	4, c3mm, coloured	
Hairs	absent	**Petals**	absent	
Stipules	lower papery, upper like leaflets, toothed	**Stamens**	4, long, crimson	
		Stigmas	1 per flower	
Leaves	on alternate sides of stem, lower with 3–7 pairs of oval or oblong leaflets, leaflet at tip, each 20–40mm, blunt, edge toothed, base heart-shaped; upper few, smaller	**Ovary**	1, 1-celled	
			FRUIT	
		Type	10–20 in head, nut-like, 4-winged, not opening, each encloses single seed	
Leaf-stalk	present	**Size**	c4mm	
		Seeds	1, not released	

Dryas octopetala Mountain Avens

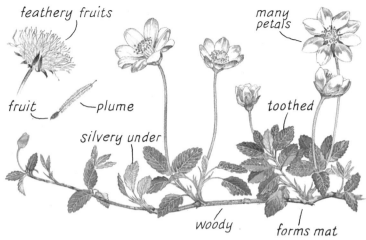

Wiry stems of Mountain Avens support a tough mat of dark green foliage which carpets rocky places or hangs down cliffs. In Summer it is dotted with anemone-like flowers of white petals encircling a boss of golden stamens. Later, it has feathery, plumed fruits like those of the distantly related Pasqueflower and Traveller's Joy. A mountain plant in the south of the area, it is found by the Atlantic shore in the north-west. This is mainly an Arctic plant, elsewhere being a relict from the last Ice Age when it covered large expanses south of the ice-sheet. Mountain Avens is often cultivated as a rockery plant in gardens, and is propagated by layering young shoots or from seed. Uses for the plant include infusion as a stomach tonic and a gargle to treat infections of the mouth and throat. *Status:* native; mountains towards south, more common at low altitudes towards Arctic. (There are no similar species.)

	MOUNTAIN AVENS		Leaf-stalk	present
Type	perennial			
Height	low-growing		**FLOWERS**	
Habitat	rock crevices, mountain ledges, sometimes near sea-level; base-rich rocks	**Position**	single, from base of leaf	
		Bracts	absent	
		Type	⚥	
Flowering	June–July	**Size**	25–40mm	
		Colour	white	
	STEMS AND LEAVES	**Stalk**	20–80mm, upright	
Stem	up to 50cm long, woody, twisted, much-branched	**Sepals**	7–10, oblong	
		Petals	8–16, 7–17mm, oblong	
Root	creeping	**Stamens**	numerous	
Hairs	dense, white beneath leaves, hairless above, flower-stalks and sepals with gland-tipped hairs	**Stigmas**	1 per ovary	
		Ovaries	numerous	
			FRUIT	
Stipules	papery, brownish	**Type**	numerous in cluster, nut-like at base, with long, feathery, whitish plume	
Leaves	on alternate sides of stem, 5–40mm, oblong or oval, evergreen, blunt, toothed, base squarish			
		Size	20–30mm	
		Seeds	not released	

Wood Avens *Geum urbanum*

Shady places are home to the small yellow, upturned flowers and hooked, animal-dispersed fruits of Wood Avens. In gardens it is awkward to remove because the brittle stems snap, leaving the roots. Faintly clove-scented, the roots were once used to flavour ale or as an insect-repellent. *Status:* native; most of area except parts of north. *Similar species:* Water Avens, in wet places, has larger, nodding, orange-pink flowers. Hybrid Avens grows near Wood Avens, with intermediate but often very variable flowers. Marsh Cinquefoil has reddish sepals and slender, purple petals.

turns upwards

hooked fruits

bristly

stipules

brittle

paired leaflets

1 Water Avens (*G. rivale*); **2** Hybrid Avens (*G. × intermedium*); **3** Marsh Cinquefoil (*Potentilla palustris*)

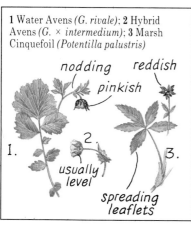

nodding

reddish

pinkish

1.

2.

usually level

3.

spreading leaflets

	WOOD AVENS		Leaf-stalk	present
Type	perennial			**FLOWERS**
Height	20–60cm		**Position**	2–5, in wide-branched heads
Habitat	shady places, woods, hedges; damp, rich soils		**Bracts**	present
			Type	⚲
Flowering	June–August		**Size**	10–15mm
			Colour	yellow
	STEMS AND LEAVES		**Stalk**	longer than flower, upright
Stem	mostly upright, brittle		**Sepals**	5, oval, pointed
Root	fibrous from short stock		**Petals**	5, 5–9mm, oval, blunt
Hairs	short, rather bristly		**Stamens**	numerous
Stipules	lower as row of bristles; upper toothed, leaflet-like		**Stigmas**	1 per ovary
			Ovaries	numerous, 1-celled
Leaves	basal or on alternate sides of stem; lower with 2–4 unequal pairs of leaflets, leaflet at tip, each 5–80mm, blunt, toothed, base wedge-shaped; upper with 3 leaflets or lobes			**FRUIT**
			Type	numerous in small head, nut-like, egg-shaped, tip hooked
			Size	3–6mm
			Seeds	not released

Tormentil *Potentilla erecta*

Four-petalled, buttercup-like flowers of Tormentil are a common sight on heaths or other grassy places. Its dried roots have many uses including treating mouth infections or sunburn, and provide a red dye. Tormentil is a larval food of the Grizzled Skipper butterfly. *Status:* native; common, throughout area. *Similar species:* stems of Creeping Cinquefoil run along the ground, regularly sending up long-stalked leaves and single flowers. Silverweed grows in the same way but its numerous, paired leaflets are silvery beneath. The silvery leaves of Hoary Cinquefoil look more like those of Tormentil.

nut-like fruits

4 petals

stipules

leaflets

1 Creeping Cinquefoil (*P. reptans*); **2** Silverweed (*P. anserina*); **3** Hoary Cinquefoil (*P. argentea*)

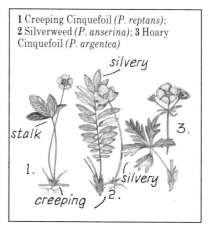

silvery

stalk

3.

1.

creeping

silvery

2.

	TORMENTIL			FLOWERS
Type	perennial		**Position**	numerous in branched head
Height	10–30cm, rarely 50cm		**Bracts**	leaf-like, upper undivided
Habitat	grassland, heaths, wood clearing; mainly acid soil		**Type**	⚲
			Size	7–15mm
Flowering	June–September		**Colour**	yellow
			Stalk	much longer than flower
	STEMS AND LEAVES		**Sepals**	4, 3–5mm, spear-shaped, pointed, surrounded by bract-like structures
Stem	low-growing to nearly upright, slender, branched			
Root	thick, woody stock		**Petals**	4, 3–6mm, tip notched
Hairs	short, pressed to surface		**Stamens**	14–20
Stipules	like leaflets, lobed		**Stigmas**	1 per ovary
Leaves	basal or on alternate sides of stem, with 3 or rarely 5 leaflets; lower 5–10mm, blunt, toothed; upper 10–20mm, narrower, lobed or toothed above		**Ovaries**	4–8, rarely to 20, 1-celled
				FRUIT
Leaf-stalk	long below, absent above		**Type**	mostly 4–8 in rounded head, nut-like, egg-shaped, rough
			Size	c2mm
			Seeds	not released

Fragaria vesca **Wild Strawberry**

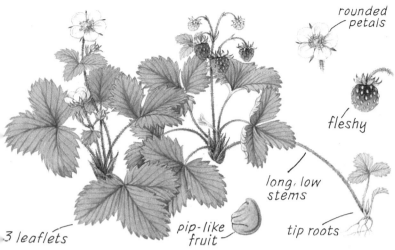

rounded petals

fleshy

long, low stems

pip-like fruit

tip roots

3 leaflets

Like a diminutive version of the Garden Strawberry, the fruits of the Wild Strawberry are less succulent but full of flavour. Plants spread by low, arching stems called runners. The fleshy part of a Strawberry is derived from the swollen base of the flower, the fruits proper being the yellowish pips on the surface. *Status:* native; common throughout area. *Similar species:* Hautbois Strawberry, mainly from the east of the area, is larger and has fruits devoid of pips at the base. Garden Strawberry is commonly naturalized. Barren Strawberry lacks the fleshy base to the nut-like fruits.

1 Hautbois Strawberry (*F. moschata*); 2 Garden Strawberry (*F. × ananassa*); 3 Barren Strawberry (*Potentilla sterilis*)

overlapping petals

no pips at base

1.

notched petals

3. dry fruit

2.

	WILD STRAWBERRY		
Type	perennial		
Height	5–30cm		
Habitat	shady places, woods, hedgerows, grassland; mainly lime-rich soils		
Flowering	April–July		
	STEMS AND LEAVES		
Stem	nearly upright or low, arching and rooting		
Root	thick, woody stock		
Hairs	spreading out on stem, silky under leaves		
Stipules	papery, often purplish		
Leaves	basal or on alternate sides of stem, with 3 leaflets, each 10–60mm, oval, blunt, toothed		
Leaf-stalk	long		

	FLOWERS	
Position	few, in branched head	
Bracts	leaf-like, upper undivided	
Type	☿	
Size	12–18mm	
Colour	white	
Stalk	longer than flower	
Sepals	5, 3–6mm, oval, pointed, bent back in fruit, 5 extra bract-like parts	
Petals	5, 5–7mm, oval, blunt	
Stamens	c20	
Stigmas	1 per ovary	
Ovaries	numerous, 1-celled	
	FRUIT	
Type	egg-shaped or spherical, red, juicy base, mainly tiny, nut-like fruits on surface	
Size	10–20mm	
Seeds	1 per fruit, not released	

Alchemilla filicaulis subsp. *vestita* **Hairy Lady's-mantle**

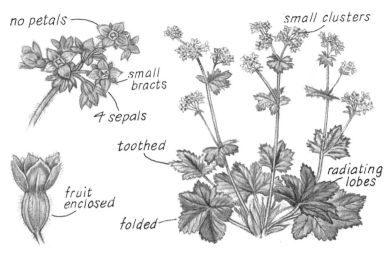

no petals

small clusters

small bracts

4 sepals

toothed

fruit enclosed

radiating lobes

folded

Although its flowers are inconspicuous, the broad leaves of this plant are lobed with fan-like folds, for which it is often grown in gardens. Water-droplets are exuded by the leaves when the air humidity is high, usually before the morning sun touches them. *Status:* native; most of area but rarer in south. *Similar species:* one of the more distinct of many related species is Alpine Lady's-mantle, its narrowly lobed leaves silvery beneath. Parsley-piert is a much smaller, annual plant of waste or cultivated ground. Sibbaldia has leaves cut into leaflets and usually has narrow, yellow petals.

1 Alpine Lady's-mantle (*A. alpina*); 2 Parsley-piert (*Aphanes arvensis*); 3 Sibbaldia (*Sibbaldia procumbens*)

narrow

tiny flowers

2.

1.

silvery under

small petals

leaflets

3.

	HAIRY LADY'S-MANTLE		
Type	perennial		
Height	5–45cm		
Habitat	open woods, rock-ledges, grassland; damp lime-rich or neutral soil		
Flowering	June–September		
	STEMS AND LEAVES		
Stem	turning or angled upwards		
Root	thick, woody stock		
Hairs	rather dense, projecting		
Stipules	papery, often purple-tinged		
Leaves	basal or few on alternate sides of stem; lower 10–150mm, circular or kidney-shaped with 7–9 toothed lobes, notch between lobes wide; upper smaller, with fewer lobes		
Leaf-stalk	long below, short above		

	FLOWERS	
Position	in small clusters on near stem-tips	
Bracts	leaf-like, toothed	
Type	☿	
Size	3–4mm	
Colour	green	
Stalk	shorter than flower	
Sepals	4, oval, broad-based	
Petals	absent	
Stamens	4, between sepals	
Stigma	1, club-shaped	
Ovary	1, 1-celled	
	FRUIT	
Type	1, nut-like, enclosed by base of flower, not opening	
Size	2–3mm	
Seeds	1, not released	

Peas

This is a large and economically important family. Native species are herbaceous or, less commonly, shrubby, but the family includes many large trees and climbers in the tropics. The leaves are commonly divided into three or have paired leaflets. There are normally two stipules at the base of each leaf and, in the Bird's-foot-trefoils and the Garden Pea (*Pisum sativum*), these are relatively large and resemble a further pair of leaflets.

All of the northern European species have remarkably similar individual flowers. Typically, the lowest pair of petals are joined to form a structure called the keel; two side petals are termed the wings; and a large upper petal is called the standard. Some species have solitary flowers while others, such as the Clovers, have compact heads of flowers. Another characteristic feature of the family is the fruit. Most are similar in shape to the familiar pea-pod, but others are short and single-seeded, as in the Clovers, or coiled, as in the Medicks.

An important feature of species of the Pea family is the presence of bacteria in small nodules on the roots. These bacteria convert nitrogen from the atmosphere into a form that can be taken up by the roots and is essential for plant growth. Farmers may grow a crop of Clover or Lucerne to enrich the soil and provide an alternative to manure or artificial fertilizers. Commercially important crops of this family provide various sorts of beans, peas and peanuts.

Smothered with spikes of tiny pea-flowers, Tufted Vetch brings a splash of vibrant colour to a grassy bank.

Lupinus arboreus **Tree Lupin**

These bushy plants form such large colonies by the sea that they appear to be a long-established native species. But they and most other Lupins have been introduced recently from North America. Seeds are flung from the explosive seed pods which, on a hot day, sound like the rattle of gunfire. *Status:* introduced; coastal areas of Britain and Ireland. *Similar species:* Garden Lupin and its hybrids are often found by roads or railways. Stems bear blue, pink or white flowers and die back after fruiting. Sweet Lupin is a Mediterranean annual, naturalized in the south of the area.

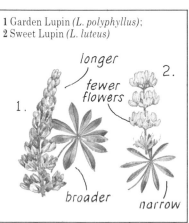

1 Garden Lupin (*L. polyphyllus*);
2 Sweet Lupin (*L. luteus*)

longer
fewer flowers
1.
2.
broader
narrow

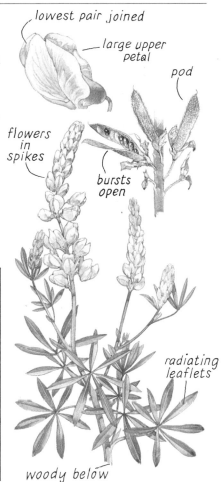

lowest pair joined
large upper petal
pod
flowers in spikes
bursts open
radiating leaflets
woody below

	TREE LUPIN			
Type	shrub	Bracts	absent
Height	up to 300cm	Type	⚥, scented
Habitat	shingle banks, waste ground	Size	14–17mm
Flowering	June–September	Colour	yellow, rarely white or tinged with blue
		Stalk	shorter than flower
	STEMS AND LEAVES	Sepals	joined into 2-lipped tube
Stem	much-branched, woody below	Petals	5, 14–17mm, lowest pair joined, overlapped by 2 side petals, upper largest
Root	fibrous from stout stock		
Hairs	leaves hairless above, silky below	Stamens	10, joined at base
Stipules	joined to leaf-stalk	Stigma	1, on curved style
Leaves	on alternate sides of stem, 7–11 radiating, spear-shaped leaflets, each 20–60mm, pointed	Ovary	1, 1-celled
Leaf-stalk	about equalling leaflets		FRUIT
		Type	1, pod, hairy, splits open, flicks seeds out
	FLOWERS	Size	c80mm
Position	numerous, spirally arranged in spike at stem-tip, stalk of spike 4–10cm	Seeds	8–12, 4–5mm, ellipsoidal

Vicia cracca **Tufted Vetch**

An elegant plant, climbing high through tall grass or hedgerow by means of branched tendrils at the tips of ladder-like leaves. The slender spires of small pea-flowers open a rather pale purple but fade deep violet-blue. *Status:* native; common, throughout area. *Similar species:* Bush Vetch is less robust, and has smaller, short-stalked spikes of duller purple flowers. Two related species frequent wooded or rocky places: Wood Vetch has fewer, larger flowers and toothed stipules; Wood Bitter-vetch lacks a tendril at the leaf-tip.

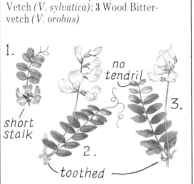

1 Bush Vetch (*V. sepium*); 2 Wood Vetch (*V. sylvatica*); 3 Wood Bitter-vetch (*V. orobus*)

1.
no tendril
3.
short stalk
2.
toothed

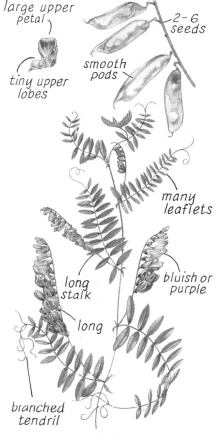

large upper petal
tiny upper lobes
2–6 seeds
smooth pods
many leaflets
long stalk
bluish or purple
long
branched tendril

	TUFTED VETCH			
Type	perennial	Bracts	absent
Height	60–200cm	Type	⚥
Habitat	among grass or bushes	Size	10–12mm
Flowering	June–August	Colour	pale purple, turning blue
		Stalk	much shorter than flower
	STEMS AND LEAVES	Sepals	5, 2–4mm, joined into tube at base, upper teeth short
Stem	climbing by tendrils		
Root	fibrous, with tiny nodules	Petals	5, 10–12mm, lowest pair joined, side pair overlap lower, upper largest
Hairs	pressed close against leaves or absent		
Stipules	half arrow-shaped, not toothed	Stamens	10, 9 joined at base
Leaves	on alternate sides of stem, branched tendril at tip, 6–15 pairs of leaflets, each 5–30mm, spear-shaped, pointed	Stigma	1, with hairy style
		Ovary	1, 1-celled
Leaf-stalk	almost absent		FRUIT
		Type	1, pod, oblong, smooth, splits lengthwise into 2
	FLOWERS	Size	10–20mm
Position	10–40, in long-stalked, dense spike from leaf-base	Seeds	2–6, c3mm, orbicular

Hairy Tare *Vicia hirsuta*

Tares have caused farmers problems for thousands of years, reducing yields and making harvesting difficult, and are mentioned as such in the Bible. Slender stems climb with twining tendrils, to bear tiny flowers and pods amidst fields of grain. *Status:* native, throughout area. *Similar species:* other Tares have short, unequal sepal-teeth. Smooth Tare has one or two flowers on a stalk and smooth, mostly four-seeded pods. Slender Tare has small flower-heads and pods usually with five or six seeds. Bird's-foot has a leaf-like bract just below the flowers, and curved, jointed pods.

1 Smooth Tare (*V. tetrasperma*);
2 Slender Tare (*V. tenuissima*);
3 Bird's-foot (*Ornithopus perpusillus*)

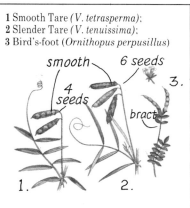

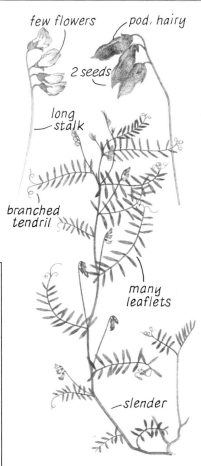

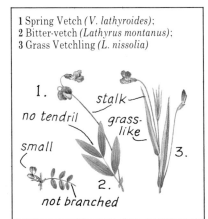

	HAIRY TARE
Type	annual
Height	20–30cm, rarely 70cm
Habitat	cultivated ground, grassy places
Flowering	May–August
	STEMS AND LEAVES
Stem	climbing, slender
Root	fibrous, with tiny nodules
Hairs	nearly hairless
Stipules	often lobed
Leaves	on alternate sides of stem, branched tendril at tip, 4–10 pairs of leaflets, each 5–12mm, narrowly oblong, tip squarish or notched
Leaf-stalk	mostly absent

	FLOWERS
Position	1–9, in short spike from leaf-base, stalk 10–30mm
Bracts	absent
Type	⚥
Size	2–4mm, rarely 5mm
Colour	dull white or purplish
Stalk	shorter than flower
Sepals	5, *c*2mm, bases joined, teeth equal, longer than tube
Petals	5, 4–5mm, lowest 2 joined, 2 side petals overlap lower
Stamens	10, 9 joined at base
Stigma	1, style hairless or hairy
Ovary	1, 1-celled
	FRUIT
Type	1, pod, splits lengthwise, oblong, hairy, black
Size	6–11 × 3–5mm
Seeds	usually 2, *c*1mm, round

Common Vetch *Vicia sativa*

This common plant twines its way through grass, bearing rather small but bright pea-flowers. There are two forms: one native, with rather pointed leaflets, small flowers and straight pods; the other, a crop or naturalized, with mostly notched leaflets, larger flowers and pods narrowed between the seeds. *Status:* native or introduced; throughout area. *Similar species:* Spring Vetch has smaller flowers and rough seeds. Two species lack tendrils and have a long stalk bearing the flowers: Bitter-vetch has several pairs of leaflets, and Grass Vetchling has odd, grass-like leaves.

1 Spring Vetch (*V. lathyroides*);
2 Bitter-vetch (*Lathyrus montanus*);
3 Grass Vetchling (*L. nissolia*)

	COMMON VETCH
Type	annual
Height	15–120cm
Habitat	hedges, grassy places
Flowering	May–September
	STEMS AND LEAVES
Stem	climbing or trailing
Root	fibrous, with tiny nodules
Hairs	short, throughout
Stipules	usually toothed, with blackish mark
Leaves	on alternate sides of stem, branched tendril at tip, 4–8 pairs of leaflets, each 6–20mm, tip pointed, blunt or notched
Leaf-stalk	short
	FLOWERS
Position	1–2, at leaf-base

Bracts	absent
Type	⚥
Size	10–30mm
Colour	purplish magenta
Stalk	shorter than flower
Sepals	5, 6–12mm, equal, bases joined, teeth equal to tube
Petals	5, 10–30mm, lowest pair joined, side pair overlap lower, upper largest
Stamens	10, 9 joined at base
Stigma	1, style hairy
Ovary	1, 1-celled
	FRUIT
Type	1, pod, splits lengthwise, narrowly oblong, tip beaked
Size	25–80mm
Seeds	4–12, 2–6.5mm, globular, smooth, mottled

Ononis repens **Common Restharrow**

Restharrow's pretty pink pea-flowers are found in dry grassy places, especially chalk-grassland. Tough, matted, underground stems of Restharrow literally arrested the harrow of ox-drawn ploughs. Farmers disliked the plant also because it gave an unpleasant taint to cow's milk, yet the underground stems were sometimes cut for chewing like Wild Liquorice. *Status:* native; most of area, rarer in north. *Similar species:* Spiny Restharrow has spine-tipped stems, with two lines of hairs. Large Yellow-restharrow, from the south of the area, is a much stickier plant, its yellow flowers pencilled red.

large upper petal
short pod
1 or 3 leaflets
hairy all round stem
stipules
curves upwards

1 Spiny Restharrow (*O. spinosa*);
2 Large Yellow-restharrow (*O. natrix*)

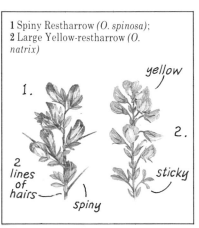

1.
yellow
2.
2 lines of hairs
spiny
sticky

COMMON RESTHARROW		Bracts	leaf-like
Type	perennial	**Type**	♀
Height	30–60cm	**Size**	10–20mm
Habitat	grassy places; dry, often lime-rich soils	**Colour**	pink or purple
		Stalk	much shorter than flower
Flowering	June–September	**Sepals**	5, bases joined, teeth equal, longer than tube, enlarged in fruit
STEMS AND LEAVES			
Stem	low-growing or angled upwards, woody, rooting below	**Petals**	5, 7–20mm, lowest pair joined, side pair overlap lower, upper largest, broad
Root	creeping underground stem	**Stamens**	10, bases joined
Hairs	long or short and sticky, hairy all round stems	**Stigma**	1, style long, hairless
		Ovary	1, 1-celled
Stipules	toothed, bases clasp stem		
Leaves	on alternate sides of stem, each up to 20mm, with 1–3 leaflets, tip blunt, edge toothed	**FRUIT**	
		Type	1, pod, splits lengthwise, shorter than sepals, oblong
Leaf-stalk	3–5mm, shorter than leaf	**Size**	5–7mm
FLOWERS		**Seeds**	1–4, 2–3mm, globular, rough
Position	1–2 at leaf-base		

Lathyrus pratensis **Meadow Vetchling**

A common plant of meadows and grassy edges of roads or paths, it has clusters of rich yellow pea-flowers. Specialized nodules on its roots turn nitrogen from the air into a form which enriches the pasture. *Status:* native; throughout area. *Similar species:* Yellow Vetchling is a rather rare native annual in dry, sandy or chalky places in the south of the area, although it is sometimes introduced further north. Its 'leaves' are the broad, arrow-shaped stipules, the true leaves being reduced to tendrils. Yellow-vetch has short-stalked, solitary flowers at the base of leaves with many paired leaflets.

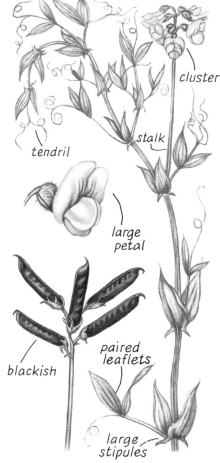

cluster
stalk
tendril
large petal
paired leaflets
large stipules

1 Yellow Vetchling (*L. aphaca*);
2 Yellow-vetch (*Vicia lutea*)

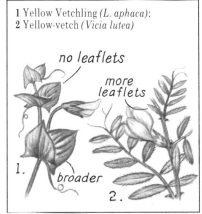

no leaflets
more leaflets
blackish
1.
broader
2.

MEADOW VETCHLING		Bracts	minute
Type	perennial	**Type**	♀
Height	30–120cm	**Size**	15–18mm
Habitat	grassland, scrub	**Colour**	yellow, greenish veins
Flowering	May–August	**Stalk**	shorter than flower
		Sepals	5, bases joined, teeth equalling tube
STEMS AND LEAVES			
Stem	climbs or trails, angled	**Petals**	5, 11–18mm, lowest pair joined, side pair overlap lower, upper largest
Root	fibrous, with tiny nodules		
Hairs	short, throughout plant		
Stipules	10–25mm, arrow-shaped	**Stamens**	10, 9 joined at base
Leaves	on alternate sides of stem, tendril at tip sometimes branched, 1 pair of leaflets, each 10–30mm, spear-shaped, pointed	**Stigma**	1, hairy on one side
		Ovary	1, 1-celled
		FRUIT	
Leaf-stalk	about equalling leaflets	**Type**	1, pod, splits lengthwise, oblong, blackish
FLOWERS		**Size**	25–35mm
Position	5–12, in long-stalked head from leaf-base	**Seeds**	5–10, 3–4mm, globular, smooth

Narrow-leaved Everlasting-pea *Lathyrus sylvestris*

This exotic-looking plant has long-stalked heads of pink pea-flowers, similar to the cultivated Sweet Pea. Its leaves have two narrow leaflets and a tendril enabling the plant to scramble over surrounding vegetation. *Status:* native; scattered through area except extreme north. *Similar species:* two southern species are sometimes naturalized further north. Broad-leaved Everlasting-pea has broader leaves and stipules. Tuberous Pea has narrow, angled stems, swollen tubers and crimson flowers. The low-growing Sea Pea has several pairs of broad leaflets and grows on dunes, shingle beaches or, rarely, lake-shores.

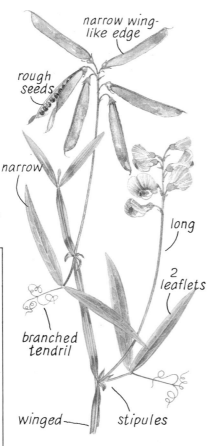

narrow wing-like edge

rough seeds

narrow

long

2 leaflets

branched tendril

winged

stipules

1 Broad-leaved Everlasting-pea (*L. latifolius*); 2 Tuberous Pea (*L. tuberosus*); 3 Sea Pea (*L. japonicus*)

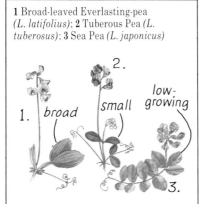

2.

1. broad small low-growing

3.

	NARROW-LEAVED EVERLASTING-PEA	**FLOWERS**	
Type	perennial	**Position**	3–12 in head on stalk 100–200mm long, from leaf-base
Height	100–200cm	**Bracts**	small, pointed
Habitat	woods, scrub, hedges, railway embankments	**Type**	♂
		Size	15–17mm
Flowering	June–August	**Colour**	rosy pink
		Stalk	shorter than flower
	STEMS AND LEAVES	**Sepals**	5, unequal, bases joined, teeth shorter than tube
Stem	climbing, broadly winged	**Petals**	5, 12–17mm, lowest pair joined, side pair overlap lower
Root	fibrous, with tiny nodules	**Stamens**	10, 9 joined at base
Hairs	absent	**Stigma**	1, style curved, hairy
Stipules	up to 20mm, slender, pointed, narrow basal lobe	**Ovary**	1, 1-celled
Leaves	on alternate sides of stem, branched tendril at tip, 2 leaflets, each 70–150mm, narrowly elliptical or spear-shaped, bluish, pointed	**FRUIT**	
		Type	1, pod, splits lengthwise, oblong, top edge winged
		Size	50–70mm
Leaf-stalk	shorter than leaflets	**Seeds**	8–14, 5–6mm, globular, rough

Lucerne *Medicago sativa*

An important crop, often grown for the tiny nodules on the roots, in which bacteria turn nitrogen from the air into nitrates. These are essential for plant growth and enrich the soil in a way similar to fertilizers. *Status:* introduced; most of area except extreme north. *Similar species:* several native plants have yellow flowers and tightly coiled, spiny fruits. Spotted Medick, with dark-spotted leaves, has three grooves on the edge of each coil of the fruit. Toothed Medick lacks spots and has only two grooves. Bur Medick has hairy leaves and tiny fruits, bristling with fine spines.

large, upper petal

rounded fruits

in heads

3 leaflets
2 stipules

blunt

toothed

1-3 coils

1 Spotted Medick (*M. arabica*); 2 Toothed Medick (*M. polymorpha*); 3 Bur Medick (*M. minima*)

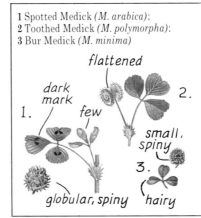

flattened

dark mark

few

2.

small, spiny

3.

globular, spiny hairy

	LUCERNE	**Bracts**	small, slender
Type	perennial	**Type**	♂
Height	30–90cm	**Size**	7–12mm
Habitat	waste and grassy places	**Colour**	purple
Flowering	June–July	**Stalk**	shorter than flower
		Sepals	5, equal, bases joined, teeth about equalling tube
	STEMS AND LEAVES	**Petals**	5, 6–12mm, lowest pair joined, side pair overlap lower, upper largest
Stem	upright or angled upwards		
Root	deep, with tiny nodules	**Stamens**	10, 9 joined at base
Hairs	short, on whole plant	**Stigma**	1, club-shaped
Stipules	narrowly spear-shaped, toothed, on leaf-stalk	**Ovary**	1, 1-celled
Leaves	on alternate sides of stem, 3 leaflets, each to 30mm, broadest near tip, blunt except for fine point, toothed above	**FRUIT**	
		Type	1, pod, rarely splitting, in spiral of 1–3 turns
Leaf-stalk	usually shorter than leaf	**Size**	4–6mm
	FLOWERS	**Seeds**	10–20, 2–3mm, smooth
Position	5–40, in spike with stalk about equalling leaf		

Trifolium campestre Hop Trefoil

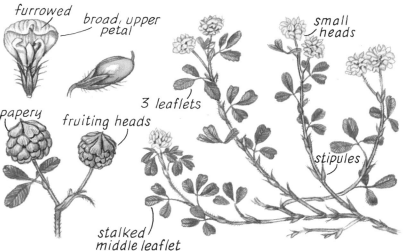

furrowed

broad, upper petal

small heads

papery

fruiting heads

3 leaflets

stipules

stalked middle leaflet

Hop Trefoil is a small, clover-like plant with tiny yellow flower-heads, and is common in short grass. The fruiting heads look like diminutive hops, owing to the dry petals which remain attached. *Status:* native; very common, most of area. *Similar species:* Lesser Trefoil has smaller fruiting heads, the dark brown upper petals lacking grooves but folded over the pod. Slender Trefoil has stalkless middle leaflets and very few flowers in a head. In flower, Black Medick is often mistaken for Hop Trefoil but has coiled black pods without remains of flowers.

1 Lesser Trefoil (*T. dubium*);
2 Slender Trefoil (*T. micranthum*);
3 Black Medick (*Medicago lupulina*)

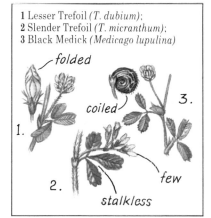

folded

coiled

3.

1.

2.

few

stalkless

	HOP TREFOIL			
Type	annual	**Bracts**	absent	
Height	5–35cm, rarely to 50cm	**Type**		
Habitat	grassy places; dryish soil	**Size**	4–6mm	
Flowering	June–September	**Colour**	yellow, turning pale brown	
		Stalk	very short	
	STEMS AND LEAVES	**Sepals**	5, unequal, bases joined, teeth about equal tube	
Stem	upright or angled upwards	**Petals**	5, 3–6mm, remaining in fruit, lowest pair joined, side pair overlap lower, upper broad, becomes grooved	
Root	fibrous, with tiny nodules			
Hairs	over whole plant			
Stipules	oval, joined to leaf-stalk, not toothed			
Leaves	on alternate sides of stem, with 3 leaflets, the end one stalked, each 6–10mm, tip blunt or notched, edge toothed	**Stamens**	10, 9 joined at base	
		Stigma	1, with curved style	
		Ovary	1, 1-celled	
Leaf-stalk	shorter than leaflets			
			FRUIT	
	FLOWERS	**Type**	1, egg-shaped pod, not opening	
Position	20–30, in head from leaf-base, stalk about equals leaf	**Size**	2–2.5mm	
		Seeds	1, 1–1.5mm, yellow	

Trifolium arvense Hare's-foot Clover

A slender, short-lived annual, often covering large areas on sand-dunes in early Summer. Attractive, pink, softly hairy flower-heads give the plant its common name. In fruit, the reddish, bristle-like sepal-teeth project from the head like a miniature bottle-brush. *Status:* native; scattered, most common in south and east. *Similar species:* the cultivated Crimson Clover is more robust, and has crimson petals, although a rarer pale form on cliff-tops is native. Two low-growing species are Knotted Clover, which has stalkless flower-heads, and Strawberry Clover, which has an inflated, reddish sepal-tube in fruit.

pink

soft hairs

long sepals

hairy

3 leaflets

stipules

elongated in fruit

1 Crimson Clover (*T. incarnatum*);
2 Knotted Clover (*T. striatum*);
3 Strawberry Clover (*T. fragiferum*)

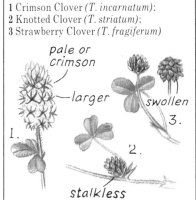

pale or crimson

larger

swollen

1.

2.

3.

stalkless

	HARE'S-FOOT CLOVER			
Type	annual or biennial	**Bracts**	absent	
Height	5–40cm	**Type**		
Habitat	arable fields, pastures, dunes; dry, sandy soil	**Size**	3.5–7mm	
Flowering	June–September	**Colour**	white or pink	
		Stalk	almost absent	
	STEMS AND LEAVES	**Sepals**	5, about equal, bases joined, bristle-like teeth, reddish, longer than tube and petals	
Stem	upright or angled upwards	**Petals**	5, remaining in fruit, 2.5–7mm, lower 2 joined, side 2 overlapping, upper largest	
Root	fibrous, with tiny nodules			
Hairs	soft, downy, white or pink, dense on sepals			
Stipules	oval, bristle-like tip			
Leaves	on alternate sides of stem, with 3 leaflets, each 10–15, oblong, blunt or sharpish	**Stamens**	10, 9 joined at base	
		Stigma	1, style-tip curved	
		Ovary	1, 1-celled	
Leaf-stalk	to 10mm, upper stalkless			
			FRUIT	
	FLOWERS	**Type**	1, pod, egg-shaped	
Position	numerous, in stalked, cylindrical heads to 25mm, from stem-tip or leaf-base	**Size**	1–1.5mm	
		Seeds	1, c0.8mm, egg-shaped	

Red Clover *Trifolium pratense*

The familiar Clover of pasture, grown to feed livestock and to enrich the pasture by virtue of tiny nodules on its roots. Many vigorous forms, often with paired heads, have been bred and frequently escape from fields. Clover leaflets fold up at night or in rain. The flowers are important to bee-keepers as a nectar-source. *Status:* native or planted; often very common, most of area. *Similar species:* Zigzag Clover has rather twisting stems; the base of the sepals is hairless. Species with white or pink flowers include White Clover, which has creeping, rooting stems, and Alsike Clover which has upright stems.

1 Zigzag Clover *(T. medium)*; **2** White Clover *(T. repens)*; **3** Alsike Clover *(T. hybridum)*

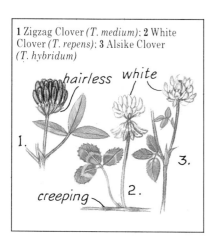

	RED CLOVER		Bracts	2 tiny leaves with broad stipules beneath head
Type	perennial		**Type**	♀
Height	5–100cm		**Size**	12–15mm
Habitat	grassy places; mostly rich, moist soil		**Colour**	usually pinkish purple
Flowering	May–September		**Stalk**	absent
			Sepals	5, bases joined, tube 10-ribbed, hairy, teeth thin
	STEMS AND LEAVES		**Petals**	5, 10–15mm, attached in fruit, lower 2 joined, side 2 hide lower, upper broad
Stem	upright or turns upright		**Stamens**	10, 9 joined at base
Root	fibrous, with tiny nodules		**Stigma**	1, style-tip curved
Hairs	short, often sparse above		**Ovary**	1, 1-celled
Stipules	oblong, bases joined, end triangular, tip slender			
Leaves	on alternate sides of stem, 3 leaflets, each 10–30mm, mostly elliptical, with V-shaped, white mark, blunt			**FRUIT**
			Type	1, pod, egg-shaped, tip breaks off, hairless
Leaf-stalk	lower longer than leaves		**Size**	2–2.5mm
			Seeds	1, 1.5–2mm, notched
	FLOWERS			
Position	many in rounded, stalkless head, 20–40mm, at stem-tip			

Tall Melilot *Melilotus altissima*

A tall, bushy plant with many branched stems bearing slender, spiky flower-heads. The whole plant has an aroma of new-mown hay, especially when dried. Melilots were once used to treat blisters, swellings and sore eyes. *Status:* native or introduced in west; most of area. *Similar species:* other Melilots have hairless fruits. White Melilot is easily identified by the white petals. Ribbed Melilot has short lower petals and blunt, ridged, brown ripe pods. Small Melilot has tiny flowers and smaller, olive-green ripe pods.

1 White Melilot *(M. alba)*; **2** Ribbed Melilot *(M. officinalis)*; **3** Small Melilot *(M. indica)*

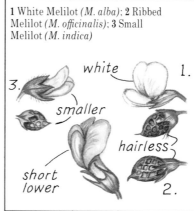

	TALL MELILOT		Bracts	hair-like
Type	biennial or perennial		**Type**	♀
Height	60–150cm		**Size**	5–6mm
Habitat	grassland, wood clearings; damp, sometimes salty soil		**Colour**	yellow
Flowering	June–August		**Stalk**	shorter than flower
			Sepals	5, bases joined, teeth longer than tube
	STEMS AND LEAVES		**Petals**	5, 5–6mm, about equal, lower 2 joined, side 2 overlap, upper broad
Stem	upright, branched		**Stamens**	10, 9 joined
Root	fibrous, with tiny nodules		**Stigma**	1, style long, curved
Hairs	under leaves, on sepals		**Ovary**	1, 1-celled
Stipules	slender, bristle-like			
Leaves	on alternate sides of stem, with 3 leaflets, each 15–30mm, oblong or oval, blunt, edge toothed			**FRUIT**
			Type	1, egg-shaped pod, most not opening, net-like pattern, hairy, pointed, black
Leaf-stalk	shorter than leaflets		**Size**	5–6mm
			Seeds	2, 2–2.5mm, notched
	FLOWERS			
Position	many, in stalked head, 20–50mm, from leaf-base			

A plant of sunny, grassy places, with wiry stems bearing yellow pea-flowers tipped or streaked with red. Of its many common names, 'Eggs and bacon' recalls the yellow and red flowers. The leaves are food to the larvae of the Silver-studded Blue butterfly and the Six-spot Burnet moth. *Status:* native; throughout area. *Similar species:* Greater Bird's-foot-trefoil, of wetter places, has tall, upright, hollow stems and creeping underground stems. Horseshoe Vetch has many leaflets and wavy pods that break into horseshoe-shaped segments. Dragon's-teeth has larger flowers and pods with 4, wing-like angles.

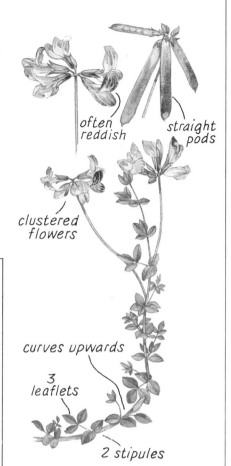
often reddish — *straight pods* — *clustered flowers* — *curves upwards* — *3 leaflets* — *2 stipules*

1 Greater Bird's-foot-trefoil (*L. uliginosus*); **2** Horseshoe Vetch (*Hippocrepis comosa*); **3** Dragon's-teeth (*Tetragonolobus maritimus*)

wavy — *2.* — *single, angled* — *1.* — *3.* — *upright, hollow* — *paired leaflets*

COMMON BIRD'S-FOOT-TREFOIL			
Type	perennial	**Bracts**	divided into 3
Height	10–40cm	**Type**	↓
Habitat	grassy places	**Size**	10–16mm
Flowering	June–September	**Colour**	yellow, often tinged or veined with red
STEMS AND LEAVES		**Stalk**	shorter than flowers
Stem	low-growing, tips turn up	**Sepals**	5, equal, bases joined, teeth about equal tube
Root	stout, woody stock	**Petals**	9–16mm, lower 2 joined, side 2 overlap, upper largest
Hairs	hairless or rarely hairy	**Stamens**	10, 9 joined at base
Stipules	minute	**Stigma**	1, style long, straight
Leaves	on alternate sides of stem, 5 leaflets, lower 2 stipule-like, each 3–10mm, oval, blunt, edge unbroken	**Ovary**	1, 1-celled
		FRUIT	
Leaf-stalk	very short	**Type**	1, pod, splits lengthwise, cylindrical, straight; partitions between seeds
FLOWERS		**Size**	15–30mm
Position	2–8 in short head, stalk up to 80mm, from leaf-base	**Seeds**	many, 1–1.5mm, kidney-shaped

A plant of sunny, grassy places, especially the short turf around tops of sea-cliffs. The flower-heads often have a dual nature, one half in flower, the other in bud or fruit. *Status:* native; widespread, most of area, most common by coast. *Similar species:* several pea-flowered species have more elongated flower-heads. Wild Liquorice has cream-coloured flowers and long, curved, hairless pods. Two yellow-flowered species that have swollen, hairy pods are Yellow Alpine Milk-vetch (tiny sepal-teeth and ellipsoidal pods) and Wild Lentil (oval, membranous pods and sepal-teeth about half as long as the tube).

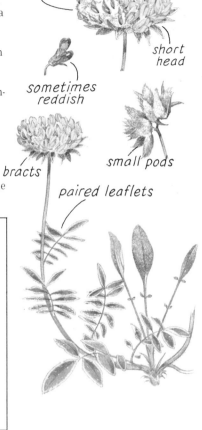
woolly — *short head* — *sometimes reddish* — *small pods* — *bracts* — *paired leaflets*

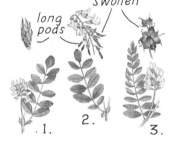
1 Wild Liquorice (*Astragalus glycyphyllos*); **2** Yellow Alpine Milk-vetch (*A. frigidus*); **3** Wild Lentil (*A. cicer*)

long pods — *swollen* — *.1.* — *2.* — *3.*

KIDNEY VETCH			
Type	perennial, rarely annual	**Bracts**	2, leafy, several leaflets
Height	5–60cm	**Type**	↓
Habitat	grassy places; dry, often lime-rich soils	**Size**	12–15mm
		Colour	yellow, rarely tinged red
Flowering	June–September	**Stalk**	mostly absent
STEMS AND LEAVES		**Sepals**	5, bases joined, inflated, woolly, teeth short, unequal
Stem	upright or turns upright	**Petals**	5, 10–15mm, lowest pair joined, side pair overlap lower, upper largest
Root	fibrous, with tiny nodules		
Hairs	short, silky	**Stamens**	10, 9 joined at base
Stipules	small, soon fall	**Stigma**	1, club-shaped
Leaves	on alternate sides of stem, to 140mm, mostly 5–15 oval to oblong leaflets, that at tip often largest, lower scattered, upper paired	**Ovary**	1, 1-celled
		FRUIT	
Leaf-stalk	short or absent	**Type**	1 nearly globular pod, not opening, sepals persist
FLOWERS		**Size**	c3mm
Position	numerous, in dense, mostly paired, long-stalked heads	**Seeds**	1–2, 2–2.5mm, notched

Sainfoin *Onobrychis viciifolia*

A spectacular plant to find in a pasture or grassy verge on a chalky hillside, its bright pink flowers lined with purple. A network of ridges and spines covers the unusual pods. The common name, borrowed from the French, simply means that this makes wholesome hay. *Status:* probably introduced; mainly southern. *Similar species:* several plants with pink or purplish pea-flowers have longer pods lacking teeth. Purple Milk-vetch has short stems and dense heads of purple flowers. Crown Vetch has a ring of pink flowers and the long pods break into segments. Goat's-rue is bushy, with lilac or white flowers.

1 Purple Milk-vetch (*Astragalus danicus*); **2** Crown Vetch (*Coronilla varia*); **3** Goat's-rue (*Galega officinalis*)

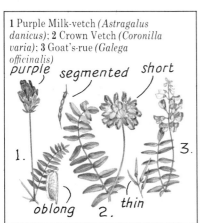

large upper petal
striped
toothed
net-like pattern
in spikes
fruits
upright
paired leaflets

purple
segmented
short
oblong
thin

	SAINFOIN		Bracts	minute
Type	perennial		**Type**	♀
Height	30–60cm		**Size**	10–12mm
Habitat	grassland; lime-rich soils		**Colour**	pink or red, purple veins
Flowering	June–August		**Stalk**	much shorter than flower
	STEMS AND LEAVES		**Sepals**	5, 5–8mm, bases joined into tube, teeth very narrow, longer than tube
Stem	upright		**Petals**	5, 4–12mm, lower 2 joined, side 2 tiny, upper broad
Root	fibrous, with tiny nodules		**Stamens**	10, 9 joined at base
Hairs	short, sparse		**Stigma**	1
Stipules	oval, papery		**Ovary**	1, 1-celled
Leaves	on alternate sides of stem, oblong or oval leaflets in 6–12 pairs, one at tip, each 10–30mm, not toothed			**FRUIT**
Leaf-stalk	short		**Type**	1, short pod, not opening, with network of ridges and bumps, 6–8 teeth on edge
	FLOWERS		**Size**	6–8mm
Position	up to 50 in long-stalked, spike-like head from leaf-base		**Seeds**	1, not released

Sainfoin's pea-like flowers are striped and suffused with pink or purple.

Crane's-bills, Spurges, Wood-sorrels and Flaxes

Plants of three of these families, the Crane's-bills, Wood-sorrels and Flaxes, may produce large, brightly coloured flowers, all having parts in multiples of five. In the majority of species the petals are equal.

Crane's-bills develop a long beak-like projection from the ovary that persists in fruit and is involved in seed dispersal. In typical Crane's-bills it splits away with a section of the fruit wall, coiling up like a clock-spring and flinging out the seed. In Stork's-bills it remains attached to part of the fruit enclosing a seed and forms a coil that drills the seed into the ground.

The Wood-sorrels are predominantly a tropical family. Many species, including our native Wood-sorrel, have leaflets which fold downwards at night or in cool weather. The seeds have an unusual swollen, fleshy appendage which at maturity suddenly turns inside out, detaching from the seed which is violently flung from the fruit. This method of dispersal, coupled with the rather brittle stems and tenacious roots, makes some of the Wood-sorrels troublesome weeds.

Flaxes include the flax of commerce, grown both for its fibres (linen) and for linseed oil.

Another plant group included here is the Spurge family. Nearly all species have distinctive milky sap.

Bright flowers of Meadow Crane's-bill develop into fruits with a long "beak" – hence its common name.

Wood-sorrel *Oxalis acetosella*

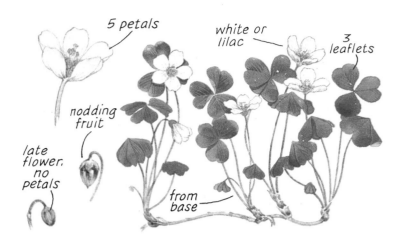

5 petals

white or lilac

3 leaflets

nodding fruit

late flower, no petals

from base

The delicate white flowers and clover-like leaves of Wood-sorrel carpet the floor of many deciduous woods in Spring. At night and in wet weather, the leaflets fold together. An elastic coat to the seeds enables them to be shot from the capsule. Most seeds develop from late, petal-less flowers. *Status:* native; throughout area. *Similar species:* several yellow-flowered species are naturalized. Procumbent Yellow-sorrel has slender, trailing, rooting stems; Upright Yellow-sorrel has thick, upright stems. Bermuda-buttercup, with large heads of flowers, occurs in the south-west.

1 Procumbent Yellow-sorrel (*O. corniculata*); 2 Bermuda-buttercup (*O. pes-caprae*); 3 Upright Yellow-sorrel (*O. europaea*)

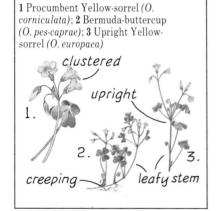

clustered

upright

1.

2.

3.

creeping

leafy stem

	WOOD-SORREL		FLOWERS	
Type	perennial	**Position**	single, at stem-tip
Height	5–15cm	**Bracts**	2, small, at middle of stem
Habitat	woods, hedgerows, among	**Type 1**	⚥, cup-shaped
	rocks; mostly acid soils	**Type 2**	late, no petals, not opening
Flowering	April–May	**Size**	15–30mm
		Colour	white, rarely lilac or purple, lilac veins
	STEMS AND LEAVES	**Stalk**	longer than flower
Stem	flowering stem upright	**Sepals**	5, 3–4mm, equal, oblong
Root	fibrous from slender, scaly, underground stem	**Petals**	5, 8–16mm, equal, notched
		Stamens	10, 2 rings of 5
Hairs	sparse, pressed to surface	**Stigmas**	5
Stipules	absent	**Ovary**	1, 1-celled
Leaves	at base of plant, with 3 leaflets, each 10–20mm, heart-shaped, yellowish green, notched, edge unbroken		
			FRUIT	
		Type	1, capsule, 5-ridged
Leaf-stalk	50–150mm	**Size**	4–7mm
		Seeds	many, 2–2.5mm, egg-shaped, ridged, with fleshy coat

Fairy Flax *Linum catharticum*

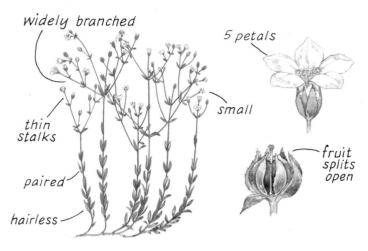

widely branched

5 petals

thin stalks

small

paired

fruit splits open

hairless

An appropriate common name for such a delicate plant, the tiny flowers seeming to float as the hair-like, dark stems are lost against the background. The plant has had many uses, one being indicated in the alternative common name 'Purging Flax'. Fairy Flax is related to the cultivated flaxes, which are the source of linen. *Status:* native; throughout area. *Similar species:* Allseed is a smaller plant which has four tiny petals and toothed sepals. Two blue-flowered species resemble the cultivated Flax: Pale Flax has pointed sepals, and Perennial Flax has blunt sepals.

1 Pale Flax (*L. bienne*); 2 Perennial Flax (*L. perenne*); 3 Allseed (*Radiola linoides*)

blue

4 petals

blunt

tiny

1.

2.

pointed

3.

	FAIRY FLAX		FLOWERS	
Type	annual	**Position**	many, wide-branched head
Height	5–25cm	**Bracts**	slender, lowest leaf-like
Habitat	grassy places, moors, dunes; dry, often lime-rich soils	**Type**	⚥, nodding in bud
		Size	5–7mm
Flowering	June–September	**Colour**	white
		Stalk	5–10mm, hair-like
	STEMS AND LEAVES	**Sepals**	5, 2–3mm, equal, spear-shaped, pointed
Stem	1 or few, slender, wiry, upright, often blackish	**Petals**	5, 4–6mm, equal, oval, edge rounded, separate
Root	fibrous	**Stamens**	5, bases joined
Hairs	absent	**Stigmas**	5, club-shaped
Stipules	absent	**Ovary**	1, 5-celled
Leaves	paired, either side of stem, 5–12mm, oblong to spear-shaped, most blunt, edge unbroken, base wedge-shaped or rounded		
			FRUIT	
		Type	1 globular, angled capsule, splits into 10 parts
Leaf-stalk	absent	**Size**	2–3mm
		Seeds	10, *c*1mm, flattened

Geranium robertianum **Herb-Robert**

Common in shady places, it attains its full glory on walls or rocks where the sun turns stems and leaves brilliant crimson. Native *Geranium* species are of a genus different from the Geraniums (*Pelargonium*) of gardens, but they are related and even smell similar. *Status:* native or introduced; south-west of area, naturalized elsewhere. *Similar species:* other species have leaves with shallower, radiating lobes. Two with notched petals are Hedgerow Crane's-bill, which has upright, perennial stems, and low-growing, annual Dove's-foot Crane's-bill. Shining Crane's-bill is almost hairless, with glossy leaves and broad, angular sepals.

1 Hedgerow Crane's-bill (*G. pyrenaicum*); 2 Dove's-foot Crane's-bill (*G. molle*); 3 Shining Crane's-bill (*G. lucidum*)

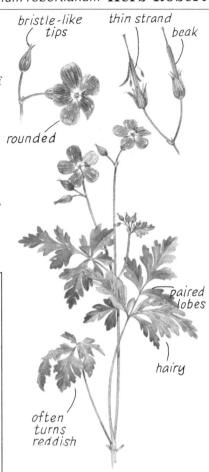

	HERB-ROBERT		
Type	annual or biennial	**Type**	
Height	10–50cm	**Size**	16–20mm
Habitat	woods, hedges, rocks, walls	**Colour**	purplish, pink, rarely white
Flowering	May–September	**Stalk**	longer than flower
		Sepals	5, 7–9mm, oval, bristle-like tip, upright
	STEMS AND LEAVES	**Petals**	5, 9–13mm, equal, oval, rounded, base stalk-like
Stem	angled upwards, branched from base, brittle	**Stamens**	10, orange or purple
Root	slender tap-root	**Stigmas**	5, slender
Hairs	dense below, sparse above	**Ovary**	1, 3–5-celled
Stipules	small, oval		
Leaves	basal or paired either side of stem, 15–65mm, deeply cut into 3–5 lobes, toothed, strong-smelling, often red-tinged		**FRUIT**
		Type	1, long-beaked capsule, strip from beak coils up with each segment
Leaf-stalk	lower long, upper short	**Size**	12–20mm
	FLOWERS	**Seeds**	1 per segment, *c*2mm, oblong, smooth
Position	1–2, from leaf-base		
Bracts	scale-like		

Geranium dissectum **Cut-leaved Crane's-bill**

One of the most common of roadside wild flowers, it is distinguished from most other sorts of Crane's-bill with small flowers by its notched petals and narrow-lobed leaves. Ripe fruits have one-seeded segments. Each splits at the base and a strip of the beak suddenly coils, hurling the seed away. *Status:* native; throughout area. *Similar species:* Long-stalked Crane's-bill has much longer flower-stalks, rounded petals and almost hairless fruits. Small-flowered Crane's-bill has less deeply divided leaves, with mostly wedge-shaped, three-lobed segments and tiny flowers.

1 Long-stalked Crane's-bill (*G. columbinum*); 2 Small-flowered Crane's-bill (*G. pusillum*)

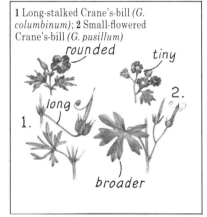

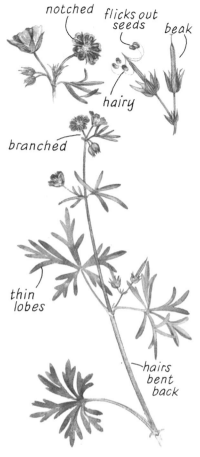

	CUT-LEAVED CRANE'S-BILL		FLOWERS
Type	annual	**Position**	1–2, from leaf-base
Height	10–60cm	**Bracts**	slender
Habitat	cultivated or waste ground, grassland; dryish soil	**Type**	
		Size	8–10mm
Flowering	May–August	**Colour**	reddish-pink
		Stalk	5–15mm
	STEMS AND LEAVES	**Sepals**	5, 5–6mm, oval, tip bristle-like, hairy
Stem	straggling, usually branched	**Petals**	5, 4–5mm, equal, oval, notched
Root	slender tap-root	**Stamens**	10
Hairs	dense, bent back	**Stigmas**	5, slender
Stipules	small, triangular	**Ovary**	1, usually 5-celled
Leaves	paired either side of stem, 20–70mm, almost circular, deeply cut into 5–7 narrow, main lobes; those of lower leaves further lobed or toothed		**FRUIT**
		Type	1, lobed, long-beaked capsule, hairy
Leaf-stalk	long below, short above	**Size**	7–12mm
		Seeds	1 per segment, 2–2.5mm, minutely pitted

Meadow Crane's-bill *Geranium pratense*

A strikingly beautiful plant of summer meadows and grassy roadsides, it has bold, deeply lobed leaves and large, bluish-violet flowers. This is one of the few native plants that finds a permanent place in gardens, often as a double form. *Status:* native, naturalized in parts of north; most of area. *Similar species:* Wood Crane's-bill, in shadier places, has smaller flowers and more finely toothed leaves. Dusky Crane's-bill often escapes from gardens and has blackish-purple petals with pointed tips. Bloody Crane's-bill is a creeping plant with reddish-purple flowers that are carried singly.

rounded

curls

beak

large, blue

branched heads

irregular lobes

1 Wood Crane's-bill (*G. sylvaticum*);
2 Dusky Crane's-bill (*G. phaeum*);
3 Bloody Crane's-bill (*G. sanguineum*)

smaller

blackish

solitary

toothed

1.

2.

3.

	MEADOW CRANE'S-BILL		
Type	perennial		
Height	30–80cm		
Habitat	grassy, sunny places; mainly lime-rich soils		
Flowering	June–September		
	STEMS AND LEAVES		
Stem	upright or angled upwards		
Root	thick rhizome		
Hairs	short, bent back below, long, dense above		
Stipules	wide, papery, upper slender		
Leaves	basal or on alternate sides of stem, 70–150mm, 3–7 deep, radiating lobes, each further toothed or lobed, tips pointed		
Leaf-stalk	lower much longer than leaf, upper very short		

	FLOWERS	
Position	stalked pair from leaf-base	
Bracts	narrowly triangular	
Type	cup-shaped	
Size	30–40mm	
Colour	bright bluish violet	
Stalk	shorter than flower	
Sepals	5, 11–15mm, oval, thin tip	
Petals	5, 15–20mm, equal, broadly oval, tip rounded	
Stamens	10	
Stigmas	5, slender	
Ovary	1, usually 5-celled	
	FRUIT	
Type	capsule, lobed, long-beaked, strip from beak coils up with each lobe	
Size	25–30mm	
Seeds	1 per segment, 3–4mm	

Common Stork's-bill *Erodium cicutarium*

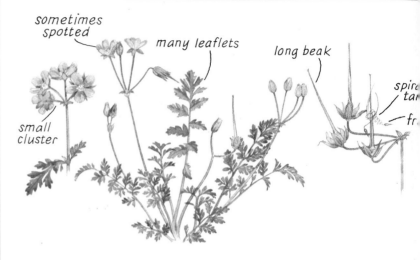

sometimes spotted

many leaflets

long beak

spiral tail

small cluster

fr...

A variable, mainly coastal species. Stickily hairy plants with slender stems and unspotted flowers are often regarded as a different subspecies, the typical version having stout stems and two dark-spotted petals. The beaked fruit of Stork's-bill splits from the top, each strip twisting spirally and parting with a one-seeded segment. This corkscrew-like structure twists and buries the seed. *Status:* native, mostly near sea. *Similar species:* the musk-scented Musk Stork's-bill has blunt stipules, sticky leaves and larger flowers. Sea Stork's-bill has shallow-lobed leaves and tiny flowers.

1 Musk Stork's-bill (*E. moschatum*);
2 Sea Stork's-bill (*E. maritimum*)

larger

tiny

1.

2.

sticky, scented

not divided

	COMMON STORK'S-BILL		
Type	annual		
Height	to 60cm, rarely 100cm		
Habitat	dunes, cultivated or waste ground; dry, sandy soil		
Flowering	June–September		
	STEMS AND LEAVES		
Stem	variable, slender to stout		
Root	slender to stout tap-root		
Hairs	sparse to dense		
Stipules	oval, papery, whitish		
Leaves	most paired either side of stem, 20–200mm, paired leaflets are deeply lobed		
Leaf-stalk	lower long, upper short		
	FLOWERS		
Position	1–9, in long-stalked head, from leaf-base		

Bracts	oval, papery, brownish	
Type		
Size	8–18mm	
Colour	pinkish purple, often black spot at base of upper 2 petals	
Stalk	longer than flower	
Sepals	5, 3–7mm, oval, tip bristle-like	
Petals	5, 4–11mm, often unequal	
Stamens	5, orange	
Stigmas	5, slender	
Ovary	1, 5-celled	
	FRUIT	
Type	1, lobed, long-beaked capsule, beak splits, each strip twists spirally, parts with 1 segment	
Size	15–40mm	
Seeds	1 per segment, 3–4mm, elongated	

Mercurialis perennis Dog's Mercury

A poisonous plant mainly of Oak, Ash or Beech woodland, where it carpets the floor with sombre green. Plants are either male or female, but because Dog's Mercury spreads more effectively by the creeping underground stems than by seed, large areas are of the same gender. The common name implies that this was a worthless version of the Annual Mercury, which was used medicinally. *Status:* native or introduced in north and Ireland; most of area except extreme north. *Similar species:* Annual Mercury lacks underground stems and is more branched. Its leaves almost lack hairs and the female flowers their stalks.

many stamens — 2 stigmas — ♂ ♀

spikes of ♂ flowers — stalk — hairy — watery sap — small teeth — paired — upright, unbranched

Annual Mercury *(Mercurialis annua)*

♀ — branched — stalkless

Euphorbia helioscopia Sun Spurge

Although the curious flowers lack sepals or petals, the bracts of Sun Spurge are yellowish and function like a large flower. This is the same structure as in the related, brightly coloured Poinsettia, most popular at Christmas. The milky sap is acrid and poisonous, and was formerly used to treat warts. *Status:* native; throughout area. *Similar species:* three other spurges have horn-like ends to the glands of the flowers. Petty Spurge has oval, green leaves, and Dwarf Spurge narrow, bluish leaves. Wood Spurge is perennial, hairy, and has joined pairs of bracts below the flowers.

1 Petty Spurge (*E. peplus*); 2 Dwarf Spurge (*E. exigua*); 3 Wood Spurge (*E. amygdaloides*)

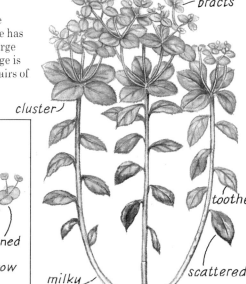

♂ ♀ — fruit opens — rounded glands — cup-like base — yellowish bracts — cluster — toothed — milky sap — scattered

1. smaller — horned glands — 3. — joined — narrow — 2.

DOG'S MERCURY		FLOWERS	
Type	perennial	Position	♂ and ♀ flowers on different plants
Height	15–40cm		
Habitat	woods, hedges; fertile, often lime-rich soils	Bracts	absent
		Type 1	many ♂ flowers in stalked spike from leaf-base
Flowering	February–April		
		Type 2	1–3 ♀ flowers on stalk from leaf-base
STEMS AND LEAVES		Size	4–5mm
Stem	upright, unbranched, watery sap	Colour	green
		Stalk	more or less absent
Root	creeping underground stem	Perianth	3
Hairs	throughout plant	Stamens	8–15
Stipules	small	Stigmas	2
Leaves	paired either side of stem, 30–80mm, more or less elliptical, pointed, edge with rounded teeth	Ovary	1, hairy, 2-celled
		FRUIT	
Leaf-stalk	3–10mm, shorter than blade	Type	capsule, broad, hairy, opening by 2 vertical splits
		Size	6–8mm
		Seeds	2, 3–3.5mm, globular, rough

SUN SPURGE		FLOWERS	
Type	annual	Position	♂ and ♀ flowers on same plant, each ♀ with several ♂ flowers and cup-like base with 4–5 oval, green glands around lip
Height	10–50cm		
Habitat	cultivated and waste ground; fertile soil		
		Bracts	leaf-like, yellowish green
Flowering	May–October	Type 1	♂ a stamen on jointed stalk
		Type 2	♀ a stalked ovary
STEMS AND LEAVES		Size	1–2mm
Stem	single, upright, with 5 branches above, sap milky	Colour	green
		Stalk	elongating in fruit
Root	vertical main root	Sepals	absent
Hairs	more or less hairless	Petals	absent
Stipules	absent	Stigmas	3, often forked
Leaves	spirally arranged around stem, 15–30mm, oval, broad above, blunt, minutely toothed, base wedge-shaped	Ovary	1, 3-celled
		FRUIT	
Leaf-stalk	absent	Type	1, broad, 3-angled, smooth capsule, opens by 3 splits
		Size	3–5mm
		Seeds	3, c2mm, brown, rough

St John's-worts, Milkworts and Balsams

The native St John's-worts are herbaceous plants or sometimes small shrubs, but the family is frequently broadly defined to include many large tropical trees. Several of the native species have characteristic, translucent dots on the paired leaves, as though they were perforated, but these are actually small glands. Similar, stalked glands around the petals appear like black dots on the flowers. In most species, the hermaphrodite flowers form branched heads, though the Rose-of-Sharon has solitary flowers.

The native species of the Milkworts are all herbaceous plants. In most, the undivided leaves are scattered on the stem and lack stipules. Asymmetrical flowers are a distinctive feature of the family, with two of usually five sepals much larger than the others and petal-like. The three petals are joined to form a tube at the base, with the lower petal largest and fringed. The family has little economic value, though some species are cultivated as alpine plants.

A somewhat smaller family of herbaceous plants, the Balsams are widespread in both the tropics and temperate regions. They include the hybrid ornamental plants known as "Busy-lizzies". The stems are characteristically rigid, bearing toothed leaves.

Introduced from the Himalayan region for its attractive flowers, Indian Balsam has escaped to colonize hundreds of miles of river banks. This annual spreads most effectively with the aid of explosive fruits.

Polygala vulgaris **Common Milkwort**

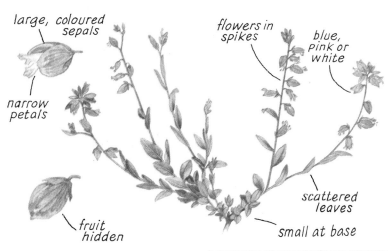

large, coloured sepals

narrow petals

flowers in spikes

blue, pink or white

fruit hidden

scattered leaves

small at base

A bright jewel of a flower, brightening grassland with patches of sky-blue, mauve, pink or white. Its colour comes more from the two large sepals than it does from the relatively small and partly hidden petals. The plant was believed to increase the milk of nursing mothers, although this effect is unsubstantiated. *Status:* native; fairly common, throughout area. *Similar species:* Heath Milkwort, mainly in lime-free soils, has leaves paired either side of the stem. Chalk Milkwort, in lime-rich soils, has large lower leaves forming a rosette.

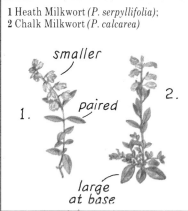

1 Heath Milkwort (*P. serpyllifolia*); 2 Chalk Milkwort (*P. calcarea*)

smaller

paired

1.

2.

large at base

COMMON MILKWORT			
Type	perennial	**Bracts**	small, translucent
Height	10–30cm	**Type**	☿
Habitat	grassland, heaths, dunes	**Size**	4–8mm
Flowering	May–September	**Colour**	blue, purplish pink, or white
		Stalk	shorter than flower
STEMS AND LEAVES		**Sepals**	5, 3 outer c3mm, 2 inner 4–7mm, oval, petal-like, coloured
Stem	upright or angled upwards	**Petals**	3, 4–8mm, unequal, narrow, lower fringed, bases joined
Root	woody stock	**Stamens**	8, partly joined
Hairs	absent or sparse	**Stigma**	1, 2-lobed, style long
Stipules	absent	**Ovary**	1, usually 2-celled
Leaves	on alternate sides of stem, 5–35mm, pointed, edge unbroken, lower oval or elliptical, small; upper spear-shaped		
		FRUIT	
Leaf-stalk	absent	**Type**	1, 2-celled capsule, heart-shaped, flattened, splits at edge, hidden by sepals
FLOWERS		**Size**	4–6mm
Position	10–40, in spike at stem-tip, often one-sided	**Seeds**	2, 2.5–3mm, oblong, hairy

Impatiens glandulifera **Indian Balsam**

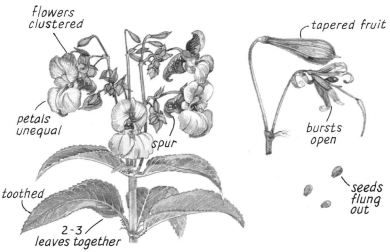

flowers clustered

tapered fruit

petals unequal

spur

bursts open

toothed

seeds flung out

2-3 leaves together

A spectacular plant that has hooded, pink flowers; stout, red-flushed stems; and purple, stalked glands at the leaf-bases. Walls of the ripe capsule are elastic and, at the slightest touch, rapidly roll back to fling out the seeds. *Status:* introduced from the Himalaya; often common, most of area. *Similar species:* the leaves of other Balsams are not paired. Orange Balsam, from North America, is fairly common in Britain and France. Touch-me-not Balsam, which has bright yellow flowers, is native. Small Balsam is Asiatic, and has much smaller, pale yellow flowers.

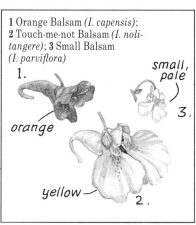

1 Orange Balsam (*I. capensis*); 2 Touch-me-not Balsam (*I. noli-tangere*); 3 Small Balsam (*I. parviflora*)

1.

orange

small, pale

3.

yellow

2.

INDIAN BALSAM			
Type	annual	**FLOWERS**	
Height	100–200cm	**Position**	5–10, spike from leaf-base
Habitat	river banks, lakesides, waste ground; damp soil	**Bracts**	oval, pointed
		Type	☿
Flowering	July–October	**Size**	24–40mm
		Colour	purplish pink, rarely white
STEMS AND LEAVES		**Stalk**	almost equalling flower
Stem	stout, fleshy, upright, often reddish	**Sepals**	3, 2 small, lower 12–27mm, hollow, tip spur-like
Root	thick, vertical main root	**Petals**	5, 2 joined each side, upper broad, 10–25mm
Hairs	more or less absent	**Stamens**	5, mostly joined
Stipules	absent	**Stigma**	1, 5-toothed
Leaves	paired or in threes, 60–150mm, spear-shaped or elliptical, pointed, sharp-toothed	**Ovary**	1, 5-celled
		FRUIT	
Leaf-stalk	shorter than blade, often with purple, stalked glands	**Type**	1, capsule, club-shaped, angled, walls elastic, sides coil back when ripe
		Size	15–30mm
		Seeds	few, 4–5mm, egg-shaped

Perforate St John's-wort *Hypericum perforatum*

A common plant of dry, grassy places, especially hedge-banks, its leaves are covered with translucent dots as if punctured, and are described in the common name. Stamens resembling a pin-cushion are gathered by their bases into three bundles. St John's-worts were long used to treat wounds and are still found in some medicines. *Status:* native; throughout area. *Similar species:* Slender St John's-wort has blunt sepals and mostly heart-shaped leaf-bases. Square-stalked St John's-wort has four-angled stems and smaller flowers. Marsh St John's-wort, in wet ground, has softly hairy stems and sepals fringed with reddish glands.

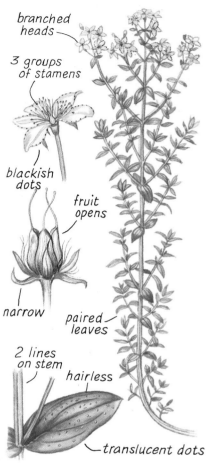

branched heads

3 groups of stamens

blackish dots

fruit opens

narrow

paired leaves

2 lines on stem

hairless

translucent dots

1 Slender St John's-wort (*H. pulchrum*); **2** Square-stalked St John's-wort (*H. tetrapterum*); **3** Marsh St John's-wort (*H. elodes*)

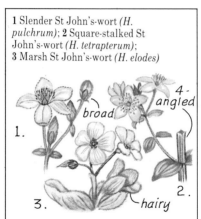

4-angled

broad

1.

2.

3.

hairy

		FLOWERS	
PERFORATE ST JOHN'S-WORT		**Position**	many in wide-branched head
Type	perennial	**Bracts**	present, lower leaf-like
Height	30–90cm	**Type**	⚥
Habitat	grassland, hedges, woods; mainly lime-rich soils	**Size**	17–25mm
		Colour	yellow, petal-edge dotted with black
Flowering	June–September	**Stalk**	shorter than flower
		Sepals	5, 5–7mm, spear-shaped
STEMS AND LEAVES		**Petals**	5, 8–14mm, rather wedge-shaped with oblique end
Stem	upright, woody at base, with 2 raised lines	**Stamens**	numerous
		Stigmas	3, on long styles
Root	creeping underground stem	**Ovary**	1, 3-celled
Hairs	absent		
Stipules	absent	**FRUIT**	
Leaves	paired either side of stem, 10–20mm, elliptical to narrowly oblong, blunt, edge unbroken, base narrowed, many translucent dots	**Type**	1, almost pear-shaped capsule, splits into 3
		Size	*c*6mm
Leaf-stalk	absent	**Seeds**	many, *c*1mm, oblong, finely pitted

Tutsan *Hypericum androsaemum*

In the centre of each yellow flower of this shrub is a prominent tuft of long stamens. The berries turn to red, then purplish black. Corrupted from French, the common name means 'all wholesome' and the leaves were widely used to treat wounds. *Status:* native; rather scattered, mainly south-west of area. *Similar species:* Stinking Tutsan has a goat-like smell, stamens longer than the petals, and the ripe fruit is red but scarcely succulent. Rose-of-Sharon is low-growing and has much larger flowers. Commonly planted, it often escapes and spreads with creeping underground stems to cover large areas.

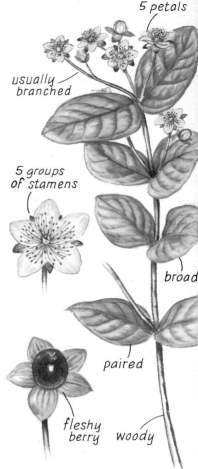

5 petals

usually branched

5 groups of stamens

broad

paired

fleshy berry

woody

1 Stinking Tutsan (*H. hircinum*); **2** Rose-of-Sharon (*H. calycinum*)

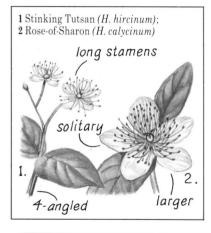

long stamens

solitary

1.

4-angled

larger

2.

TUTSAN		**Bracts**	present
Type	shrub	**Type**	⚥
Height	40–100cm	**Size**	12–23mm
Habitat	woods, hedges; damp soils	**Colour**	yellow
Flowering	June–August	**Stalk**	about equalling flower
		Sepals	5, 8–15mm, oval, blunt, unequal, often reddish-tinged, remaining in fruit
STEMS AND LEAVES		**Petals**	5, 6–12mm, oval
Stem	woody, branched, with 2 raised lines	**Stamens**	many, about equalling petals
		Stigmas	3, on curved styles
Root	woody stock	**Ovary**	1, partly 3-celled
Hairs	absent		
Stipules	absent	**FRUIT**	
Leaves	paired either side of stem, 50–100mm, oval, blunt, edge unbroken, base heart-shaped, partly evergreen	**Type**	1, ellipsoidal to globular berry, fleshy, turning red then purplish black
Leaf-stalk	absent	**Size**	7–12mm
		Seeds	numerous, *c*1mm, oblong, narrowly winged
FLOWERS			
Position	few, in branched cluster from leaf-base		

Violets, Mallows, Rock-roses and Cucumbers

The native Violets are all small herbs. They have undivided leaves, generally scattered around the stem, with stipules at the base. Unequal petals, often with face-like markings, are typical of the European Violets, and the lower pair of petals forms a spur at the base. Though of little economic value, the family includes ornamental plants such as the garden Pansy, and Sweet Violet, which is cultivated for use in perfumery, flavourings, and cake decoration.

Mallows are easily recognized by the distinctive arrangement of numerous stamens, joined at the base into a tube surrounding the long style. Hollyhocks, *Hibiscus* and cotton (*Gossypium* species) all belong to this family.

Rock-roses, and their larger relatives the Sun-roses (*Cistus*), are commonly grown as ornamental plants. When in bud, the flowers are characteristically crumpled like tissue-paper. The numerous, separate stamens of the Rock-roses are sensitive to touch and move apart when touched by an insect, to expose the stigma lobes.

The only native species of the Cucumber family is White Bryony. Cultivated species include Cucumber, Gourds, Loofah, Melons, Marrows and Watermelon. A distinguishing feature of White Bryony is the tendrils that twine from the stalk base of each broad leaf.

Clumps of Common Dog-violets thrive on a shady bank. Unlike the cultivated Sweet Violet, this species lacks scent.

Common Dog-violet *Viola riviniana*

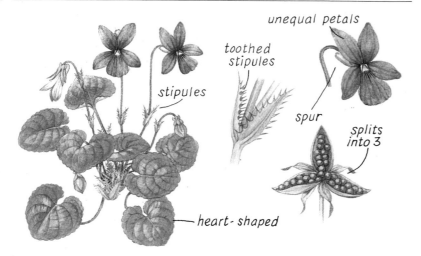

unequal petals

toothed stipules

stipules

spur

splits into 3

heart-shaped

One of the most attractive wild flowers of shady hedge-banks or the edges of woodland. The reference to 'dog' in the name probably means that this was thought to be inferior to the scented violet. *Status:* native; throughout area. *Similar species:* Sweet Violet is the familiar, sweetly-scented Violet of gardens and has all its leaves at the base of the plant. Heath Dog-violet, which has clear blue flowers, has narrower leaves and smaller short-toothed stipules. Marsh Violet, of wet places, has kidney-shaped leaves from underground, creeping stems and lilac, dark-veined flowers.

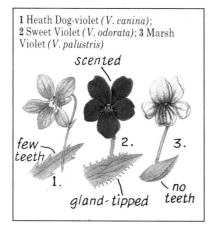

1 Heath Dog-violet (*V. canina*); 2 Sweet Violet (*V. odorata*); 3 Marsh Violet (*V. palustris*)

scented

few teeth

2.

3.

1.

gland-tipped

no teeth

COMMON DOG-VIOLET		FLOWERS	
Type	perennial	**Position**	single, from leaf-base
Height	2–40cm	**Bracts**	2, slender
Habitat	woods, hedges, heaths, mountain rocks	**Type**	⚥, not scented
		Size	14–22mm
Flowering	April–June	**Colour**	blue-violet, spur whitish
		Stalk	much longer than flower
STEMS AND LEAVES		**Sepals**	5, 7–12mm, spear-shaped, lobed at base
Stem	main, non-flowering stem short, side-shoots longer	**Petals**	5, 8–18mm, spur 3–5mm, oval, overlapping, lowest with backward-pointing spur
Root	slender, short, upright, some shoots from root-buds		
Hairs	absent or sparse, short	**Stamens**	5, 2 lower with spur
Stipules	short, spear-shaped, fringed	**Stigma**	1, style hook-like at tip
Leaves	basal or on alternate sides of stem, 5–80mm, heart-shaped, blunt to sharpish, edge with rounded teeth	**Ovary**	1, 1-celled
		FRUIT	
		Type	1, 3-angled, pointed capsule, splits into 3
Leaf-stalk	often longer than leaf	**Size**	6–13mm
		Seeds	many, 2–2.5mm, egg-shaped

Wild Pansy *Viola tricolor* subsp. *tricolor*

Face-like markings on the flowers of Wild Pansy have long made it a favourite, the wild species of Pansy being developed as the familiar garden plants. Pansies differ from Violets mainly in the large, leaf-like stipules and flatter flowers with side petals angled upwards. *Status:* native; throughout area. *Similar species:* Seaside Pansy is a low-growing perennial found by the coast. Field Pansy, usually a weed, has small petals about equalling the sepals. Mountain Pansy is a perennial of hilly areas, spreading by underground stems to form large clumps on fairly lime-rich soils.

splits into 3

short spur

lobed stipules

often 3-coloured

broad petals

narrow leaves

1 Seaside Pansy (*V. tricolor* subsp. *curtisii*); 2 Field Pansy (*V. arvensis*); 3 Mountain Pansy (*V. lutea*)

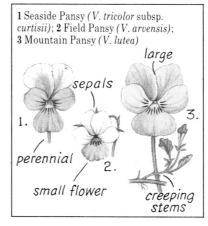

large

sepals

3.

1.

perennial

2.

small flower

creeping stems

WILD PANSY		FLOWERS	
Type	usually annual	**Position**	solitary, from leaf-base
Height	15–30cm, rarely 45cm	**Bracts**	2, tiny
Habitat	cultivated and waste ground, grassland; mainly lime-free soils	**Type**	⚥
		Size	15–25mm, rarely 35mm
Flowering	April–September	**Colour**	petals violet, yellow, pink or white with purplish marks
STEMS AND LEAVES		**Stalk**	long
Stem	usually many-branched	**Sepals**	5, 5–14mm, spear-shaped
Root	fibrous, rarely with short underground stems	**Petals**	5, 7–17mm, unequal, oval, flattish, side petals turn upwards, lowest with spur
Hairs	absent or very short		
Stipules	large, with paired lobes	**Stamens**	5, 2 lower with spur
Leaves	on alternate sides of stem, 10–50mm, oval, spear-shaped or elliptical, blunt, with rounded teeth	**Stigma**	1, club-shaped
		Ovary	1, 1-celled
		FRUIT	
Leaf-stalk	lower long, upper short	**Type**	1, 3-angled capsule, splits into 3
		Size	6–10mm
		Seeds	many, 1.5–2mm, egg-shaped

Malva moschata Musk Mallow

These attractive, large, pink flowers resemble those of the related Hollyhock or Hibiscus, and have stamens joined into a club-shaped cluster. Mallows make copious mucilage, formerly used in cough-mixtures, poultices or to treat wasp-stings. *Status:* native or naturalized in north; widespread except for much of north. *Similar species:* other Mallows have leaves less divided. Common Mallow has purplish, dark-striped flowers. Dwarf Mallow is a low-growing annual with small pale flowers. Marsh-mallow, in marshy places near the sea, has soft, velvety leaves, pale pink flowers and more bracts beneath the sepals.

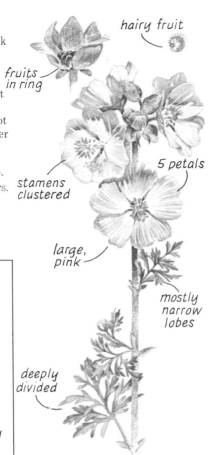

hairy fruit

fruits in ring

5 petals

stamens clustered

large, pink

mostly narrow lobes

1 Common Mallow (*M. sylvestris*);
2 Dwarf Mallow (*M. neglecta*);
3 Marsh-mallow (*Althaea officinalis*)

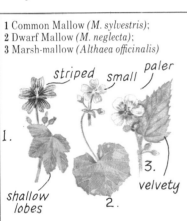

striped   small   paler

1.

3.

shallow lobes

2.

velvety

deeply divided

	MUSK MALLOW	
Type	perennial	
Height	30–80cm	
Habitat	grassy places; mainly fertile soils	
Flowering	July–August	
	STEMS AND LEAVES	
Stem	upright, rounded	
Root	thick, branched stock	
Hairs	sparse	
Stipules	small, spear-shaped	
Leaves	basal or on alternate sides of stem, variable, 50–80mm, 3–7 lobes, toothed, lower kidney-shaped, upper mostly cut into thin lobes	
Leaf-stalk	lower long, upper short	
	FLOWERS	
Position	single from leaf-base or irregular head at stem-tip	

Bracts	3 beneath base of sepals
Type	♂
Size	30–60mm
Colour	rose-pink, rarely white, veins crimson
Stalk	shorter than flower
Sepals	5, 6–12mm, oval, pointed
Petals	5, 14–25mm, twisted together in bud, equal, oval, squarish and notched
Stamens	many, in club-shaped head
Stigmas	numerous, slender
Ovary	1, usually many-celled
	FRUIT
Type	a ring of wedge-shaped, hairy, nut-like segments
Size	*c*2mm
Seeds	1 per segment, nearly circular, flattened

Pastel-coloured Marsh-mallow inhabits marshy areas near the sea.

Common Rock-rose *Helianthemum nummularium*

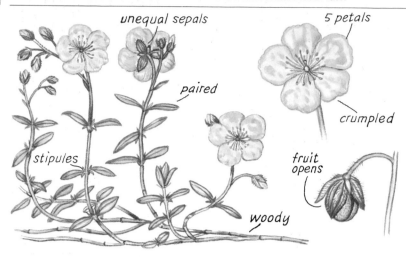

unequal sepals · paired · stipules · 5 petals · crumpled · fruit opens · woody

A wiry-stemmed plant, its yellow petals crumpled like tissue-paper, opening in sunny weather and falling within a few hours. The flowers open with a tuft of stamens in the centre, so the first insect visitor is dusted with pollen. Once touched, the stamens move apart so that the flower can receive pollen from the next visitor. *Status:* native; often common, absent from much of north, west and many islands. *Similar species:* White Rock-rose has narrow, greyish, woolly leaves and white flowers. Spotted Rock-rose is an annual with a rosette of leaves at the base and smaller petals, often with a red spot at the base.

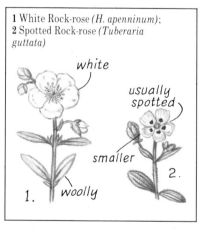

1 White Rock-rose (*H. apenninum*);
2 Spotted Rock-rose (*Tuberaria guttata*)

white · usually spotted · smaller · woolly · 1. · 2.

	COMMON ROCK-ROSE		
Type	perennial	**Bracts**	narrowly spear-shaped
Height	5–30cm	**Type**	♂
Habitat	grassland, scrub; lime-rich soils	**Size**	14–25mm, rarely 30mm
Flowering	June–September	**Colour**	usually bright yellow
		Stalk	about equalling flower
	STEMS AND LEAVES	**Sepals**	5, 2 slender, *c*2mm; 3 oval, *c*6mm
Stem	many, woody below, low-growing or angled upwards	**Petals**	5, 6–12mm, equal, oval, crumpled, soon falling
Root	thick, woody stock, vertical tap-root	**Stamens**	numerous, moving apart when touched
Hairs	sparse or short; dense, whitish beneath leaves	**Stigma**	1, 3-lobed on S-shaped style
Stipules	narrowly spear-shaped	**Ovary**	1, 1-celled
Leaves	paired either side of stem, 5–20mm, oblong or oval, blunt, edge unbroken		**FRUIT**
Leaf-stalk	much shorter than blade	**Type**	1, capsule, almost globular, splits into 3
	FLOWERS	**Size**	*c*6mm
Position	1–12, in 1-sided, spike-like head from stem-tip	**Seeds**	many, *c*2mm, egg-shaped

White Bryony *Bryonia cretica* subsp. *dioica*

Most noticeable in fruit, the stems bearing clusters of red berries hang like festoons in a leafless Autumn hedgerow. Although attractive, the berries are poisonous and can be fatal. White Bryony was cultivated for the massive rootstock; its uses included the treatment of rheumatic and arthritic pain. *Status:* native or naturalized in north; sometimes common, rare in north. *Similar species:* Black Bryony is unrelated, although in fruit and with withered leaves the two look similar. This plant has twining stems, glossy, heart-shaped leaves, and six-petalled flowers, the males in long spikes.

male · female · ovary · bristly · lobed leaves · tendril · fleshy berries

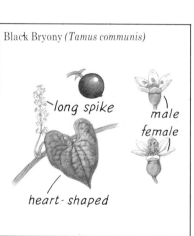

Black Bryony (*Tamus communis*)

long spike · male · female · heart-shaped

	WHITE BRYONY		
Type	perennial	**Bracts**	absent
Height	up to 400cm	**Type 1**	♂, 3–8 in long-stalked head
Habitat	hedgerows, scrub, woods; mainly well-drained soils	**Type 2**	♀, 2–5 in stalkless cluster from leaf-base, 10–12mm
Flowering	May–September	**Size**	12–18mm
		Colour	greenish white
	STEMS AND LEAVES	**Stalk**	present
Stem	long, angled, bristly; climbs with coiled tendrils at base of leaf-stalks	**Sepals**	5, triangular, bases joined
		Petals	5, oblong, hairy, bases joined
Root	large, swollen, stock	**Stamens**	5, 4 joined in pairs
Hairs	stiff, swollen-based	**Stigmas**	3, 2-lobed, on thick style
Stipules	absent	**Ovary**	1, globular, beneath petals, 3-celled
Leaves	spirally placed around stem, 50–100mm, most with 5 radiating lobes, wavy-toothed		
Leaf-stalk	shorter than blade		**FRUIT**
		Type	1, berry, globular, smooth, red when ripe
	FLOWERS	**Size**	5–8mm
Position	♂ and ♀ flowers on different plants	**Seeds**	3–6, 4–5mm, flattened, black and yellow mottled

Willowherbs, Loosestrifes and Water-milfoils

The Willowherbs form a moderately large, widespread family, most abundant in North America, and include ornamental garden plants such as Clarkias, Evening-primroses and Fuchsias. There are many native species in northern Europe, and several more are naturalized. One of the most characteristic features of the family is the ovary situated beneath the sepals and petals. In the Willowherb genus, it develops into a four-angled capsule which eventually splits open lengthwise to reveal rows of fluffy seeds.

Loosestrifes form a small family of little economic importance, though it includes the dye-plant *Lawsonia inermis*, the source of henna. Loosestrife flowers have four or sometimes six sepals and petals. There are usually twice as many stamens as petals and, in the Purple-loosestrife, these show a characteristic pattern with five longer and five shorter stamens.

Water-milfoils are aquatic plants with finely divided leaves and spikes of tiny flowers. Each flower has four petals and the ripe fruit splits into four, nut-like parts. They are usually classified with *Gunnera*, plants of moist places but with very different habit.

With horizontally creeping roots, Rosebay Willowherb can spread rapidly and sends up extensive clumps of flowering shoots. It prefers cleared land, especially where the vegetation has been burned.

Purple-loosestrife *Lythrum salicaria*

An elegant plant with tall spikes of purple flowers. Each plant has one of three sorts of flowers. The style is either shorter than, about equal to, or much longer than the sepals, and the stamens are equally different in length. This ensures that a flower receives pollen from a different plant. *Status:* native; more or less throughout area, rare or absent towards north. *Similar species:* two related plants of wet places are smaller annuals with each flower at a leaf-base. Grass-poly is upright with oblong leaves; creeping Water-purslane has spoon-shaped leaves and tiny flowers.

long, medium or short style

flowers in spike

fruit opens

6 petals

upright

4 angled

broad

paired

1 Grass-poly *(L. hyssopifolia)*;
2 Water-purslane *(L. portula)*

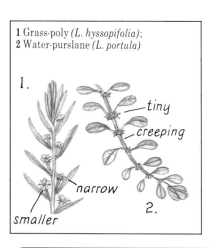

tiny

creeping

narrow

smaller

2.

1.

PURPLE-LOOSESTRIFE			FLOWERS	
Type	perennial		**Position**	numerous, in rings towards stem-tip, in spike-like head
Height	60–120cm		**Bracts**	slender, soon falling
Habitat	edges of lakes or rivers, fens; wet ground		**Type**	♀
Flowering	June–August		**Size**	10–15mm
			Colour	reddish-purple
STEMS AND LEAVES			**Stalk**	shorter than flower
Stem	upright, 4-angled, usually unbranched		**Sepals**	6, *c*6mm, teeth 2–3mm, bases joined into ribbed, hairy tube
Root	thick stock		**Petals**	6, 8–10mm, nearly oval
Hairs	short, often sparse		**Stamens**	12, 2 different lengths
Stipules	absent		**Stigma**	1, club-shaped, style short, medium or long
Leaves	most paired or in threes, 40–70mm, spear-shaped to oval, pointed, edge unbroken, base heart-shaped		**Ovary**	1, 2-celled
			FRUIT	
Leaf-stalk	absent		**Type**	1, capsule, splits into 2, egg-shaped, in sepal-tube
			Size	3–4mm
			Seeds	numerous, *c*1mm, flattened

Large-flowered Evening-primrose *Oenothera erythrosepala*

A tall, rather bushy plant, originally only a garden plant. At dusk the flowers open so rapidly that the petals move visibly. Within minutes, sepals split and petals unfurl. A delicate scent, like orange-blossom, and almost luminous, pale petals attract night-flying moths. *Status:* introduced; often common, absent from north. *Similar species:* Fragrant Evening-primrose lacks red-based hairs and has more strongly scented flowers which turn red. Common Evening-primrose lacks red-based hairs and has smaller flowers with green sepals.

fruit splits into 4

large

wavy-edged

bend back

red-striped

red-based hairs

1 Common Evening-primrose *(O. biennis)*; 2 Fragrant Evening-primrose *(O. stricta)*

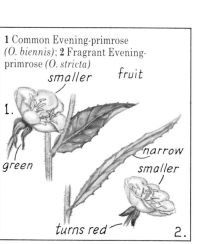

smaller

fruit

1.

green

narrow
smaller

turns red

2.

LARGE-FLOWERED EVENING-PRIMROSE			Bracts	leaf-like below
Type	biennial		**Type**	♀, scented
Height	50–100cm		**Size**	80–100mm
Habitat	waste ground, banks of roads and railways, dunes		**Colour**	pale yellow
			Stalk	shorter than flower
Flowering	June–September		**Sepals**	4, 35–50mm, bases joined, tubular, red-striped, bending back on opening
STEMS AND LEAVES			**Petals**	4, 40–50mm, twisted together in bud, broad, overlapping, notched
Stem	upright, stout, leafy		**Stamens**	8, bases curved
Root	thick, white tap-root		**Stigma**	1, 4-lobed, on long style
Hairs	mostly short, some long with swollen, red bases		**Ovary**	1, below sepals, 4-celled
Stipules	absent			
Leaves	spirally arranged, 40–250mm, elliptical to spear-shaped, midrib white or pink, tip pointed, edge wavy, slightly toothed		**FRUIT**	
			Type	1, capsule, splits into 4, oblong, tapered, hairy
Leaf-stalk	short or almost absent		**Size**	25–40mm
FLOWERS			**Seeds**	numerous, 1–2mm, oblong
Position	in loose spike at stem-tip			

Circaea lutetiana **Enchanter's-nightshade**

An easily overlooked plant with small, two-petalled, white flowers, it is better known for its bur-like fruits, which become entangled in socks or pet's fur. This is the plant's method of dispersal, courtesy of passing animals. *Status:* native; throughout area except parts of north. *Similar species:* Upland Enchanter's-nightshade is a hybrid between the above and Alpine Enchanter's-nightshade. Like the latter, it has a tiny bract below each flower but its fruits never mature. Alpine Enchanter's-nightshade has heart-shaped leaf-bases, open flowers clustered at the tops of the stems and hairless sepals.

1 Upland Enchanter's-nightshade (*C. × intermedia*); **2** Alpine Enchanter's-nightshade (*C. alpina*)

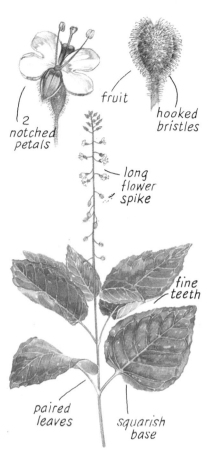

fruit

2 notched petals

hooked bristles

long flower spike

fine teeth

paired leaves

squarish base

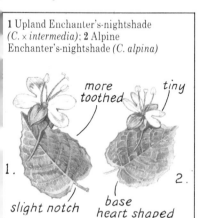

more toothed

tiny

1.

2.

slight notch

base heart shaped

	ENCHANTER'S-NIGHTSHADE		**FLOWERS**
Type	perennial	**Position**	numerous, in loose spike at stem-tip
Height	20–70cm		
Habitat	woods, hedges, scrub; damp, fertile soils	**Bracts**	few at base of spike
		Type	♀
Flowering	June–August	**Size**	4–8mm
		Colour	white or pinkish
	STEMS AND LEAVES	**Stalk**	long, bent down in fruit
Stem	upright, or angled upwards, swollen at leaf-bases	**Sepals**	2, 2–3.5mm, equal, bases joined into short tube, soon falling
Root	slender, creeping, underground stems	**Petals**	2, 2–4mm, deeply notched
		Stamens	2
Hairs	sparse, short, gland-tipped	**Stigma**	1, 2-lobed, on long style
Stipules	absent	**Ovary**	1, below sepals, 2-celled
Leaves	paired either side of stem, 40–100mm, oval, pointed, edge minutely toothed, base usually rounded		
		FRUIT	
		Type	1, capsule, ovoid, with dense, hooked bristles
Leaf-stalk	usually shorter than blade, furrowed above	**Size**	3–4mm
		Seeds	1–2, 2–2.5mm, elongated

Chamerion angustifolium **Rosebay Willowherb**

Spreading underground to form vast clumps, this plant bears slender spikes of rose-purple flowers. In Autumn it has fluffy masses of plumed seeds. Formerly rarer, the species has spread with the creation of railway embankments and demolition sites. *Status:* native; throughout area, often common, rarer in Ireland and north. *Similar species:* other Willowherbs have mostly paired leaves and upright, equal-petalled flowers. Great Willowherb has hairy leaves which clasp the stem. Two species with smaller flowers are Hoary Willowherb, which has hairy leaves, and Broad-leaved Willowherb which has almost hairless leaves.

1 Great Willowherb (*Epilobium hirsutum*); **2** Hoary Willowherb (*E. parviflorum*); **3** Broad-leaved Willowherb (*E. montanum*)

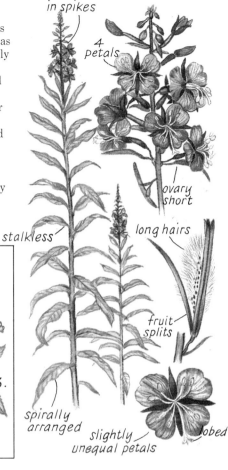

in spikes

4 petals

ovary short

long hairs

stalkless

fruit splits

spirally arranged

slightly unequal petals

lobed

almost hairless

paired, hairy

1.

smaller

3.

stalked

2.

hairy

	ROSEBAY WILLOWHERB		**FLOWERS**
Type	perennial	**Position**	many, in spike at stem-tip
Height	30–120cm, rarely 250cm	**Bracts**	leaf-like below
Habitat	woodland clearings, scree, waste ground; mostly stony soils, often on burnt ground	**Type**	♀
		Size	20–30mm
		Colour	deep pinkish purple
Flowering	July–September	**Stalk**	10–15mm
		Sepals	4, 8–12mm, slender, purple
	STEMS AND LEAVES	**Petals**	4, 10–16mm, oval, notched, upper 2 broader than lower 2
Stem	upright, leafy		
Root	woody, horizontal, creeping roots make new stems	**Stamens**	8
		Stigma	1, 4-lobed, on long style
Hairs	absent below, short above	**Ovary**	1, below sepals, 4-celled
Stipules	absent		
Leaves	spirally arranged around stem, 50–150mm, narrowly spear-shaped or elliptical, pointed, edge unbroken or minutely toothed, wavy	**FRUIT**	
		Type	1, capsule, 4-angled, slender, split into 4
		Size	25–80mm
Leaf-stalk	almost stalkless	**Seeds**	many, 1–2mm, egg-shaped, with plume of long bristles

Short-fruited Willowherb *Epilobium obscurum*

One of the commonest Willowherbs but easily overlooked because it lacks showy flowers. In poorly-drained, cultivated ground it can be a troublesome weed as creeping stems root to make new plants. Willowherbs are larval food-plants for the Elephant Hawk-moth. *Status:* native; often common, most of area except parts of north and some islands. *Similar species:* two common species of similar wet places have rather smaller flowers. Pale Willowherb has stalked leaves and whitish, pink-streaked flowers. Marsh Willowherb has rounded stems without any raised lines. Its creeping stems end in bulb-like buds.

1 Pale Willowherb (*E. roseum*);
2 Marsh Willowherb (*E. palustre*)

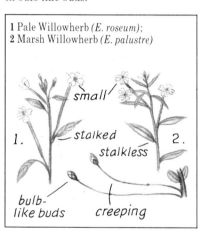

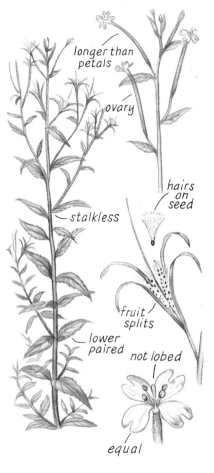

	SHORT-FRUITED WILLOWHERB		FLOWERS	
Type	perennial		Position	many, in loose spike at stem-tip
Height	30–60cm, rarely 80cm		Bracts	present, lowest leaf-like
Habitat	banks of streams, ditches, marshes; wet ground		Type	♀
			Size	7–9mm
Flowering	July–August		Colour	pinkish purple
			Stalk	shorter than flower
	STEMS AND LEAVES		Sepals	4, 3–4mm, spear-shaped, bases joined into tube
Stem	upright, 4 raised lines		Petals	4, 5–6mm, deeply notched
Root	creeping, rooting stems at or below ground-level		Stamens	8
			Stigma	1, on short style
Hairs	absent below, sparse above, pressed to surface		Ovary	1, 4-celled
Stipules	absent		FRUIT	
Leaves	lower paired, upper spirally arranged, 30–70mm, spear-shaped, edge with few, small teeth, base rounded, runs into lines on stem		Type	slender, 4-angled capsule, downy, splits into 4
			Size	40–60mm
Leaf-stalk	absent		Seeds	many, base *c*1mm, rough, with long plume of hairs

Spiked Water-milfoil *Myriophyllum spicatum*

A submerged aquatic plant with feathery leaves mostly carried in fours. It is most noticeable in flower, when the slender, reddish flower-spikes appear above the water's surface. *Status:* native; most of area, absent from some islands. *Similar species:* Alternate-flowered Water-milfoil has leaf-like lower bracts and the upper flowers are not in rings. Whorled Water-milfoil has leaves in fives and toothed upper bracts. It overwinters in the form of club-shaped resting buds called 'turions'. Rigid Hornwort is unrelated and has rigid, repeatedly forked leaves. Each flower or spiny fruit is at the base of a leaf.

1 Whorled Water-milfoil (*M. verticillatum*); 2 Alternate-flowered Water-milfoil (*M. alterniflorum*); 3 Rigid Hornwort (*Ceratophyllum demersum*)

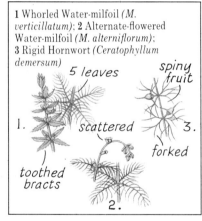

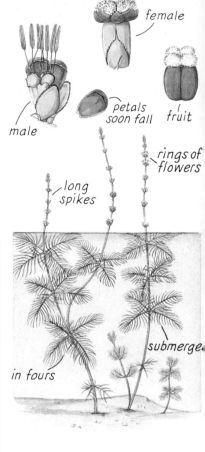

	SPIKED WATER-MILFOIL		Bracts	nearly all not toothed, shorter than flowers
Type	perennial		Type	lowest ♀, next ♂, upper ♂
Height	50–250cm		Size	2–4mm
Habitat	lakes, ponds, ditches; still water, especially in lime-rich areas		Colour	pinkish or dull red
			Stalk	absent
Flowering	June–July		Sepals	4, ♀ minute, ♂ *c*0.5mm
			Petals	4, minute on ♀ flowers; ♂ *c*3mm, soon falling
	STEMS AND LEAVES		Stamens	8
Stem	slender, branched, leafless towards base		Stigmas	4, without a style
Root	creeping underground stems		Ovary	1, below sepals, 4-celled
Hairs	absent			
Stipules	absent		FRUIT	
Leaves	usually rings of 4 around stem, 15–30mm, deeply cut either side into 15–35 thin segments		Type	1, almost globular, splits into 4 nut-like parts
Leaf-stalk	absent		Size	2–3mm
			Seeds	1 per segment, not released
	FLOWERS			
Position	mostly rings of 4, in spike towards stem-tip			

Carrots and Ivy

The large, widespread Carrot family contains several crop-plants and many native species. They can be recognized easily by their umbrella-shaped flower-heads. The family has unusual chemistry, reflected in the characteristic odour, flavour or toxicity of many of the species. Familiar products of the family include the herbs caraway, coriander, cumin, dill, fennel and parsley, plus the vegetables carrots, celery and parsnips. The other claim to fame, or rather infamy, of the family is the poisonous Hemlock. It provided the state poison of ancient Greece and was used to execute Socrates.

Stems of the Carrot family are often hollow as generations of children have discovered, cutting them for "pea-shooters". The flower-head has many branches at the same level, then each of these commonly branches again at a higher level, ultimately bearing single flowers. Bracts may be present beneath each branch and provide a useful way of identifying species. The fruit may also aid identification. It can be elongated, swollen or flattened. Each half typically has five ridges, some of which may be enlarged and wing-like or spiny.

Like plants of the Carrot family, Ivy has flower-heads with many branches at the same level. It belongs to a mainly tropical family, consisting predominantly of trees and shrubs. Ivies are often grown as ornamental plants and the family includes the source of ginseng (*Panax quinquefolia*).

Stems of the naturalized Giant Hogweed soar to several metres tall. Its broad, umbrella-shaped flower-heads are characteristic of the Carrot family.

Ivy *Hedera helix*

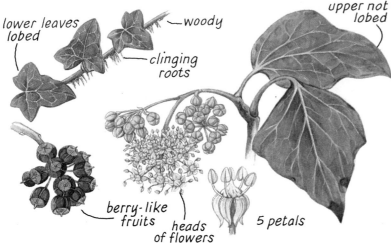

lower leaves lobed — *woody* — *clinging roots* — *upper not lobed*

berry-like fruits *heads of flowers* *5 petals*

A woody climber with sombre, glossy leaves, Ivy is associated with death and decay because it needs a support to climb up on and there is none better than an old, crumbling wall or a dying tree. Ivy has gained a reputation for killing trees – an unfounded slander, for it has little effect other than to increase the weight on the branches and trunk or to shade some leaves. The yellowish flowers are rather insignificant, but produce copious nectar at a time when little else is in flower and so are visited by large numbers of insects, particularly wasps and hornets. The berries are eaten by birds, such as thrushes and blackbirds, and the plant makes a favoured nesting-site. Ivy is a food-plant for caterpillars of both butterflies and moths, including the Holly Blue and the Swallow-tailed Moth. Many horticultural forms of Ivy are grown, differing greatly in habit and in form and colour of the leaves. *Status:* native; common except in northernmost part of area. (There are no similar species.)

	IVY		
Type	biennial	**Leaf-stalk**	shorter than blade
Height	up to 30cm		**FLOWERS**
Habitat	woods, hedges, rocks, walls; most soils	**Position**	many in compact, stalked heads towards stem-tip
Flowering	September–November	**Bracts**	absent
		Type	☿
	STEMS AND LEAVES	**Size**	5–8mm
Stem	woody, up to 25cm across, climbs with clinging roots	**Colour**	yellowish green
		Stalk	about equalling flower
Root	woody stock; stem roots	**Sepals**	5 minute, triangular teeth
Hairs	mostly hairless; young shoots with branched hairs	**Petals**	5, 3–4mm, equal, oval
		Stamens	5
Stipules	paired either side of stem	**Stigma**	1, slender
Leaves	spirally arranged, 40–100mm, most with 3–5 triangular, radiating lobes, glossy, evergreen, base heart-shaped; oval or diamond-shaped on flowering stems, not lobed, base rounded or wedge-shaped	**Ovary**	1, below sepals, 5-celled
			FRUIT
		Type	1, berry-like, leathery, almost globular, black
		Size	6–8mm
		Seeds	2–5, whitish, papery coat

Sanicle *Sanicula europaea*

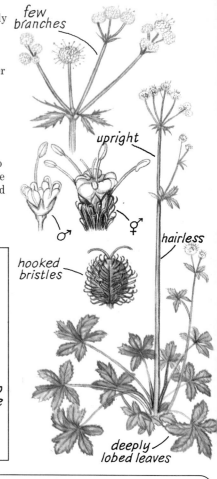

few branches — *upright* — *hairless* — *hooked bristles* — *deeply lobed leaves*

An unusual species of the Carrot family with radiating lobes to the leaves and very few flowers in each head. Especially common in Beech and Oak woods, it carpets the ground in summer with glossy, dark green leaves. Like several other species of the woodland floor, it is animal-dispersed and has fruits with hooked bristles. *Status:* native; wooded parts of region, often common; absent from many of islands. *Similar species:* Marsh Pennywort also has few flowers in a head. Its leaves are nearly circular, the long stalk attached at the centre and arising from a creeping stem, often hidden among moss.

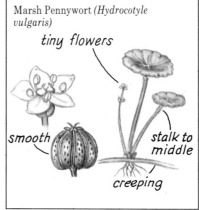

Marsh Pennywort (*Hydrocotyle vulgaris*)

tiny flowers — *smooth* — *stalk to middle* — *creeping*

	SANICLE		
Type	perennial	**Bracts**	lower often lobed, toothed; upper narrow, edge unbroken
Height	20–60cm		
Habitat	woods, hedges; rich soils	**Type**	♂ and ☿ in same flower-head, outer ♂
Flowering	May–September		
		Size	2–3.5mm
	STEMS AND LEAVES	**Colour**	pink or white
Stem	upright	**Stalk**	shorter than flower
Root	stout stock	**Sepals**	5, 1–2mm, pointed, bases joined
Hairs	absent	**Petals**	5, 1.5–2mm, notched, curved inwards
Stipules	absent		
Leaves	mostly basal, few on stem, 20–60mm, with 3–5 radiating lobes, each wedge-shaped, glossy, edge toothed	**Stamens**	5
		Stigmas	2, slender
		Ovary	1, below sepals, 2-celled
Leaf-stalk	lower 50–250mm, base broad, clasping stem; upper short		**FRUIT**
		Type	1, splits into 2, egg-shaped, covered with hooked bristles, dry
	FLOWERS		
Position	few, in 3 or more long-stalked heads at stem-tip	**Size**	4–5mm
		Seeds	1 per half, not released

A beautiful plant with a pale blue waxiness to both leaves and stems. Most unusually for a species of the Carrot family, the leaves have holly-like, spine-tipped teeth, and the flower-heads are compact and thistle-like. The thick, fleshy roots were peeled and boiled with sugar to make candied eryngoes. *Status:* native; coasts except for extreme north. *Similar species:* Field Eryngo, from southern parts, has more divided, greener leaves and narrow, often toothless bracts. Astrantia is often naturalized and has flattened flower-heads encircled by greenish-white or pink, petal-like bracts.

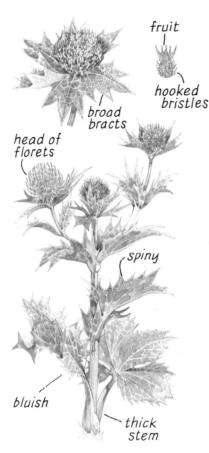

fruit

hooked bristles

broad bracts

head of florets

spiny

bluish

thick stem

1 Field Eryngo (*E. campestre*);
2 Astrantia (*Astrantia major*)

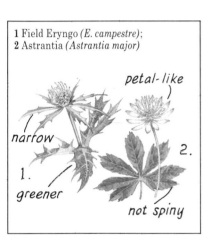

petal-like

narrow

greener

1.

2.

not spiny

Seemingly ubiquitous, this is the plant that forms the walls of white flanking many a country lane in the Spring. Fern-like foliage supports the broad, umbrella-shaped heads of tiny, five-petalled flowers. Although several species are rather similar, Cow Parsley is the earliest and most common, at least in the southern half of the area. *Status:* native; throughout area. *Similar species:* Bur Chervil is a related annual, which has egg-shaped fruits covered with hooked spines. Rough Chervil, with smooth fruits, has hairy, purple-spotted, solid stems and flowers later than Cow Parsley.

few bracts under flowers

no bracts

hairless

outer flower

ridged, hollow

many leaflets

slender, smooth

1 Bur Chervil (*A. caucalis*); 2 Rough Chervil (*Chaerophyllum temulentum*)

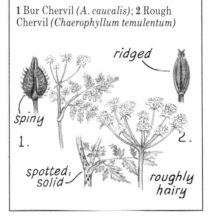

ridged

spiny

1.

spotted, solid

2.

roughly hairy

SEA-HOLLY			**FLOWERS**	
Type	perennial		**Position**	many in almost globular, stalked head, 15–30mm long
Height	15–60cm		**Bracts**	leaf-like, spiny below head; 3-toothed below flowers
Habitat	sand-dunes, shingle banks		**Type**	☿
Flowering	July–August		**Size**	6–8mm
			Colour	whitish or pale blue
STEMS AND LEAVES			**Stalk**	absent
Stem	more or less upright, thick, branched, hollow		**Sepals**	5, 4–5mm, thin, spine-tipped
Root	long, thick, fleshy		**Petals**	5, 3–4mm, narrow, notched
Hairs	absent		**Stamens**	5, curved inwards
Stipules	absent		**Stigmas**	2, slender
Leaves	basal or on alternate sides of stem, 40–120mm, with radiating lobes and spine-tipped teeth, pale bluish-green or purple-tinged, base heart-shaped, upper leaves clasp stem		**Ovary**	1, below sepals, 2-celled
			FRUIT	
			Type	1, dry, egg-shaped, corky-walled, covered with hooked spines, splits into 2
Leaf-stalk	present or upper absent		**Size**	5–6mm
			Seeds	1 per half, not released

COW PARSLEY			**Bracts**	none below head; few below flower-stalks, 2–5mm, oval
Type	biennial or perennial		**Type**	☿
Height	60–100cm		**Size**	3–5mm
Habitat	hedges, woods, waste ground		**Colour**	white
Flowering	April–June		**Stalk**	2–5mm
			Sepals	5, minute
STEMS AND LEAVES			**Petals**	5, 1–2.5mm, equal except on outer flowers, notched
Stem	upright, furrowed, hollow		**Stamens**	5
Root	tap-root, often stout		**Stigmas**	2, slender
Hairs	absent below, downy above		**Ovary**	1, below sepals, 2-celled
Stipules	absent			
Leaves	basal or alternate sides of stem, up to 300mm, divided 2–3 times, lobes 15–25mm, oval, toothed		**FRUIT**	
			Type	1, splits into 2, oblong, narrow above, dry, smooth, blackish brown, short, beak-like tip
Leaf-stalk	long below, short above, base broad		**Size**	5–10mm
			Seeds	1 per half, not released
FLOWERS				
Position	many in umbrella-shaped head 20–60mm wide, 8–16 branches, at stem-tip			

Sweet Cicely *Myrrhis odorata*

On a hot summer's day this plant is usually smelled before seen, the air perfused with a cloying, aniseed-like smell. Sweet Cicely was widely cultivated because it is almost entirely edible. Surprisingly sweet, mildly aniseed-flavoured leaves are pleasant on their own or in mixed salads. Roots substitute for Parsnips, and the fruits are still used in liqueurs. *Status:* naturalized; mainly hilly or mountain districts in northern part of area. *Similar species:* Shepherd's-needle also has elongated fruits, but these are usually much longer and thinner. It is a more delicate, annual plant and often a weed.

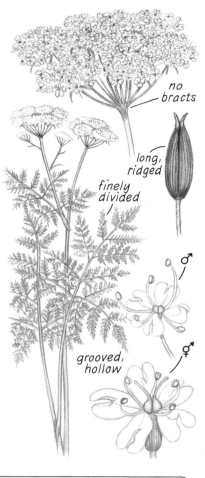

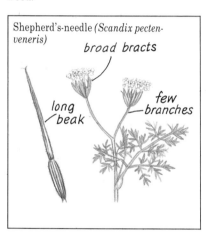

Shepherd's-needle (*Scandix pecten-veneris*)

broad bracts

long beak

few branches

no bracts

long, ridged

finely divided

♂

♀

grooved, hollow

	SWEET CICELY	Bracts	none below head; c5 below flower-stalks, spear-shaped
Type	perennial	Type	♂ and ♀ in same head
Height	60–100cm	Size	2–5mm
Habitat	hedges, woods, grassy places	Colour	white
Flowering	May–June	Stalk	longest on ♂ flowers
		Sepals	5, minute
	STEMS AND LEAVES	Petals	5, 1–3mm, equal except on outer flowers, oval, notched
Stem	upright, grooved, hollow		
Root	thick tap-root	Stamens	5
Hairs	short	Stigmas	2, slender
Stipules	absent	Ovary	1, below sepals, 2-celled
Leaves	basal or on alternate sides of stem, to 300mm, divided 2–3 times, lobes oblong, toothed; strong-smelling		**FRUIT**
		Type	1, splits into 2, oblong, tapered, dry, sharply ridged, brown, tip beaked
Leaf-stalk	lower long, upper short, bases broad, sheathing	Size	20–25mm
	FLOWERS	Seeds	1 per half, not released
Position	many, heads 10–50mm across, umbrella-shaped at stem-tips; main branches 5–20		

Alexanders *Smyrnium olusatrum*

A robust plant of coastal districts, with glossy, dark green foliage, umbrella-shaped, greenish-yellow flower-heads and almost globular, blackish fruits. Probably brought by the Romans as a pot-herb, it was long used for the celery-like leaf-bases. *Status:* introduced, or native in extreme south; mostly near southern coasts. *Similar species:* Scots Lovage is native on northern coasts. A smaller plant, with fewer leaflets, whitish flowers and flattened fruits, it is also edible. Lovage, a garden herb that often escapes, has leaves with fewer, coarser teeth and smaller fruits.

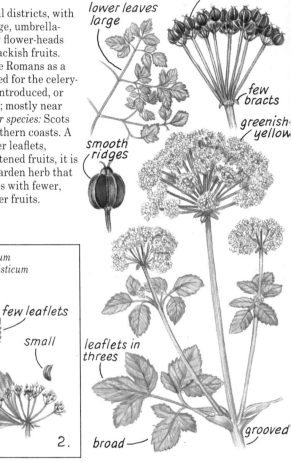

lower leaves large

blackish

few bracts

greenish yellow

smooth ridges

1 Scots Lovage (*Ligusticum scoticum*); 2 Lovage (*Levisticum officinale*)

white

few leaflets

small

leaflets in threes

1.

flattened

few teeth

2.

broad

grooved

	ALEXANDERS		FLOWERS
Type	biennial	Position	many in umbrella-shaped head, 7–20 branches, at stem-tip
Height	50–150cm		
Habitat	grassy banks, hedges, cliffs	Bracts	few or absent
Flowering	April–June	Type	♀
		Size	1.5–3.5mm
	STEMS AND LEAVES	Colour	greenish yellow
Stem	upright, stout, solid or oldest hollow, furrowed	Stalk	about equalling flower
		Sepals	absent
Root	tap-root	Petals	5, 0.7–1.5mm, spear-shaped, tip curved in
Hairs	absent		
Stipules	absent	Stamens	5
Leaves	basal, scattered or upper paired, up to 300mm, divided 1–3 times, leaflets in 3s, oval, glossy dark green, toothed or lobed	Stigmas	2, slender
		Ovary	1, below petals, 2-celled
			FRUIT
		Type	1, splits into 2, nearly globular, dry, smooth or 3-ridged, almost black
Leaf-stalk	broad base sheaths stem, long or upper short		
		Size	7–8mm
		Seeds	1 per half, not released

Crithmum maritimum **Rock Samphire**

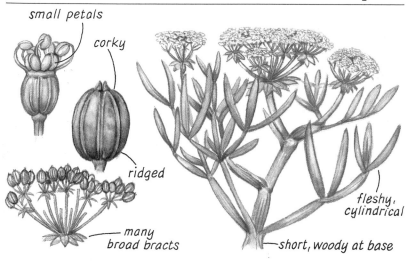

small petals

corky

ridged

many broad bracts

fleshy, cylindrical

short, woody at base

A curious member of the Carrot family, with the normal umbrella-shaped heads of flowers but swollen, succulent, aromatic leaves. These leaves can be made into a pickle or sauce, uses that were formerly commonplace but are now rarely tried. Rock Samphire commonly inhabits inaccessible ledges of sea-cliffs and its collection was an exceedingly hazardous and often lethal trade. Eating the plant was believed to aid digestion and have beneficial effects on the kidneys and bladder. Rock Samphire was sometimes grown as a vegetable on well-drained soils, especially in England and France. The succulent leaves, with a thick, translucent coat, are an adaptation to drought, for even though the plant may be drenched by spray from a rough sea, the salt in the water tends to dry out an unprotected leaf and makes it difficult for roots to take up usable water. *Status:* native; coastal, from Scotland southwards. (There are no similar species.)

	ROCK SAMPHIRE		
Type	perennial	**Position**	many, in umbrella-shaped head 30–60mm across, 8–20 branches, at stem-tip
Height	15–30cm		
Habitat	cliffs, rocks, shingle	**Bracts**	many, spear-shaped, below head and flower-stalks
Flowering	June–August		
		Type	☿
	STEMS AND LEAVES	**Size**	1.5–2.5mm
Stem	angled upwards, solid, fleshy, woody at base	**Colour**	yellowish green
		Stalk	about equalling flower
Root	woody stock	**Sepals**	5, minute
Hairs	absent	**Petals**	5, 0.6–1mm, heart-shaped
Stipules	absent	**Stamens**	5
Leaves	on alternate sides of stem, divided 1–2 times into slender, smoothly rounded, fleshy, pointed segments, each 10–40mm, edge unbroken	**Stigmas**	2, slender
		Ovary	1, below petals, 2-celled
			FRUIT
		Type	1, splits into 2, corky, egg-shaped, angled, sometimes purplish
Leaf-stalk	short with broad base sheathing stem		
		Size	5–6mm
	FLOWERS	**Seeds**	1 per half, not released

Pimpinella saxifraga **Burnet-saxifrage**

Like a curious mixture of other plants, this has umbrella-shaped flower-heads like Wild Carrot but lower leaves like Salad Burnet. Like true Saxifrages, it was used to treat kidney stones. The root has a goat-like smell. *Status:* native; most of area except extreme north and many islands. *Similar species:* Greater Burnet-saxifrage is larger, and has ridged, hollow stems, longer, pointed lower leaflets, and grows in shadier places. Two grassland species have lumpy edible tubers. Pignut has hollow stems, long styles and narrow-beaked fruits. Great Pignut has solid stems, short styles and fruits with a short, bent beak.

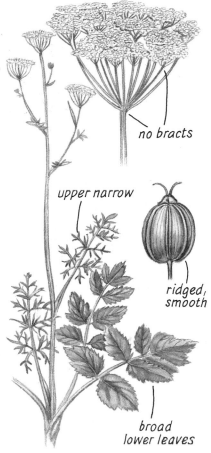

no bracts

upper narrow

ridged, smooth

broad lower leaves

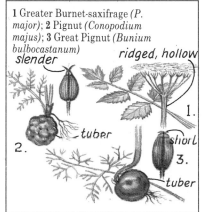

1 Greater Burnet-saxifrage (*P. major*); **2** Pignut (*Conopodium majus*); **3** Great Pignut (*Bunium bulbocastanum*)

slender

ridged, hollow

tuber

short

tuber

	BURNET-SAXIFRAGE		**FLOWERS**
Type	perennial	**Position**	many, in umbrella-shaped heads 20–50mm wide, 10–20 branches, at stem-tip
Height	30–100cm		
Habitat	grassy places; mostly dry, lime-rich soils		
		Bracts	absent
Flowering	July–August	**Type**	mostly ☿
		Size	2–3mm
	STEMS AND LEAVES	**Colour**	white
Stem	upright, mostly solid, slightly ridged	**Stalk**	longer than flower
		Sepals	5, minute
Root	slender stock, fibres from old leaves, strong-smelling	**Petals**	5, 0.8–1.5mm, tip curved in
		Stamens	5
Hairs	short, often sparse	**Stigmas**	2, slender, short styles
Stipules	absent	**Ovary**	1, below sepals, 2-celled
Leaves	basal with 6–14 leaflets, mostly paired, each 10–25mm, oval, toothed; stem-leaves scattered, cut 1–2 times into thin leaflets		**FRUIT**
		Type	1, splits into 2, dry, nearly globular, ridged
Leaf-stalk	lower long, upper with base sheathing stem	**Size**	2–3mm
		Seeds	1 per half, not released

Ground-elder *Aegopodium podagraria*

Creeping, underground stems spring up, making a new plant at a distance from the original, and lead gardeners many a chase. Often a persistent weed, Ground-elder was formerly cultivated as a pot-herb and used to treat gout and arthritis. *Status:* native, introduced to Britain and Ireland; most of area. *Similar species:* also spreading by long, rooting stems but with mostly paired leaflets, are several species of damp soil or still water. Fool's Water-cress has short-stalked flower-heads. Lesser Marshwort has narrow-lobed lower leaves. Lesser Water-parsnip has leaf-like bracts.

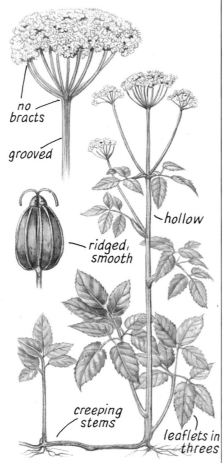

1 Fool's Water-cress (*Apium nodiflorum*); **2** Lesser Marshwort (*A. inundatum*); **3** Lesser Water-parsnip (*Berula erecta*)

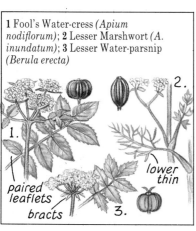

	GROUND-ELDER			FLOWERS	
Type	perennial		**Position**	many, in umbrella-shaped heads, 20–60mm wide, 15–20 branches, at stem-tip	
Height	40–100cm				
Habitat	cultivated or waste ground, often a weed		**Bracts**	usually absent	
Flowering	May–July		**Type**	♂	
			Size	1–3mm	
	STEMS AND LEAVES		**Colour**	white	
Stem	upright, stout, grooved, hollow		**Stalk**	longer than flower	
Root	long, creeping, rooting, underground stems		**Sepals**	absent	
			Petals	5, 0.5–1.5mm, slightly unequal, tip curved in	
Hairs	absent				
Stipules	absent		**Stamens**	5	
Leaves	basal or scattered on stem, 100–200mm, divided 1–2 times, leaflets in 3s, 40–80mm, oval, pointed, toothed		**Stigmas**	2, slender	
			Ovary	1, below sepals, 2-celled	
			FRUIT		
Leaf-stalk	lower long, 3-angled, upper short, base sheathing stem		**Type**	1, splits into 2, dry, egg-shaped, beak bent back	
			Size	3–4mm	
			Seeds	1 per half, not released	

Hemlock Water-dropwort *Oenanthe crocata*

A robust plant of wet places, with large, much-divided lower leaves and umbrella-shaped flower-heads, it is extremely poisonous and often kills livestock. The tubers are attached to the base of the plant by thread-like roots, and this is the origin of the name 'dropwort'. *Status:* native; fairly common, south-west of region. *Similar species:* Fine-leaved Water-dropwort has tiny leaflets and no bracts. Parsley Water-dropwort has bracts but few, slender leaflets. Tubular Water-dropwort has curious, swollen stem-segments and flower-heads with few branches and no bracts.

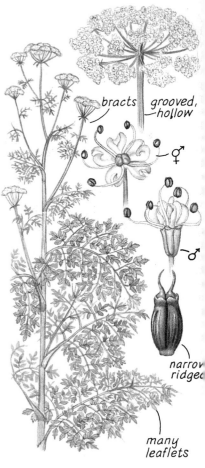

1 Fine-leaved Water-dropwort (*O. aquatica*); **2** Parsley Water-dropwort (*O. lachenalii*); **3** Tubular Water-dropwort (*O. fistulosa*)

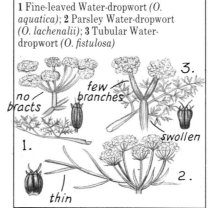

	HEMLOCK WATER-DROPWORT			FLOWERS	
Type	perennial		**Position**	many, in umbrella-shaped heads 50–100mm wide, 12–40 branches, at stem-tip	
Height	50–150cm				
Habitat	wet ditches, edge of water		**Bracts**	many, slender, below head and flower-stalks	
Flowering	June–July				
			Type	♂ and ♀ in same head	
	STEMS AND LEAVES		**Size**	2–4mm	
Stem	upright, stout, grooved, hollow		**Colour**	white	
Root	elongated tubers		**Stalk**	longer than flower	
Hairs	absent		**Sepals**	5, small, pointed	
Stipules	absent		**Petals**	5, 1–2mm, notched, unequal on outer flowers	
Leaves	basal or scattered on stem, up to 400mm, divided 2–4 times; leaflets many, oval to narrowly spear-shaped, toothed or lobed		**Stamens**	5, anthers crimson	
			Stigmas	2, slender	
			Ovary	1, below sepals, 2-celled	
Leaf-stalk	base sheathing stem, lower long, upper short		**FRUIT**		
			Type	1, splits into 2, dry, nearly cylindrical, ridged	
			Size	4–6mm	
			Seeds	1 per half, not released	

Conium maculatum Hemlock

A tall, rather elegant plant with fern-like foliage, purple-spotted stems and white, lacy flower-heads. Marring this image is a strong smell which hints at the extremely poisonous nature of the plant. Its powerful alkaloids can paralyse the respiratory system of animals or humans. In ancient times, preparations were made as a method of execution and, apparently, used by the Greeks to kill Socrates. Children should be warned of this plant: hollow stems cut for use as pea-shooters have proved fatal, although the toxicity of the plant varies greatly between different areas. Hemlock has been used as a drastic antidote to strychnine. In times long past it was used as an external treatment for herpes and breast tumours, and in controlled doses, equally misguidedly, to treat epilepsy and certain nervous afflictions; this practice has ceased because such usage can lead to paralysis or death. There are no plants quite like Hemlock, although several others, such as Rough Chervil, have purple-spotted stems. *Status:* native; throughout area, rarer in north. (There are no similar species.)

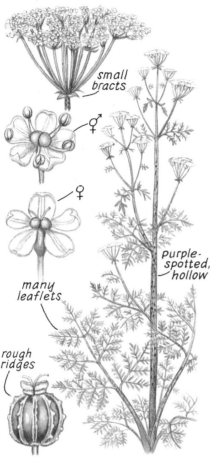

small bracts

♂

♀

many leaflets

purple-spotted, hollow

rough ridges

Pastinaca sativa Wild Parsnip

Yellow, umbrella-shaped flower-heads and coarse, hairy foliage of Wild Parsnip are common by many roadsides in high Summer. The whole plant has a strong smell of Parsnips, for this is the same species as the cultivated plant. Wild roots are slender and often woody. *Status:* native, escaped from cultivation in north; often common, most of area. *Similar species:* two yellow-flowered species have finely divided, hairless leaves and oblong, wingless fruits. Fennel is more robust, the aniseed-scented foliage having almost hair-like segments. Pepper-saxifrage has spear-shaped segments and fruits with the beak curved back.

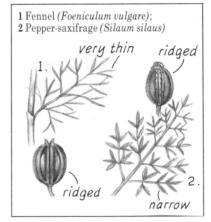

1 Fennel *(Foeniculum vulgare);*
2 Pepper-saxifrage *(Silaum silaus)*

very thin

ridged

1.

ridged

narrow

2.

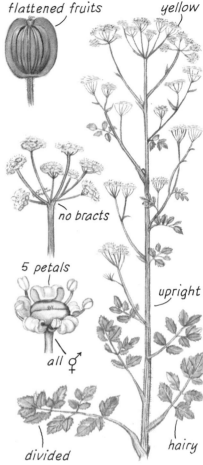

flattened fruits

yellow

no bracts

5 petals

upright

all ♂

divided

hairy

<table>
<tr><td colspan="2">HEMLOCK</td><td colspan="2">FLOWERS</td></tr>
<tr><td>Type</td><td>perennial</td><td>Position</td><td>many in umbrella-shaped heads 20–50mm wide, 10–20 branches</td></tr>
<tr><td>Height</td><td>50–250cm</td><td></td><td></td></tr>
<tr><td>Habitat</td><td>woodland edges, waste ground; mostly damp soils</td><td></td><td></td></tr>
<tr><td></td><td></td><td>Bracts</td><td>few, bent back, below head and flower-stalks</td></tr>
<tr><td>Flowering</td><td>June–July</td><td></td><td></td></tr>
<tr><td></td><td></td><td>Type</td><td>♀ in head at stem-tip, ♂ in head from leaf-base</td></tr>
<tr><td colspan="2">STEMS AND LEAVES</td><td></td><td></td></tr>
<tr><td>Stem</td><td>upright, grooved, smooth, purple-spotted, hollow</td><td>Size</td><td>2–3mm</td></tr>
<tr><td></td><td></td><td>Colour</td><td>white</td></tr>
<tr><td>Root</td><td>stout tap-root</td><td>Stalk</td><td>longer than flower</td></tr>
<tr><td>Hairs</td><td>absent</td><td>Sepals</td><td>absent</td></tr>
<tr><td>Stipules</td><td>absent</td><td>Petals</td><td>5, 1–1.5mm, oval, notched</td></tr>
<tr><td>Leaves</td><td>basal or scattered on stem, up to 300mm, divided 2–3 times; leaflets 10–20mm, spear-shaped to triangular, coarsely toothed</td><td>Stamens</td><td>5</td></tr>
<tr><td></td><td></td><td>Stigmas</td><td>2, on slender styles</td></tr>
<tr><td></td><td></td><td>Ovary</td><td>1, below petals, 2-celled</td></tr>
<tr><td></td><td></td><td colspan="2">FRUIT</td></tr>
<tr><td>Leaf-stalk</td><td>lower long, upper very short, base broad</td><td>Type</td><td>1, splits into 2, nearly globular</td></tr>
<tr><td></td><td></td><td>Size</td><td>3–4mm</td></tr>
<tr><td></td><td></td><td>Seeds</td><td>1 per half, not released</td></tr>
</table>

<table>
<tr><td colspan="2">WILD PARSNIP</td><td colspan="2">FLOWERS</td></tr>
<tr><td>Type</td><td>biennial</td><td>Position</td><td>many in umbrella-shaped heads 30–100mm wide, 5–15 unequal branches, at stem-tip</td></tr>
<tr><td>Height</td><td>30–150cm</td><td></td><td></td></tr>
<tr><td>Habitat</td><td>grassy and waste ground; mainly lime-rich soil</td><td></td><td></td></tr>
<tr><td></td><td></td><td>Bracts</td><td>absent or few, soon falling</td></tr>
<tr><td>Flowering</td><td>July–August</td><td>Type</td><td>♀</td></tr>
<tr><td></td><td></td><td>Size</td><td>1.5–2.5mm</td></tr>
<tr><td colspan="2">STEMS AND LEAVES</td><td>Colour</td><td>yellow</td></tr>
<tr><td>Stem</td><td>upright, ridged, hollow</td><td>Stalk</td><td>little longer than flower</td></tr>
<tr><td>Root</td><td>tap-root, strong-smelling</td><td>Sepals</td><td>absent</td></tr>
<tr><td>Hairs</td><td>straight, throughout plant</td><td>Petals</td><td>5, oval, curved inwards</td></tr>
<tr><td>Stipules</td><td>absent</td><td>Stamens</td><td>5</td></tr>
<tr><td>Leaves</td><td>basal or scattered on stem, up to 300mm, divided 1–2 times; leaflets oval, lobed, toothed</td><td>Stigmas</td><td>2, styles short</td></tr>
<tr><td></td><td></td><td>Ovary</td><td>1, below petals, 2-celled</td></tr>
<tr><td>Leaf-stalk</td><td>mostly short, base sheathing stem</td><td colspan="2">FRUIT</td></tr>
<tr><td></td><td></td><td>Type</td><td>1, splits into 2, broad, flattened with encircling wing, ridged, dark-lined</td></tr>
<tr><td></td><td></td><td>Size</td><td>5–8mm</td></tr>
<tr><td></td><td></td><td>Seeds</td><td>1 per half, not released</td></tr>
</table>

Hogweed *Heracleum sphondylium*

A robust, bristly plant that has coarse foliage and almost flat-topped flower-heads with larger petals around the edges. These broad flower-heads attract many insects, especially the orange or brownish Soldier Beetle. Hollow stems are frequently used as pea-shooters by children, and the leaves are edible. *Status:* native; throughout area. *Similar species:* often naturalized in damp places, Giant Hogweed is distinguished by its great size, some stems growing over 5 metres tall and having flower-heads half a metre across. Wild Angelica has smoother, purplish stems and more divided, hairless leaves.

1 Giant Hogweed
(*H. mantegazzianum*); 2 Wild
Angelica (*Angelica sylvestris*)

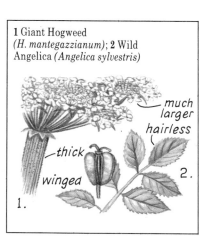

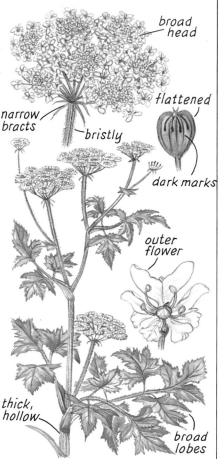

broad head

narrow bracts

bristly

flattened

dark marks

outer flower

thick, hollow

broad lobes

much larger hairless

thick

winged

1.

2.

HOGWEED		Bracts	slender, usually below head and flower-stalks
Type	biennial	**Type**	☿
Height	50–200cm	**Size**	5–10mm
Habitat	grassland, hedges, woods	**Colour**	white or pink
Flowering	June–September	**Stalk**	longer than flower
		Sepals	5, small, unequal
STEMS AND LEAVES		**Petals**	5, 2–7mm, notched, very unequal on outer flowers
Stem	upright, stout, ridged, hollow	**Stamens**	5
Root	stout tap-root	**Stigmas**	2, styles short
Hairs	stiff, over whole plant	**Ovary**	1, below sepals, 2-celled
Stipules	absent		
Leaves	basal or scattered on stem, 150–600mm, divided; leaflets 50–150mm, broad, irregularly lobed, toothed, paired	**FRUIT**	
		Type	1, splits into 2, nearly circular, flattish, winged, ridged, dark-lined
Leaf-stalk	lower longest, bases broad, sheathing stem	**Size**	7–8mm
		Seeds	1 per half, not released
FLOWERS			
Position	many, in umbrella-shaped heads at stem-tips, 50–150mm wide, 7–25 branches		

Upright Hedge-parsley *Torilis japonica*

One of the later-flowering hedgerow species of the Carrot family, with lacy umbrella-shaped heads of pinkish flowers. Spiny fruits and many slender bracts distinguish it from most other native species of the family. *Status:* native; often very common, most of area except extreme north. *Similar species:* Knotted Hedge-parsley has almost stalkless flower-heads with few branches. Spreading Hedge-parsley has heads with fewer branches and usually one bract. Fool's Parsley has long, downward-pointing bracts below the flower-stalks, and smoothly ridged fruits.

1 Knotted Hedge-parsley (*T. nodosa*);
2 Spreading Hedge-parsley
(*T. arvensis*); 3 Fool's Parsley
(*Aethusa cynapium*)

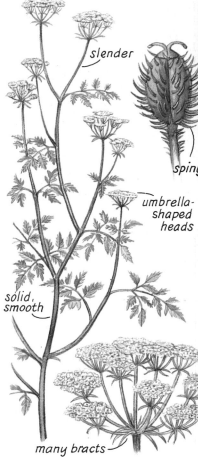

slender

spiny

umbrella-shaped heads

solid, smooth

few branches

stemless head

half spiny

smooth, ridged

long

3.

2.

many bracts

UPRIGHT HEDGE-PARSLEY		Bracts	many, unequal, thin, below head and flower-stalks
Type	annual	**Type**	☿
Height	5–125cm	**Size**	2–3mm
Habitat	hedges, grassy places	**Colour**	white tinged pink or purple
Flowering	July–August	**Stalk**	longer than flower
		Sepals	5, small, triangular
STEMS AND LEAVES		**Petals**	5, 1–1.5mm, unequal, notched, tip curved in
Stem	more or less upright, solid	**Stamens**	5
Root	slender tap-root	**Stigmas**	2, styles short
Hairs	short, pressed to surface	**Ovary**	1, below sepals, 2-celled
Stipules	absent		
Leaves	on alternate sides of stem, divided 1–3 times; leaflets 10–20mm, oval to spear-shaped, lobed or toothed	**FRUIT**	
		Type	1, splits into 2, egg-shaped, ridged, covered with spines, beak-like tips curved back
Leaf-stalk	lower longest	**Size**	3–4mm
		Seeds	1 per half, not released
FLOWERS			
Position	many, in umbrella-shaped heads 15–40mm wide, 5–12 branches, most at stem-tip		

Distinct among the many species of the family because of the conspicuous, divided bracts beneath the flower-heads. In the middle of the white flower-head there is usually a single purple flower. The fruiting head curls up like a ball and bristles with spiny fruits. Cultivated Carrot belongs to a different subspecies. *Status:* native or introduced in extreme north; throughout area. *Similar species:* Sea Carrot, from the Atlantic coasts of Britain and France, is often short-stemmed, with more triangular leaves having broader, fleshier segments, and the fruiting heads are flat or slightly domed.

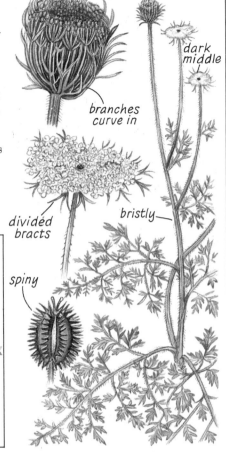

branches curve in

dark middle

divided bracts

bristly

spiny

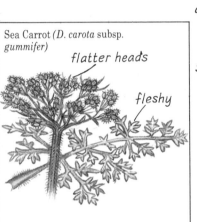

Sea Carrot (*D. carota* subsp. *gummifer*)

flatter heads

fleshy

WILD CARROT			
Type	biennial	**Bracts**	7–13 below head, deeply cut into thin lobes, undivided below flowers, edges papery
Height	30–100cm, rarely 150cm		
Habitat	grassland, often lime-rich soils	**Type**	♀
Flowering	June–August	**Size**	2–4mm
		Colour	white, middle flower usually purple or red
STEMS AND LEAVES		**Stalk**	about equalling flower
Stem	upright, ridged, solid	**Sepals**	5, small
Root	usually thin tap-root	**Petals**	5, 1–2mm, notched, unequal on outer flowers
Hairs	stems stiffly hairy		
Stipules	absent	**Stamens**	5
Leaves	on alternate sides of stem, divided 2–3 times; leaflets 4–7mm, slender, lobed	**Stigmas**	2, styles short
		Ovary	1, below sepals, 2-celled
Leaf-stalk	lower longest, base sheathing stem	**FRUIT**	
		Type	1, splits into 2, nearly oblong, ridged, spiny
FLOWERS			
Position	many, in umbrella-shaped heads at stem-tips 30–70mm wide, many branches	**Size**	2.5–4mm
		Seeds	1 per half, not released

A most peculiar member of the Carrot family, its stems appear to pass straight through the bluish, undivided leaves, as referred to in the common name. Broad bracts and dull yellow flowers look rather like some sort of Spurge. Once a common cornfield weed, it became extinct in many areas with seed-cleaning and selective herbicides. *Status:* native or introduced; uncommon, south of area. *Similar species:* warty fruits are found on False Thorow-wax, with narrower leaves, and Slender Hare's-ear, with grass-like leaves. Sickle-leaved Hare's-ear is perennial, and has smooth fruits and narrow, often curved leaves.

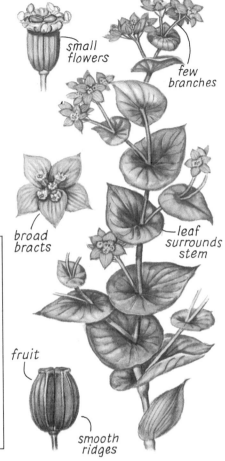

small flowers

few branches

broad bracts

leaf surrounds stem

fruit

smooth ridges

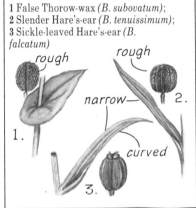

1 False Thorow-wax (*B. subovatum*);
2 Slender Hare's-ear (*B. tenuissimum*);
3 Sickle-leaved Hare's-ear (*B. falcatum*)

rough

rough

narrow

2.

1.

curved

3.

THOROW-WAX			
Type	annual	**FLOWERS**	
Height	15–30cm	**Position**	few, umbrella-shaped heads 10–30mm wide, 3–8 branches, at stem-tip or leaf-base
Habitat	cornfields, waste ground; mostly dry soils		
Flowering	June–July	**Bracts**	none below head, large below flower-stalks, oval, yellowish
		Type	♀
STEMS AND LEAVES		**Size**	1.5–2mm
Stem	upright, smooth, hollow	**Colour**	yellow
Root	fibrous	**Stalk**	about equalling flower
Hairs	absent	**Sepals**	absent
Stipules	absent	**Petals**	5, 0.5–0.8mm, equal, oval
Leaves	scattered around stem, 20–50mm, elliptical to almost circular, bluish green, edge unbroken, upper with stem passing through blade	**Stamens**	5
		Stigmas	2, styles slender
		Ovary	1, below petals, 2-celled
Leaf-stalk	absent or short on lower	**FRUIT**	
		Type	1, splits into 2, egg-shaped, ridged, blackish
		Size	2–3mm
		Seeds	1 per half, not released

Primroses, Heathers, Wintergreens and Thrift

Most of the plants in this group have hermaphrodite flowers with five, equal sepals and petals, at least the latter of which are joined by their bases to form a tube. The solitary ovary is generally positioned above the base of the sepals.

The Primrose family contains many popular ornamental plants such as Cyclamens, Shooting Star (*Dodecatheon*) and species of *Primula* (Auriculas, Polyanthus and Primroses).

The Heather family features prominently in the vegetation of moorland and heath. Amongst many ornamental species are *Pernettya*, Rhododendrons and Strawberry Trees (*Arbutus* species), in addition to the cultivated heathers. A curious aspect of this family is that they all have some degree of dependence on a fungus. Edible fruits of the Heather family include bilberries, blueberries and cranberries.

Wintergreens are sometimes included in the Heather family, but are herbaceous plants with the ovary incompletely divided. These plants also derive their nutrition partly from decomposing leaves, with the aid of a fungus.

Thrift and Sea-lavender belong to a moderately large family of herbs and shrubs, the native species of which are mostly found near the sea. A distinctive feature of these species is the five sepals, joined to form a funnel-shaped, papery structure.

Cowslips brighten a sunny bank with lop-sided heads of tubular flowers.

Pyrola minor Common Wintergreen

From a cluster of broad, glossy leaves, long, scaly stems arise bearing the nodding, globular flowers. Wintergreen leaves were used to treat wounds and kidney or bladder infections, because they have both diuretic and disinfectant properties. *Status:* native; scattered over much of area, rarer in south, absent from many islands. *Similar species:* other species have a projecting style with a thickened tip. Intermediate Wintergreen has a straight style. Round-leaved Wintergreen has more open flowers, a curved style and longer leaf-stalks. Serrated Wintergreen has one-sided flower-heads, a straight style and sharp-toothed leaves.

1 Intermediate Wintergreen (*P. media*); 2 Round-leaved Wintergreen (*P. rotundifolia*); 3 Serrated Wintergreen (*Orthilia secunda*)

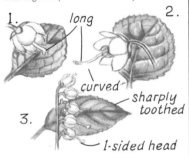

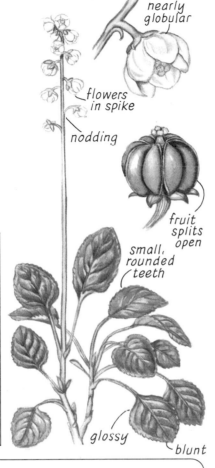

	COMMON WINTERGREEN		FLOWERS	
Type	perennial	**Position**	5–17, in crowded spike-like head at stem-tip	
Height	5–30cm	**Bracts**	slender, pointed	
Habitat	woods, moors, rocks, dunes; mostly damp soils	**Type**	♀, globular, nodding	
Flowering	May–June	**Size**	5–6.5mm	
		Colour	whitish pink	
	STEMS AND LEAVES	**Stalk**	almost equalling flower	
Stem	short, leafy; flowering stems upright, scaly	**Sepals**	5, 1.5–2mm, bases joined	
Root	creeping underground stem	**Petals**	5, 5–6.5mm, equal, not joined, overlapping	
Hairs	absent	**Stamens**	10	
Stipules	absent	**Stigma**	1, 5-lobed, style straight, shorter than petals	
Leaves	basal or scattered on stem, often a rosette, 25–40mm, oval, mostly blunt with tiny, rounded teeth, base wedge-shaped or squarish	**Ovary**	1, 5-celled	
		FRUIT		
Leaf-stalk	shorter than blade	**Type**	1, capsule, globular, splits into 5	
		Size	4–5mm	
		Seeds	numerous, minute	

Erica cinerea Bell Heather

A wiry, evergreen, dwarf shrub with needle-like leaves and nodding, bell-shaped flowers. Garden forms have varying flowering times and colours. Species of Heathers can be so prolific that they change the colour of vast tracts of land as flowering commences. *Status:* native; most of area, commoner in west. *Similar species:* Cross-leaved Heath has leaves in fours, edged with long, gland-tipped hairs. Cornish Heath is larger with long flower-stalks and projecting stamens. Heather, or Ling, has small, closely-packed leaves and the large, purple sepals are longer than the petals.

1 Cross-leaved Heath (*E. tetralix*); 2 Cornish Heath (*E. vagans*); 3 Heather (*Calluna vulgaris*)

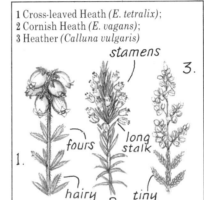

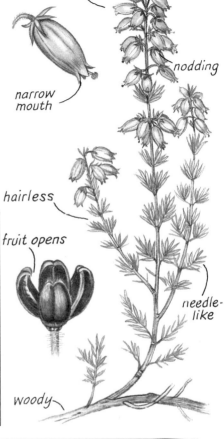

	BELL HEATHER			
Type	dwarf, evergreen shrub	**Bracts**	3 tiny bracts below sepals	
Height	15–75cm	**Type**	♀, nodding	
Habitat	heaths, moors, woodland edges; dryish, acid soils	**Size**	4–7mm	
		Colour	reddish purple	
Flowering	July–September	**Stalk**	shorter than flower	
		Sepals	4, 2–3mm, pointed, bases joined	
	STEMS AND LEAVES	**Petals**	4, 4–7mm, joined except at tips, bell-shaped with narrow mouth	
Stem	many, branched, woody, rooting, almost upright	**Stamens**	8, not projecting	
Root	woody stock	**Stigma**	1, club-shaped, on long style, projecting	
Hairs	only on young shoots	**Ovary**	1, 4-celled	
Stipules	absent			
Leaves	rings of 3, 5–7mm, slender, straight-sided, pointed, edges curved under	**FRUIT**		
		Type	1, capsule, splits open, enclosed by dry petals	
Leaf-stalk	very short	**Size**	1.5–2mm	
		Seeds	numerous, minute	
	FLOWERS			
Position	many in head, 10–70mm, at stem-tip			

Bilberry *Vaccinium myrtillus*

A small deciduous shrub of moors and heaths, with globular pink flowers followed by globular black fruits. The berries have a bluish 'bloom', as on black grapes. Although small and rather watery, they are edible and often eaten in pies, tarts or with cream. *Status:* native; most of area, on mountains in south. *Similar species:* Cowberry is evergreen with glossy leaves, bell-shaped flowers and red fruits. Cranberry has long-stalked, red fruits, and petals bent sharply back revealing purple stamens. Although with blue-black fruits, Crowberry is unrelated, having heather-like leaves and six-petalled flowers.

1 Cowberry (*V. vitis-idaea*);
2 Cranberry (*V. oxycoccos*);
3 Crowberry (*Empetrum nigrum*)

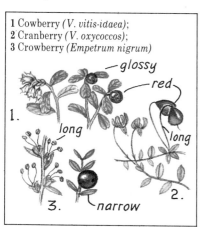

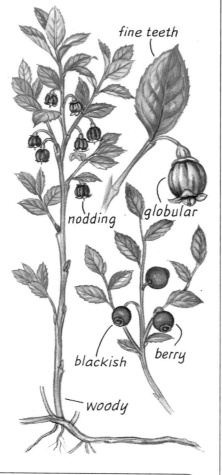

	BILBERRY			FLOWERS
Type	deciduous shrub		**Position**	mostly single, at leaf-base
Height	15–60cm		**Bracts**	2, scale-like
Habitat	moors, heaths, woods; acid soils		**Type**	♂, nodding
			Size	4–6mm
Flowering	July–September		**Colour**	pink, sometimes greenish
			Stalk	about equalling flower
	STEMS AND LEAVES		**Sepals**	4–5, joined, forming scarcely lobed ring
Stem	upright, many, young shoots 3-angled		**Petals**	4–5, 4–6mm, joined, globular, tips bent back
Root	creeping underground stem		**Stamens**	8–10
Hairs	absent		**Stigma**	1, club-shaped, long style
Stipules	absent		**Ovary**	1, below sepals, 4–5-celled
Leaves	on alternate sides of stem, 10–30mm, oval, pointed, finely toothed			**FRUIT**
			Type	1, berry, globular, black with bluish, waxy bloom, edible
Leaf-stalk	shorter than blade		**Size**	6–10mm
			Seeds	many, small

Primrose *Primula vulgaris*

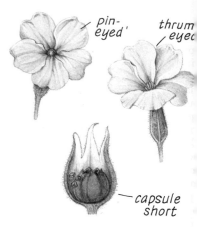

Few sights are more welcome after a bleak Winter, than a bank covered with the soft yellow flowers of Primroses. Two forms of flower differ by the look of the tube-mouth. One has five stamens ('thrum-eyed'), the other a stigma ('pin-eyed'), an arrangement enhancing the chances of cross-pollination. *Status:* native; most parts except extreme north. *Similar species:* other species have stalked flower-clusters. Cowslip has small, often darker petals; Oxlip has large, whitish-yellow petals and a long capsule. Bird's-eye Primrose has floury-looking leaves and lilac flowers.

1 Cowslip (*P. veris*); 2 Oxlip (*P. elatior*); 3 Bird's-eye Primrose (*P. farinosa*)

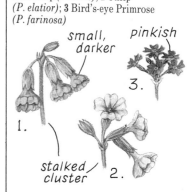

	PRIMROSE			FLOWERS
Type	perennial		**Position**	in cluster at base or on very short stem
Height	10–20cm			
Habitat	woods, hedgerows, grassy banks; damp soils		**Bracts**	present
			Type	♀, facing upwards
Flowering	December–May		**Size**	width 20–40mm
			Colour	pale yellow, deeper marks around throat, rarely pink
	STEMS AND LEAVES		**Stalk**	50–200mm, with long hairs
Stem	very short		**Sepals**	5, joined into tube, 15–17mm, teeth 4–6mm
Root	short underground stem; thick, white roots		**Petals**	5, 20–40mm, base forms tube
			Stamens	5, at tube-mouth or middle
Hairs	few below leaves, none above; long on flower-stalks and sepals		**Stigma**	1, club-shaped, style long, at mouth of tube or middle
Stipules	absent		**Ovary**	1, 1-celled
Leaves	rosette at base, 80–200mm, oval to spoon-shaped, widest above middle, blunt, irregularly toothed			**FRUIT**
			Type	1, capsule, nearly globular
Leaf-stalk	short or absent		**Size**	5–7mm
			Seeds	numerous, c1mm, angular

Cyclamen hederifolium **Cyclamen**

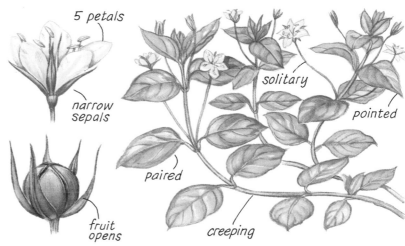

bent back
fruit opens
small lobes
stem coils

A delightful little plant, the upswept petals of its nodding, pink flowers spotted purple at the base. Leaves arise singly from the underground stem and only as the flowers fade, and are often marked with silver above and tinged purple below. The young capsule's stalk spirals from the tip until it lies on the ground, looking like a coil-spring. Cyclamen multiplies readily by seed and becomes naturalized. *Status:* introduced from southern Europe; scattered, mainly southern. *Similar species:* one species is native in the south-eastern part of the area. It has scented flowers, rounded leaves, and purplish petals lacking basal lobes.

nodding
long stalk
some angled
swollen stem

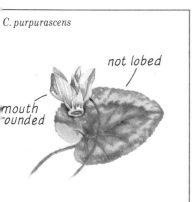

C. purpurascens

not lobed
mouth rounded

	CYCLAMEN		Bracts	absent
Type	perennial		Type	♂, nodding
Height	10–30cm		Size	15–25mm
Habitat	woods, hedges, near gardens		Colour	pink with purple blotches at base, rarely white
Flowering	August–September		Stalk	10–30mm, nearly upright
			Sepals	5, 4–8mm, oval, bases joined
	STEMS AND LEAVES		Petals	5, 15–25mm, equal, elliptical, bases joined into 5-angled tube, each petal bent back, 2 small lobes at base
Stem	very short			
Root	underground, swollen stem to 100mm wide, globular or hollow upper face			
			Stamens	5, forming short cone
Hairs	more or less absent		Stigma	1, scarcely projecting
Stipules	absent		Ovary	1, 1-celled
Leaves	at base, 30–140mm, oval to kidney-shaped, 5–9-angled, often pale marks above and purple below, blunt, finely toothed, appearing after flowers			**FRUIT**
			Type	1, capsule, globular, splits from middle, purple-flecked, centre sticky; stalk coiled
Leaf-stalk	often longer than blade			
			Size	10–18mm
	FLOWERS		Seeds	many, 2–4mm, angular
Position	single, from base			

Lysimachia nemorum **Yellow Pimpernel**

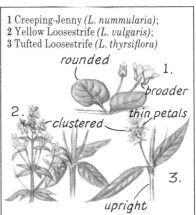

5 petals
narrow sepals
fruit opens
solitary
pointed
paired
creeping

Rather a delicate, trailing plant with starry, yellow flowers dotted over a shady woodland floor. Paired oval leaves and long-stalked flowers look rather like those of the Scarlet Pimpernel. *Status:* native; most of area except extreme north. *Similar species:* often escaping from cultivation, Creeping-Jenny has rounded leaves and larger flowers with much broader sepals. Two related species with upright stems are Yellow Loosestrife, with clusters of flowers towards the stem-tips, and Tufted Loosestrife with spikes of narrow-petalled flowers from the upper leaf-bases.

1 Creeping-Jenny (*L. nummularia*);
2 Yellow Loosestrife (*L. vulgaris*);
3 Tufted Loosestrife (*L. thyrsiflora*)

rounded
broader
thin petals
clustered
upright

	YELLOW PIMPERNEL		Bracts	absent
Type	perennial		Type	♂
Height	10–45cm		Size	6–8.5mm
Habitat	woods, hedges; mostly damp soils		Colour	yellow
			Stalk	much longer than flower, hair like
Flowering	May–September			
			Sepals	5, 3.5–6mm, very slender, pointed
	STEMS AND LEAVES		Petals	5, 6–8.5mm, equal, bases joined, wide-spreading
Stem	slender, low-growing			
Root	fibrous			
Hairs	absent		Stamens	5
Stipules	absent		Stigma	1, slender, style long
Leaves	paired either side of stem, 20–40mm, oval, evergreen, pointed, edge unbroken, base rounded		Ovary	1, 1-celled
				FRUIT
Leaf-stalk	shorter than blade		Type	1, capsule, globular, splits into 5
	FLOWERS		Size	3–4mm
Position	solitary, at leaf-base		Seeds	many, 1.5–2mm, circular, flattened

Scarlet Pimpernel *Anagallis arvensis*

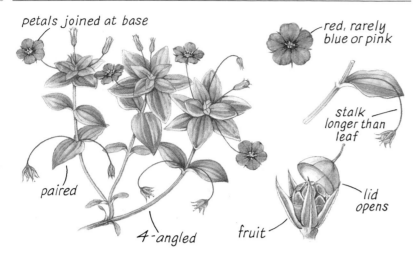

petals joined at base

red, rarely blue or pink

stalk longer than leaf

paired

lid opens

4-angled

fruit

Although commonly a weed, Scarlet Pimpernel has jewel-like flowers of scarlet, sometimes deep blue, or rarely other, colours. Petals close in the afternoon, or when overcast, and soon drop, falling as a joined ring. *Status:* native; almost throughout area, rarer in north. *Similar species:* Blue Pimpernel usually has shorter-stalked, blue flowers, lacking hairs on the petal-edges. Bog Pimpernel, in marshy places, has narrow-petalled, pink flowers. Sea-milkwort also has pink flowers, although short-stalked, and has succulent leaves like many other plants from the upper fringe of sea-shores.

1 Blue Pimpernel (*A. foemina*); **2** Bog Pimpernel (*A. tenella*); **3** Sea-milkwort (*Glaux maritima*)

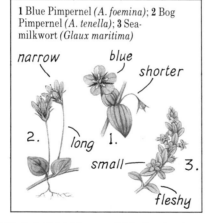

narrow

blue

shorter

2.

long

1.

small

3.

fleshy

	SCARLET PIMPERNEL
Type	annual
Height	6–30cm, rarely 90cm
Habitat	cultivated and waste ground, dunes; most soils
Flowering	June–August
	STEMS AND LEAVES
Stem	low-growing, 4-angled
Root	fibrous
Hairs	absent
Stipules	absent
Leaves	paired either side of stem, 15–18mm, oval or spear-shaped, black-dotted below, edge unbroken
Leaf-stalk	absent
	FLOWERS
Position	solitary, at leaf-base
Bracts	absent

Type	♂
Size	5–14mm
Colour	red, sometimes blue, rarely paler colours
Stalk	3–35mm, slender, curved back in fruit
Sepals	5, 3.5–5mm, narrow, pointed
Petals	5, 2–6mm, oval, equal, bases joined, edges usually with many small hairs
Stamens	5, stalks hairy
Stigma	1, slender, style long
Ovary	1, 1-celled
	FRUIT
Type	1, capsule, globular, top splits off
Size	2.5–4mm
Seeds	12–45, 1–1.5mm, nearly circular, slightly flattened

Water Violet *Hottonia palustris*

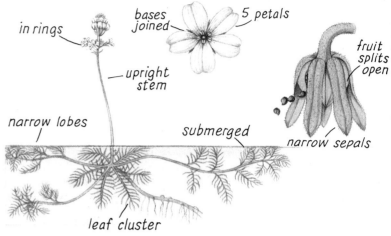

in rings

bases joined

5 petals

upright stem

fruit splits open

narrow lobes

submerged

narrow sepals

leaf cluster

A most attractive plant that has rings of lilac, yellow-eyed flowers quite like those of some garden Primulas, but with very different foliage. This water-plant has feathery leaves on submerged stems which turn up at the tip and emerge from the water before flowering. *Status:* native, introduced to Ireland and elsewhere; scattered through much of area except parts of north. *Similar species:* no species is quite like Water Violet but Bogbean is also aquatic and has stalked spikes of pale flowers, although pink, with fringed petals. The leaves have three broad leaflets and are carried above the water.

Bogbean (*Menyanthes trifoliata*)

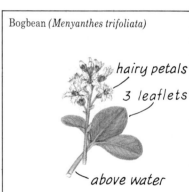

hairy petals

3 leaflets

above water

	WATER VIOLET
Type	perennial
Height	30–90cm
Habitat	ponds, ditches; shallow, still, fresh water
Flowering	May–June
	STEMS AND LEAVES
Stem	submerged or floating, turns upright to flower above water
Root	fibrous; stems root
Hairs	absent except for flowers
Stipules	absent
Leaves	in rings or scattered around stem, 20–130mm, cut 1–2 times into very slender lobes, some float
Leaf-stalk	shorter than blade

	FLOWERS
Position	3–8 in a ring, 3–9 rings around stem
Bracts	5–10mm, thin, pointed
Type	♂
Size	20–25mm
Colour	lilac with yellow centre
Stalk	about equalling flower
Sepals	5, 5–10mm, narrowly oblong
Petals	5, 12–17mm, bases joined into slender tube
Stamens	5, attached to petals
Stigma	1, club-shaped, style short or long
Ovary	1, 1-celled
	FRUIT
Type	1, capsule, globular, splits into 5 except at tip
Size	3–6mm
Seeds	numerous, *c*1mm, angular

A plant mostly of mountain and moorland, Chickweed Wintergreen has white flowers rather like Anemones, above a ring of broad leaves. Slender stems spring up singly from a creeping underground stem. The plant was formerly applied to wounds and has been used to counteract blood-poisoning. *Status:* native; common in north, mostly in mountains in south or often absent. *Similar species:* although no species looks quite alike, Brookweed has flowers of similar construction although much smaller, with five petals, and in spike-like heads. It also occurs in damp places, often in coastal areas.

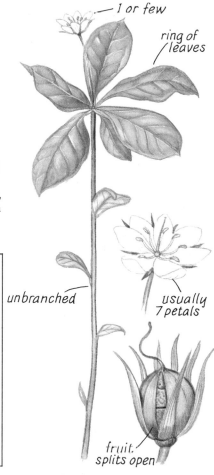

1 or few

ring of leaves

unbranched

usually 7 petals

fruit splits open

Brookweed (*Samolus valerandi*)

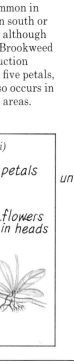

leaves at base

5 petals

flowers in heads

	CHICKWEED WINTERGREEN		FLOWERS	
Type	perennial	**Position**	1–few, from upper leaf-base
Height	5–30cm	**Bracts**	absent
Habitat	among grass or moss, often in pine-woods; damp places	**Type**	☿
		Size	11–19mm
Flowering	June–July	**Colour**	white
		Stalk	10–70mm, thin, upright
	STEMS AND LEAVES	**Sepals**	usually 7, 4–7mm, very narrow, pointed
Stem	single, unbranched, upright	**Petals**	usually 7, 11–19mm, oval, joined at extreme base
Root	creeping, underground stems	**Stamens**	7
Hairs	absent	**Stigma**	1, club-shaped; style long
Stipules	absent	**Ovary**	1, 1-celled
Leaves	few small, scattered below, ring of 5–6 leaves above, 10–90mm, oval or spear-shaped, broadest above, glossy, edge unbroken or finely toothed above		
			FRUIT	
		Type	1, capsule, globular, usually splits into 5
Leaf-stalk	short or absent	**Size**	4–6mm
		Seeds	7–11, 1.5–2mm, circular, flattened, black

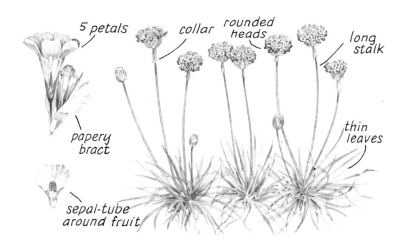

5 petals

collar

rounded heads

long stalk

papery bract

thin leaves

sepal-tube around fruit

A distinctive plant of coastal areas. On exposed cliff-tops, the leaves disappear among grassy tufts so that the pink heads, held aloft above the short turf, provide the first indication of the plant's presence. The only common *Armeria* in the area. *Status:* native; common in coastal areas, sometimes on inland mountains. *Similar species:* although at first sight rather different, Sea-lavenders grow in similar places, have much the same growth-habit and similar flowers. Common Sea-lavender prefers muddy salt-marshes and has bluish-purple flowers in widely-branched heads.

Common Sea-lavender (*Limonium vulgare*)

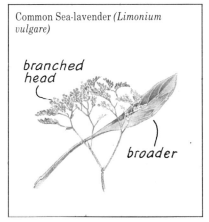

branched head

broader

	THRIFT		Bracts	lowest form tubular sheath up to 20mm long, around stalk-tip; innermost papery
Type	perennial			
Height	5–30cm	**Type**	☿, slightly scented
Habitat	coastal cliffs, rocks, salt-marshes	**Size**	7–10mm; heads 15–25mm
		Colour	pink, rarely red or white
Flowering	April–October	**Stalk**	shorter than flower
		Sepals	5, 5–10mm, joined, papery, funnel-shaped, 5 hairy ribs
	STEMS AND LEAVES	**Petals**	5, equal, oval, bases joined
Stem	leafy part very short; stalk of flower-head upright, unbranched	**Stamens**	5
		Stigmas	5, slender; long styles
Root	woody, branched stock	**Ovary**	1, 1-celled
Hairs	short or absent		
Stipules	absent		**FRUIT**	
Leaves	basal, forming rosette, 20–150mm, grass-like, rather thick, edge unbroken	**Type**	1, oblong capsule, opening irregularly, surrounded by sepals and withered petals
Leaf-stalk	absent	**Size**	2.5–3mm
		Seeds	1, 2–2.5mm, egg-shaped
	FLOWERS		
Position	small clusters grouped into rounded head at stalk-tip		

Bedstraws, Gentians and Periwinkles

Gentians are mainly herbaceous plants, with few shrubby species. Most have five petals and separate stamens. Many species are grown as garden plants and extracts of some species are used as bitter flavourings or in medicines. Two native aquatic plants that are sometimes included in this family are the Bogbean (see page 110) and the Fringed Water-lily (see page 42).

Neither Gentians nor Periwinkles have stipules, but they are present in Bedstraws and often resemble extra leaves. There are four or five petals and the same number of separate stamens. Bedstraws form a very large, widespread family, occurring mostly in the tropics and often forming large trees. The economic importance of the family lies mainly with Coffee (*Coffea* species), though it includes the plants that yield quinine (*Cinchona* species). Ornamental plants include Gardenias and Woodruffs.

Though the plants of the Periwinkle family included here are all herbaceous, this is atypical and there are many large trees in the tropics. Most species have five petals. A quite distinctive feature is the way the five stamens are joined above, forming a ring. Some species of the family have medicinal value, providing an important source of anti-cancer drugs. In northern Europe, probably all Periwinkles encountered are relics of earlier cultivation, though they are native farther south.

A rare native of wet heaths, the Marsh Gentian is as attractive as any of its garden relatives.

A delicate plant with slender stems, glossy leaves and pink petals. It is very variable in height, branching, and the size and number of the flowers. Common Centaury is a bitter-tasting herb, formerly taken to stimulate appetite and to treat digestive disorders. It was also used to combat fevers and treat anaemia. *Status:* native; absent from much of north. *Similar species:* Lesser Centaury has distinctly stalked flowers in less crowded heads; Seaside Centaury has narrower, oblong leaves. Yellow-wort is more distantly related, has the upper leaves joined, and flowers with six to eight yellow petals.

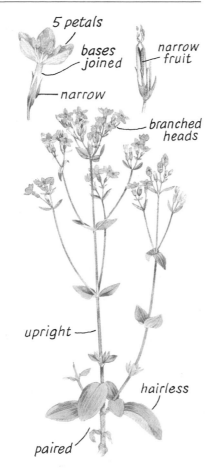

5 petals
bases joined
narrow fruit
narrow
branched heads
upright
hairless
paired

1 Lesser Centaury (*C. pulchellum*);
2 Seaside Centaury (*C. littorale*);
3 Yellow-wort (*Blackstonia perfoliata*)

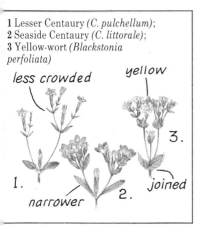

less crowded
yellow
3.
1.
narrower
2.
joined

A small-flowered relative of the garden Gentians, with clusters of purplish, tubular flowers. Field Gentian is bitter-tasting and one of several plants used to flavour ales before the introduction of Hops. Native species were sometimes made into a tonic used medicinally and to stimulate appetite. *Status:* native; common, especially in north. *Similar species:* Autumn Gentian has narrower, equal, non-overlapping sepals. True Gentians have non-fringed petal-lobes separated by small lobes. Of these, Marsh Gentian has a broad, green-striped petal-tube, and Spring Gentian has a slender, deep-blue petal-tube.

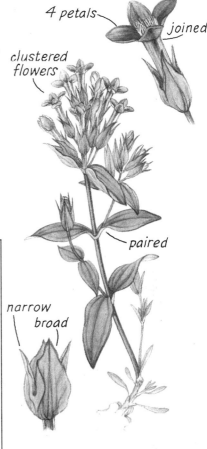

4 petals
joined
clustered flowers
paired
narrow
broad

1 Autumn Gentian (*G. amarella*);
2 Marsh Gentian (*Gentiana pneumonanthe*); 3 Spring Gentian (*G. verna*)

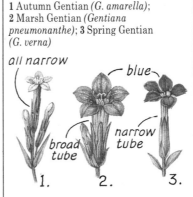

all narrow
blue
broad tube
narrow tube
1.
2.
3.

COMMON CENTAURY

Type	annual or biennial
Height	2–50cm
Habitat	mostly grassy places or dunes; dry soils
Flowering	June–October

STEMS AND LEAVES

Stem	1–few, upright, often branched
Root	small tap-root
Hairs	absent
Stipules	absent
Leaves	basal forming rosette or paired either side of stem, 10–50mm, oval or elliptical 3–7 main veins, blunt or sharpish, edge unbroken; upper smaller
Leaf-stalk	absent

FLOWERS

Position	many in branched, crowded, flattish-topped heads
Bracts	present
Type	♀, facing upwards
Size	10–14mm
Colour	pink, rarely white
Stalk	short or absent
Sepals	5, 5–8mm, narrow, pointed, bases joined
Petals	5, lobes 5–6mm, equal, bases joined into tube
Stamens	5, at top of petal-tube
Stigmas	2; style forked
Ovary	1, 1-celled

FRUIT

Type	1, slender capsule, pointed
Size	8–12mm
Seeds	many, 0.8–1mm, rounded

FIELD GENTIAN

Type	annual or biennial
Height	10–30cm
Habitat	grassy places, dunes; mostly lime-free soils
Flowering	July–October

STEMS AND LEAVES

Stem	upright, branched above
Root	fibrous
Hairs	absent
Stipules	absent
Leaves	basal or paired either side of stem, 10–30mm, oval to oblong, blunt or pointed, edge unbroken
Leaf-stalk	absent

FLOWERS

Position	many, in branched heads
Bracts	present
Type	♀
Size	15–30mm
Colour	bluish lilac, rarely white
Stalk	shorter than flower
Sepals	4, 10–18mm, very unequal, bases joined, 2 outer oval, widest below middle, pointed, 2 inner narrow
Petals	4, 15–30mm, equal, joined into long tube, the oblong lobes fringed at base
Stamens	4
Stigmas	2, somewhat flattened
Ovary	1, 1-celled

FRUIT

Type	1, elongated capsule, splits lengthwise
Size	20–25mm
Seeds	many, 0.8–1mm, globular

Lesser Periwinkle *Vinca minor*

An evergreen, carpeting shady bank-sides with glossy leaves and a sprinkling of bluish-purple, white-eyed blooms. Cultivated for many centuries, it has often escaped. Species of Periwinkle have had many medicinal uses, including staunching bleeding and reducing blood-pressure; other members of the family provide anti-cancer drugs. *Status:* native, introduced in north-west; scattered through area except extreme north. *Similar species:* Greater Periwinkle is more robust, with larger leaves and flowers. The stems arch over and root at the tips, springing up again as a new plant.

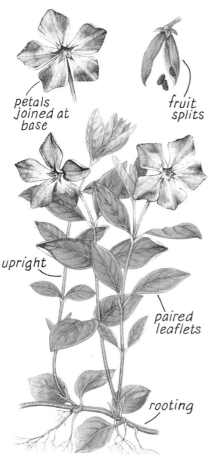

petals joined at base

fruit splits

upright

paired leaflets

rooting

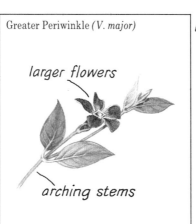

Greater Periwinkle (*V. major*)

larger flowers

arching stems

LESSER PERIWINKLE			
Type	evergreen perennial	**Type**	♀
Height	300–600cm	**Size**	25–32mm
Habitat	woods, hedges; often dry, lime-rich soils	**Colour**	bluish purple, rarely white or pink
Flowering	March–May	**Stalk**	about equalling flower
		Sepals	5, 4–5mm, spear-shaped
STEMS AND LEAVES		**Petals**	5, 12–16mm, equal, bases joined into tube, lobes broad, twisted together in bud, spreading widely, tip asymmetrical
Stem	trailing with short, upright flowering stems		
Root	woody stock; stems root		
Hairs	absent	**Stamens**	5, joined to petal-tube
Stipules	absent	**Stigmas**	forming broad head; styles joined
Leaves	paired either side of stem, 25–40mm, oval to elliptical, pointed or blunt, edge unbroken	**Ovaries**	2, 1-celled
Leaf-stalk	shorter than blade	**FRUIT**	
		Type	2, dry, pointed, spreading apart, splitting lengthwise
FLOWERS		**Size**	20–25mm
Position	1, rarely 2, at leaf-base	**Seeds**	1–4, 5–6mm, oblong, grooved
Bracts	absent		

Cleavers *Galium aparine*

A plant known better for its foliage than for its tiny flowers, Cleavers (or Goosegrass) has stiff, backward-curving hairs on stems and leaves with which it clings tenaciously to the least support. The fruits are covered with hooked hairs and are dispersed by animals. *Status:* native; very common, throughout area. *Similar species:* Woodruff is smaller, upright and glossy-leaved, with larger, sweetly-scented flowers. Two species with larger flower-heads and smooth fruits are Heath Bedstraw, which has smooth stems, and Common Marsh-bedstraw, which has roughish stem-angles and blunt leaves.

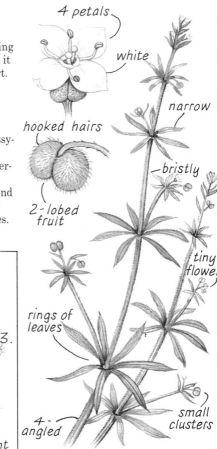

4 petals

white

narrow

bristly

hooked hairs

2-lobed fruit

tiny flower

rings of leaves

small clusters

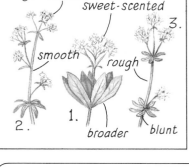

1 Woodruff (*G. odoratum*); 2 Heath Bedstraw (*G. saxatile*); 3 Common Marsh-bedstraw (*G. palustre*)

larger heads

sweet-scented

smooth

rough

3.

2.

1.

broader

blunt

4-angled

CLEAVERS			
Type	annual	**FLOWERS**	
Height	15–120cm	**Position**	2–5 in cluster at leaf-base
Habitat	hedges, waste ground, rocks and shingle	**Bracts**	leaf-like
		Type	♀
Flowering	June–August	**Size**	1.5–2mm
		Colour	white
STEMS AND LEAVES		**Stalk**	about equalling flower
Stem	trailing or climbing by means of stiff, hook-like hairs, 4-angled	**Sepals**	4, minute, forming ridge
		Petals	4, 0.6–1mm, oval, wide-spreading, bases joined
Root	fibrous		
Hairs	stiff, curved, mostly backward-pointing	**Stamens**	4, projecting
		Stigmas	2, club-shaped
Stipules	like the leaves	**Ovary**	1, below petals, 2-celled
Leaves	rings of 6–8 leaves and stipules on stem, 12–50mm, narrowly spear-shaped or elliptical, with slender point, edge unbroken	**FRUIT**	
		Type	1, dry, 2-lobed, splits in half, with hooked bristles
Leaf-stalk	absent	**Size**	4–6mm
		Seeds	1 per half, not released

Galium verum Lady's Bedstraw

Rather a delicate plant, with slender stems bearing rings of needle-like leaves and golden heads of tiny, four-petalled flowers. The plant has a pleasant smell of new-mown hay when dried and was formerly used for making bedding. Bedstraws are food-plants for caterpillars of the Broad-bordered Bee Hawk-moth, a remarkable bee-mimic with transparent wings. *Status:* native; common, most of area. *Similar species:* Crosswort has hairy leaves in fours and flowers clustered at the leaf-bases. Wild Madder is much larger, with greenish-yellow five-petalled flowers and hooked teeth around the broad leaves.

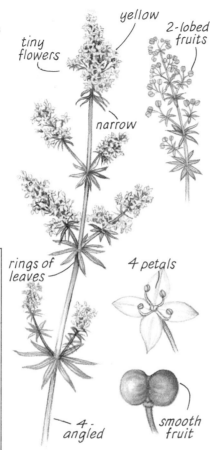
yellow
tiny flowers
2-lobed fruits
narrow
rings of leaves
4 petals
4-angled
smooth fruit

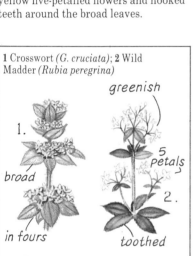
1 Crosswort (*G. cruciata*); **2** Wild Madder (*Rubia peregrina*)
greenish
5 petals
broad
in fours
1.
2.
toothed

LADY'S BEDSTRAW

Type	perennial
Height	15–100cm
Habitat	grassy places, dunes; all but poorest soils
Flowering	July–August

STEMS AND LEAVES

Stem	upright or angled upwards, 4-angled, much-branched
Root	fibrous; creeping underground stems
Hairs	absent or sparse
Stipules	resembling leaves
Leaves	8–12 leaves and stipules in ring, 6–25mm, narrow, straight-sided, rough, with thin point, edge unbroken
Leaf-stalk	absent

FLOWERS

Position	many, in branched cluster at tip of stem or branch
Bracts	present
Type	☿
Size	2–4mm
Colour	bright yellow
Stalk	about equalling flower
Sepals	4, minute, forming ridge
Petals	4, 1–2mm, oval, wide-spreading, bases joined
Stamens	4, projecting
Stigmas	2, club-shaped
Ovary	1, below petals, 2-celled

FRUIT

Type	1, 2-lobed, smooth, dry, becomes black, splits in half
Size	2.5–3mm
Seeds	1 per half, not released

Sherardia arvensis Field Madder

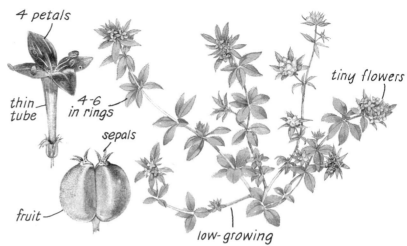
4 petals
thin tube
4–6 in rings
sepals
tiny flowers
fruit
low-growing

A diminutive annual species with leaves in rings and small heads of tubular, lilac flowers, Field Madder often turns up in gardens as a weed, in flowerbeds and lawns. *Status:* native; common throughout region. *Similar species:* Squinancywort, mainly on chalk grassland, is a more slender, hairless plant with branched heads of pink flowers. Dune Squinancywort is similar but has orange underground stems, smaller, slightly fleshy leaves and stalkless flowers. Pink Woodruff is a larger, broad-leaved plant with heads of whitish pink flowers and is sometimes naturalized.

1 Squinancywort (*Asperula cynanchica*); **2** Dune Squinancywort (*A. occidentalis*); **3** Pink Woodruff (*A. taurina*)
stalkless
many flowers
orange
narrow
1.
2.
3.
broad

FIELD MADDER

Type	annual
Height	5–40cm
Habitat	cultivated and waste ground
Flowering	May–October

STEMS AND LEAVES

Stem	many, low-growing, 4-angled
Root	slender, reddish
Hairs	sparse, pointing backwards on stem-angles, forwards on leaves
Stipules	resembling leaves
Leaves	rings of 4–6 leaves and stipules on stem, 5–18mm, oval or elliptical, pointed, edge unbroken
Leaf-stalk	absent

FLOWERS

Position	4–8, in head at tip of stem or branch
Bracts	8–10 in ring beneath head
Type	☿
Size	4–5mm
Colour	pale, pinkish purple
Stalk	shorter than flower
Sepals	4–6, 0.7–1.5mm, spear-shaped, fringed with hairs
Petals	4, 4–5mm, equal, bases form thin tube, lobes oval
Stamens	4, protruding
Stigmas	2; style long, forked
Ovary	1, below sepals, 2-celled

FRUIT

Type	1, 2-lobed, splits in half, bristly, sepals at tip
Size	2–7mm
Seeds	1 per half, not released

Bindweeds, Jacob's-ladder and Water-starworts

Bindweeds are commonly climbing plants, though they include non-climbing herbaceous plants and a few shrubs. From an economic point of view, the most important species of the family is the Sweet Potato (*Ipomoea batatas*), which is widely cultivated as a vegetable in the tropics. The same genus includes many ornamental species, such as Morning Glory. The leaves of the Bindweeds are undivided, arranged on alternate sides of the stem and rarely have stipules. In this family the petal-tube is characteristically broad and funnel-shaped, with the petals folded together in bud. Only a few seeds develop in each capsule. Sometimes regarded as a separate family, Dodders are parasitic with reduced, scale-like leaves and compact clusters of flowers.

There are many ornamental plants in the Jacob's-ladder family, such as species of *Phlox* and *Polemonium* grown in gardens. The leaves are sometimes divided into many leaflets and are carried in pairs or scattered on the stem. In bud, the petal-lobes are commonly twisted together and unfurl as the flower opens.

Water-starworts, included here for convenience though more properly placed next to the Mints, are aquatic plants. They produce tiny, unisexual, petal-less flowers, but their four-lobed ovaries are similar to the Mints.

Sea Bindweed's trailing stems bear kidney-shaped leaves and trumpets of candy-striped pink and white.

Polemonium caeruleum Jacob's-ladder

A handsome plant with long heads of hazy-blue showy flowers and finely divided foliage. When ripe, each anther bursts, releasing a mass of bright orange pollen, contrasting vividly with the blue of the petals. Creeping underground stems propagate the plant so that, given time, it forms extensive clumps. The common name derives from the ladder-like pattern made by the numerous parallel, narrow leaflets. A distant relative of the garden Phlox, Jacob's-ladder is widely cultivated for ornament, although many plants are the rarer white form or an introduced variant with larger flowers. Until the last century in some parts of Europe, the species was thought to be effective in the treatment of syphilis and rabies. It was used in more ancient times against dysentery and toothache. *Status:* native or often introduced; scattered, mostly north and east of area. (There are no similar species.)

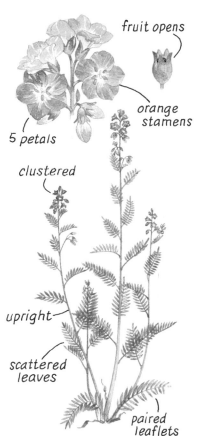

fruit opens

orange stamens

5 petals

clustered

upright

scattered leaves

paired leaflets

	JACOB'S-LADDER		FLOWERS	
Type	perennial	**Position**	many, in branched clusters at leaf-base or stem-tip
Height	30–90cm	**Bracts**	few
Habitat	grassy places, rocks and scree; mostly lime-rich, often damp soils	**Type**	♂ or rarely some ♀
		Size	20–30mm
Flowering	June–July	**Colour**	blue, rarely white
	STEMS AND LEAVES	**Stalk**	shorter than flower
Stem	1–few, upright, unbranched	**Sepals**	5, 5–9mm, bases joined
Root	creeping underground stem	**Petals**	5, 8–15mm, broadly oval, bases form short tube, lobes widely spreading
Hairs	gland-tipped in flower-head		
Stipules	absent	**Stamens**	5, protruding; pollen orange
Leaves	spirally placed on stem, 100–400mm, 3–25 mostly paired leaflets, each 20–40mm, oval to oblong, pointed, edge unbroken	**Stigmas**	3, slender, on long style
		Ovary	1, 3-celled
			FRUIT
		Type	1, capsule, splits into 3, globular, hidden by sepals
Leaf-stalk	lower long, upper short	**Size**	5–7mm
		Seeds	12–18, 2.5–3mm, angular

Petals of Jacob's-ladder unfurl after being twisted together in bud.

Hedge Bindweed *Calystegia sepium*

A spectacular climber with funnel-shaped flowers of pure white, just as large as those of many treasured garden plants. Gardeners shun Hedge Bindweed because it has long, creeping underground stems which sprout up all around, and its vigorous growth swamps all but the most robust plants. This rampant vine is beneficial in that it covers abandoned ruins, refuse tips, even a scrapped car or telegraph pole. *Status:* native; throughout area except for extreme north. *Similar species:* Large Bindweed has larger flowers and larger, balloon-like bracts. Hairy Bindweed has pink flowers and short hairs on young stems, stalks and bracts.

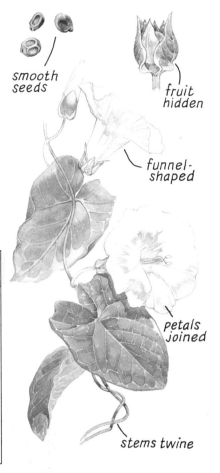

smooth seeds

fruit hidden

funnel-shaped

petals joined

stems twine

1 Large Bindweed (*C. silvatica*);
2 Hairy Bindweed (*C. pulchra*)

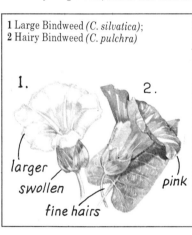

larger
swollen
fine hairs
pink

	HEDGE BINDWEED		FLOWERS	
Type	perennial	Position	solitary, at leaf-base	
Height	100–300cm	Bracts	2 below sepals, 10–30mm, broad, nearly flat	
Habitat	hedges, woods, waste and cultivated ground	Type	☿	
Flowering	April–July	Size	30–55mm	
		Colour	white	
	STEMS AND LEAVES	Stalk	shorter than flower	
Stem	climbs by twining anticlockwise, some creeping	Sepals	5, 9–12mm, oval, bases joined, enclosed by bracts	
Root	long, white, rooting, underground stems	Petals	5, 30–50mm, equal, almost completely joined into tube	
Hairs	absent	Stamens	5, at base of petal-tube	
Stipules	absent	Stigmas	2, broad; style forked	
Leaves	spirally placed on stem, to 150mm, heart- or arrow-shaped, blunt or with small point, edge unbroken	Ovary	1, 1-celled	
			FRUIT	
		Type	1, capsule, globular, hidden by sepals	
Leaf-stalk	mostly shorter than blade	Size	7–12mm	
		Seeds	4, 4–7mm, angular brown	

Field Bindweed *Convolvulus arvensis*

A climber with delightful pink and white, candy-striped flowers; its funnel-shaped petal-tube is pleated and opens fan-like by day, attracting many sorts of insect. On bare ground, such as railway ballast, long, radiating stems of Field Bindweed spread in a circle and sometimes twist together, using each other for support. This species is unwelcome in gardens because it has extremely invasive underground stems. *Status:* native; throughout area, rarer in north. *Similar species:* Sea Bindweed is a trailing plant from sand-dunes and shingle, with kidney-shaped leaves and larger flowers.

rough seeds

fruit exposed

lobed base

petals joined

pink and white

twining

Sea Bindweed (*Calystegia soldanella*)

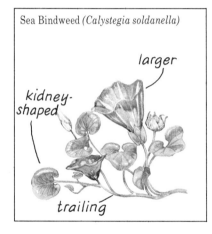

larger

kidney-shaped

trailing

	FIELD BINDWEED		FLOWERS	
Type	perennial	Position	1–3, in stalked cluster at leaf-base	
Height	20–100cm, rarely to 200cm	Bracts	2, small, below flower-stalks	
Habitat	cultivated and waste ground, often near sea	Type	☿, scented	
Flowering	June–September	Size	10–30mm	
		Colour	pink and white	
	STEMS AND LEAVES	Stalk	shorter than flower	
Stem	trailing or climbing by twisting anticlockwise	Sepals	5, 4–6mm, bases joined	
Root	long, creeping, underground stems	Petals	5, 9–25mm, almost completely joined, funnel-shaped	
Hairs	absent or on young shoots	Stamens	5, at base of petal-tube	
Stipules	absent	Stigmas	2, slender; style forked	
Leaves	on alternate sides of stem, 20–50mm, oblong, oval or arrow-shaped, blunt, edge more or less unbroken	Ovary	1, 2-celled	
			FRUIT	
		Type	1, capsule, almost globular	
Leaf-stalk	shorter than blade	Size	3–5mm	
		Seeds	2–4, 2.5–4mm, angular, rough	

Cuscuta epithymum Dodder

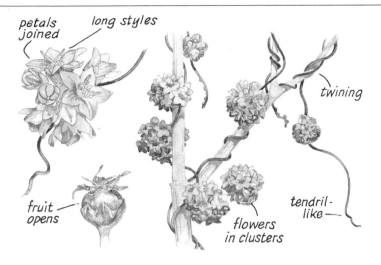

petals joined

long styles

twining

fruit opens

flowers in clusters

tendril-like

A most curious plant, with leafless, tendril-like stems. Individually scarcely noticeable, these stems can swamp a clump of Heather or Dwarf Gorse with a tangled mass of lurid pink and yellow threads. Dodder lacks green pigment because it is a parasite, drawing nourishment through sucker-like, modified roots which are firmly attached to the stem of another plant. It is rooted in the ground only as a seedling. *Status:* native; common in many localities, scattered through area except extreme north. *Similar species:* Greater Dodder usually attacks nettles or hops and has larger petals.

Greater Dodder *(C. europaea)*

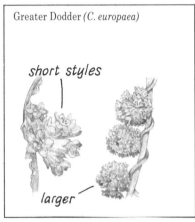

short styles

larger

DODDER		FLOWERS	
Type	annual, parasite	Position	8–17, crowded in rounded heads 5–10mm wide
Height	15–120cm		
Habitat	mainly on species of Heather, Gorse and Clover	Bracts	minute, below each flower
		Type	♂
Flowering	July–September	Size	2.5–5mm
		Colour	white tinged pink or red
STEMS AND LEAVES		Stalk	absent
		Sepals	5, 1–2mm, joined below
Stem	thread-like, white or yellow tinged with red or purple, twining, branched	Petals	5, 2.5–4mm, joined, lobes pointed, spreading, with scales at base closing mouth of tube
Root	sucker-like, on stem, attached to other plants	Stamens	5, between petal-lobes
		Stigmas	2, slender
Hairs	absent	Ovary	1, 2-celled
Stipules	absent		
Leaves	on alternate sides of stem, 0.5–2mm, scale-like, pointed, edge unbroken	**FRUIT**	
		Type	1, capsule, globular, splits near base, hidden by withered petals
Leaf-stalk	absent	Size	1.5–2mm
		Seeds	2–4, 1–1.5mm, angled

Callitriche stagnalis Common Water-starwort

A plant usually noticed as fresh green rosettes of small leaves, floating on the surface of a pond or stream. It is very variable, the shape of the leaves changing with the depth and speed of the water and the flowering or fruiting state. Plants growing on mud look very different. Closely related species are identified only with difficulty, and if ripe fruit is present. *Status:* native; common, most of area. *Similar species:* other aquatic plants include Canadian Waterweed, with leaves in threes and long-stalked flowers, and Nuttall's Waterweed with narrower, pointed leaves. Mare's-tail has leaves in rings of six to twelve.

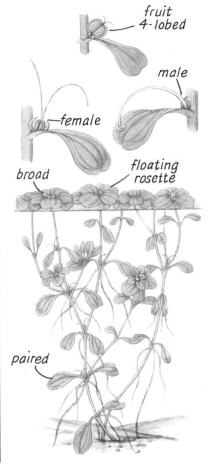

fruit 4-lobed

male

female

broad

floating rosette

paired

1 Canadian Waterweed *(Elodea canadensis)*; **2** Nuttall's Waterweed *(E. nuttallii)*; **3** Mare's-tail *(Hippuris vulgaris)*

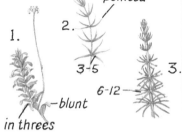

pointed

3-5

6-12

blunt

in threes

COMMON WATER-STARWORT		FLOWERS	
Type	annual or perennial	Position	solitary, at base of upper leaf, separate ♂ and ♀
Height	10–60cm		
Habitat	ponds, streams; shallow fresh water or wet mud	Bracts	2, curved
		Type 1	♂, with stamen
Flowering	May–September	Type 2	♀, with ovary
		Size	1.5–2mm
STEMS AND LEAVES		Colour	white or green
Stem	submerged or low-growing	Stalk	shorter than flower
Root	fibrous; stems root	Sepals	absent
Hairs	absent	Petals	absent
Stipules	absent	Stamen	1, c2mm
Leaves	paired or in rosette at stem-tip, 10–20mm, rounded or notched, edge unbroken; lower usually submerged, elliptical or spoon-shaped; upper usually floating, broader, forming rosette	Stigmas	2; styles curved, 2–3mm
		Ovary	1, 4-celled
		FRUIT	
		Type	1, splits into 4, nearly circular, 4 ridged
Leaf-stalk	shorter than blade	Size	1.6–2mm
		Seeds	4, 1.4–1.8mm, winged

Mints, Vervains and Forget-me-nots

These two large and widespread families share a number of features. The flowers usually have five sepals and petals, each joined by their bases to form a tube. In the Mints the petals tend to be unequal whereas they are equal in most species of the Forget-me-not family. At maturity, in the majority of species, the fruit splits into four, single-seeded, nut-like parts.

The Mint family is the source of many culinary herbs and flavourings, such as basil, marjoram, mint, oregano, rosemary, sage, thyme, peppermint and spearmint. In addition, there are many ornamental garden and house-plants, such as *Coleus*, Lavender (*Lavandula* species) and *Salvia*. A further three characteristics readily distinguish the Mints: the stems are usually square in cross-section with paired leaves; the foliage is frequently scented; and the two upper petals of the asymmetrical flowers are often joined to form a hood-like structure.

The Vervains are generally regarded as closely related to the Mints. The mainly tropical family usually has flowers with only slightly unequal petals, as in the garden Verbenas.

Forget-me-nots often have bristly hairs on the stems, leaves and in the flower-heads. The latter are commonly coiled, bearing the flowers on one side, and uncoiling as the fruits develop. Garden plants include *Anchusa, Echium* and Heliotrope.

Yellow Archangel demonstrates the characteristic hooded flowers and paired leaves of the Mint family.

Lithospermum arvense **Field Gromwell**

A stiffly upright plant with narrow, bristly leaves and white flowers, rather like those of Forget-me-not. Predominantly a cornfield weed, this plant has become much rarer in recent years with the increased use of selective weed-killers and more effective methods of cleaning the seeds of crops. *Status:* native or introduced; scattered through area, most common in south. *Similar species:* Common Gromwell is a perennial with a thick stock bearing many stems. It differs in the broader leaves with distinct side-veins, and shiny, smooth, white fruits.

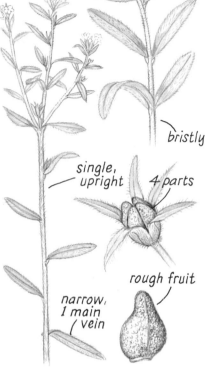

5 equal petals joined

bristly

single, upright

4 parts

narrow, 1 main vein

rough fruit

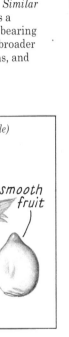

Common Gromwell (*L. officinale*)

smooth fruit

broader

	FIELD GROMWELL		Bracts	lower leaf-like
Type	annual		**Type**	♀
Height	10–50cm, rarely to 90cm		**Size**	6–9mm
Habitat	cultivated and waste ground; mostly dry places		**Colour**	white, rarely tinged blue
			Stalk	shorter than flower
Flowering	May–July		**Sepals**	5, 4.5–8mm, narrow, pointed, bases joined
	STEMS AND LEAVES		**Petals**	5, 6–9mm, equal, joined into narrow tube; lobes oblong, spreading widely
Stem	single, upright, sometimes branched, rough		**Stamens**	5, at base of petal-tube
Root	fibrous		**Stigma**	1, club-shaped
Hairs	bristly, close to surface		**Ovary**	1, 2-celled, each half 2-lobed
Stipules	absent			
Leaves	on alternate sides of stem, 30–50mm, oval to narrowly spear-shaped, blunt to sharp, edge unbroken			**FRUIT**
			Type	splits into 4, each nut-like, 3-angled, rough, greyish brown
Leaf-stalk	only on lower leaves		**Size**	3–4mm
			Seeds	1 per segment, not released
	FLOWERS			
Position	head at stem-tip, curved in bud, lengthening in fruit			

Symphytum officinale **Common Comfrey**

This bristly plant has blades of the upper leaves running down the stem as wings. Curved heads of tubular, nodding flowers are variously cream, pink, red or purple. Leaves were once used to dress cuts or bruises and roots made into cough-medicine. *Status:* native, or naturalized in north; throughout region. *Similar species:* Russian Comfrey, a hybrid with the next species, has almost wingless stems and usually blue flowers. Tuberous Comfrey has thick, underground stems and cream-coloured flowers. White Comfrey has soft, hairy leaves and white flowers with short, blunt sepals.

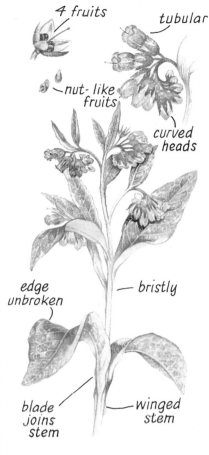

4 fruits

tubular

nut-like fruits

curved heads

edge unbroken

bristly

blade joins stem

winged stem

1 Russian Comfrey (*S. × uplandicum*); **2** Tuberous Comfrey (*S. tuberosum*); **3** White Comfrey (*S. orientale*)

cream coloured

1.

2.

white

not winged

soft hairs

3.

	COMMON COMFREY		Bracts	absent
Type	perennial		**Type**	♀, nodding
Height	30–120cm		**Size**	15–18mm
Habitat	grassland, river-banks; damp soil		**Colour**	yellowish white, variably tinged red, purple or pink
Flowering	May–June		**Stalk**	shorter than flower
			Sepals	5, 7–8mm, narrow, pointed, bases joined
	STEMS AND LEAVES		**Petals**	5, 15–18mm, equal, joined into tube; lobes short
Stem	upright, branched, winged		**Stamens**	5, inside tube
Root	thick stock; roots fleshy		**Stigma**	1; style long
Hairs	stiff, dense, throughout		**Ovary**	1, 2-celled, each 2-lobed
Stipules	absent			
Leaves	on alternate sides of stem, 40–250mm, oval or upper spear-shaped, the blade joining wings on stem, pointed, edge unbroken			**FRUIT**
			Type	splits into 4, each part nut-like, almost egg-shaped, smooth shiny, black
Leaf-stalk	lower long, absent above		**Size**	5–6mm
			Seeds	1 per segment, not released
	FLOWERS			
Position	many, in curved heads			

Green Alkanet *Pentaglottis sempervirens*

Widely grown for its bright blue, white-eyed flowers, bristly-leaved Green Alkanet often escapes from gardens. It is native to the extreme south-west of Europe, but is naturalized further north. The roots yield a reddish dye that may have been an early reason for cultivation. *Status:* introduced; south-western part of area. *Similar species:* Bugloss is annual, with narrower leaves and a curved petal-tube. Borage has blackish stamens, projecting as a spike beyond the petal-tube. Viper's-bugloss has many curved flower-heads towards the stem-tip and some stamens project beyond the unequal petal-lobes.

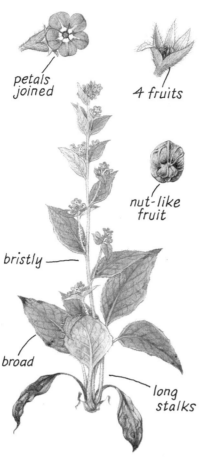

petals joined

4 fruits

nut-like fruit

bristly

broad

long stalks

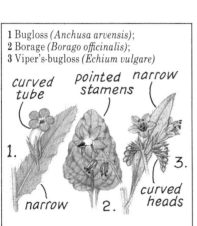

1 Bugloss *(Anchusa arvensis)*;
2 Borage *(Borago officinalis)*;
3 Viper's-bugloss *(Echium vulgare)*

curved tube

pointed stamens

narrow

1.

narrow

2.

3.

curved heads

	GREEN ALKANET		Bracts	leaf-like, below head
Type	perennial		**Type**	☿
Height	30–100cm		**Size**	8–10mm
Habitat	woods, hedges, mainly near houses; damp soils		**Colour**	bright blue
			Stalk	almost absent
Flowering	May–June		**Sepals**	5, 2.5–8mm, narrowly spear-shaped
	STEMS AND LEAVES		**Petals**	5, 6–8mm, equal, joined into tube at base, lobes broad, spreading widely
Stem	angled upwards or upright			
Root	underground creeping stem		**Stamens**	5, not protruding
Hairs	bristly throughout		**Stigma**	1, club-shaped
Stipules	absent		**Ovary**	1, deeply 4-lobed
Leaves	basal or on alternate sides of stem, 30–400mm, oval, tip pointed, edge unbroken or slightly wavy			**FRUIT**
			Type	splits into 4 nut-like parts, egg-shaped with ring-like base, rough
Leaf-stalk	lower stalked			
	FLOWERS		**Size**	1.5–2mm
Position	5–15, in head at leaf-base		**Seeds**	1 per segment, not released

Hound's-tongue *Cynoglossum officinale*

This greyish, softly hairy plant with dull red flowers has a strong smell rather like places where mice have been. Rabbits find it distasteful, so the plants are among the few untouched in the close-grazed turf surrounding their burrows. *Status:* native; rather scattered through area, mainly near coasts. *Similar species:* Green Hound's-tongue has greener leaves, nearly hairless above, and the fruit lacks a thickened edge. Other species do not have spiny fruits. Lungwort has white-spotted leaves and flowers opening pink, turning blue or purple. Oysterplant, mainly from northern seashores, is hairless with rough dots.

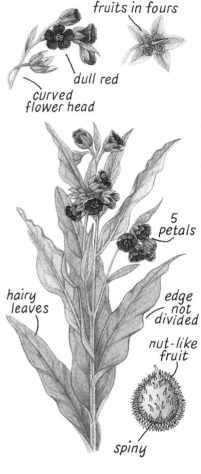

fruits in fours

dull red

curved flower head

5 petals

hairy leaves

edge not divided

nut-like fruit

spiny

1 Green Hound's-tongue *(C. germanicum)*; 2 Lungwort *(Pulmonaria officinalis)*; 3 Oysterplant *(Mertensia maritima)*

nearly hairless

pink to blue

3.

grey, hairless

1.

spotted

2.

	HOUND'S-TONGUE		**Type**	☿
Type	biennial		**Size**	6–10mm
Height	30–90cm		**Colour**	purplish red, rarely white
Habitat	grassy places or wood edges; mostly dry soils		**Stalk**	about equalling flower
			Sepals	5, bases joined, 4–8mm, oblong or oval, bluntish
Flowering	June–August			
			Petals	5, 7–11mm, equal, bases form tube, lobes with scales closing tube-mouth
	STEMS AND LEAVES			
Stem	upright			
Root	tap-root		**Stamens**	5, not protruding
Hairs	long, soft, grey		**Stigma**	1; style thick
Stipules	absent		**Ovary**	1, deeply 4-lobed
Leaves	basal or scattered around stem, 30–300mm, spear-shaped to oval, usually pointed, edge unbroken			**FRUIT**
			Type	splits into 4 nut-like parts, flattened, oval, covered with barbed spines, edge thickened
Leaf-stalk	lower long, upper stalkless			
	FLOWERS		**Size**	5–6mm
Position	long heads at stem-tips		**Seeds**	1 per segment, not released
Bracts	few, lower leaf-like			

Myosotis arvensis Field Forget-me-not

A Spring-flowering plant with pink buds opening into pale blue, yellow-eyed flowers. Young flower-heads are coiled, but straighten and lengthen as the fruits develop. Forget-me-nots are popular garden plants, in varying shades of blue or pink. *Status:* native; common throughout area. *Similar species:* Wood Forget-me-not has larger flowers with flat petal-lobes; those of the Field Forget-me-not are slightly hollow. Two small-flowered, annual species are Changing Forget-me-not, which has tiny flowers turning from yellow to blue, and Early Forget-me-not, which has short flower-stalks.

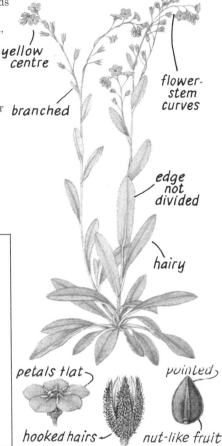

1 Wood Forget-me-not (*M. sylvatica*); 2 Changing Forget-me-not (*M. discolor*); 3 Early Forget-me-not (*M. ramosissima*)

larger
short stalks
tiny
yellow to blue
1.
2.
3.

yellow centre
branched
flower-stem curves
edge not divided
hairy
petals flat
hooked hairs
nut-like fruit
pointed

	FIELD FORGET-ME-NOT		
Type	biennial	**Bracts**	absent
Height	15–30cm, rarely 60cm	**Type**	♂
Habitat	woods, hedges, cultivated ground, dunes; dryish soils	**Size**	3–5mm
		Colour	blue with yellow centre, buds pinkish
Flowering	April–September	**Stalk**	about equalling flower, longer in fruit
	STEMS AND LEAVES	**Sepals**	5, 2.5–7mm, bases joined, covered with hooked hairs
Stem	upright, branched	**Petals**	5, 1.5–3mm, equal, bases form tube, lobes spreading
Root	fibrous	**Stamens**	5, inside tube
Hairs	short, throughout plant	**Stigma**	1, tip swollen
Stipules	absent	**Ovary**	1, deeply 4-lobed
Leaves	basal or scattered around stem, 6–80mm, oblong to spear-shaped, mostly blunt, edge unbroken		
			FRUIT
Leaf-stalk	only on lower leaves	**Type**	splits into 4 nut-like parts, angled, brown
	FLOWERS	**Size**	c1.5mm
Position	many in heads at stem-tips, coiled in bud, lengthening	**Seeds**	1 per segment, not released

Myosotis laxa subsp. *caespitosa* Tufted Forget-me-not

This species has coiled heads of small, sky-blue, yellow-eyed flowers like other Forget-me-nots, but grows in damp or wet places. The Forget-me-nots of wet places have straight hairs on the sepals, whereas those of dry places have distinctly hooked hairs. *Status:* native; common, throughout area. *Similar species:* two other species of damp or wet places are perennials with creeping stems. Water Forget-me-not has broad sepals joined for at least two-thirds of their length. Creeping Forget-me-not has narrower sepals joined to the middle, and long, projecting hairs near the base of the stems.

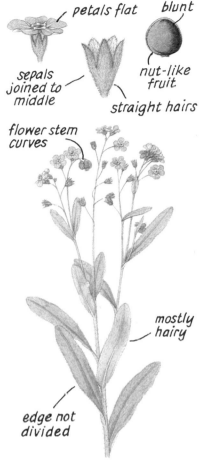

1 Water Forget-me-not (*M. scorpioides*); 2 Creeping Forget-me-not (*M. secunda*)

petals flat
blunt
sepals joined to middle
nut-like fruit
straight hairs
flower stem curves
mostly hairy
edge not divided

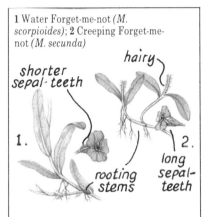

shorter sepal-teeth
hairy
rooting stems
long sepal-teeth
1.
2.

	TUFTED FORGET-ME-NOT		
Type	annual or biennial	**Bracts**	absent or few at base
Height	20–40cm	**Type**	♂
Habitat	streams, ponds, marshes; damp soil	**Size**	2–4mm
		Colour	light blue with yellow centre; buds pink
Flowering	May–August	**Stalk**	about equalling flower, longer in fruit
	STEMS AND LEAVES	**Sepals**	5, 2.5–4mm, up to 8mm in fruit, joined to middle
Stem	sometimes branched, upright	**Petals**	5, 2–4mm, forming tube at base, lobes rounded
Root	fibrous	**Stamens**	5, inside petal-tube
Hairs	on most of plant, pointing towards stem- or leaf-tip	**Stigma**	1, tip swollen
Stipules	absent	**Ovary**	1, deeply 4-lobed
Leaves	on alternate sides of stem, 10–80mm, oblong or spear-shaped, blunt, edge unbroken, base narrowed		
			FRUIT
Leaf-stalk	absent	**Type**	splits into 4 nut-like parts, oval, glossy brown
	FLOWERS	**Size**	1.3–1.8mm
Position	many in heads at stem-tips, coiled, becoming straight	**Seeds**	1 per segment, not released

Vervain *Verbena officinalis*

A tall plant with stiffly upright, tough stems and slender spikes of tiny lilac and pink flowers. It belongs to a family which includes the Verbenas of gardens, yet it is similar in many respects to species of the Mint family. Vervain had many herbal uses and was attributed magical properties. *Status:* native, introduced in north; rather scattered through region except for extreme north. *Similar species:* Gipsywort is a species of the Mint family and is found in wet places, often partly submerged. It has clusters of small flowers at the base of the upper leaves.

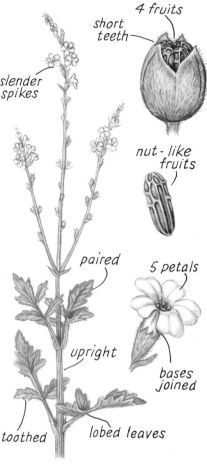

4 fruits
short teeth
slender spikes
nut-like fruits
paired
5 petals
upright
bases joined
toothed
lobed leaves

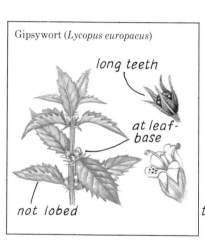

Gipsywort (*Lycopus europaeus*)

long teeth
at leaf-base
not lobed

	VERVAIN		FLOWERS	
Type	perennial	**Position**	many in long, spike-like heads at stem-tips	
Height	30–60cm	**Bracts**	small, pointed	
Habitat	waste ground or roadsides; mostly dry soils	**Type**	♂	
Flowering	July–September	**Size**	4–6mm	
		Colour	lilac, tube pink	
	STEMS AND LEAVES	**Stalk**	almost absent	
Stem	usually several, upright, branched, 4-angled	**Sepals**	5, 2–3mm, joined forming 5-ribbed tube, teeth short	
Root	woody stock	**Petals**	5, 4–6mm, bases form tube, lower lobes longest	
Hairs	stiff, on leaves	**Stamens**	4, rarely 2, inside tube	
Stipules	absent	**Stigma**	1, tip swollen, slightly 2-lobed	
Leaves	paired on stem, 20–75mm, deeply lobed, the lobes mostly paired, dull green, sharp or blunt, toothed	**Ovary**	1, 4-celled	
			FRUIT	
Leaf-stalk	stalked or upper stalkless	**Type**	splits into 4 nut-like parts, oblong, ridged, reddish-brown	
		Size	1.5–2mm	
		Seeds	1 per segment, not released	

Water Mint *Mentha aquatica*

A soft-leaved, lilac-flowered relative of Garden Mint, with broad leaves having a similar aroma. Water Mint makes a refreshing herbal tea. *Status:* native; suitable places throughout area. *Similar species:* Peppermint has almost hairless leaves and oblong heads of flower-clusters. A hybrid with the following species, it does not produce fruit. Many variants are known, differing in leaf-shape, hairiness and scent. Spear Mint has stalkless leaves and flower-clusters in a slender spike. Corn Mint is found in drier places and has small, widely spaced clusters of flowers at the base of the upper leaves.

pointed, equal teeth
nut-like fruits
10–13 veins
flowers towards stem-tip
clust of flow
toothed
hairy
4-angled
stalked pairs

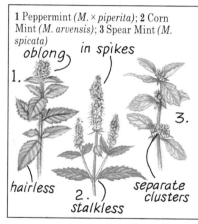

1 Peppermint (*M.* × *piperita*); **2** Corn Mint (*M. arvensis*); **3** Spear Mint (*M. spicata*)

oblong
in spikes
1.
3.
hairless
2.
stalkless
separate clusters

	WATER MINT		Bracts	lowest leaf-like; small bracts beneath each flower
Type	perennial, strongly scented		**Type**	♂ or some ♀
Height	15–90cm		**Size**	5–8mm
Habitat	marshes, rivers, wet woods		**Colour**	pinkish lilac
Flowering	July–October		**Stalk**	shorter than flower
			Sepals	5, 2.5–4mm, forming tube with 10–13 veins, teeth pointed, almost equal
	STEMS AND LEAVES			
Stem	upright, some branched, 4-angled, often red-tinged		**Petals**	5, 5–8mm, bases form tube, upper 2 lobes nearly joined, lower 3 lobes separate
Root	creeping underground stems			
Hairs	over most of plant, soft		**Stamens**	4, protruding
Stipules	absent		**Stigmas**	2 on forked style
Leaves	paired, 20–90mm, most oval, blunt or pointed, toothed, base slightly heart-shaped		**Ovary**	1, deeply 4-lobed
Leaf-stalk	shorter than blade			**FRUIT**
			Type	splits into 4 nut-like parts, egg-shaped, brown
	FLOWERS		**Size**	1–1.5mm
Position	many in 2–6 rounded clusters towards stem-tip		**Seeds**	1 per segment, not released

Teucrium scorodonia Wood Sage

A mint relative with vaguely sage-like, crinkly leaves and one-sided spikes of greenish-yellow flowers. In spite of its name, this is more a plant of sunny, grassy places than woodland, where it grows on the margins or in clearings. The flowers have very short upper petal-lobes. *Status:* native; most of area except parts of north. *Similar species:* the related Wall Germander has purple flowers of a similar form. Native in the south-east of the area, it is naturalized in Britain. Yellow Archangel is a yellow-flowered mint relative with nettle-like leaves and long upper lobes to the petal-tube.

1 Wall Germander (*T. chamaedrys*);
2 Yellow Archangel (*Lamiastrum galeobdolon*)

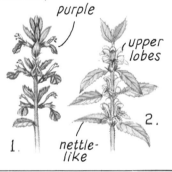

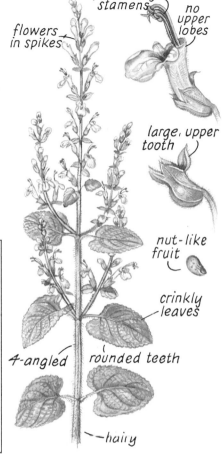

	WOOD SAGE			FLOWERS	
Type	perennial		**Position**	many, in spikes at stem-tips	
Height	15–50cm		**Bracts**	oval, shorter than flowers	
Habitat	grassland, heaths, dunes, woods; mostly dry soils		**Type**	⚥	
			Size	9–12mm	
Flowering	July–September		**Colour**	greenish yellow	
			Stalk	shorter than flower	
	STEMS AND LEAVES		**Sepals**	5, 4 6mm, joined, with pointed teeth, upper often largest	
Stem	upright, branched, woody at base		**Petals**	5, 9–12mm, bases joined into narrow tube, lower lobe largest, upper 2 very short	
Root	creeping underground stem				
Hairs	short, over most of plant				
Stipules	absent		**Stamens**	4, protruding	
Leaves	paired on stem, 30–70mm, oval, rough, blunt to sharpish, with rounded teeth, base heart-shaped		**Stigmas**	2 on long, forked style	
			Ovary	1, deeply 4-lobed	
			FRUIT		
Leaf-stalk	shorter than blade		**Type**	splits into 4 nut-like parts, egg-shaped, smooth	
			Size	1.5–2mm	
			Seeds	1 per segment, not released	

Galeopsis tetrahit Common Hemp-nettle

A bristly plant with nettle-like leaves and purple, mint-like flowers with spiny sepal-teeth. The brittle stems usually have distinct swellings below the attachment of each leaf-pair, and a tuft of reddish, gland-tipped hairs. The lower three petals have two cone-shaped projections at the base, which are not found in related genera. *Status:* native; common, throughout area. *Similar species:* Red Hemp-nettle is softly hairy, without swellings on the stems, and with narrower leaves. Its pinkish-purple flowers have yellow markings. Large-flowered Hemp-nettle has larger, pale yellow, purple-spotted flowers.

1 Red Hemp-nettle (*G. angustifolia*);
2 Large-flowered Hemp-nettle (*G. speciosa*)

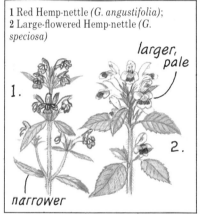

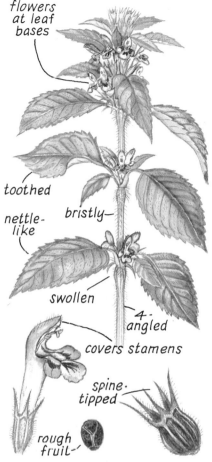

	COMMON HEMP-NETTLE			Bracts	leaf-like but most smaller
Type	annual			**Type**	⚥
Height	10–100cm			**Size**	15–20mm, rarely to 28mm
Habitat	cultivated ground, hedges, woods			**Colour**	purple or pink marked with purple, rarely white
Flowering	July–September			**Stalk**	much shorter than flower
				Sepals	5, 12–14mm, joined into tube, teeth spine-tipped
	STEMS AND LEAVES				
Stem	angled upwards, 4-angled, swollen below leaf-pairs			**Petals**	5, 15–28mm, bases form tube, upper 2 lobes joined, hood-like, lower 3 bent back, with 2 swellings
Root	fibrous				
Hairs	stiff, over most of plant				
Stipules	absent			**Stamens**	4, under upper petal-lobes
Leaves	paired on stems, 25–100mm, oval, pointed, toothed, base wedge-shaped			**Stigmas**	2 on long, forked style
				Ovary	1, deeply 4-lobed
Leaf-stalk	shorter than blade			**FRUIT**	
				Type	splits into 4 nut-like parts, rounded, 3-angled
	FLOWERS				
Position	clusters at leaf-bases and near stem-tip			**Size**	3–4mm
				Seeds	1 per segment, not released

White Dead-nettle *Lamium album*

Nettle-like foliage but with softer, stingless hairs and clusters of white, two-lipped flowers identify the White Dead-nettle. Long-tongued insects, such as bees, pollinate the flowers. The faintly aromatic leaves were once used in the north to make herbal teas. *Status:* mostly native, introduced to Ireland; common in most of area except parts of north. *Similar species:* Cat-mint has grey-green foliage with a mint-like scent. This is closely related to the garden Cat-mint, with low-growing stems and blue flowers, that cats find irresistible. White Horehound has rounded, white-haired leaves and ten hooked sepal-teeth.

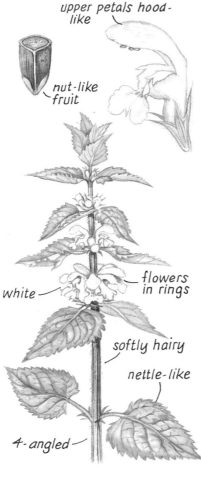

upper petals hood-like

nut-like fruit

white

flowers in rings

softly hairy

nettle-like

4-angled

1 Cat-mint *(Nepeta cataria)*; 2 White Horehound *(Marrubium vulgare)*

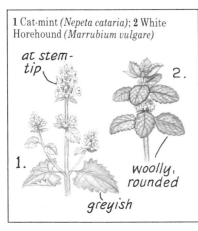

at stem-tip

1.

2.

greyish

woolly, rounded

	WHITE DEAD-NETTLE		Bracts	present
Type	perennial		Type	♀♂
Height	20–80cm		Size	20–25mm
Habitat	roadsides, hedges, waste ground		Colour	white
			Stalk	much shorter than flower
Flowering	May–December		Sepals	5, 9–13mm, forming tube, teeth long, slender
	STEMS AND LEAVES		Petals	5, 20–25mm, bases form tube; upper 2 lobes joined, hood-like, lowest lobe large, bent back, side lobes small, toothed
Stem	upright			
Root	creeping underground stems			
Hairs	long, fairly soft			
Stipules	absent		Stamens	4, under upper petal-lobes
Leaves	paired, 25–120mm, oval, with slender point, coarsely toothed, base heart-shaped		Stigmas	2 on long, forked style
			Ovary	1, deeply 4-lobed
Leaf-stalk	shorter than blade		**FRUIT**	
	FLOWERS		Type	splits into 4 nut-like parts, 3-angled, tip squarish
Position	many, in clusters at upper leaf-bases		Size	2.5–3mm
			Seeds	1 per segment, not released

Red Dead-nettle *Lamium purpureum*

A vaguely nettle-like plant but with stingless hairs on the leaves and four-angled stems, with flowers and clusters of four nut-like fruits typical of the Mint family. The creeping, rooting, basal parts of the plant were formerly used as pig-feed. In complete contrast, the flowers were crystallized in sugar and eaten as sweets. *Status:* native; very common, throughout area. *Similar species:* Henbit Dead-nettle has stalkless upper leaves. Cut-leaved Dead-nettle has deeply lobed leaves with few teeth. Black Horehound is a more robust perennial, with short, broad sepal-teeth.

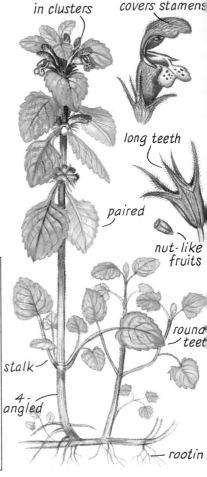

in clusters

covers stamens

long teeth

paired

nut-like fruits

round teeth

stalk

4-angled

rooting

1 Henbit Dead-nettle *(L. amplexicaule)*; 2 Cut-leaved Dead-nettle *(L. hybridum)*; 3 Black Horehound *(Ballota nigra)*

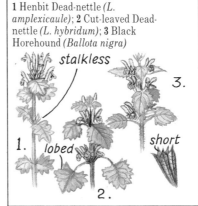

stalkless

1.

3.

lobed

short

2.

	RED DEAD-NETTLE		Bracts	similar to leaves
Type	annual		Type	♀♂
Height	10–45cm		Size	10–18mm
Habitat	cultivated and waste ground		Colour	pinkish purple
Flowering	March–October		Stalk	very short
			Sepals	5, 5–7mm, bases joined, teeth long, pointed
	STEMS AND LEAVES		Petals	5, 10–18mm, bases form tube, upper 2 lobes joined, hood-like, lowest large, 2-lobed, side 2 short, toothed
Stem	base branched, often rooting, upper parts upright, 4-angled, purplish			
Root	fibrous			
Hairs	short, over most of plant		Stamens	4, under upper petal-lobes
Stipules	absent		Stigmas	2 on long, forked style
Leaves	paired on stem, 10–50mm, oval, blunt, with rounded teeth, base heart-shaped		Ovary	1, deeply 4-lobed
Leaf-stalk	lowest long, upper short		**FRUIT**	
	FLOWERS		Type	splits into 4 nut-like parts, 3-angled, tip square
Position	few, in clusters towards stem-tip		Size	2–2.5mm
			Seeds	1 per segment, not released

Stachys officinalis **Betony**

Almost leafless stems of Betony arise from a basal tuft of long-stalked leaves, and each bears a fairly compact, cylindrical head of reddish-purple flowers at the tip. To Betony was attributed many properties, both medicinal and magical, and it was used in herbal tea and herbal tobacco. *Status:* native; common in south, absent from parts of north. *Similar species:* related species lack leaves at the base but have many on the stems. Stem-leaves of Hedge Woundwort are long-stalked, whereas those of Marsh Woundwort are stalkless. Field Woundwort is a small-flowered annual with broad stem-leaves.

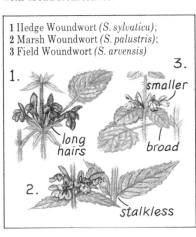

1 Hedge Woundwort (*S. sylvatica*);
2 Marsh Woundwort (*S. palustris*);
3 Field Woundwort (*S. arvensis*)

3. smaller
1. long hairs broad
2. stalkless

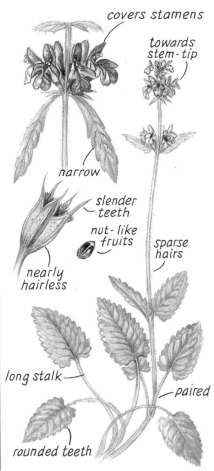

covers stamens
towards stem-tip
narrow
slender teeth
nut-like fruits
sparse hairs
nearly hairless
long stalk
paired
rounded teeth

	BETONY	**Bracts**	lowest leaf-like
Type	perennial	**Type**	☿
Height	15–60cm	**Size**	12–18mm
Habitat	woods, hedges, grassy places; light soils	**Colour**	bright reddish purple
		Stalk	much shorter than flower
Flowering	June–September	**Sepals**	5, 5–9mm, bases form tube, teeth sharply pointed
	STEMS AND LEAVES	**Petals**	5, 12–18mm, bases form tube, upper 2 lobes joined, hood-like, other lobes bent back
Stem	upright, mostly unbranched		
Root	woody underground stem		
Hairs	sparse	**Stamens**	4, under upper lobes
Stipules	absent	**Stigmas**	2 on long, forked style
Leaves	most basal, 2–4 pairs on stem, 30–70mm, oval to oblong, blunt, with rounded teeth, base heart-shaped	**Ovary**	1, deeply 4-lobed
		FRUIT	
		Type	splits into 4 nut-like parts, 3-angled, tip rounded
Leaf-stalk	lowest twice as long as blade, uppermost stalkless	**Size**	2.5–3mm
		Seeds	1 per segment, not released
	FLOWERS		
Position	many, in clusters around stem, towards stem-tip		

Salvia verbenaca **Wild Clary**

A very variable plant, usually with spikes of violet, 2-lipped flowers and pairs of rough, lobed leaves. Some specimens produce flowers which never open fully, being pollinated in bud and setting a full crop of nut-like fruits. Height, lobing of the leaves and size of the flowers vary considerably. The fruits swell and become sticky when wet. *Status:* native; scattered localities, mainly in south-west of area, north to Scotland. *Similar species:* Meadow Clary has larger flowers with long, curved, hood-like upper petal-lobes, and lacks white hairs on the sepal-tube.

Meadow Clary (*S. pratensis*)

larger, sticky
not lobed

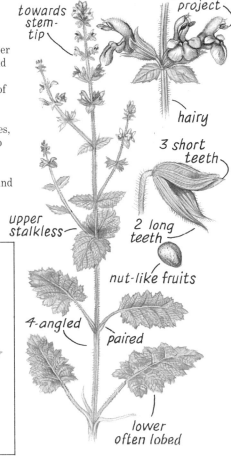

towards stem-tip
stamens project
hairy
3 short teeth
upper stalkless
2 long teeth
nut-like fruits
4-angled
paired
lower often lobed

	WILD CLARY	**Bracts**	oval, shorter than sepals
Type	perennial	**Type**	☿ or ♀, some not opening
Height	30–80cm	**Size**	6–15mm
Habitat	grassy places; dry soils	**Colour**	bluish violet
Flowering	May–August	**Stalk**	much shorter than flower
		Sepals	5, 6–8mm, with long, white hairs, bases form tube; 3 upper lobes nearly joined, lower 2 longer than tube
	STEMS AND LEAVES		
Stem	upright, hardly branched, 4-angled		
Root	tough stock	**Petals**	5, 6–15mm, bases form tube, upper 2 lobes joined, hood-like, lower lobes bent back
Hairs	short, gland-tipped above		
Stipules	absent		
Leaves	basal or 2–3 pairs on stem, 40–120mm, oblong or oval, rough, blunt, toothed, lowest often deeply lobed	**Stamens**	2, under upper petal-lobes
		Stigmas	2 on long, forked style
		Ovary	1, deeply 4-lobed
Leaf-stalk	lowest long, upper absent	**FRUIT**	
	FLOWERS	**Type**	splits into 4 nut-like parts, egg-shaped
Position	6–10, in rings, clustered in spikes at stem-tips	**Size**	1.5–2mm
		Seeds	1 per segment, not released

Ground-ivy *Glechoma hederacea*

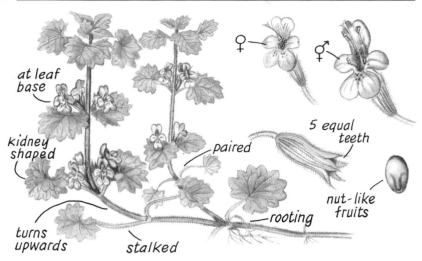

at leaf base

kidney shaped

paired

5 equal teeth

nut-like fruits

turns upwards

stalked

rooting

A charming plant with violet-coloured, two-lipped flowers, creeping beneath hedgerows and over woodland floors. It is sometimes grown in gardens, often as a variegated form used to trail over hanging baskets. Ground-ivy was formerly known best as a bitter herb used for flavouring ale, although it also had medicinal uses. *Status:* native; common, most of area. *Similar species:* Skullcap also has violet, two-lipped flowers. It has elongated leaves, a swelling on the upper side of the sepal-tube, and grows in wet, sunny places. Lesser Skullcap has smaller, pinkish flowers and sparsely toothed leaves.

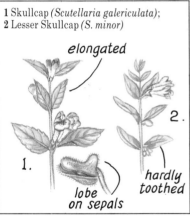

1 Skullcap (*Scutellaria galericulata*); 2 Lesser Skullcap (*S. minor*)

elongated

hardly toothed

lobe on sepals

GROUND-IVY	
Type	perennial
Height	10–50cm
Habitat	hedges, woods, grassy places; usually damp soil
Flowering	March–May
STEMS AND LEAVES	
Stem	creeping, rooting, angled upwards to flower
Root	fibrous, stems root
Hairs	soft, fairly long
Stipules	absent
Leaves	paired on stem, 5–35mm, kidney-shaped to nearly oval, blunt, coarsely-toothed, base heart-shaped
Leaf-stalk	most longer than blade
FLOWERS	
Position	clusters of 2–4 towards stem-tips
Bracts	resembling leaves
Type	♂ or sometimes ♀
Size	15–22mm
Colour	bluish violet, spotted reddish purple
Stalk	much shorter than flower
Sepals	5, 5–6.5mm, bases joined, teeth nearly equal, pointed
Petals	5, 15–22mm, bases joined; upper 2 lobes nearly joined, hood-like, lower 3 larger
Stamens	4, under upper petal-lobes
Stigmas	2 on long, forked style
Ovary	1, deeply 4-lobed
FRUIT	
Type	splits into 4 nut-like parts, egg-shaped, smooth
Size	2–3mm
Seeds	1 per segment, not released

Selfheal *Prunella vulgaris*

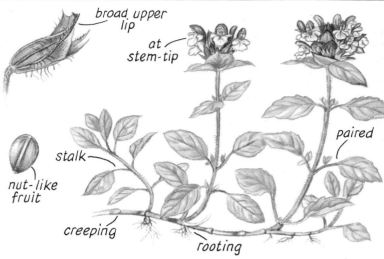

broad upper lip

at stem-tip

paired

stalk

nut-like fruit

creeping

rooting

A grassland plant, often thriving in close-grazed or mown turf, from which it raises its compact, cylindrical heads of deep violet-coloured flowers. It was much prized as a herb for treating wounds and also taken for sore throats. *Status:* native; very common, throughout area. *Similar species:* Cut-leaved Selfheal has divided upper leaves and cream-coloured flowers. It is native only in the south of the area but is naturalized in Britain. Bugle has more widely spaced clusters of flowers with larger bracts, often tinged with blackish violet and contrasting vividly with the bluish flowers.

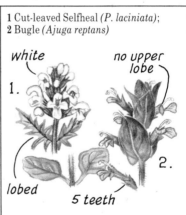

1 Cut-leaved Selfheal (*P. laciniata*); 2 Bugle (*Ajuga reptans*)

white

no upper lobe

lobed

5 teeth

SELFHEAL	
Type	perennial
Height	5–50cm
Habitat	grassland, woodland clearings; most soils
Flowering	June–September
STEMS AND LEAVES	
Stem	angled upwards or upright
Root	short underground stem
Hairs	sparse, short
Stipules	absent
Leaves	paired on stem, 20–50mm, oval or diamond-shaped, edge toothed or unbroken
Leaf-stalk	shorter than blade
FLOWERS	
Position	rings of 6, in compact, oblong head at stem-tip
Bracts	circular, stalkless, often purple-tinged
Type	♂
Size	10–15mm
Colour	violet, rarely pink or white
Stalk	much shorter than flower
Sepals	5, 8–9mm, bases joined, upper 3 teeth almost joined, lower 2 longer
Petals	5, 10–15mm, bases form tube, upper 2 lobes joined, hood-like, lower 3 bent back
Stamens	4, under upper petal-lobes
Stigmas	2 on long, forked style
Ovary	1, deeply 4-lobed
FRUIT	
Type	splits into 4 nut-like parts, oblong, smooth
Size	2–2.5mm
Seeds	1 per segment, not released

Origanum vulgare **Marjoram**

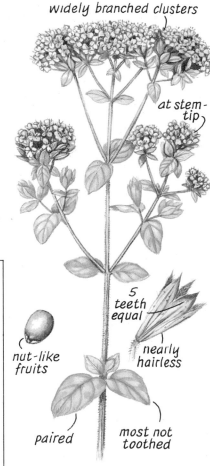

widely branched clusters

at stem-tip

5 teeth equal

nut-like fruits

nearly hairless

paired

most not toothed

Usually found among tall grasses, this rather bushy plant has branched heads of pink flowers and contrasting purple bracts. It is sometimes used as a pot-herb and is related to Oregano, which derives from Mediterranean plants. Native plants were widely used to treat coughs and headaches. *Status:* native; most of area, most common in south. *Similar species:* two other species have longer, less crowded heads of larger flowers and unequal, hairier sepal-teeth. Wild Basil has almost stalkless flower-clusters and a curved sepal-tube, whereas Common Calamint has stalked clusters of flowers.

1 Wild Basil (*Clinopodium vulgare*); **2** Common Calamint (*Calamintha sylvatica* subsp. *ascendens*)

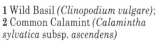

hairy

1.

2) thinner stalked

2.

	MARJORAM		FLOWERS
Type	perennial	Position	many, in widely branched clusters of short spikes
Height	30–90cm		
Habitat	grassy places, scrub; dry, often lime-rich soils	Bracts	oval, smaller than leaves, usually purple
Flowering	July–September	Type	♂ or sometimes ♀
		Size	4–8mm
	STEMS AND LEAVES	Colour	pinkish purple or white
Stem	upright, usually branched	Stalk	much shorter than flower
Root	woody, creeping underground stem	Sepals	5, 2–4mm, bases joined, teeth nearly equal
Hairs	usually scattered	Petals	5, 4–8mm, bases joined, lower 3 lobes longer than upper 2
Stipules	absent		
Leaves	paired on stem, 10–45mm, oval, strongly scented, blunt or sharp, edge unbroken or hardly toothed	Stamens	4, usually protruding
		Stigmas	2 on long, forked style
		Ovary	1, deeply 4-lobed
Leaf-stalk	shorter than blade	FRUIT	
		Type	splits into 4 nut-like parts
		Size	1.5–2mm
		Seeds	1 per segment, not released

Thymus praecox subsp. *arcticus* **Wild Thyme**

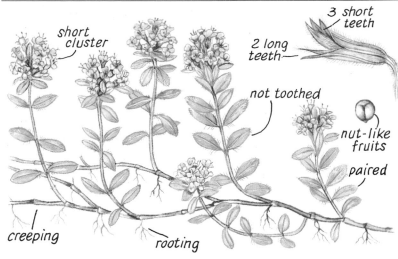

short cluster

3 short teeth

2 long teeth

not toothed

nut-like fruits

paired

creeping

rooting

A mat-forming plant of dry places, that has short flowering stems bearing compact heads of purple flowers. The leaves have a faint but distinctive aroma of Thyme as used in the kitchen. Species of Thyme formerly had medicinal as well as culinary uses. *Status:* native; common in south, absent from much of north. *Similar species:* Large Thyme usually has much taller stems, with cylindrical heads of larger flowers. The stems are more upright, sharply four-angled, and the whole plant is more strongly scented. Basil Thyme is a much hairier plant, with toothed leaves and larger flowers.

1 Large Thyme (*T. pulegioides*); **2** Basil Thyme (*Acinos arvensis*)

larger head

1.

2.

toothed

more upright

curved base

	WILD THYME		FLOWERS
Type	perennial, aromatic	Position	short heads at stem-tips
Height	1–8cm	Bracts	lowest leaf-like
Habitat	grasslands, heaths, dunes, rocks; dry soils	Type	♂ or ♀
		Size	4–7mm
Flowering	May–August	Colour	pinkish purple
		Stalk	much shorter than flower
	STEMS AND LEAVES	Sepals	5, 3–4mm, bases form tube, upper 3 teeth short, lower 2 long
Stem	long, creeping, forming mats, branches angled upwards to flower		
		Petals	5, 4–7mm, bases joined, upper 2 lobes nearly joined
Root	woody stock; stems root		
Hairs	on 2 sides of stem, long on leaf-edges	Stamens	4, protruding on ♂ flowers
		Stigmas	2 on long, forked style
Stipules	absent	Ovary	1, deeply 4-lobed
Leaves	paired on stem, 4–8mm, elliptical or oval, blunt, edge unbroken	FRUIT	
		Type	splits into 4 nut-like parts, egg-shaped, smooth
Leaf-stalk	very short		
		Size	0.7–1mm
		Seeds	1 per segment, not released

Figworts, Nightshades and Broomrapes

The Figwort family includes many garden plants grown for their attractive flowers, including Foxgloves, *Hebe*, Snapdragons, Speedwells and Toadflaxes. Though the family has relatively little economic importance, the Foxglove is the source of a glucoside used in treating heart disorders. In Figworts there are usually five sepals and petals, but only four in the Speedwells. Many Figwort species, such as the Hay-rattle, are partially parasitic and derive some of their nutrition from other plants.

The Broomrapes, sometimes included in the Figwort family, take the partially parasitic mode of nutrition common in that family to an extreme, with all species totally dependent on their host-plants. The leaves do not contain chlorophyll and are mere brown scales.

Vegetables like the aubergine (*Solanum melongena*), chillies or peppers of various sorts (*Capsicum* species) and tomatoes (*Lycopersicon esculentum*) belong to the Nightshade family, but the most important crop is the potato (*Solanum tuberosum*). The genus *Nicotiana* includes tobacco, but there are also plants grown for their sweetly-scented flowers. While there are many highly toxic species in the family, some, such as Deadly Nightshade, are valuable in medicine. Garden plants include Petunias and *Schizanthus*.

A frequent inhabitant of hedge-banks, Common Toadflax has Snapdragon-like flowers, each bearing a slender spur.

Atropa belladonna **Deadly Nightshade**

A powerful narcotic plant; even a few berries can prove fatal. It has bushy stems, rather dull purple flowers, and black, cherry-like fruits. Although toxic, Deadly Nightshade has long been cultivated for medicinal purposes. An alkaloid extract from the plant is used in hospitals to dilate the pupil of the eye. *Status:* native in south, naturalized in north and Ireland; scattered, absent from most of north. *Similar species:* Henbane is stickily hairy; the yellow flowers, veined purple are clustered in long heads and each capsule is hidden within its sepal-tube. It is also poisonous but used medicinally.

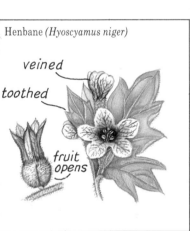

Henbane (*Hyoscyamus niger*)

veined
toothed
fruit opens

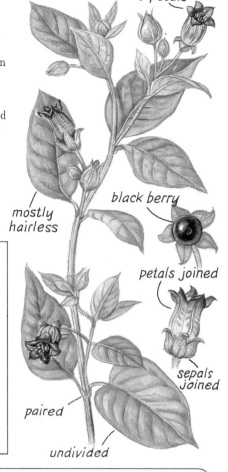

5 petals
mostly hairless
black berry
petals joined
sepals joined
paired
undivided

Solanum dulcamara **Bittersweet**

This woody plant threads its way through hedgerows or clambers over plants and rocks. Related to both Tomato and Potato, the flowers similarly have five petals curved back, but of purple with contrasting yellow stamens. The red berries are far less poisonous than those of Deadly Nightshade. *Status:* native; common, most of area. *Similar species:* related species are annual, with white flowers and almost globular fruits. Black Nightshade has black or green fruits; those of Hairy Nightshade are yellow, orange or red; Green Nightshade has green or rarely black fruits, partly hidden by the enlarged sepals.

1 Black Nightshade (*S. nigrum*); **2** Green Nightshade (*S. sarrachoides*); **3** Hairy Nightshade (*S. luteum*)

1. pale
2. large sepals
ripen black
hairy
3.
ripen yellow

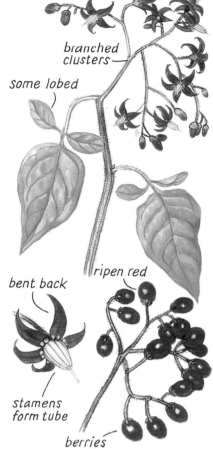

branched clusters
some lobed
ripen red
bent back
stamens form tube
berries

DEADLY NIGHTSHADE		**FLOWERS**	
Type	perennial	**Position**	solitary, from leaf-base
Height	50–150cm, rarely 200cm	**Bracts**	absent
Habitat	woods, scrub, hedges; lime-rich soils	**Type**	⚥
		Size	25–30mm
Flowering	June–August	**Colour**	violet or greenish
		Stalk	shorter than flower, drooping
STEMS AND LEAVES		**Sepals**	5, 10–15mm, joined, bell-shaped, spreading in fruit
Stem	upright, many-branched	**Petals**	5, 25–30mm, equal, joined into broad tube
Root	fibrous		
Hairs	absent or short, gland-tipped	**Stamens**	5, shorter than petals
Stipules	absent	**Stigma**	1, tip swollen, style long
Leaves	mostly on alternate sides of stem, 25–200mm, oval, pointed, edge unbroken, base wedge-shaped	**Ovary**	1, 2-celled
		FRUIT	
Leaf-stalk	shorter than blade	**Type**	1, globular berry, glossy, black
		Size	15–20mm
		Seeds	many, 1.5–2mm, egg-shaped

BITTERSWEET		**Bracts**	absent
Type	perennial	**Type**	⚥
Height	30–200cm	**Size**	10–15mm
Habitat	hedges, woods, rocks, shingle, waste ground	**Colour**	purple, rarely white
		Stalk	about equalling flower
Flowering	June–September	**Sepals**	5, 2–3mm, joined, teeth shorter than tube
STEMS AND LEAVES		**Petals**	5, 4–7mm, equal, bases joined, lobes spear-shaped, curved back
Stem	trailing or clambering, woody below		
Root	woody stock	**Stamens**	5, protruding, yellow
Hairs	absent or sometimes dense	**Stigma**	1, style long
Stipules	absent	**Ovary**	1, 2-celled
Leaves	most on alternate sides of stem, 30–90mm, oval, often 1–4 lobes at base, pointed, edge unbroken	**FRUIT**	
		Type	1, berry, egg-shaped, glossy, red
Leaf-stalk	shorter than blade	**Size**	10–15mm
FLOWERS		**Seeds**	many, 1.7–2mm, rounded
Position	10–25 in stalked, branched cluster opposite leaf-base		

Great Mullein *Verbascum thapsus*

A stiffly upright plant that has slender, crowded spikes of yellow flowers and is clothed with whitish wool. Innumerable branched hairs give the leaves a softness and warmth. Dried tops of plants were used to make tapers for burning; leaves provided shoe-liners; and flowers a cough medicine. *Status:* native; most of area except north. *Similar species:* White Mullein has wide-spaced, whitish, smaller flowers, and all stamens are hairy. Two species have stamens with purple hairs: Dark Mullein has dark green, rather hairy leaves; Moth Mullein has almost hairless leaves and long-stalked, widely-spaced flowers.

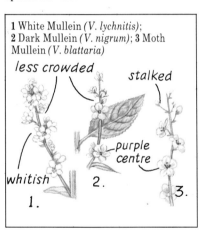

1 White Mullein (*V. lychnitis*); 2 Dark Mullein (*V. nigrum*); 3 Moth Mullein (*V. blattaria*)

less crowded / stalked / whitish / purple centre / 1. / 2. / 3.

flowers in spike / short-stalked / 5 petals / crowded / blade joins stem / whitish hairs on stamens / fruit splits open / thick hairs / lower large

GREAT MULLEIN			
Type	biennial	**Bracts**	narrowly triangular, pointed
Height	30–200cm	**Type**	☿
Habitat	grassy banks, waste ground; dry, often sandy soil	**Size**	12–30mm
		Colour	yellow
Flowering	June–August	**Stalk**	much shorter than flowers
		Sepals	5, 8–12mm, bases joined, lobes equal, oval, pointed
STEMS AND LEAVES		**Petals**	5, 6–14mm, almost equal, bases joined, lobes rounded, spreading widely
Stem	upright, usually unbranched		
Root	tap-root		
Hairs	dense, woolly, whitish	**Stamens**	5, upper 3 with long, white hairs, lower 2 hairless
Stipules	absent		
Leaves	basal rosette or spirally placed on stem, 40–500mm, oval to oblong, most pointed, edge unbroken or fine-toothed, upper blades run down stem as wings	**Stigma**	1, tip swollen
		Ovary	1, 2-celled
		FRUIT	
		Type	1, egg-shaped capsule, splits lengthwise
Leaf-stalk	lowest short, upper absent	**Size**	7–10mm
FLOWERS		**Seeds**	many, 0.8–1mm, oblong, pitted
Position	in dense spike at stem-tip		

Common Figwort *crophularia nodosa*

A tall, perhaps sombre plant, with broad, dark leaves and dull, brownish-purple flowers. Small flowers, rather unpleasantly scented, are pollinated mainly by wasps. Leaves of Figwort were used as poultices for skin complaints. *Status:* native; common, almost throughout area. *Similar species:* two Figworts have wing-like angles to the stems and broader papery edges to the sepals. Water Figwort has blunt leaves with rounded teeth and often two lobes at the base. Green Figwort has more pointed leaves with pointed teeth and lacks lobes. Yellow Figwort is softly hairy, and has pointed sepals and yellow flowers.

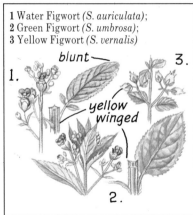

1 Water Figwort (*S. auriculata*); 2 Green Figwort (*S. umbrosa*); 3 Yellow Figwort (*S. vernalis*)

blunt / 3. / 1. / yellow winged / 2.

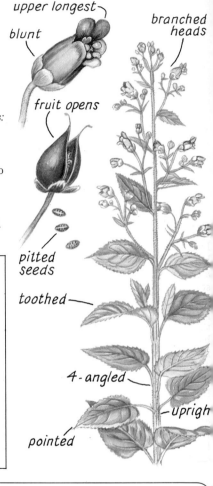

upper longest / branched heads / blunt / fruit opens / pitted seeds / toothed / 4-angled / upright / pointed

COMMON FIGWORT			
Type	perennial	**Bracts**	small or lowest leaf-like
Height	30–80cm	**Type**	☿
Habitat	woods, hedges; damp soils	**Size**	7–10mm
Flowering	June–September	**Colour**	green below, reddish brown on upper petal-lobes
		Stalk	2–3 times length of flower
STEMS AND LEAVES		**Sepals**	5, 2–3.5mm, joined, lobes oval, blunt, edge papery
Stem	upright, 4-angled		
Root	short, irregularly swollen, underground stem	**Petals**	5, 7–10mm, bases joined, nearly globular, upper 2 lobes rounded, lower shorter
Hairs	absent below, gland-tipped in flower-head		
		Stamens	4 normal, 1 broad, sterile
Stipules	absent	**Stigma**	1, tip swollen, style short
Leaves	paired on stem, 60–130mm, oval, pointed, with uneven teeth, base squarish	**Ovary**	1, 2-celled
		FRUIT	
Leaf-stalk	shorter than blade	**Type**	1, capsule, egg-shaped, pointed, splits lengthwise
FLOWERS		**Size**	5–10mm
Position	5–7 in branched heads, clustered towards stem-tip	**Seeds**	many, *c*1mm, oblong, pitted

Cymbalaria muralis Ivy-leaved Toadflax

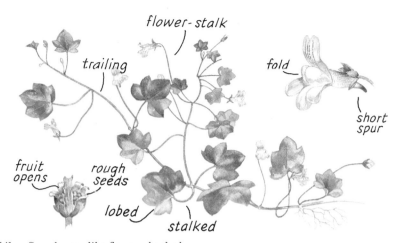

flower-stalk
trailing
fold
short spur
fruit opens
rough seeds
lobed
stalked

Lilac, Snapdragon-like flowers, backed by broad, lobed, glossy leaves make this a charming plant. In full sun, stems, stalks and the base of the flowers have a purple tinge which is lacking in shady places. Long stalks hold flowers clear of the foliage but, in fruit, curve round to bury the seeds in crevices. *Status:* introduced, from southern Europe; most common in south. *Similar species:* Fluellens, of cornfields or waste ground, have capsules with circular lids and pitted seeds. Sharp-leaved Fluellen has arrow-shaped leaves, with backward-pointing lobes; Round-leaved Fluellen lacks the lobes and has sepals that enlarge in fruit.

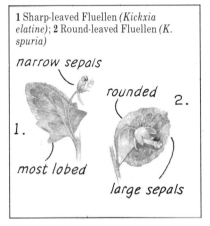

1 Sharp-leaved Fluellen (*Kickxia elatine*); **2** Round-leaved Fluellen (*K. spuria*)

narrow sepals
rounded
2.
1.
most lobed
large sepals

	IVY-LEAVED TOADFLAX		
Type	perennial	Bracts	absent
Height	5–15cm	Type	♀
Habitat	walls, rocks, shingle, railway ballast; dry places	Size	9–15mm
		Colour	lilac, yellow on fold of lower petals, violet veins
Flowering	May–September	Stalk	much longer than flower, bends down in fruit
STEMS AND LEAVES		Sepals	5, 2–2.5mm, spear-shaped, pointed, bases joined
Stem	trailing, hanging, to 80cm long, often tinged purple	Petals	5, 9–15mm, bases form tube, spur at base, lower 3 lobes with fold closing tube
Root	fibrous, stems root		
Hairs	absent	Stamens	4, inside petal-tube
Stipules	absent	Stigma	1, tip swollen
Leaves	most on alternate sides of stem, lowest paired, 7–25mm, kidney-shaped, 5–9 rounded or triangular lobes	Ovary	1, 2-celled
		FRUIT	
Leaf-stalk	longer than blade	Type	capsule, sides split open
		Size	2.5–4mm
FLOWERS		Seeds	many, 0.8–1mm, globular, irregularly ridged, black
Position	single from base of leaf		

Antirrhinum majus Snapdragon

A popular garden plant that has often escaped, known to generations of children for the mouth-like flower which snaps open when the sides are pressed. Snapdragon originated in the western Mediterranean region, but the exact location has been obscured by many centuries of cultivation outside its original range. *Status:* introduced; mainly south of area, often near coasts. *Similar species:* Lesser Snapdragon is a native annual that has small flowers, long sepals and seeds with one face smooth, the other encircled by a ridge. Asarina is sometimes naturalized and has large, yellow flowers, trailing stems and kidney-shaped, lobed leaves.

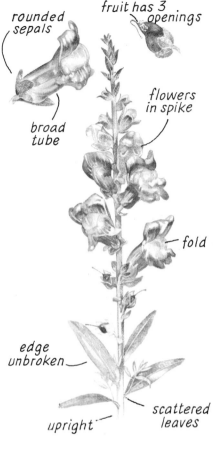

rounded sepals
fruit has 3 openings
flowers in spike
broad tube
fold
edge unbroken
upright
scattered leaves

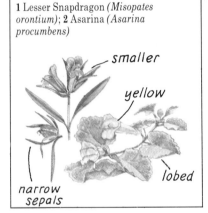

1 Lesser Snapdragon (*Misopates orontium*); **2** Asarina (*Asarina procumbens*)

smaller
yellow
lobed
narrow sepals

	SNAPDRAGON		
Type	perennial	Type	♀
Height	30–80cm	Size	30–40mm
Habitat	walls, cliffs; dry soils	Colour	reddish purple with yellow mark, some pink or white
Flowering	July–September	Stalk	much shorter than flower
STEMS AND LEAVES		Sepals	5, 6–8mm, slightly unequal, bases joined, lobed oval
Stem	upright, base woody	Petals	5, bases form broad tube, lower 3 lips with fold closing mouth of tube
Root	fibrous		
Hairs	absent below, sticky, gland-tipped in flower-head		
Stipules	absent	Stamens	4, inside petal-tube
Leaves	spirally placed on stem or lowest paired, 30–50mm, spear-shaped or oblong, edge unbroken, base tapered	Stigma	1, tip swollen
		Ovary	1, 2-celled
		FRUIT	
Leaf-stalk	absent	Type	1, egg-shaped capsule, sides unequal, 3 pores at tip
FLOWERS		Size	10–14mm
Position	many, in spike at stem-tip	Seeds	many, 1–1.2mm, egg-shaped, with net-like ridges
Bracts	oval, smaller than leaves		

Small Toadflax *Chaenorhinum minus*

A delicate annual, Small Toadflax has tiny flowers like those of Snapdragon but with a small spur at the base. Mainly a weed of arable fields, it thrives on railway ballast although recent use of weedkillers has led to a decline. *Status:* native or introduced; mainly south of region. *Similar species:* other small-flowered Toadflaxes from the south of the area have spikes of flowers, capsules with equal halves and seeds with an encircling wing. Sand Toadflax, on sand-dunes, is stickily hairy, with yellow flowers. Field Toadflax, an almost hairless weed of cultivation, has blue flowers with a slender, curved spur.

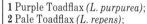
fold
short spur
fruit has 2 openings
ridged seeds
long stalk
from leaf-base

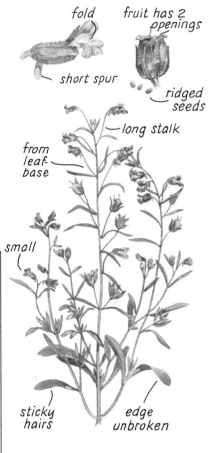
small
sticky hairs
edge unbroken

1 Sand Toadflax *(Linaria arenaria)*;
2 Field Toadflax *(L. arvensis)*

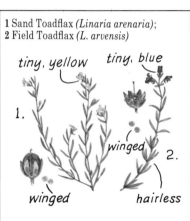
tiny, yellow
tiny, blue
1.
winged
2.
winged
hairless

	SMALL TOADFLAX		Bracts	absent
Type	annual		Type	♂♀
Height	8–25cm		Size	6–9mm
Habitat	cultivated and waste ground, railway ballast		Colour	whitish, lobes and veins purple
			Stalk	mostly longer than flower
Flowering	May–October		Sepals	5, 2–5mm, unequal, narrow, blunt, bases joined
	STEMS AND LEAVES		Petals	5, 6–9mm, bases form tube, with spur, fold of lower 3 lobes closes tube-mouth
Stem	upright, branched			
Root	fibrous			
Hairs	short, gland-tipped		Stamens	4, inside petal-tube
Stipules	absent		Stigma	1, tip swollen
Leaves	lower paired, upper on alternate sides of stem, 5–25mm, narrow, spear-shaped to oblong, blunt, edge unbroken, tapered		Ovary	1, 2-celled
				FRUIT
			Type	1, egg-shaped capsule, sides unequal, 2 pores at tip
Leaf-stalk	short		Size	3–6mm
	FLOWERS		Seeds	many, 0.5–0.8mm, egg-shaped, ridged lengthwise
Position	each at base of upper leaf			

Common Toadflax *Linaria vulgaris*

Flowering in late Summer, commonly on grassy banks, many stems arise from creeping roots. Pollination is almost solely by bees, which have enough weight and strength to open the flower, and a long tongue to reach the nectar at the base. *Status:* native; common, most of area. *Similar species:* two species have purplish flowers and wingless seeds. Purple Toadflax has long spikes of flowers each with a slender, curved spur. Pale Toadflax has fewer flowers with a short, straight spur; it sometimes forms hybrids with Common Toadflax. Prostrate Toadflax is low-growing, its pale yellow flowers with longer petal-lobes than those of Common Toadflax.

fold
fruit open
thin spur
in spikes
narrow
edge unbroken
scattered around stem
stalkless
upright

1 Purple Toadflax *(L. purpurea)*;
2 Pale Toadflax *(L. repens)*;
3 Prostrate Toadflax *(L. supina)*

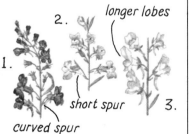
2.
longer lobes
1.
curved spur
short spur
3.

	COMMON TOADFLAX			FLOWERS
Type	perennial		Position	5–30, in crowded spike
Height	30–80cm		Bracts	small, oval, pointed
Habitat	grassy and waste places, railway embankments		Type	♂♀
			Size	20–33mm
Flowering	July–October		Colour	yellow, darker fold at base of lower petal-lobes
	STEMS AND LEAVES		Stalk	shorter than flower
Stem	many, upright, branched		Sepals	5, 3–6mm, oval, pointed
Root	fibrous, long, creeping roots produce new stems		Petals	5, 20–33mm, forming tube, spur at base, fold of lower 3 lobes closes tube-mouth
Hairs	absent or sticky hairs above			
Stipules	absent		Stamens	4, paired
Leaves	spirally around stem, lowest in ring or paired, 20–60mm, narrow, straight-sided or spear-shaped, pointed, edge unbroken		Stigma	1, style slender
			Ovary	1, 2-celled
				FRUIT
Leaf-stalk	absent		Type	1, oblong capsule, 2 pores at tip
			Size	5–11mm
			Seeds	many, 2–3mm, flattened, encircling wing, black

In partial shade, Foxglove bears handsome spires of tubular flowers.

Digitalis purpurea Foxglove

A tall, majestic plant, with long spikes of purple, tubular flowers, it is widely grown for ornament, in varying shades of purple, pink or white, and with more flowers all around the stem. Species of Foxglove yield the drug digitalis, which speeds and strengthens the heart-beat. *Status:* native, sometimes introduced; common, most of area. *Similar species:* two Foxgloves with yellowish flowers and almost hairless leaves, are native in the south-east of the area. Large Yellow-foxglove has a broad petal-tube; Small Yellow-foxglove has a narrow tube with almost equal petal-lobes.

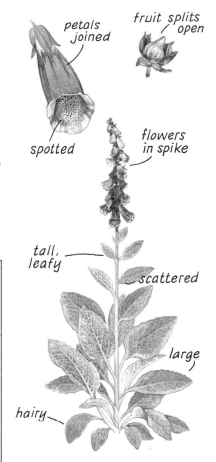

1 Large Yellow-foxglove (*D. grandiflora*); 2 Small Yellow-foxglove (*D. lutea*)

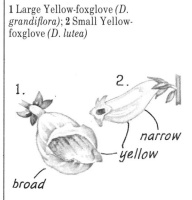

FOXGLOVE		**Bracts**	spear-shaped, not toothed
Type	biennial, rarely perennial	**Type**	☿
Height	50–150cm	**Size**	40–50mm
Habitat	wood clearings, heaths, among rocks; lime-free soils	**Colour**	pinkish purple, usually purple spots inside tube
Flowering	June–September	**Stalk**	much shorter than flower
		Sepals	5, 10–13mm, oval, upper spear-shaped, bases joined
STEMS AND LEAVES		**Petals**	5, 40–50mm, forming broad tube; lower lobe largest
Stem	upright, stout, unbranched	**Stamens**	4, inside tube, paired
Root	rather woody tap-root	**Stigma**	1, 2 flat lobes; style long
Hairs	long, greyish	**Ovary**	1, 2-celled
Stipules	absent		
Leaves	basal rosette or spirally placed on stem, 150–300mm, oval to spear-shaped, blunt or pointed, with rounded teeth	**FRUIT**	
		Type	1, egg-shaped capsule, splits lengthwise
Leaf-stalk	shorter than blade	**Size**	14–18mm
FLOWERS		**Seeds**	many, 0.8–1mm, oblong, net-like pattern
Position	20–80, in one-sided spike		

Monkeyflower *Mimulus guttatus*

Large, bright yellow flowers of Monkeyflower brighten many a stream and look so well established that they appear native. But this is an introduced plant that has often escaped from cultivation and spread widely along water-courses. Other species and hybrids are often cultivated in gardens. *Status:* introduced from North America; common, much of area. *Similar species:* Blood-drop-emlets has large, red blotches on the flowers and is almost hairless. The hybrid with Monkeyflower is often more common than either species. Musk has smaller, unspotted flowers and stickily hairy foliage.

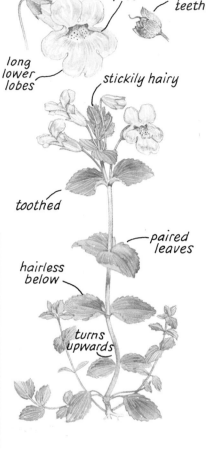

small red spots
unequal teeth
long lower lobes
stickily hairy
toothed
paired leaves
hairless below
turns upwards

1 Blood-drop-emlets (*M. luteus*);
2 Musk (*M. moschatus*)

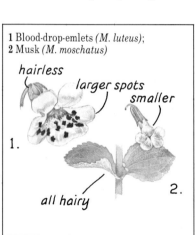

hairless
larger spots
smaller
1.
all hairy
2.

Germander Speedwell *Veronica chamaedrys*

Brilliant blue, white-eyed flowers of Speedwells gleam on grassy banks and lawns in Spring and early Summer. The four petals are joined in a ring at the base and soon fall together. Speedwells are related to the shrubby species of *Hebe*, much grown in gardens and often escaping. *Status:* native; very common, most of area. *Similar species:* two species have a capsule longer than the sepals. Wood Speedwell has stems hairy all round and longer leaf-stalks. Heath Speedwell has crowded heads of short-stalked flowers. Spiked Speedwell has upright stems ending in a crowded spike of deep blue flowers.

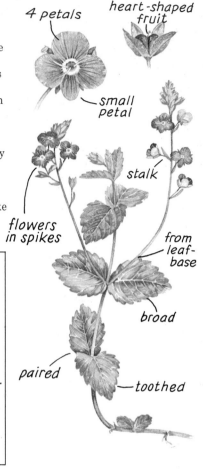

4 petals
heart-shaped fruit
small petal
stalk
flowers in spikes
from leaf-base
broad
paired
toothed

1 Wood Speedwell (*V. montana*);
2 Heath Speedwell (*V. officinalis*);
3 Spiked Speedwell (*V. spicata*)

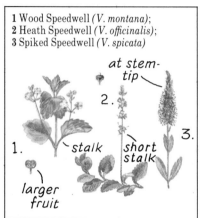

at stem-tip
2.
1.
stalk
short stalk
3.
larger fruit

MONKEYFLOWER

Type	perennial
Height	5–50cm
Habitat	streams, slow rivers; wet ground or shallow water
Flowering	July–September

STEMS AND LEAVES

Stem	low-growing, angled upwards, hollow
Root	fibrous; stems root
Hairs	absent below, stickily hairy in flower-head
Stipules	absent
Leaves	paired on stem, 10–70mm, oval to circular, blunt to pointed, irregularly toothed
Leaf-stalk	lower short, upper absent

FLOWERS

Position	few to many, in heads towards stem-tips
Bracts	leaf-like or upper smaller
Type	♀♂
Size	25–45mm
Colour	yellow, red-spotted in tube
Stalk	nearly equalling flower
Sepals	5, 15–20mm, bases form 5-angled tube, inflated in fruit, teeth unequal
Petals	5, 25–45mm, bases form tube, lower 3 lobes longer, folds nearly close tube-mouth
Stamens	4, paired, inside tube
Stigma	1, 2 flat lobes; style long
Ovary	1, 2-celled

FRUIT

Type	1, oblong capsule, splits lengthwise
Size	8–12mm
Seeds	many, 0.7–0.9mm, oblong

GERMANDER SPEEDWELL

Type	perennial
Height	20–40cm
Habitat	grassland, woods, hedges
Flowering	March–July

STEMS AND LEAVES

Stem	low-growing, angled upwards
Root	fibrous; stems root
Hairs	long, white, in 2 lines on stem
Stipules	absent
Leaves	paired on stem, 10–25mm, oval, blunt, toothed, base almost heart-shaped
Leaf-stalk	absent or short

FLOWERS

Position	10–20, in spike from upper leaf-base
Bracts	about equal to flower-stalk
Type	♂
Size	7–11mm
Colour	bright blue, white-eyed
Stalk	nearly equalling flower
Sepals	4, 4–6mm, spear-shaped, hairy
Petals	4, 4–6mm, bases joined, upper 3 lobes broad, lowest narrow
Stamens	2, protruding
Stigma	1, tip swollen; style long
Ovary	1, 2-celled

FRUIT

Type	1, broadly heart-shaped capsule, flattened
Size	3–5mm
Seeds	few, 1.5–2mm, oblong, flattened

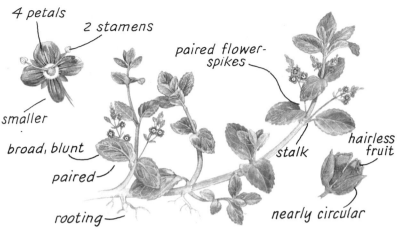

4 petals

2 stamens

paired flower-spikes

smaller

broad, blunt

paired

stalk

hairless fruit

rooting

nearly circular

Spikes of deep blue flowers, set against glossy dark foliage, make this an attractive plant often cultivated in ornamental ponds. It is one of the Speedwells, of which species in wet places are more robust than their counterparts of dry grassland, and are mostly hairless. *Status:* native; common, throughout area. *Similar species:* three species have elongated, stalkless leaves. Blue Water-speedwell has long heads of flowers from both leaves of a pair. Pink Water-speedwell is similar but with smaller, pink flowers on widely spreading stalks. Marsh Speedwell has sparsely-flowered heads from only one leaf of a pair.

1 Blue Water-speedwell (*V. anagallis-aquatica*); 2 Pink Water-speedwell (*V. catenata*); 3 Marsh Speedwell (*V. scutellata*)

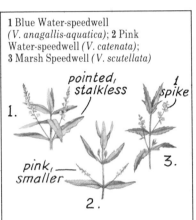

pointed, stalkless

1 spike

1.

pink, smaller

3.

2.

BROOKLIME		Bracts	small, narrow, pointed
Type	perennial	Type	☿
Height	20–60cm	Size	5–8mm
Habitat	streams, ponds, wet meadows; wet places	Colour	usually deep blue
		Stalk	nearly equal to flower
Flowering	May–September	Sepals	4, 2–4mm, unequal, oval, pointed
STEMS AND LEAVES		Petals	4, 2.5–4mm, bases joined, lobes flat, upper largest
Stem	creeping, angled upwards, fleshy	Stamens	2, protruding
Root	fibrous; stems root	Stigma	1, tip swollen; style long
Hairs	absent	Ovary	1, 2-celled
Stipules	absent		
Leaves	paired on stem, 30–60mm, oval or oblong, thick, tip blunt, edge shallow-toothed, base rounded	**FRUIT**	
		Type	1, nearly circular capsule, flattened, notched
Leaf-stalk	shorter than blade	Size	2–4mm
FLOWERS		Seeds	few, 0.8–1mm, oblong, flattened
Position	10–30, in spike at base of both leaves of pair		

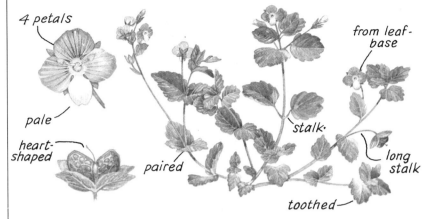

4 petals

from leaf-base

pale

heart-shaped

stalk

paired

long stalk

toothed

Sky-blue flowers with the lowest petal white make this an attractive weed for the short time that the flowers endure. Seeds germinate and flowers open in almost any month of the year. Introduced from Asia nearly two centuries ago, in many parts of Europe this is now the most common of all Speedwells. *Status:* introduced; common weed, throughout area. *Similar species:* Wall Speedwell has short-stalked flowers clustered in a rather lax spike at the stem-tip. Green Field-speedwell has small, pale flowers with shorter stalks. Ivy-leaved Speedwell has leaves with few, large lobes and broad-based sepals.

1 Wall Speedwell (*V. arvensis*); 2 Green Field-speedwell (*V. agrestis*); 3 Ivy-leaved Speedwell (*V. hederifolia*)

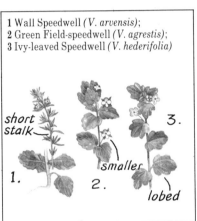

short stalk

3.

1.

smaller

2.

lobed

COMMON FIELD-SPEEDWELL		Type	♂
Type	annual	Size	8–12mm
Height	10–40cm	Colour	bright blue, lower petal paler or white
Habitat	arable fields, gardens		
Flowering	January–December	Stalk	longer than leaf at base, bent down in fruit
STEMS AND LEAVES		Sepals	4, 5–7mm, unequal, oval, enlarging in fruit
Stem	low-growing, branches angled upwards	Petals	4, 4–6mm, bases joined, upper broadest
Root	fibrous	Stamens	2, protruding
Hairs	almost throughout plant	Stigma	1, tip swollen; style long
Stipules	absent	Ovary	1, 2-celled
Leaves	on alternate sides of stem or lower paired, 10–30mm, oval, blunt, coarsely toothed, base squarish	**FRUIT**	
		Type	2-lobed, flattened capsule, lobes spread apart
Leaf-stalk	shorter than blade	Size	5–10mm
FLOWERS		Seeds	few, 1.5–1.8mm, oblong, one face hollow
Position	solitary, from leaf-base		
Bracts	absent		

Common Eyebright *Euphrasia nemorosa*

An attractive grassland plant, the white flowers are blotched with deep yellow and veined with purple. Eyebrights are partly parasitic, their roots latching on to those of other plants and drawing sustenance. They also make food by using green pigment in their leaves and sunlight. *Status:* native; common, most of area. *Similar species:* the many Eyebrights are mostly identified only with difficulty. One of the most distinctive species is Irish Eyebright, which has narrow leaves with few, slender teeth and hairless capsules. Red Bartsia has reddish-purple flowers with longer, hood-like upper petal-lobes.

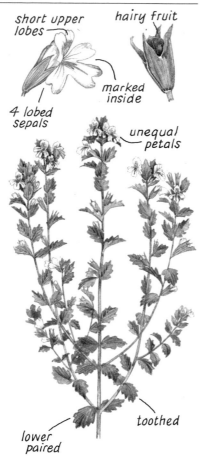

short upper lobes — hairy fruit — marked inside — 4 lobed sepals — unequal petals — toothed — lower paired

1 Irish Eyebright (*E. salisburgensis*);
2 Red Bartsia (*Odontites verna*)

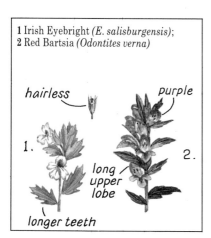

hairless — purple — long upper lobe — longer teeth — 1. — 2.

	COMMON EYEBRIGHT		Type	♂
Type	annual, partly parasitic		**Size**	5–8mm
Height	10–35cm		**Colour**	white or purple-tinged, deep yellow blotch, veins purple
Habitat	grassland, woods, heaths		**Stalk**	much shorter than flower
Flowering	July–September		**Sepals**	4, 3–6mm, bases form tube, teeth pointed
	STEMS AND LEAVES		**Petals**	5, bases form tube, lobes notched, 3 lower longer
Stem	upright, branched		**Stamens**	4, inside tube
Root	fibrous, attached to roots of other plants		**Stigma**	1, tip swollen; style long
			Ovary	1, 2-celled
Hairs	short, usually sparse			
Stipules	absent			**FRUIT**
Leaves	paired or upper spirally placed on stem, 6–12mm, oblong or oval, blunt or upper pointed, edge with few pointed teeth		**Type**	1, oblong capsule, hairy at tip, splits lengthwise
			Size	4–6mm
Leaf-stalk	absent		**Seeds**	numerous, 1.5–2mm, grooved, ends narrowed
	FLOWERS			
Position	in loose spike towards stem-tip			
Bracts	leaf-like but smaller			

Marsh Lousewort *Pedicularis palustris*

A striking plant, especially in water-meadows, where its purplish, finely-divided foliage and pink flowers stand out. The species is partly parasitic, attaching itself to roots of grasses and deriving nourishment from them. Grazing animals were thought to catch liver-fluke from Louseworts but it is now known that both fluke and plant just flourish in the same places. *Status:* native; fairly common, most of area. *Similar species:* the perennial Lousewort, of moors and heaths, is generally smaller with hairless sepals. Leafy Lousewort, from mountains in the south-east of the area, has leafy spikes of pale yellow flowers.

lobed sepals — hood-like — fruit splits open — 4 teeth — broad lower petals — hairy sepals — flowers towards stem-tip — hairless

1 Lousewort (*P. sylvatica*); **2** Leafy Lousewort (*P. foliosa*)

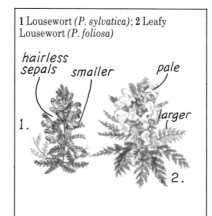

hairless sepals — smaller — pale — larger — 1. — deeply lobed — 2.

	MARSH LOUSEWORT		Type	♀
Type	biennial or annual, partly parasitic		**Size**	20–25mm
			Colour	purplish pink
Height	8–60cm		**Stalk**	much shorter than flower
Habitat	meadows, heaths; wet places		**Sepals**	5, joined, hairy, lobes unequal, toothed, tube swollen in fruit
Flowering	May–September		**Petals**	5, 18–25mm, upper 2 lobes joined, hood-like, 2 teeth each side
	STEMS AND LEAVES			
Stem	single, branched below		**Stamens**	4, under upper petal-lobes
Root	fibrous, attached to roots of other plants		**Stigma**	1, tip swollen; style long
			Ovary	1, 2-celled
Hairs	almost absent			
Stipules	absent			**FRUIT**
Leaves	on alternate sides of stem, 20–40mm, deeply divided into paired, toothed lobes, often tinged purple		**Type**	1; capsule, curved, flattened, pointed
			Size	10–12mm
Leaf-stalk	shorter than blade		**Seeds**	few, 2–3mm, oblong, with net-like pattern
	FLOWERS			
Position	many in spike at stem-tip			
Bracts	leaf-like but smaller			

Rhinanthus minor **Yellow-rattle**

A plant of sunny, grassy places, with yellow, hooded flowers, but best known in fruit when the seeds rattle inside the capsule and papery sepal-tube. This is another partial parasite, some of its nourishment coming from grasses and other herbs through joined roots. *Status:* native; common, most of area. *Similar species:* Greater Yellow-rattle is a larger plant of arable fields, and has yellowish, long-toothed bracts and a curved petal-tube with longer upper lobes. Yellow Bartsia is stickily hairy and the sepal-tube is not swollen. Common Cow-wheat, a woodland plant, also has a slender sepal-tube but the leaves are not toothed.

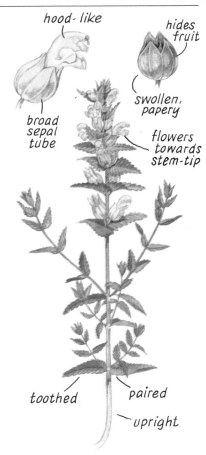

1 Greater Yellow-rattle (*R. angustifolius*); **2** Yellow Bartsia (*Parentucellia viscosa*); **3** Common Cow-wheat (*Melampyrum pratense*)

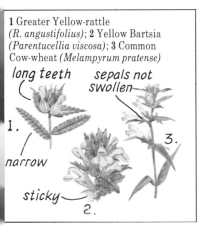

Orobanche rapum-genistae **Greater Broomrape**

This curious plant is a parasite, deriving all sustenance from its host, usually a shrub of Broom or Gorse. It has no need of green pigment, so stems and scale-like leaves are a lurid yellow or purple, and give an impression of unhealthiness. *Status:* native; fairly common, from south to southern Scotland. *Similar species:* Common Broomrape, mainly on Clovers, is usually smaller, with fewer flowers and purple stigmas. Toothwort, mainly on Hazel or Elm, has one-sided heads of pinkish flowers, broad bracts and equal sepal-teeth. Yellow Bird's-nest has yellow, nodding flowers and grows on decaying leaves in woodland.

1 Common Broomrape (*O. minor*); **2** Toothwort (*Lathraea squamaria*); **3** Yellow Bird's-nest (*Monotropa hypopitys*)

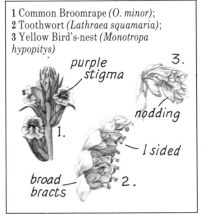

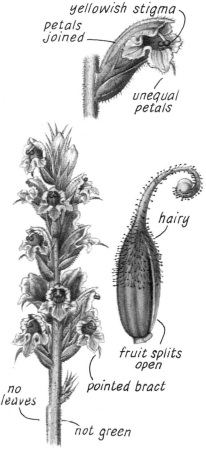

YELLOW-RATTLE			
Type	annual, partly parasitic	**Type**	⚥
Height	12–50cm	**Size**	12–15mm
Habitat	grassland, marshes, mountains	**Colour**	yellow or purple-tinged
Flowering	May–August	**Stalk**	much shorter than flower
		Sepals	4, 12–18mm, bases joined, flattened, enlarged in fruit, almost hairless
STEMS AND LEAVES			
Stem	upright, usually black-spotted, sometimes branched	**Petals**	5, 12–15mm, bases form tube, upper 2 lobes joined, hood-like
Root	fibrous, attached to those of other plants	**Stamens**	4, under upper petal-lobes
Hairs	short, rough	**Stigma**	1, tip swollen; style long
Stipules	absent	**Ovary**	1, 2-celled
Leaves	paired on stem, 10–50mm, oblong, toothed		
Leaf-stalk	absent	**FRUIT**	
		Type	1, rounded, flattened capsule, splits lengthwise
FLOWERS		**Size**	10–12mm
Position	in spike at stem-tip	**Seeds**	few, 4–5mm, flattened, with encircling wing
Bracts	triangular, leaf-like		

GREATER BROOMRAPE			
Type	perennial, parasite	**FLOWERS**	
Height	20–80cm	**Position**	many in long, crowded spike at stem-tip
Habitat	heaths, woodland clearings; mainly on Gorse or Broom	**Bracts**	long, slender, pointed
Flowering	May–July	**Type**	⚥
		Size	20–25mm
STEMS AND LEAVES		**Colour**	pale yellow, tinged purple
Stem	single, unbranched, stout, yellowish or purple-tinged	**Stalk**	almost absent
Root	swollen, scaly; fibrous roots attach to other plants	**Sepals**	4, 8–15mm, bases joined, teeth unequal, slender
Hairs	sticky, gland-tipped	**Petals**	5, 20–25mm, bases form curved tube, lower 3 lobes bent downwards, upper short
Stipules	absent	**Stamens**	4, inside petal-tube
Leaves	spirally around stem, 15–25mm, scale-like, spear-shaped, yellowish, pointed, edge unbroken	**Stigma**	1, 2-lobed, pale yellow
		Ovary	1, 1-celled
Leaf-stalk	absent		
		FRUIT	
		Type	capsule, splits lengthwise
		Size	10–14mm
		Seeds	many, 0.3–0.4mm, dust-like

Butterworts and Plantains

Butterworts have hermaphrodite flowers similar to those of the Figworts and Broomrapes. Butterworts commonly have undivided leaves in a rosette at the base of the plants, but in the aquatic species of Bladderwort they are scattered along the stems and finely divided, or modified to form minute, animal-catching traps. Species of both families are all insectivorous, the Butterworts catching insects with sticky leaves that roll up to engulf the prey. The flowers have a spur at the base of the petal-tube and bear a resemblance to those of Toadflaxes, in the Figwort family.

Though at first sight very different, the Plantains are sometimes placed close to the Broomrapes and Figworts. Most of the obvious differences in the flowers arise from the fact that most Plantains are wind-pollinated. Generally, the flowers are densely clustered into heads, which may be very long. Each flower has four papery petals, joined beneath to form a short tube, and four separate stamens project from the flower, where the wind can dislodge the pollen. The fruit takes the form of a lidded capsule that opens to release the few seeds. In the aquatic Shoreweed there are separate male and female flowers and the fruit does not open.

Restricted to areas of high rainfall, Common Butterwort makes up for soils poor in nutrients by catching insects with its sticky leaves. The edges of the leaves roll up to engulf the prey.

Pinguicula vulgaris Common Butterwort

Beautiful violet flowers arising from a cluster of glistening, yellowish leaves characterize the Common Butterwort. This plant of peat-bogs is carnivorous. Sticky leaves capture unwary insects that alight, then slowly roll up while digestive enzymes are secreted to dissolve the tissues. In this way the plant makes up for mineral deficiencies in the soil. *Status:* native; fairly common, most of area. *Similar species:* two species occur in the south-west of the area. Large-flowered Butterwort has flowers almost twice as large with overlapping petal-lobes. Pale Butterwort is much smaller, with grey-green leaves and lilac flowers.

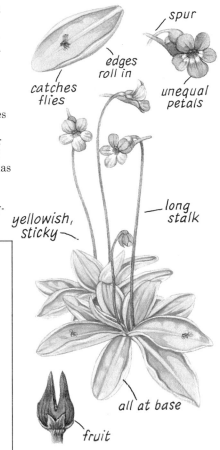

spur
edges roll in
catches flies
unequal petals
long stalk
yellowish, sticky
all at base
fruit

1 Large-flowered Butterwort (*P. grandiflora*); **2** Pale Butterwort (*P. lusitanica*)

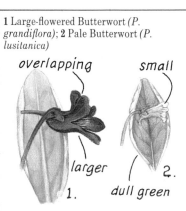

overlapping
small
larger
dull green
1.
2.

COMMON BUTTERWORT			
Type	perennial	**Type**	☿
Height	5–20cm	**Size**	15–22mm
Habitat	bogs, wet rocks or heath; wet places	**Colour**	violet, paler in petal-tube
		Stalk	50–200mm, much longer than flower
Flowering	May–July	**Sepals**	5, 3–4mm, unequal, oval, bases joined
STEMS AND LEAVES		**Petals**	5, 15–22mm, bases form tube, slender spur at base, lower 3 lobes longer
Stem	almost absent, 1–6 long flower-stalks		
Root	fibrous	**Stamens**	2, inside petal-tube
Hairs	leaves with sticky hairs	**Stigma**	1 broad lobe, 1 narrow; style very short
Stipules	absent		
Leaves	rosette at base, 20–80mm, oblong, yellowish-green, blunt, edge unbroken, folds inwards	**Ovary**	1, 1-celled
		FRUIT	
Leaf-stalk	absent	**Type**	1, egg-shaped capsule, splits lengthwise into 2
FLOWERS		**Size**	5–9mm
Position	solitary, from base	**Seeds**	numerous, 0.8–1mm, oblong
Bracts	absent		

Utricularia vulgaris Greater Bladderwort

Spikes of rich yellow flowers mark where this aquatic plant floats near the surface of the water. Finely-cut leaves bear small bladders, each a trap sprung when a tiny water-animal touches a bristle. A trap-door springs open and shut, sucking in the prey which is gradually digested. *Status:* native; scattered, most of area. *Similar species:* flowering is sporadic, making identification difficult. Bladderwort has flowers with a long upper lip and flatter lower lip. Other species have two sorts of leaf. Lesser Bladderwort lacks leaf-bristles and has a broad spur. Intermediate Bladderwort has bristle-edged leaves and a slender spur.

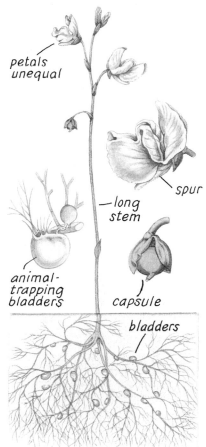

petals unequal
spur
long stem
animal-trapping bladders
capsule
bladders

1 Bladderwort (*U. australis*); **2** Lesser Bladderwort (*U. minor*); **3** Intermediate Bladderwort (*U. intermedia*)

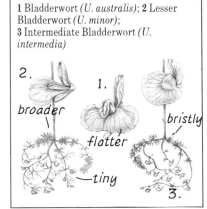

2.
broader
1.
flatter
bristly
tiny
3.

GREATER BLADDERWORT			
Type	perennial	**FLOWERS**	
Height	15–100cm	**Position**	2–8 in spike-like head above water, stalk 100–200mm
Habitat	ponds, lakes, ditches; still, often deep water	**Bracts**	shorter than flower-stalks
		Type	☿
Flowering	July–August	**Size**	12–18mm
		Colour	deep yellow
STEMS AND LEAVES		**Stalk**	shorter than flower
Stem	long, leafy, submerged, floats near surface	**Sepals**	2, oval, slightly toothed
		Petals	bases joined, with conical spur, lobes form 2 lips, fold of lower lip about equalling upper lip
Root	absent		
Hairs	absent		
Stipules	absent	**Stamens**	2, inside petal-tube
Leaves	spirally placed on stem, 20–25mm, finely cut, edges slightly toothed, bristly, some with tiny bladders	**Stigma**	flattened lobe and much smaller lobe; style short
		Ovary	1, 1-celled
Leaf-stalk	shorter than blade	**FRUIT**	
		Type	1, capsule, globular
		Size	3–5mm
		Seeds	many, 0.5–0.7mm, angular

Shoreweed   *Littorella uniflora*

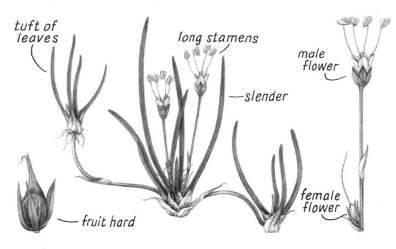

tuft of leaves

long stamens

male flower

—slender

fruit hard

female flower

A number of superficially similar plants form a turf-like sward around the edges of northern lakes, sometimes submerged to a depth of several metres as the water-level fluctuates. Wind-pollinated flowers of Shoreweed, a relative of the Plantains, only appear on exposed plants. *Status:* native; most of area, more common in north. *Similar species:* Mudwort has five petals and short stamens. Awlwort, a relative of the Cabbage, has spike-like heads of four-petalled flowers and pod-like fruits. The most attractive of these plants is Water Lobelia, the long-stalked heads of white or lilac flowers with unequal petals.

1 Mudwort (*Limosella aquatica*);
2 Awlwort (*Subularia aquatica*);
3 Water Lobelia (*Lobelia dortmanna*)

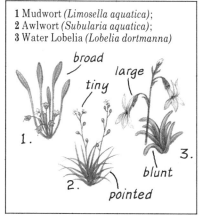

broad

tiny

large

1.

2.

3.

blunt

pointed

	SHOREWEED		Bracts	oval, papery
Type	perennial		**Type 1**	♂ with stamens
Height	15–100mm, rarely 250mm		**Type 2**	♀ stalkless, with ovary
Habitat	lakes, ponds; in or by lime-free water		**Size**	5–6mm
			Colour	whitish, translucent
Flowering	June–August		**Stalk**	longer than flower
			Sepals	3–4, edges papery, 3–5mm, oval or slender
	STEMS AND LEAVES		**Petals**	3–4, 4–6mm, bases joined
Stem	creeping, producing upright tufts of leaves		**Stamens**	4, protruding, 10–20mm
Root	rather thick		**Stigma**	1; style long
Hairs	absent		**Ovary**	1, 1-celled
Stipules	absent			
Leaves	in rosette, 15–100mm, rarely 250mm, slender, almost cylindrical, edge unbroken, base broad, sheaths stem		**FRUIT**	
			Type	1, dry, hard, oblong, enclosed by petal-tube
Leaf-stalk	absent		**Size**	1.5–2mm
			Seeds	1, not released
	FLOWERS			
Position	single ♂, sometimes several ♀ near base of stalked head			

Greater Plantain   *Plantago major*

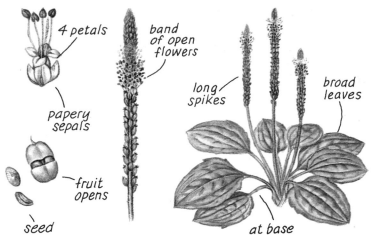

4 petals

band of open flowers

papery sepals

long spikes

broad leaves

fruit opens

seed

at base

A rosette of broad, tough leaves and long spikes of insignificant flowers are characteristic of the Greater Plantain. It is often a weed of lawns. The flowers are pollinated by the wind: anthers dangle from the flowers to shed pollen, and a long, roughened stigma catches airborne pollen. Sparrows and Finches eagerly seek the seeds in the long fruiting-heads. *Status:* native; common, throughout area. *Similar species:* Hoary Plantain, a more attractive plant, has leaves of similar shape but with soft, whitish hairs and shorter, creamy-white flower-heads with lilac stamens.

Hoary Plantain (*P. media*)

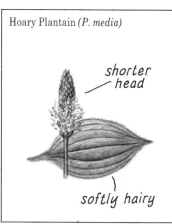

shorter head

softly hairy

	GREATER PLANTAIN		Bracts	shorter than flower, brown
Type	perennial		**Type**	♂
Height	10–15cm, rarely to 50cm		**Size**	2–3mm
Habitat	cultivated and waste ground, grassy places		**Colour**	yellowish-white
			Stalk	absent
Flowering	May–September		**Sepals**	4, 1.5–2.5mm, oval, almost equal, edges papery
	STEMS AND LEAVES		**Petals**	4, 2–3mm, bases form tube, lobes oval
Stem	very short, stout; flower-stalks long		**Stamens**	4, protruding
Root	thick, whitish		**Stigma**	1, slender
Hairs	absent or short		**Ovary**	1, 2-celled
Stipules	absent			
Leaves	rosette at base, 100–300mm, oval or elliptical, blunt, edge unbroken or slightly toothed, base squarish		**FRUIT**	
			Type	1, capsule, oblong, top splits away
Leaf-stalk	about equalling blade		**Size**	2–4mm
			Seeds	6–13, 1–1.5mm, elliptical, flattened
	FLOWERS			
Position	numerous, in long, slender, stalked, often curved spike			

Plantago lanceolata **Ribwort**

A very common plant, distinctive in its long leaves with several almost parallel veins, and compact, blackish-brown flower-heads borne on very long stalks. It is familiar to children , for many games are played with the tough-stalked flower-heads and passed on or re-invented by successive generations. *Status:* native; common, throughout area. *Similar species:* several narrow-leaved Plantains grow by the coast or in sandy and rocky places inland. Leaves of Buck's-horn Plantain have paired lobes. Those of Sea Plantain are almost parallel-sided. Branched Plantain has long, branched, leafy stems and many flower-heads.

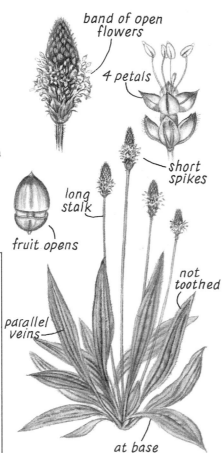

band of open flowers

4 petals

short spikes

long stalk

fruit opens

not toothed

parallel veins

at base

---

1 Buck's-horn Plantain *(P. coronopus)*; **2** Sea Plantain *(P. maritima)*; **3** Branched Plantain *(P. arenaria)*

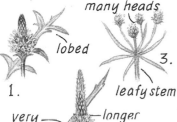

many heads

lobed

3.

leafy stem

1.

very narrow

longer

2.

	RIBWORT		FLOWERS	
Type	perennial	**Position**	many, in crowded spike on long, grooved stalk
Height	10–45cm		
Habitat	grassland; all but most acid soils	**Bracts**	oval, long-pointed
		Type	☿
Flowering	April–August	**Size**	3–4mm; head 10–20mm, rarely to 50mm
	STEMS AND LEAVES	**Colour**	pale brown
Stem	short, sometimes branched; flower-stalks long	**Stalk**	absent
		Sepals	4, 2.5–3mm, partly joined
Root	fibrous	**Petals**	4, 3–4mm, bases form tube, lobes oval
Hairs	sparse, pressed to surface		
Stipules	absent	**Stamens**	4, 3–5mm, protruding
Leaves	rosette at base, 100–300mm, narrowly to broadly spear-shaped, 3–5 main veins, pointed, edge unbroken or slightly toothed, base tapered	**Stigma**	1, slender
		Ovary	1, 2-celled
			FRUIT	
		Type	1, capsule, oblong
Leaf-stalk	about half length of blade	**Size**	3–5mm
		Seeds	2, 2–3mm, elliptical, flattened

Like a tiny bottle-brush, Hoary Plantain's stamens project outwards.

Valerians, Teasels, Honeysuckles and Moschatel

Plants in all four of these families can have compact, sometimes Daisy-like, flower-heads. In both Valerians and Teasels, the ovary has one cavity and develops into a dry, nut-like fruit that does not open. There are many similarities between these two families and the Daisy family, but they are easily distinguished by their separate stamens.

Valerians form a relatively small family of mostly herbaceous plants. The petals are somewhat unequal, with a spur on one side of the base of the tube in some species. The sepals are scarcely visible in flower but in fruit they sometimes form a feathery parachute.

Teasel has long been used for raising the nap on cloth. All species have compact flower-heads surrounded by prominent, often spiny bracts. The sepals are surrounded by modified bracts that can form a rim around the fruit.

Though Honeysuckle is a climber, the family includes many trees and shrubs. Most produce berries, and in Elder (*Sambucus niger*) these are edible. Several species of Honeysuckle, *Viburnum* and *Weigelia* are grown as decorative garden plants.

Moschatel is an unusual plant, with a single species in the family. The most distinctive feature is its compact flower-head comprised of four flowers facing away from each other at the same level and a fifth flower at the top.

Rings of opening florets progress from the middle of Teasel's spiky head, towards the base and tip.

Sweet-scented Honeysuckle is a favourite hedgerow plant, its compact heads of creamy, trumpet-shaped flowers often flushed with red or purple. In Autumn it is also conspicuous, with its clusters of crimson berries. Night-flying moths are attracted by the scent, which is strongest at dusk, and pollinate the flowers as they seek nectar. *Status:* native; common, most of area except extreme north. *Similar species:* Perfoliate Honeysuckle, a garden plant that has often escaped, differs in its joined pairs of upper leaves and stalkless flower-heads. Fly Honeysuckle is a native, upright shrub with much shorter flowers.

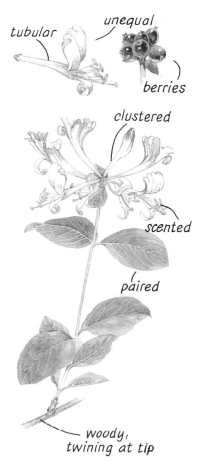
tubular · *unequal* · *berries* · *clustered* · *scented* · *paired* · *woody, twining at tip*

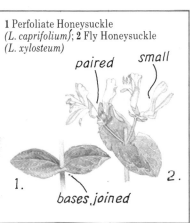

1 Perfoliate Honeysuckle (*L. caprifolium*); **2** Fly Honeysuckle (*L. xylosteum*)

paired · *small* · 1. · 2. · *bases joined*

	HONEYSUCKLE		
Type	climber	**Type**	♀
Height	up to 600cm	**Size**	40–50mm
Habitat	woods, hedges, rocks	**Colour**	creamy white or yellowish, often tinged red or purple
Flowering	June–September		
		Stalk	much shorter than flower
	STEMS AND LEAVES	**Sepals**	5, 2–5mm, bases joined
Stem	long, twining clockwise or trailing, woody below	**Petals**	5, 40–50mm, bases form long tube, upper 4 lobes joined into broad lip, lower lobe curved back
Root	woody stock		
Hairs	absent or sparse		
Stipules	absent	**Stamens**	5, protruding
Leaves	paired on stem, 30–70mm, oval to oblong, bluish green beneath, usually pointed, edge unbroken	**Stigma**	tip swollen; style long
		Ovary	1, 2-celled
Leaf-stalk	shorter than blade or absent	**FRUIT**	
		Type	1, cluster of red, globular berries
	FLOWERS	**Size**	7–10mm
Position	4–30, in short, stalked head	**Seeds**	2–8, 4–5mm, oblong
Bracts	shorter than flowers		

This curious species often lurks unnoticed at the base of a hedgerow, its greenish-yellow flowers lost against the delicate, rather Fern-like foliage. It is worth searching out the plant because the flower-heads have a unique arrangement: four flowers face outwards and a single flower faces upwards. Such an unusual arrangement has earned this species the picturesque alternative common name of 'Townhall Clock'. The top flower has four petals but the side flowers have five. The flowers have a musk-like scent, particularly in the evening. No native plant resembles Moschatel at all closely, so its relationship to other species is obscure. Some place it with the Fumitories because of a vague similarity in the foliage, but the form of the flowers is closer to that of Honeysuckle. *Status:* native; rather scattered, most of area except many islands, mainly in mountains in south. (There are no similar species.)

stalk droops · *4 petals* · *5 petals* · *berry-like fruits* · *5 flowers* · *leaflets in threes* · *long stalk*

	MOSCHATEL		
		Bracts	absent
Type	perennial	**Type**	♀, slightly scented
Height	5–10cm	**Size**	6–8mm
Habitat	woods, hedges, rocks	**Colour**	yellowish green
Flowering	April–May	**Stalk**	absent
		Sepals	2–3, 1.5–2mm, oval
	STEMS AND LEAVES	**Petals**	4–5, 2–3.5mm, bases joined, lobes oval, spreading widely
Stem	upright, unbranched		
Root	creeping, scaly, underground stem	**Stamens**	4–5, divided and appearing as 8 or 10
Hairs	absent		
Stipules	absent	**Stigmas**	4–5; styles short
Leaves	basal with 2–3 on stem, 8–30mm, divided into threes, leaflets often 3–lobed, pale green, blunt	**Ovary**	1, partly below sepals, 3–5-celled
Leaf-stalk	basal long, upper short	**FRUIT**	
		Type	1, globular, berry-like, green, rarely produced
	FLOWERS	**Size**	3–5mm
Position	5, head 6–9mm, long-stalked, at stem-tip	**Seeds**	1, 2–3mm, oval, flattened

145

Common Cornsalad *Valerianella locusta*

An easily overlooked, rather weedy plant that has compact heads of tiny flowers. The plant was formerly used and sometimes cultivated as a salad plant, especially in France. *Status:* native; scattered through most of area, rarer in north. *Similar species:* other sorts of Cornsalad are rather difficult to tell apart but differ in the shape of the fruit. Keeled-fruited Cornsalad has an oblong, grooved fruit. Broad-fruited Cornsalad has an egg-shaped fruit with distinct sepals at the tip. Narrow-fruited Cornsalad has a similar-shaped fruit but the sepals are very unequal, with one long tooth.

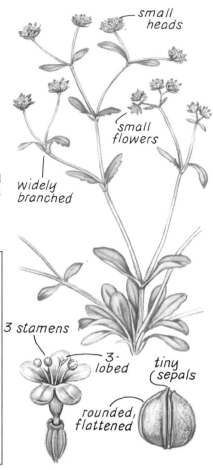

small heads
small flowers
widely branched

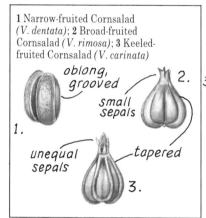

1 Narrow-fruited Cornsalad (*V. dentata*); 2 Broad-fruited Cornsalad (*V. rimosa*); 3 Keeled-fruited Cornsalad (*V. carinata*)

oblong, grooved
small sepals
unequal sepals
tapered
1.
2.
3.

3 stamens
3-lobed
tiny sepals
rounded, flattened

	COMMON CORNSALAD		FLOWERS
Type	annual	Position	compact heads at stem-tips, sometimes single flowers in forks of branches
Height	7–40cm		
Habitat	cultivated or waste ground, rocks, dunes; dry soils	Bracts	smaller than leaves
		Type	☿
Flowering	April–June	Size	2–3mm
		Colour	pale lilac
	STEMS AND LEAVES	Stalk	absent
		Sepals	5, 0.1–0.3mm, indistinct
Stem	upright, slender, brittle, angular, widely branched	Petals	5, 2–3mm, bases joined, funnel-shaped, lobes spreading widely
Root	fibrous		
Hairs	stem minutely bristly	Stamens	3, protruding
Stipules	absent	Stigma	3-lobed; style long
Leaves	basal or paired on stem, 20–70mm, oblong to spoon-shaped, mostly blunt, edge unbroken or some toothed	Ovary	1, below petals, 3-celled
			FRUIT
		Type	1, dry, nearly circular, flattened, smooth
Leaf-stalk	shorter than blade	Size	2–2.5mm
		Seeds	1, not released

Common Valerian *Valeriana officinalis*

A tall, conspicuous plant of river banks and damp ditches, its leaves cut into narrow leaflets and broad heads of lilac flowers. This plant still has several medicinal uses. Extracts from the roots have a sedative effect and were used for epilepsy, headaches and insomnia, although the drug can be addictive. *Status:* native; throughout area. *Similar species:* Marsh Valerian has rounded lower leaves on the separate male and female plants. Red Valerian is an introduced plant which is very common on cliffs and walls in the west of the area. It has broad, bluish leaves and spurred flowers with one stamen.

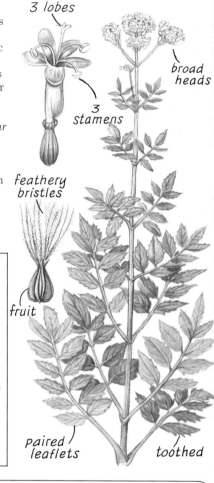

3 lobes
broad heads
3 stamens
feathery bristles
fruit
paired leaflets
toothed

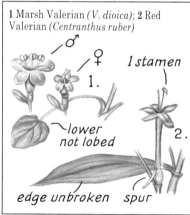

1 Marsh Valerian (*V. dioica*); 2 Red Valerian (*Centranthus ruber*)

♂
♀
1.
1 stamen
2.
lower not lobed
edge unbroken
spur

	COMMON VALERIAN		Bracts	shorter than flowers
Type	perennial		Type	☿
Height	20–150cm, rarely 240cm		Size	4–5mm
Habitat	grassy places, scrub; mostly damp soils		Colour	pinkish lilac
			Stalk	more or less absent
Flowering	June–August		Sepals	15 lobes, up to 6mm, rolled inwards, enlarging, becoming feathery in fruit
	STEMS AND LEAVES			
Stem	upright, rarely short, creeping stems at base		Petals	5, 4–5mm, bases form tube, side swollen, lobes oblong
Root	short underground stem			
Hairs	mostly below, absent above		Stamens	3, protruding, white
Stipules	absent		Stigma	1, 3-lobed; style long
Leaves	paired on stem, 25–200mm, paired, spear-shaped, toothed leaflets, leaflet at tip		Ovary	1, apparently 1-celled
				FRUIT
Leaf-stalk	shorter than blade, upper almost absent		Type	nut-like, oval, flattish, with feathery parachute
	FLOWERS		Size	2.5–4mm
Position	many, in compact, branched, rounded heads at stem-tips		Seeds	1, not released

Dipsacus fullonum **Teasel**

A striking plant, with large, spiny heads that bear rings of rosy-purple flowers. Bases of the stem-leaves are joined and fill with water, often drowning small insects. It has been speculated that the Teasel could benefit from these animals and might be carnivorous, although tropical plants use similar water-traps to protect flowers from insect attack. Spiny heads of Teasels have long been used to raise the nap on fabric. *Status:* native; often common, most of area except parts of north. *Similar species:* Small Teasel has stalked leaves and rounded flower-heads bearing white flowers.

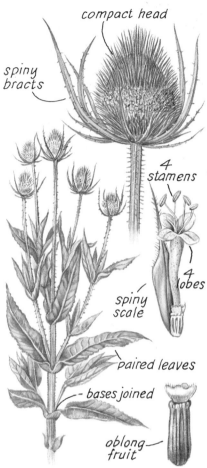
compact head
spiny bracts
4 stamens
4 lobes
spiny scale
paired leaves
bases joined
oblong fruit

Small Teasel (*D. pilosus*)
round head
white
bases not joined

Knautia arvensis **Field Scabious**

An attractive Summer-flowering meadow plant, its broad, bluish flower-heads are visible from a distance. Species of Scabious were used to treat scabies, hence the common name, and many other afflictions of the skin including sores caused by bubonic plague. *Status:* native; most of area except many northern islands, most common in south. *Similar species:* other species have more elongated heads with tiny bracts between the flowers and only five sepal-teeth. Small Scabious has five-lobed flowers and divided leaves; Devil's-bit Scabious has four-lobed flowers, all of the same size, and most leaves with unbroken edges.

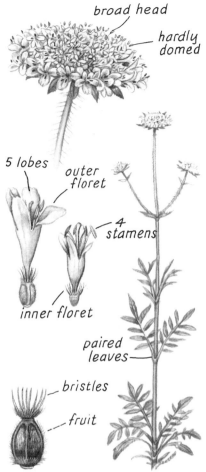
broad head
hardly domed
5 lobes
outer floret
4 stamens
inner floret
paired leaves
bristles
fruit

1 Small Scabious (*Scabiosa columbaria*); **2** Devil's-bit Scabious (*Succisa pratensis*)
more domed
5 bristles
1.
unbroken edge
rounded head
2.
5 bristles

	TEASEL			FLOWERS	
Type	biennial		**Position**	numerous in conical, blunt, upright, long-stalked heads	
Height	up to 200cm		**Bracts**	long, spiny under head; spine-tipped under flower	
Habitat	grassy places, river banks; often on clay soils		**Type**	☿	
Flowering	July–August		**Size**	8–12mm; heads 30–80mm	
	STEMS AND LEAVES		**Colour**	rosy purple, rarely white	
Stem	short in first year, then upright, with prickly angles, branched above		**Stalk**	absent	
			Sepals	1–1.5mm, joined, fringed	
Root	stout, yellowish tap-root		**Petals**	4, 8–12mm, bases form long tube; lobes unequal	
Hairs	only scattered prickles		**Stamens**	4, protruding	
Stipules	absent		**Stigma**	1; style long	
Leaves	rosette at base or paired on stem, oblong to spear-shaped, edge unbroken or toothed, bases of upper stem-leaves joined		**Ovary**	1, under petals, 1-celled	
				FRUIT	
			Type	1, nut-like, oblong, 4-angled, with sepals at tip	
Leaf-stalk	only on basal leaves		**Size**	4–5mm	
			Seeds	1, not released	

	FIELD SCABIOUS			FLOWERS	
Type	perennial		**Position**	numerous, in rounded, flattish, long-stalked heads	
Height	25–100cm		**Bracts**	oval, only under head, shorter than flowers	
Habitat	grassy places; dry soils		**Type**	☿ or ♀, outer larger	
Flowering	July–September		**Size**	8–14, heads 30–40mm	
	STEMS AND LEAVES		**Colour**	bluish lilac	
Stem	upright, branched		**Stalk**	absent beneath flowers, long under heads	
Root	tap-root		**Sepals**	2–4mm, 8 slender teeth	
Hairs	long, stiffish, throughout, angled downwards on stem		**Petals**	4, 7–14mm, bases form tube, lobes unequal	
Stipules	absent		**Stamens**	4, protruding, pink	
Leaves	basal rosette or paired on stem, lowest to 300mm long, spear-shaped, upper smaller, with paired lobes, pointed, edge unbroken or toothed		**Stigma**	1, notched; style long	
			Ovary	1, below petals, 1-celled	
				FRUIT	
Leaf-stalk	shorter than blade		**Type**	1, nut-like, cylindrical, hairy	
			Size	5–6mm	
			Seeds	1, not released	

Daisies and Bellflowers

Daisies form one of the largest of all flowering plant families, with around 25,000 species. Aside from the familiar garden Chrysanthemums, *Dahlia* and Marigolds, the family includes vegetables such as lettuce (*Lactuca sativa*) and Jerusalem artichoke (*Helianthus tuberosus*), and Sunflowers (*Helianthus annuus*) grown for the edible oil contained in the fruits. The most distinctive feature of the family is the form of the flower-head. Many small flowers (florets) are clustered in a compact head, surrounded by bracts at the base producing the overall effect of a single, complex flower.

Many species of the Bellflowers have relatively large, often bell-shaped flowers of a beautiful clear blue and are popular as garden plants. Like Daisies, Bellflowers are most abundant in temperate regions.

The floral parts of both families are usually in fives, with the petals joined to form a tube. Bellflowers have joined but otherwise fairly normal sepals. In the Daisies, they are heavily modified and may form a parachute or barbed spines on the fruit. In Daisies and some Bellflowers, the stamens are joined above to form a tube. The style pushes the pollen out. Later the forked tip opens to expose the stigmas. In Daisies the solitary ovary develops into a single-seeded, dry fruit, which does not open. Bellflowers usually have a capsule that opens by pores to release many seeds.

In the soft light of a setting sun, flowers of Oxeye Daisy intermingle with summer-flowering grasses.

Campanula trachelium **Nettle-leaved Bellflower**

A tall plant of hedgerows and woodland margins, with toothed, nettle-like leaves and a spike of bluish, bell-shaped flowers. It was widely used for treating throat infections. *Status:* native; scattered throughout most of area, except many islands. *Similar species:* Clustered Bellflower is an attractive plant of lime-rich grassland, and has stalkless flowers more or less clustered in heads. Giant Bellflower has the largest flowers of these species, bluntly angled stems and the lower leaves tapered or rounded at the base. Creeping Bellflower has nodding flowers with widely spreading sepal-teeth.

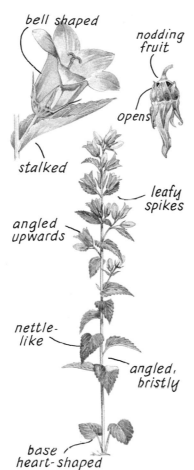

bell shaped

nodding fruit

opens

stalked

leafy spikes

angled upwards

nettle-like

angled, bristly

base heart-shaped

1 Clustered Bellflower (*C. glomerata*); **2** Giant Bellflower (*C. latifolia*); **3** Creeping Bellflower (*C. rapunculoides*)

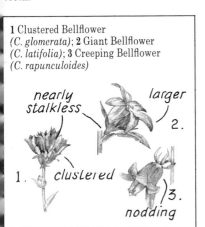

nearly stalkless

larger

2.

1.

clustered

3.

nodding

	NETTLE-LEAVED BELLFLOWER		FLOWERS	
Type	perennial	**Position**	long head, 1–4 on branches	
Height	50–100cm	**Bracts**	narrow	
Habitat	woods, hedges; usually clay soils	**Type**	♀, angled upwards	
		Size	25–50mm	
Flowering	July–September	**Colour**	purplish blue	
		Stalk	shorter than flower	
	STEMS AND LEAVES	**Sepals**	5, 13–15mm, bases joined, teeth triangular, pointed	
Stem	upright, sharply angled, sometimes branched, red-tinged, with yellowish sap	**Petals**	5, 25–50mm, equal, joined, bell-shaped, lobes pointed	
		Stamens	5, long, soon withering	
Root	tap-root	**Stigmas**	3; style long	
Hairs	stiff, leaves rough	**Ovary**	1, below sepals, 3-celled	
Stipules	absent			
Leaves	spirally placed on stem, up to 100mm, coarsely toothed; lower oval or triangular, base heart-shaped, upper oblong, pointed	**FRUIT**		
		Type	nodding capsule, half spherical, pores at base	
		Size	6–8mm	
Leaf-stalk	shorter than blade	**Seeds**	numerous, 0.6–0.8mm, oblong	

Campanula rotundifolia **Harebell**

Dainty, nodding, pale blue bells of the Harebell are a common sight on dry, grassy banks in Summer. In Scotland the plant is called 'Bluebell', although a different species bears the name in England. Upper and lower leaves of this plant are so different that they appear to belong to different species. *Status:* native; usually common, most of area. *Similar species:* the smaller relatives of the Bellflowers include Venus's-looking-glass, a cornfield annual with upright, purplish flowers and long, cylindrical capsules. Ivy-leaved Bellflower is a creeping plant of boggy places, with small, Ivy-shaped leaves and nodding, pale blue flowers.

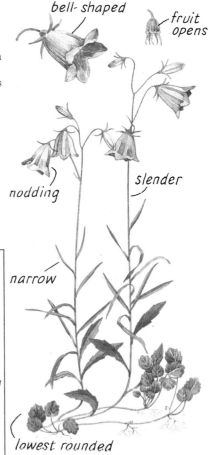

bell-shaped

fruit opens

nodding

slender

narrow

lowest rounded

1 Venus's-looking-glass (*Legousia hybrida*); **2** Ivy-leaved Bellflower (*Wahlenbergia hederacea*)

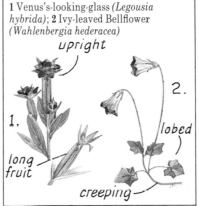

upright

2.

1.

long fruit

lobed

creeping

	HAREBELL		FLOWERS	
Type	perennial	**Position**	solitary at stem-tip or few in widely branched head	
Height	15–40cm, rarely 70cm	**Bracts**	small, straight-sided	
Habitat	grassy places, dunes; mostly dry soils	**Type**	♀	
		Size	10–20mm	
Flowering	July–September	**Colour**	blue, rarely white	
		Stalk	long, slender, nodding	
	STEMS AND LEAVES	**Sepals**	5, 5–8mm, slender, spreading apart	
Stem	low-growing, turning upright to flower	**Petals**	5, 10–20mm, joined, bell-shaped, lobes broadly oval	
Root	creeping underground stems	**Stamens**	5, inside tube	
Hairs	absent above, short below	**Stigmas**	3; style long	
Stipules	absent	**Ovary**	1, below sepals, 3-celled	
Leaves	on alternate sides of stem; lower 5–15mm, oval to nearly circular, toothed, base heart-shaped; upper narrow, straight-sided	**FRUIT**		
		Type	capsule, cone-shaped, nodding, pores at base	
Leaf-stalk	lower much longer than blade; upper absent	**Size**	4–6mm	
		Seeds	numerous, 0.6–0.8mm, oblong	

Sheep's-bit *Jasione montana*

On dry, grassy banks and heathland, Sheep's-bit bears its rounded heads of pale blue flowers at the end of almost leafless stems. Although the flower-heads resemble those of Scabious species, this is a relative of the Bellflowers, and has joined stamens and capsules that release seeds. *Status:* native; scattered throughout area, often common. *Similar species:* Rampions have similar flower-heads but with curved buds and almost hairless stems and leaves. Round-headed Rampion has short heads of violet flowers and occurs in the south of the area. Spiked Rampion is more widespread and has longer heads of yellowish flowers.

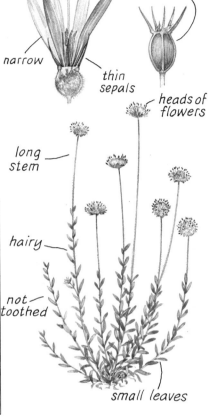

5 petals
narrow
fruit opens
thin sepals
heads of flowers
long stem
hairy
not toothed
small leaves

1 Round-headed Rampion (*Phyteuma orbiculare*); 2 Spiked Rampion (*P. spicatum*)

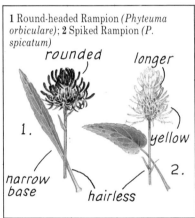

rounded
longer
1.
yellow
2.
narrow base
hairless

	SHEEP'S-BIT		Bracts	many, oval below head
Type	biennial, sometimes annual		**Type**	☿
Height	5–50cm		**Size**	4–6mm; head 5–35mm
Habitat	grassy places, heaths, cliffs; lime-free soils		**Colour**	blue, rarely white
			Stalk	absent; head long-stalked
Flowering	May–August		**Sepals**	5, 1.5–2.5mm, bases joined, teeth thin
	STEMS AND LEAVES		**Petals**	5, 4–6mm, bases joined, narrow lobes spread apart
Stem	low-growing, turns upright to flower, some branched		**Stamens**	5, elongated, joined
Root	fibrous		**Stigmas**	2; style long, protruding
Hairs	more or less throughout		**Ovary**	1, below petals, 2-celled
Stipules	absent			
Leaves	spirally placed on lower part of stem, to 50mm, narrowly oblong or spear-shaped, mostly blunt, edge straight or wavy			**FRUIT**
			Type	1, capsule, egg-shaped, sepals attached, opens by 2 short teeth
Leaf-stalk	lower short, upper absent		**Size**	3–4mm
			Seeds	numerous, c0.5mm, glossy
	FLOWERS			
Position	up to 200 in almost globular head at stem-tip			

Sea Aster *Aster tripolium*

This handsome, purple and yellow Daisy is commonly encountered in salt-marshes, where it covers extensive areas. Most plants have strap-shaped outer florets, but some only have the yellow inner florets. Sea Aster was formerly cultivated and used as a wound-herb. *Status:* native; common around coasts of region. *Similar species:* several species of Michaelmas-daisy are grown in gardens and commonly escape. Perhaps the most common is *Aster novi-belgii*, with broad-based leaves and mostly bluish outer florets. *A. lanceolatus* has narrower leaves with tapered bases and thin, white or bluish outer florets.

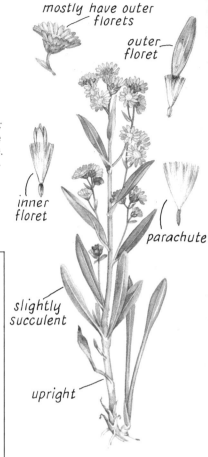

mostly have outer florets
outer floret
inner floret
parachute
slightly succulent
upright

1 Michaelmas-daisy (*A. novi-belgii*); 2 Michaelmas-daisy (*A. lanceolatus*)

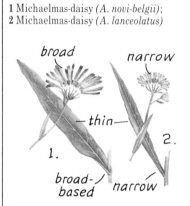

broad
narrow
thin
1.
2.
broad-based
narrow

	SEA ASTER		Bracts	papery-edged around head; none between florets
Type	perennial		**Type 1**	inner ☿, 7–8mm, tubular
Height	15–100cm		**Type 2**	outer florets ♀ usually 10–30, 9–12mm, strap-shaped
Habitat	salt-marsh, sea-cliffs, rocks; salty soils		**Size**	heads 8–20mm
Flowering	July–October		**Colour**	yellow and purplish blue
			Stalk	absent; short under heads
	STEMS AND LEAVES		**Sepals**	a ring of hairs
Stem	upright, stout, branched		**Petals**	5, 8–12mm, joined, tubular, lobes equal or very unequal
Root	short underground stem		**Stamens**	5, joined into tube
Hairs	mostly absent		**Stigma**	1, 2-lobed; style long
Stipules	absent		**Ovary**	1, below petals, 1-celled
Leaves	spirally placed on stem, 70–120mm, fleshy, edge unbroken or hardly toothed, lower spear-shaped, tapered upper oblong, broad-based			**FRUIT**
			Type	nut-like, flattened, hairy, with parachute of hairs
Leaf-stalk	long below, absent above		**Size**	5–6mm
			Seeds	1, not released
	FLOWERS			
Position	daisy-like heads of florets surrounded by bracts			

Eupatorium cannabinum **Hemp-agrimony**

A tall plant of riverbanks, with broad, fluffy heads of reddish or pink flowers. Hemp-agrimony has its small flower-heads clustered together and in sunny weather the whole top of the plant becomes alive with butterflies. *Status:* native; common, most of area except far north. *Similar species:* several species with small flower-heads have spirally-arranged undivided leaves and tiny, elongated florets around the heads. Canadian Fleabane has loose clusters of yellowish heads. Blue Fleabane has few, larger heads with purplish outer florets. Ploughman's-spikenard has toothed lower leaves and purplish bracts around the flower-heads.

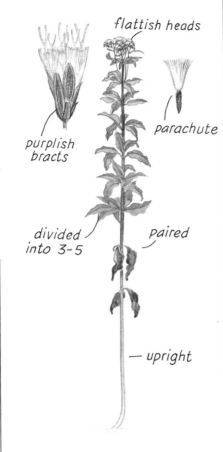

flattish heads

parachute

purplish bracts

divided into 3-5

paired

upright

1 Canadian Fleabane (*Erigeron canadensis*); 2 Blue Fleabane (*E. acer*); 3 Ploughman's-spikenard (*Inula conyza*)

tiny heads

few

1.

2.

3.

long toothed

HEMP-AGRIMONY		FLOWERS	
Type	perennial	**Position**	heads of 5–6 tiny flowers (florets) surrounded by bracts, in broad, flattish clusters
Height	30–120cm, rarely 175cm		
Habitat	banks of rivers, streams, marshes, woods; damp places	**Bracts**	purplish around head; none between florets
Flowering	July–September	**Type**	florets ⚥, 4.5–7mm, tubular
		Size	heads 5–8mm
STEMS AND LEAVES		**Colour**	pale reddish purple or pink
Stem	upright, few branches	**Stalk**	absent; short under heads
Root	woody stock	**Sepals**	a ring of hairs
Hairs	short, almost throughout	**Petals**	5, joined, tubular, lobes equal
Stipules	absent	**Stamens**	5, joined into tube
Leaves	paired on stem, to 100mm, divided into 3, rarely 5, elliptical parts, pointed, toothed; lowest undivided	**Stigma**	1, 2-lobed; style long
		Ovary	1, below petals, 1-celled
		FRUIT	
Leaf-stalk	much shorter than blade	**Type**	1, dry, nut-like, 5-angled, with parachute of hairs
		Size	2.5–3mm
		Seeds	1, not released

Solidago virgaurea **Goldenrod**

This late-flowering plant is common in hilly places on dry grassland, cliffs and among rocks, but is rarely seen in lowland areas of the south. Long clusters of golden-yellow flower-heads contrast with the dark foliage and often blackish stems. Goldenrod was widely used as a wound-herb and was formerly in great demand. *Status:* native; almost throughout area, sometimes common. *Similar species:* Canadian Goldenrod has many more, smaller flower-heads, arranged on almost horizontal branches. This garden plant has often escaped and can be abundant around towns on railway embankments and disused sidings.

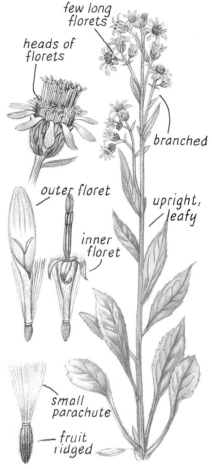

few long florets

heads of florets

branched

outer floret

upright, leafy

inner floret

small parachute

fruit ridged

Canadian Goldenrod (*S. canadensis*)

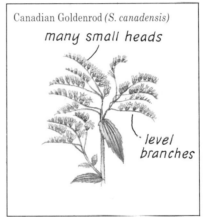

many small heads

level branches

GOLDENROD			green around head; none between florets
Type	perennial	**Type 1**	inner florets ⚥, 10–30, 4–6mm, tubular
Height	5–75cm, rarely 100cm		
Habitat	grassy places, cliffs, rocks, woods; dry soils	**Type 2**	outer florets ♀, 6–12, 6–9mm, strap-shaped
Flowering	July–September	**Size**	heads 0–20mm
		Colour	yellow
STEMS AND LEAVES		**Stalk**	absent; short under heads
Stem	upright, branched above	**Sepals**	a ring of hairs
Root	stout stock	**Petals**	5, joined, tubular, lobes equal or very unequal
Hairs	absent or short		
Stipules	absent	**Stamens**	5, joined into tube
Leaves	spirally placed on stem, 20–100mm, rarely 300mm, oval to elliptical, pointed, toothed	**Stigma**	1, 2-lobed; style long
		Ovary	1, below petals, 1-celled
Leaf-stalk	short or absent	**FRUIT**	
FLOWERS		**Type**	1, dry, nut-like, ribbed, with parachute of hairs
Position	daisy-like heads of tiny flowers (florets) surrounded by bracts, in long clusters	**Size**	3–4mm
		Seeds	1, not released
Bracts	4.5–8mm, narrow, yellowish		

Daisy *Bellis perennis*

- inner floret
- many outer florets
- no parachute
- all from base
- outer floret
- from base

Familiar to children as a favourite flower for picking, and the raw material for daisy-chains, this plant is also known to gardeners as a pernicious weed that is almost impossible to eradicate from lawns. The flower-heads, carried singly above a rosette of leaves, close at night or in dull weather and provide the origin of the common name ('day's-eye'). *Status:* native; very common, throughout area. *Similar species:* Mexican Fleabane has flower-heads similar to the Daisy, but longer, branched stems with small leaves. Often escaping from cultivation, this plant forms small, bushy mounds on old walls.

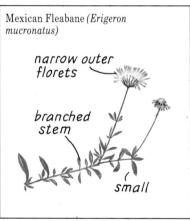

Mexican Fleabane (*Erigeron mucronatus*)

- narrow outer florets
- branched stem
- small

	DAISY		Type 1	inner florets ♂, 2–3mm, tubular
Type	perennial		Type 2	outer florets ♀, 4–8mm, strap-shaped
Height	3–20cm			
Habitat	short grassland		**Size**	heads 16–25mm
Flowering	March–October		**Colour**	inner florets yellow, outer white, often tinged red
	STEMS AND LEAVES		**Stalk**	absent; 3–20mm under heads
Stem	short; flower-heads stalked		**Sepals**	a ring of hairs
Root	stout, fibrous; short stock		**Petals**	5, joined, tubular, lobes equal or very unequal
Hairs	rather sparse			
Stipules	absent		**Stamens**	5, joined into tube
Leaves	rosette at base, 20–40mm, rarely 80mm, oval to spoon-shaped, rounded, toothed		**Stigma**	1, 2-lobed; style long
			Ovary	1, below petals, 1-celled
Leaf-stalk	shorter than blade			**FRUIT**
	FLOWERS		**Type**	dry, nut-like, flattened, hairy, without parachute
Position	solitary heads of tiny flowers (florets) surrounded by bracts		**Size**	1.5–2mm
Bracts	3–5mm, oblong, blunt around head; none between florets		**Seeds**	1, not released

Gallant Soldier *Galinsoga parviflora*

Tiny white and yellow flower-heads of Gallant Soldier resemble miniature Daisies. This weed of gardens, arable fields and waste ground is so widespread that it appears native, although it was introduced from South America to botanic gardens in Europe during the latter part of the eighteenth century. The common name is merely a corruption of the botanical name. *Status:* introduced, naturalized; common weed, much of area. *Similar species:* Shaggy Soldier has a similar history and appearance, but can be distinguished by the hairy stems and spear-shaped scales between the florets.

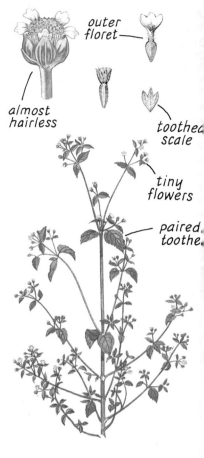

- outer floret
- almost hairless
- toothed scale
- tiny flowers
- paired toothe.

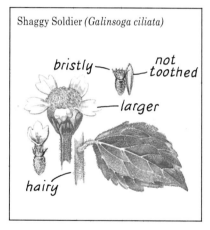

Shaggy Soldier (*Galinsoga ciliata*)

- bristly
- not toothed
- larger
- hairy

	GALLANT SOLDIER		Type 1	inner florets ♂, few, 2–3mm, tubular
Type	annual		Type 2	outer florets ♀, 4–8, 3–4.5mm, broad, 3-toothed
Height	10–75cm			
Habitat	cultivated and waste ground		**Size**	heads 3–5mm
Flowering	May–October		**Colour**	inner florets yellow, outer white
	STEMS AND LEAVES		**Stalk**	absent; short under heads
Stem	upright, many-branched		**Sepals**	8–20, narrow, scale-like
Root	fibrous		**Petals**	5, joined, tubular, lobes equal or very unequal
Hairs	almost absent			
Stipules	absent		**Stamens**	5, joined into tube
Leaves	paired on stem, 50–90mm, oval, pointed, toothed		**Stigma**	1, 2-lobed; style long
Leaf-stalk	shorter than blade		**Ovary**	1, below petals, 1-celled
	FLOWERS			**FRUIT**
Position	few, daisy-like heads of tiny flowers (florets) surrounded by bracts		**Type**	1, dry, nut-like, egg-shaped, with silvery, scale-like sepals at tip
Bracts	2.5–4mm, oval, under head; 3-lobed scales between florets		**Size**	1–1.5mm
			Seeds	1, not released

Filago vulgaris Common Cudweed

A curious member of the Daisy family, it has woolly stems and clusters of tiny yellowish flower-heads. On robust plants, the stem branches immediately below a flower-cluster and the branch turns upright to bear a second cluster of heads. The common name derives from the practice of feeding the plant to cattle. *Status:* native; fairly common, most of area except extreme north. *Similar species:* Small Cudweed has narrower leaves and few flower-heads in a cluster. Two species have larger, spreading leaves. Marsh Cudweed has several leaves surrounding each cluster of heads; and Heath Cudweed is a perennial with spikes of heads.

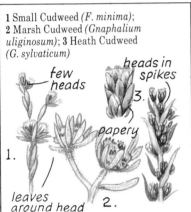

1 Small Cudweed (*F. minima*); **2** Marsh Cudweed (*Gnaphalium uliginosum*); **3** Heath Cudweed (*G. sylvaticum*)

few heads

heads in spikes

3.

papery

1.

2.

leaves around head

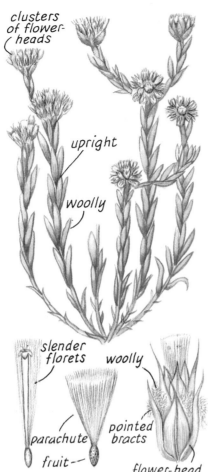

clusters of flower-heads

upright

woolly

slender florets

woolly

parachute

fruit

pointed bracts

flower-head

COMMON CUDWEED		Bracts	4–4.5mm under head, outer woolly, inner yellowish, papery; none between florets
Type	annual		
Height	5–39cm, rarely 45cm	**Type 1**	inner florets ♂, 1–4, 3–4mm, tubular
Habitat	grassy places; dry soils	**Type 2**	outer florets ♀, 20–25, 4–4.5mm, tubular, very thin
Flowering	July–August	**Size**	heads 4–5mm wide; clusters 10–12mm
STEMS AND LEAVES		**Colour**	yellow
Stem	upright, some branched	**Stalk**	absent, heads stalkless
Root	fibrous	**Sepals**	a ring of hairs
Hairs	woolly, whitish	**Petals**	5, joined, lobes equal
Stipules	absent	**Stamens**	5, joined into tube
Leaves	spirally around stem, 10–30mm, spear-shaped, blunt, upright, edge often wavy	**Stigma**	1, 2-lobed; style long
		Ovary	1, below petals, 1-celled
Leaf-stalk	absent		
FLOWERS		**FRUIT**	
Position	heads of flowers (florets) enclosed by bracts, 20–35 in cluster at stem-tip	**Type**	nut-like, some with parachute
		Size	0.6–0.7mm
		Seeds	1, not released

Antennaria dioica Mountain Everlasting

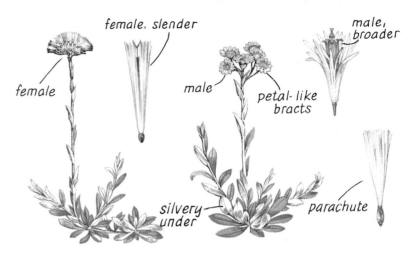

female, slender

male, broader

female

male

petal-like bracts

silvery under

parachute

A small plant of mountains, or lower altitudes in the north. The flower-heads are enclosed by pink or white papery bracts which keep their form and colour after drying, hence the common name. Male and female flowers are on separate plants. *Status:* native; much of area, most common in north, mostly in mountains in south. *Similar species:* other species do not have male and female plants. Everlasting, of dry, sandy places in the south-east, has almost globular, yellow or orange flower-heads. Pearly Everlasting, an escaped garden plant, is more robust and has pearly-white bracts.

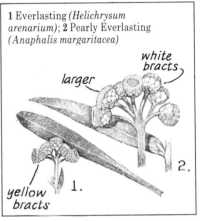

1 Everlasting (*Helichrysum arenarium*); **2** Pearly Everlasting (*Anaphalis margaritacea*)

white bracts

larger

yellow bracts

1.

2.

MOUNTAIN EVERLASTING		Bracts	many under head, woolly-based, papery, ♂ broad, petal-like; ♀ narrow; none between florets
Type	perennial		
Height	5–20cm	**Type 1**	♂, 4–5mm, funnel-shaped
Habitat	grassland, rocky slopes; dry, sandy or stony places	**Type 2**	♀, 6–7mm, very slender
Flowering	June–July	**Size**	♂ heads 8–12mm; ♀ 5–7mm
		Colour	white or pink
STEMS AND LEAVES		**Stalk**	absent; short under heads
Stem	creeping, mat-forming; flowering stems upright	**Sepals**	hair-like; ♂ thick-tipped
Root	woody stock, stems root	**Petals**	5, tubular, lobes equal
Hairs	woolly except above leaves	**Stamens**	5, joined into tube
Stipules	absent	**Stigma**	1, 2-lobed; style long
Leaves	basal or spiral on stem, 5–40mm, lower oval, broad-tipped, upper narrow, upright, edge unbroken	**Ovary**	1, below petals, 1-celled
		FRUIT	
Leaf-stalk	short or absent	**Type**	nut-like, with parachute
		Size	1–1.5mm
FLOWERS		**Seeds**	1, not released
Position	♂ and ♀ on different plants; 2–8 daisy-like heads of florets		

Common Fleabane *Pulicaria dysenterica*

A common, yellow, daisy-like plant of places where water stands for some of the year. Common Fleabane was used to repel fleas, and stems of the plant were strewn on floors for this purpose. Dried and burned, it acted as an insecticide against midges. The plant was also used to treat dysentery. *Status:* native; common, most of area. *Similar species:* Small Fleabane is annual, and has smaller flower-heads with very short outer florets. Elecampane has broad leaves and much larger flower-heads with broad bracts. Leopard's-bane has heart-shaped, long-stalked lower leaves and large flower-heads with fewer, long bracts.

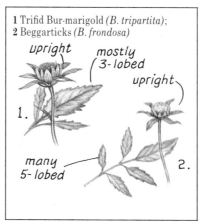

broad head of florets

bracts

parachute of hairs

fruit

hairy

outer floret

inner floret

slightly toothed

1 Small Fleabane (*P. vulgaris*);
2 Elecampane (*Inula helenium*);
3 Leopard's-bane (*Doronicum pardalianches*)

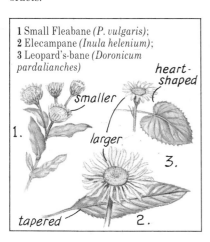

smaller

heart-shaped

larger

1.

3.

2.

tapered

COMMON FLEABANE		Bracts	many around head, thin, hairy; none between florets
Type	perrenial	**Type 1**	inner ♀, 5–6mm, tubular
Height	20–60cm	**Type 2**	outer florets ♀, numerous, 8–11mm, very narrow, flat
Habitat	stream banks, meadows, marshes; damp places	**Size**	heads 15–30mm
Flowering	August–September	**Colour**	yellow
		Stalk	absent; to 25mm under heads
STEMS AND LEAVES		**Sepals**	a ring of hairs
Stem	upright, branched above	**Petals**	5, joined, tubular, lobes equal or very unequal
Root	fibrous; stems rooting	**Stamens**	5, joined into tube
Hairs	sparse on stem, dense under leaves	**Stigma**	1, 2-lobed; style long
Stipules	absent	**Ovary**	1, below petals, 1-celled
Leaves	spirally around stem, 30–80mm, oblong, edge hardly toothed; upper spear-shaped, broad-based	**FRUIT**	
		Type	nut-like, oblong, ribbed, inner with parachute
Leaf-stalk	short below, absent above	**Size**	1.5–2mm
		Seeds	1, not released
FLOWERS			
Position	daisy-like heads of florets surrounded by bracts		

Nodding Bur-marigold *Bidens cernua*

A waterside plant, often disregarded because the flower-heads lack the usual outer florets of daisy-relatives, and soon fade to brown. A variant with outer florets is much more attractive, and has flower-heads almost twice as large. Small, barbed bristles on the fruits stick to passing animals and are spread to new localities. *Status:* native; most of area, rarer in north. *Similar species:* two other species have divided leaves, upright flowers and fruits with two bristles. Trifid Bur-marigold has mostly three-lobed leaves and barbed angles on the fruits. Beggarticks has mostly five-lobed leaves and almost smooth-angled fruits.

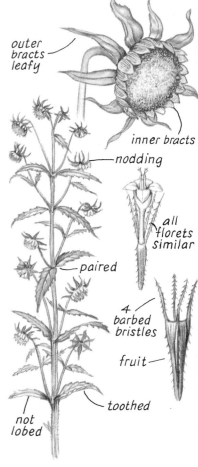

outer bracts leafy

inner bracts

nodding

all florets similar

paired

4 barbed bristles

fruit

toothed

1 Trifid Bur-marigold (*B. tripartita*);
2 Beggarticks (*B. frondosa*)

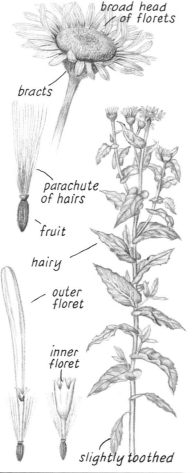

upright

mostly 3-lobed

upright

1.

2.

many 5-lobed

not lobed

NODDING BUR-MARIGOLD		Type 1	inner florets ♀, many, 6–7mm, tubular
Type	annual	**Type 2**	outer rarely present, sterile, 10–12mm, flattened
Height	8–60cm	**Size**	heads 15–25mm, rarely 45mm
Habitat	ponds, streams; wet places	**Colour**	yellow
Flowering	July–September	**Stalk**	absent; long under heads
		Sepals	4, bristle-like
STEMS AND LEAVES		**Petals**	5, joined, tubular, lobes equal, rarely very unequal
Stem	upright, branched above	**Stamens**	5, joined into tube
Root	fibrous	**Stigma**	1, 2-lobed; style long
Hairs	absent or sparse	**Ovary**	1, below petals, 1-celled
Stipules	absent		
Leaves	paired on stem, 40–150mm, spear-shaped, pointed, toothed	**FRUIT**	
		Type	nut-like, 4-angled, tip with 4 barbed bristles
Leaf-stalk	absent	**Size**	5–6mm
		Seeds	1, not released
FLOWERS			
Position	daisy-like heads of florets enclosed by bracts, nodding		
Bracts	2 rows around head, outer leaf-like, inner oval, papery, dark-streaked; scale-like between florets		

Achillea millefolium **Yarrow**

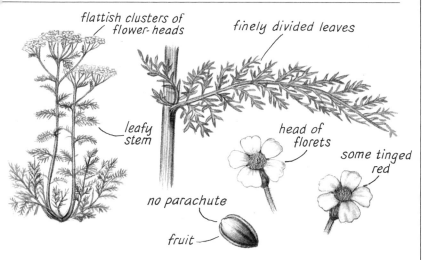

A common plant of road-verges, easily identified by the broad, flat clusters of small daisy-like flower-heads and feathery foliage. The cluster of heads functions as a single, large flower and attracts many insects, including beetles, butterflies and hover-flies. It has had many medicinal uses. Related species are grown in gardens for use as 'everlasting' flowers. *Status:* native; common, throughout area. *Similar species:* Sneezewort is readily distinguished by its undivided leaves and less numerous, much larger flower-heads. Acrid leaves were used as a form of snuff and to relieve toothache.

Sneezewort (*A. ptarmica*)

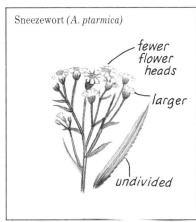

	YARROW		Bracts	dark-edged around heads; scale-like between florets
Type	perennial		**Type 1**	inner ♀, 2–3mm, tubular
Height	8–65cm		**Type 2**	outer florets ♀, 4–5mm, broad, 3-toothed
Habitat	grassy places; most soils		**Size**	heads 4–6mm wide
Flowering	June–August		**Colour**	white or tinged red
			Stalk	absent; short under heads
	STEMS AND LEAVES		**Sepals**	absent
Stem	upright, grooved, branched above, strongly scented		**Petals**	5, joined, tubular, lobes equal or very unequal
Root	tap-root; stems root		**Stamens**	5, joined into tube
Hairs	more or less woolly		**Stigma**	1, 2-lobed; style long
Stipules	absent		**Ovary**	1, below petals, 1-celled
Leaves	spirally arranged on stem, 50–160mm, oblong in outline, finely divided 2–3 times			
Leaf stalk	shorter than blade or absent above			**FRUIT**
			Type	nut-like, flattened, shiny, blunt, without parachute
	FLOWERS		**Size**	1.5–2mm
Position	flat-topped clusters, many daisy-like heads of florets enclosed by bracts		**Seeds**	1, not released

Artemisia vulgaris **Mugwort**

A tall plant with deeply divided dark-green leaves, silvery beneath, and branched clusters of insignificant reddish-brown flower-heads. Common along roadsides, it often has a dusty, neglected look. In ancient times it was believed to have powerful magical properties. Mugwort had many uses, as a herbalist medicine, to repel insects, to flavour ale, or as a herb for stuffing ducks and geese. *Status:* native; common, throughout area. *Similar species:* Wormwood has silky hairs on both sides of the leaves and wider flower-heads. Sea Wormwood has strongly scented woolly leaves, cut into very narrow segments.

1 Wormwood (*A. absinthium*); 2 Sea Wormwood (*A. maritima*)

	MUGWORT		Bracts	2.5–3mm around head, papery-edged; none between florets
Type	perennial		**Type 1**	inner florets ♂, 2–3mm, tubular, broader above
Height	60–120cm, rarely 210cm		**Type 2**	outer florets ♀, 2–3mm, very narrowly tubular
Habitat	waste ground, hedgerows		**Size**	heads 3–4mm
Flowering	July–September		**Colour**	reddish brown
			Stalk	absent; short under heads
	STEMS AND LEAVES		**Sepals**	absent
Stem	upright, grooved, reddish		**Petals**	5, tubular, lobes equal
Root	branched stock		**Stamens**	5, joined into tube
Hairs	white; woolly under leaves		**Stigma**	1, 2-lobed; style long
Stipules	absent		**Ovary**	1, below petals, 1-celled
Leaves	spirally arranged on stem, 50–80mm, deeply lobed and toothed, lower broad, upper smaller, broad-based			
Leaf-stalk	short or absent			**FRUIT**
			Type	nut-like, cylindrical, smooth, without parachute
	FLOWERS		**Size**	1–1.5mm
Position	large, branched clusters of daisy-like heads with florets enclosed by bracts		**Seeds**	1, not released

Scentless Mayweed *Tripleurospermum inodorum*

One of the Daisies of cornfields, that has large white and yellow flowers above finely divided leaves. Common on waste ground, it also colonizes new road-verges. *Status:* native; common, most of area. *Similar species:* Sea Mayweed is a low-growing coastal plant with shorter, fleshier leaf-segments. Both species have two brown oil-bearing glands on each fruit, but in this plant they are elongated, not round. Two species have flower-heads with a dome-shaped, hollow base and five-ribbed fruits. Scented Mayweed has pleasantly scented leaves. Pineappleweed has strong-smelling leaves and no outer florets.

1 Sea Mayweed (*T. maritimum*);
2 Scented Mayweed (*Matricaria recutita*); 3 Pineappleweed (*M. matricarioides*)

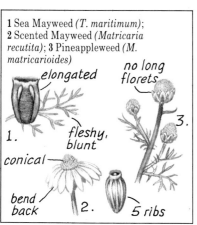

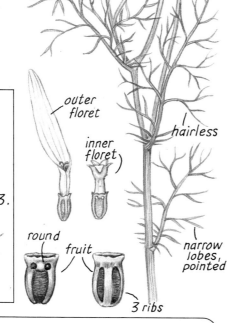

	SCENTLESS MAYWEED		
Type	annual		papery-edged; none between florets
Height	15–80cm	**Type 1**	inner florets ♂, 3–4mm, tubular
Habitat	cultivated and waste ground; most soils	**Type 2**	outer florets ♀, 12–22, 10–18mm, strap-shaped
Flowering	July–September	**Size**	heads 15–45mm
		Colour	yellow and white
	STEMS AND LEAVES	**Stalk**	absent; long under heads
Stem	upright, often branched	**Sepals**	an inconspicuous rim
Root	fibrous	**Petals**	5, joined, tubular, lobes equal or very unequal
Hairs	absent	**Stamens**	5, joined into tube
Stipules	absent	**Stigma**	1, 2-lobed; style long
Leaves	spirally placed on stem, 20–100mm, finely divided 2–3 times into thin segments	**Ovary**	1, below petals, 1-celled
Leaf-stalk	short or absent		**FRUIT**
		Type	nut-like, oblong, 3-ribbed, without parachute
	FLOWERS	**Size**	2–3mm
Position	daisy-like heads of florets surrounded by bracts	**Seeds**	1, not released
Bracts	2 rows around head, oblong,		

Corn Chamomile *Anthemis arvensis*

One of several white and yellow Daisies of the cornfield, distinguished from the Mayweeds by the scales betweeen the florets. Another distinction is in the short, relatively broad leaf-segments, which are almost woolly beneath when young. *Status:* native; most of area, sometimes common. *Similar species:* Stinking Chamomile is strong-smelling, and has narrow scales between the florets and rough fruits. It was a hated weed in the days of hand-scythes because it blistered the hands at harvest-time. Chamomile is a perennial with sparsely-ribbed fruits rounded at the top. It is widely used to make Chamomile tea.

1 Stinking Chamomile (*A. cotula*);
2 Chamomile (*Chamaemelum nobile*)

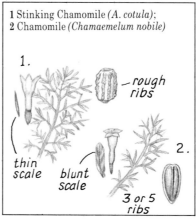

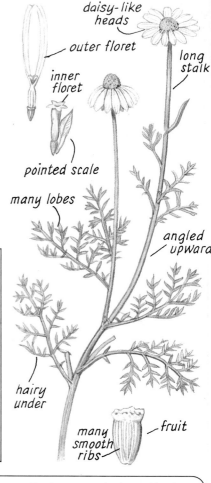

	CORN CHAMOMILE		
Type	annual, slightly scented	**Bracts**	papery-edged around head; spear-shaped, long-pointed between florets
Height	12–80cm	**Type 1**	inner ♂, 3–4mm, tubular
Habitat	cultivated and waste ground; lime-rich soils	**Type 2**	outer florets ♀, 5–14mm, strap-shaped
Flowering	June–July	**Size**	heads 20–30mm
		Colour	yellow and white
	STEMS AND LEAVES	**Stalk**	absent; long under heads
Stem	angled upwards, many-branched	**Sepals**	an inconspicuous rim
Root	fibrous	**Petals**	5, joined, tubular, lobes equal or very unequal
Hairs	fairly dense under leaves	**Stamens**	5, joined into tube
Stipules	absent	**Stigma**	1, 2-lobed; style long
Leaves	spirally arranged, 15–50mm, divided 1–3 times into short, narrow segments	**Ovary**	1, below petals, 1-celled
Leaf-stalk	short or absent		**FRUIT**
		Type	nut-like, oblong, 10-ribbed, without parachute
	FLOWERS	**Size**	2–3mm
Position	daisy-like heads of florets surrounded by bracts	**Seeds**	1, not released

Tanacetum vulgare **Tansy**

A tall perennial, commonly seen by roadsides, with deeply-cut dark-green leaves and flattish clusters of button-like flower-heads. It was formerly used as an insecticide, rubbed over meat to keep flies away or strewn on floors. Medicinally, it was taken to destroy roundworms. It is still widely grown both for ornament and as a pot-herb. *Status:* native, naturalized in Ireland; most of area, most common in south. *Similar species:* Feverfew has broader lobes to the leaves and less dense clusters of flower-heads with white outer florets. It is sometimes taken for relief from migraines.

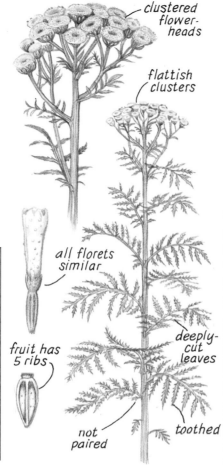

clustered flower-heads

flattish clusters

all florets similar

deeply-cut leaves

fruit has 5 ribs

not paired

toothed

Feverfew (*T. parthenium*)

daisy-like

inner floret

outer floret

shallowly cut

	TANSY		Type 1	inner ♀, 4–5mm, tubular
Type	perennial, strong-smelling		**Type 2**	outer florets ♀, 3.5–4mm, tubular or short flat part
Height	30–150cm		**Size**	heads 7–12mm
Habitat	hedge-banks, waste ground		**Colour**	deep yellow
Flowering	July–September		**Stalk**	absent; short under heads
			Sepals	inconspicuous rim
	STEMS AND LEAVES		**Petals**	5, joined, tubular, lobes equal or slightly unequal
Stem	upright, often reddish		**Stamens**	5, joined into tube
Root	creeping stock		**Stigma**	1, 2-lobed; style long
Hairs	almost absent		**Ovary**	1, below petals, 1-celled
Stipules	absent			
Leaves	spirally on stem, 150–250mm, cut 1–2 times into paired, narrow, toothed lobes			**FRUIT**
			Type	nut-like, 5-ribbed, blunt-tipped, without parachute
Leaf-stalk	short or absent		**Size**	1.5–1.8mm
			Seeds	1, not released
	FLOWERS			
Position	flattish clusters of daisy-like heads, the florets enclosed by bracts			
Bracts	papery-edged around head; none between florets			

Leucanthemum vulgare **Oxeye Daisy**

One of the most familiar of all Summer flowers, the large white and yellow Daisies adorning mile after mile of roadside, railway embankment and meadows. The long, unbranched stems make it a favourite ingredient in a bunch of wild flowers. It is related to the larger Shasta Daisy, originally from the Pyrenees and widely cultivated in gardens. *Status:* native; almost throughout area, very common in south. *Similar species:* Corn Marigold has branched stems and more deeply lobed leaves, but is most easily distinguished by the bright yellow outer florets. The fruits of the outer florets are flattened, with wing-like sides.

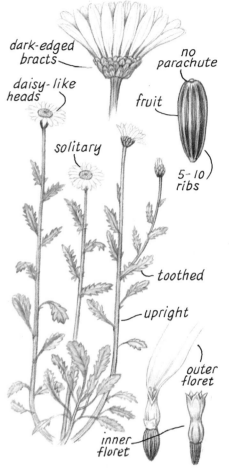

dark-edged bracts

no parachute

daisy-like heads

fruit

solitary

5–10 ribs

toothed

upright

outer floret

inner floret

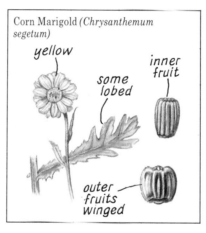

Corn Marigold (*Chrysanthemum segetum*)

yellow

some lobed

inner fruit

outer fruits winged

	OXEYE DAISY		**Bracts**	dark, papery-edged around head; none between florets
Type	perennial		**Type 1**	inner ♀, 4–5mm, tubular
Height	20–100cm		**Type 2**	outer florets ♀, 10–20mm, strap-shaped
Habitat	grassland; most soils		**Size**	heads 25–50mm
Flowering	June–August		**Colour**	white and yellow
			Stalk	absent; long under heads
	STEMS AND LEAVES		**Sepals**	absent or scale-like
Stem	upright, rarely branched		**Petals**	5, joined, tubular, lobes equal or very unequal
Root	woody stock		**Stamens**	5, joined into tube
Hairs	sparse or almost absent		**Stigma**	1, 2-lobed; style long
Stipules	absent		**Ovary**	1, below petals, 1-celled
Leaves	spirally arranged on stem, 15–120mm, lower rounded or oval, upper oblong, toothed or lobed, broad-based			
				FRUIT
Leaf-stalk	long on non-flowering stems, absent above		**Type**	nut-like, cylindrical or slightly flattened, with 5–10 ribs, without parachute
			Size	2–3mm
	FLOWERS		**Seeds**	1, not released
Position	solitary, daisy-like heads, florets enclosed by bracts			

Colt's-foot *Tussilago farfara*

One of the earliest Spring flowers with clumps of scaly, purplish stems, each ending in a yellow flower-head. It rivals bulbous plants for early flowering because it has thick underground stems that store food. Large leaves arise direct from the ground after the flowers, each initially covered with thick, felt-like hairs and opening to make a dense, shady canopy beneath which few other plants survive. *Status:* native; very common, most of area. *Similar species:* Butterbur has thick flowering stems with many pink flower-heads and even larger, Rhubarb-like leaves. Winter Heliotrope has few, larger, vanilla-scented flower-heads.

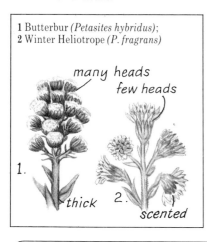

1 Butterbur *(Petasites hybridus)*;
2 Winter Heliotrope *(P. fragrans)*

many heads
few heads
1.
thick   2.   scented

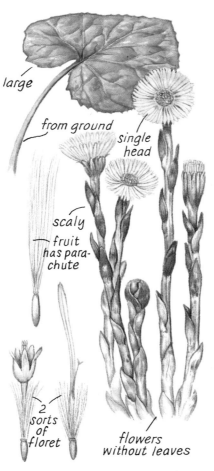

large
from ground
single head
scaly
fruit has para-chute
2 sorts of floret
flowers without leaves

	COLT'S-FOOT		Bracts	mostly 1 row around head, blunt; none between florets
Type	perennial		**Type 1**	few inner ♂, 7–8mm, tubular
Height	5–15cm		**Type 2**	outer florets ♀, up to 300, 6–15mm, flattened, narrow
Habitat	cultivated or waste ground, shingle; often clay soils		**Size**	heads 15–35mm
Flowering	March–April		**Colour**	bright yellow
			Stalk	absent; short under head
	STEMS AND LEAVES		**Sepals**	a ring of hairs
Stem	flowering stem upright, scaly, leafless, purplish		**Petals**	5, joined, tubular, lobes equal or very unequal
Root	creeping, underground stem		**Stamens**	5, joined into tube
Hairs	stems woolly; felt-like hairs mainly under leaves		**Stigma**	1, 2-lobed; style long
Stipules	absent		**Ovary**	1, below petals, 1-celled
Leaves	from ground after flowers, 100–300mm, rounded or 5–12 angles, base heart-shaped			**FRUIT**
Leaf-stalk	about equals blade, grooved		**Type**	nut-like, cylindrical, with parachute of long hairs
	FLOWERS		**Size**	5–10mm
Position	solitary daisy-like head of florets enclosed by bracts		**Seeds**	1, not released

Lesser Burdock *Arctium minus*

A rather coarse-textured plant with dull, purplish flowers, although it is familiar to children for the flowering and fruiting heads. These cling with equal efficiency to woolly clothing or to the fur of animals, the latter being the plant's normal mode of dispersal. *Status:* native; common, throughout area. *Similar species:* two very similar plants have slightly larger flower-heads, the florets of which are not longer than the bracts. *A. pubens* has stalked heads with pale bracts, and *A. nemorosum* has more globular, darker, almost stalkless heads. Greater Burdock has larger, long-stalked heads but does not have hollow leaf-stalks.

florets all similar
florets longer than bracts
hooked bracts
short stalk
bristle

1 Greater Burdock *(A. lappa)*;
2 Lesser Burdock *(A. pubens)*;
3 Lesser Burdock *(A. nemorosum)*

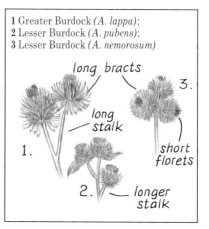

long bracts
long stalk
3.
short florets
1.
2.   longer stalk
hollow stalk
large lob le

	LESSER BURDOCK		Bracts	hooked, many under head, 10–13mm, shorter than florets; thin scales between florets
Type	biennial		**Type**	florets ⚥, 12–15mm, tubular
Height	60–130cm		**Size**	heads 15–18mm
Habitat	waste ground, hedges, woods		**Colour**	reddish purple
Flowering	July–September		**Stalk**	absent; short or absent under heads
			Sepals	bristle-like
	STEMS AND LEAVES		**Petals**	5, joined, lobes equal
Stem	upright, grooved, often reddish, many-branched		**Stamens**	5, joined into tube
Root	stout tap-root		**Stigma**	1, 2-lobed; style long
Hairs	on stems and under leaves		**Ovary**	1, below petals, 1-celled
Stipules	absent			
Leaves	spirally on stem, 30–400mm, most oval, pointed, often toothed, base heart-shaped			**FRUIT**
Leaf-stalk	lower long, hollow, upper short		**Type**	nut-like, oblong, mottled, short bristles at tip
	FLOWERS		**Size**	5–7mm
Position	clusters of almost globular, thistle-like heads of florets enclosed by bracts		**Seeds**	1, not released

Senecio jacobaea Common Ragwort

This relative of the Daisy causes problems in pasture because it is toxic to livestock. One of the few creatures to tolerate the poison is the Cinnabar moth, whose black and yellow caterpillars take over the plant's chemical defence, making them distasteful to birds. *Status:* native; most of area, often very common. *Similar species:* Hoary Ragwort has hairier leaves with more pointed lobes. Two plants with wider-branched clusters of flowers are Oxford Ragwort, an introduced species on waste ground, which has black-tipped bracts, and Marsh Ragwort, in wet places and with green bracts.

1 Oxford Ragwort (*S. squalidus*);
2 Marsh Ragwort (*S. aquaticus*);
3 Hoary Ragwort (*S. erucifolius*)

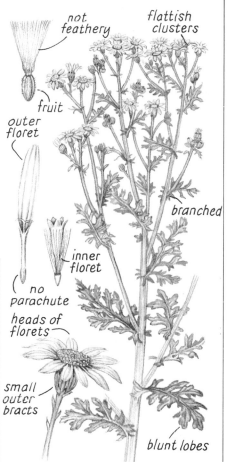

Senecio vulgaris Groundsel

One of the most familiar of garden weeds, multiplying rapidly by fruits which form even in the absence of pollinating insects and then survive many years in the soil. Silky parachutes carry tiny fruits aloft to colonize any piece of cleared ground. Some plants have a few strap-shaped florets at the edges of the flower-heads. *Status:* native; very common, throughout region, often a problematic weed. *Similar species:* Sticky Groundsel has sticky, strong-smelling foliage and fruit with hairless ribs. Heath Groundsel has outer bracts about half as long as the inner, and the fruit has stiffly hairy ribs.

1 Sticky Groundsel (*S. viscosus*);
2 Heath Groundsel (*S. sylvaticus*)

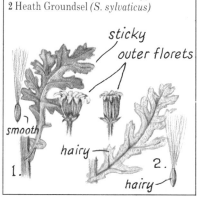

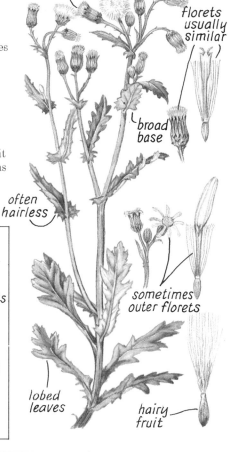

COMMON RAGWORT			
Type	biennial or perennial	**Bracts**	oblong, pointed around head; none between florets
Height	30–150cm	**Type 1**	inner ♂, 5–6mm, tubular
Habitat	grassy places, waste ground, dunes; most soils	**Type 2**	outer florets ♀, 12–15, 6–11mm, strap-shaped
Flowering	June–October	**Size**	heads 15–25mm
		Colour	deep yellow
STEMS AND LEAVES		**Stalk**	absent; short under heads
Stem	upright, branched above	**Sepals**	a ring of hairs
Root	short, upright stock	**Petals**	5, joined, tubular, lobes equal or very unequal
Hairs	none or sparse under leaves	**Stamens**	5, joined into tube
Stipules	absent	**Stigma**	1, 2-lobed; style long
Leaves	basal or spirally around stem, 25–200mm, cut into mostly blunt, toothed lobes, dark green	**Ovary**	1, below petals, 1-celled
Leaf-stalk	short or absent	**FRUIT**	
		Type	nut-like, 8-ribbed, inner with parachute of hairs
FLOWERS		**Size**	1.5–2mm
Position	dense, flat-topped clusters of daisy-like heads with florets enclosed by bracts	**Seeds**	1, not released

GROUNDSEL			
Type	annual	**Bracts**	black-tipped around head; none between florets
Height	8–45cm	**Type 1**	florets usually ♂, 5–7mm, tubular
Habitat	cultivated and waste ground	**Type 2**	outer florets sometimes present, ♀, up to 12, 8–10mm, strap-shaped
Flowering	January–December		
		Size	heads 8–10mm, rarely 14mm
STEMS AND LEAVES		**Colour**	yellow
Stem	usually upright, rather succulent, few branches	**Stalk**	absent; short under heads
Root	fibrous	**Sepals**	a ring of hairs
Hairs	absent or slightly cottony	**Petals**	5, tubular, lobes usually equal
Stipules	absent	**Stamens**	5, joined, tube-like
Leaves	spirally on stem, oblong, irregular, toothed lobes, blunt; upper broad-based	**Stigma**	1, 2-lobed; style long
Leaf-stalk	absent or short	**Ovary**	1, below petals, 1-celled
		FRUIT	
FLOWERS		**Type**	dry, cylindrical, with hairy ribs, parachute of hairs
Position	cylindrical heads of florets, enclosed by bracts	**Size**	1.5–2mm
		Seeds	1, not released

Welted Thistle *Carduus acanthoides*

One of the small-flowered Thistles, this one is found most commonly in damp meadows, shady wood-margins and hedgerows. The flower-heads are popular with butterflies. *Status:* native; most common in south of area, absent from much of north. *Similar species:* Slender Thistle has long flower-heads with broader bracts, the whole head falling when the fruits ripen. Two other Thistles have fruits with feathery hairs to the parachute. Marsh Thistle has spiny-winged stems and rather narrow, sharply pointed leaves. Creeping Thistle is a problematic weed, with long, creeping, underground stems.

1 Slender Thistle (*C. tenuiflorus*);
2 Marsh Thistle (*Cirsium palustre*);
3 Creeping Thistle (*C. arvense*)

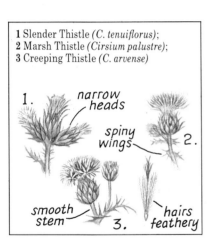

narrow heads
spiny wings
1.
2.
smooth stem
3.
hairs feathery

hairs not feathery
single floret
globular heads
clustered heads
spiny wings
spiny

WELTED THISTLE		Bracts	many around head, narrow, spine-tipped; bristle-like between florets
Type	biennial	Type	florets ♂, 16–18mm, tubular
Height	30–150cm	Size	heads 20–25mm
Habitat	grassland, hedges, waste ground; damp soils	Colour	reddish purple or white
Flowering	June–August	Stalk	absent; absent or short under heads
STEMS AND LEAVES		Sepals	a ring of hairs
Stem	upright, branched, with wavy, spine-tipped wings	Petals	5, joined, tubular, lobes slightly unequal
Root	slender tap-root	Stamens	5, joined into tube
Hairs	sparse, on stems and bracts	Stigma	1, 2-lobed; style long
Stipules	absent	Ovary	1, below petals, 1-celled
Leaves	basal or spirally on stem, lobed, wavy, spiny; blade of upper joins stem-wings	**FRUIT**	
Leaf-stalk	short below, upper absent	Type	nut-like, oblong, grooved, parachute of hairs 11–13mm
FLOWERS		Size	3–4mm
Position	almost globular heads of florets enclosed by bracts, mostly in small clusters	Seeds	1, not released

Spear Thistle *Cirsium vulgare*

A handsome plant with large, reddish-purple flower-heads above sharply spiny leaves. This is probably the plant adopted as a national emblem by Scottish kings. Thistle-down is light because the parachute usually detaches from the heavy nut-like base and floats away without effecting dispersal. *Status:* native; common, throughout area. *Similar species:* two other species have long, smooth stems below the flower-heads and softly prickly leaves with whitish hairs beneath. Melancholy Thistle has broad, rather blunt bracts; Meadow Thistle has smaller heads with spiny outer bracts. Musk Thistle has nodding flower-heads.

1 Melancholy Thistle (*C. helenioides*); 2 Meadow Thistle (*C. dissectum*); 3 Musk Thistle (*Carduus nutans*)

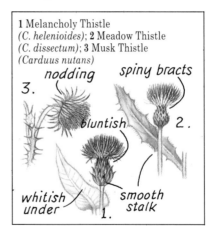

3.
nodding
spiny bracts
bluntish
2.
whitish under
smooth stalk
1.

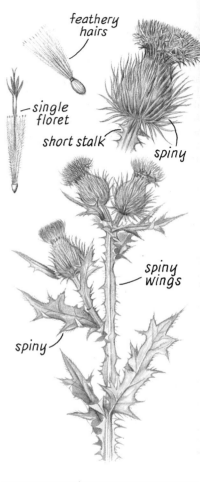

feathery hairs
single floret
short stalk
spiny
spiny wings
spiny

SPEAR THISTLE		Bracts	many around head, spiny, slightly hairy; bristle-like between florets
Type	biennial	Type	florets ♂ or ♀, 26–36mm
Height	30–150cm, rarely 300cm	Size	heads 30–50mm
Habitat	grassland, hedges, waste ground	Colour	reddish purple
Flowering	July–October	Stalk	absent; short under heads
STEMS AND LEAVES		Sepals	a ring of hairs
Stem	upright, with spiny wings	Petals	5, joined, tubular, lobes slightly unequal
Root	long tap-root	Stamens	5, joined into tube
Hairs	sparse under leaves, prickly hairs above	Stigma	1, 2-lobed; style long
Stipules	absent	Ovary	1, below petals, 1-celled
Leaves	basal or spirally on stem, 150–300mm, lobed, wavy, strongly spiny, end lobe spear-shaped; blade of upper joins stem-wings	**FRUIT**	
Leaf-stalk	lower short; upper absent	Type	nut-like, oblong, parachute of hairs 20–30mm, feathery
FLOWERS		Size	3.5–5mm
Position	upright heads of florets surrounded by bracts	Seeds	1, not released

Carlina vulgaris Carline Thistle

An unusual Thistle, the flower-heads have a ring of long, yellowish bracts, resembling the strap-shaped outer florets of Daisies. A more or less stemless species with larger flower-heads is grown for use in dried flower displays. *Status:* native; most of area, sometimes common. *Similar species:* another small Thistle is the native perennial Dwarf Thistle. This has a rosette of leaves and one to three reddish-purple flower-heads on short stems. The plant is familiar to people who take picnics in the country as the tufts of spiny leaves that abound in closely-grazed turf.

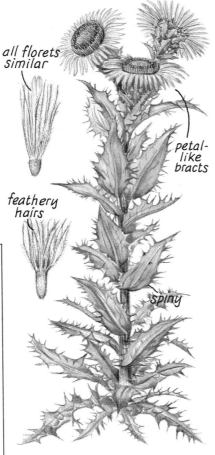

all florets similar

petal-like bracts

feathery hairs

spiny

Dwarf Thistle (*Cirsium acaule*)

short bracts

on ground

no stem

Onopordum acanthium Cotton Thistle

A tall Thistle that has broadly winged stems and leaves covered with silvery-white hairs, it is biennial, spending the first Winter as a large rosette of leaves and producing purple flowers in the second year. The fruiting heads are eagerly sought by flocks of Goldfinches, which tear out the down to get at the nut-like seeds at the base. *Status:* native in south-east, naturalized elsewhere; absent from much of north. *Similar species:* the leaves of Woolly Thistle are only woolly beneath, the upper surface being dark green. The stem lacks wings and the parachute of the fruits has feathery hairs.

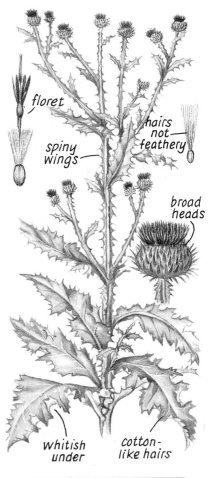

floret

spiny wings

hairs not feathery

broad heads

whitish under

cotton-like hairs

Woolly Thistle (*Cirsium eriophorum*)

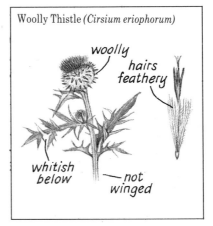

woolly

hairs feathery

whitish below

not winged

CARLINE THISTLE
Type	biennial
Height	10–30cm, rarely 60cm
Habitat	grassland; lime-rich soils
Flowering	July–October

STEMS AND LEAVES
Stem	upright, branched, purplish
Root	tap-root
Hairs	sparse, cotton-like
Stipules	absent
Leaves	basal or spirally arranged on stem, 70–130mm, oblong or spear-shaped, pointed, edge wavy, spiny, slightly lobed; upper broad-based
Leaf stalk	absent

FLOWERS
Position	2–5 heads of florets enclosed by bracts

Bracts	many around head, outer spiny, inner long, narrow, yellowish; bristle-like between florets
Type	florets ♂, 10–12mm, tubular
Size	heads 20–40mm
Colour	reddish purple
Stalk	absent; short under heads
Sepals	ring of branched hairs
Petals	5, joined, tubular, lobes equal
Stamens	5, joined into tube
Stigma	1, 2-lobed; style long
Ovary	1, below petals, 1-celled

FRUIT
Type	nut-like, cylindrical, with reddish hairs, parachute of feathery hairs 7–8mm
Size	2–4mm
Seeds	1, not released

COTTON THISTLE
Type	biennial
Height	45–300cm
Habitat	roadsides, hedges, waste ground
Flowering	July–September

STEMS AND LEAVES
Stem	upright, with spiny wings
Root	stout tap-root
Hairs	dense, white, cotton-like
Stipules	absent
Leaves	basal or spirally on stem, to 550mm, elliptical, with wavy lobes, spiny; blade of upper joins stem-wings
Leaf-stalk	lower short, upper absent

FLOWERS
Position	almost globular heads of florets surrounded by bracts

Bracts	many around head, narrow, spiny; none between florets
Type	florets ♂, 14–25mm, tubular
Size	heads 30–50mm
Colour	pale purple, rarely white
Stalk	absent; sometimes long under heads
Sepals	a ring of hairs
Petals	5, joined, tubular, lobes slightly unequal
Stamens	5, joined into tube
Stigma	1, 2-lobed; style long
Ovary	1, below petals, 1-celled

FRUIT
Type	nut-like, oblong, 4-angled, wrinkled, parachute of toothed hairs, 7–9mm
Size	4–5mm
Seeds	1, not released

Saw-wort *Serratula tinctoria*

A wiry plant with small thistle-like flower-heads in loose, branched clusters above deep-lobed and sharp-toothed leaves. Saw-wort was used as a wound-herb and for treating ruptures. Its leaves were the source of a strong, greenish-yellow dye. The common name derives from the saw-like teeth on the edges of the leaves. *Status:* native; much of area except for north. *Similar species:* Alpine Saw-wort has toothed or unlobed leaves with woolly hairs beneath. Its small clusters of flower-heads are scented rather like Sweet Violet or vanilla. A mountain plant in the south, it is found at low altitudes in the north.

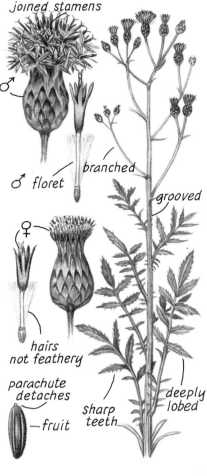

joined stamens

♂

♂ *floret*

branched

grooved

♀

hairs not feathery

parachute detaches

sharp teeth

deeply lobed

fruit

Alpine Saw-wort (*Saussurea alpina*)

small cluster

feathery hairs

white under

not lobed

	SAW-WORT		Bracts	many around head, pointed, purple-tipped; scales between florets
Type	perennial			
Height	30–90cm		Type 1	♂ florets, 10–12mm, tubular
Habitat	wood edges, grassland; damp, often lime-rich soil		Type 2	♀ florets, 7–10mm, tubular
			Size	heads 15–20mm
Flowering	July–September		Colour	purple, rarely white
			Stalk	absent; often long under heads
	STEMS AND LEAVES		Sepals	a ring of hairs
Stem	upright, slender, grooved		Petals	5, joined, lobes equal
Root	short, stout stock		Stamens	5, joined into tube
Hairs	absent		Stigma	1, 2-lobed; style long
Stipules	absent		Ovary	1, below petals, 1-celled
Leaves	spirally arranged, 120–250mm, oval or spear-shaped, lobed, with sharp, bristle-tipped teeth			
				FRUIT
Leaf-stalk	lower short, upper absent		Type	nut-like, oblong, smooth, parachute soon detached
			Size	5–6mm
	FLOWERS		Seeds	1, not released
Position	thistle-like heads of florets enclosed by bracts; ♂ and ♀ on separate plants			

Greater Knapweed *Centaurea scabiosa*

An attractive flower of Summer meadows, with large reddish-purple flowers that are thistle-like in construction but often confused with species of Scabious. Around the base of each flower-head are bracts which have a papery, blackish, horseshoe-shaped margin divided into feathery lobes. The flowers are much visited by butterflies. *Status:* native; most of area, more common in south. *Similar species:* Common Knapweed has a similar but smaller flower-head with narrower bracts tipped by a feathery, blackish lobe. The leaves are mostly undivided. Cornflower, a cornfield species that has become rare, has bright blue flowers and is grown in gardens.

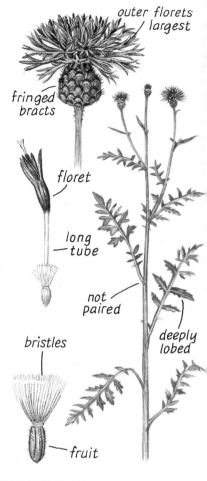

outer florets largest

fringed bracts

floret

long tube

not paired

bristles

deeply lobed

fruit

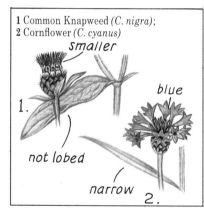

1 Common Knapweed (*C. nigra*);
2 Cornflower (*C. cyanus*)

smaller

not lobed

1.

blue

narrow

2.

	GREATER KNAPWEED		Bracts	broad around head, each with feathery, blackish tip; bristle-like between florets
Type	perennial			
Height	30–150cm, rarely 200cm		Type	florets ♀, 12–23mm, tubular, outer often larger, sterile
Habitat	grassland, hedges, cliffs; dry, often lime-rich soils			
			Size	heads 30–50mm
Flowering	July–September		Colour	reddish purple
			Stalk	absent; long under heads
	STEMS AND LEAVES		Sepals	a ring of hairs
Stem	upright, branched above		Petals	5, joined, tubular, lobes slightly unequal
Root	stout, woody stock			
Hairs	short, rough on leaves		Stamens	5, joined into tube
Stipules	absent		Stigma	1, 2-lobed; style long
Leaves	basal or spirally on stem, 50–250mm, mostly divided into paired lobes, toothed		Ovary	1, below petals, 1-celled
				FRUIT
Leaf-stalk	lower shorter than blade, upper absent		Type	nut-like, oblong, slightly flattened, parachute 4–5mm
			Size	4–5mm
	FLOWERS		Seeds	1, not released
Position	thistle-like heads of florets enclosed by bracts			

Cichorium intybus **Chicory**

The bright blue flowers of Chicory are a beautiful sight along roadsides in late Summer. Opening early in the day, the flowers close soon after midday. Chicory has been cultivated for medicinal purposes, as a vegetable or as a coffee substitute, the roots being dried, roasted and ground. *Status:* native or often introduced; most of area, rare in extreme north and Ireland. *Similar species:* two Dandelion-relatives have stalked, deep-blue flower-heads. Alpine Blue-sow-thistle, an uncommon mountain plant, has reddish hairs above; Blue Lettuce, found only in the south-east of the area, is hairless.

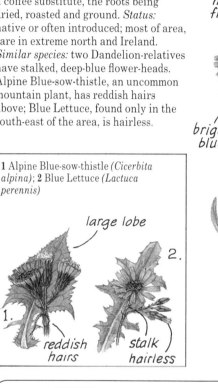

1 Alpine Blue-sow-thistle (*Cicerbita alpina*); 2 Blue Lettuce (*Lactuca perennis*)

large lobe

1. reddish hairs / stalk hairless / 2.

no parachute
all long florets
fruit
heads of florets
2 sorts of bract
bright blue
nearly stalkless head
mostly lobed
hairy

CHICORY		FLOWERS	
Type	perennial	Position	dandelion-like heads of florets enclosed by bracts
Height	30–120cm		
Habitat	roadsides, grassland, waste ground; often lime-rich soil	Bracts	2 rows under head, inner long; none between florets
Flowering	July October	Type	florets ♂♀, 12–18mm
STEMS AND LEAVES		Size	heads 25–40mm
Stem	upright, grooved, sap milky	Colour	bright blue
Root	long, stout tap-root	Stalk	absent; very short under heads
Hairs	stiff on stems, gland-tipped among flowers	Sepals	a scaly rim
		Petals	5, joined, flattened above, 5-toothed
Stipules	absent	Stamens	5, joined into tube
Leaves	basal or spirally on stem, 70–300mm, spear-shaped, most lobed or toothed, upper clasp stem	Stigma	1, 2-lobed; style long
		Ovary	1, below petals, 1-celled
Leaf-stalk	lower short, upper absent	**FRUIT**	
		Type	nut-like, almost egg-shaped, mottled, without parachute
		Size	2–3mm
		Seeds	1, not released

Tragopogon pratensis **Goat's-beard**

A familiar roadside plant, not for the pale yellow flowers, but for the fruiting heads which look like enormous dandelion-clocks. The greyish parachutes have feathery bristles, the fine hairs distinctly interwoven. The common name derives from these conspicuous fruits. Unlike the Dandelion, Goat's-beard has narrow, almost grass-like leaves, without lobes. Its long tap-roots were formerly used as a vegetable. *Status:* native; most of area, often common. *Similar species:* Viper's-grass has broader basal leaves and the oval bracts are much shorter than the florets.

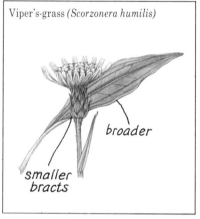

Viper's-grass (*Scorzonera humilis*)

broader
smaller bracts

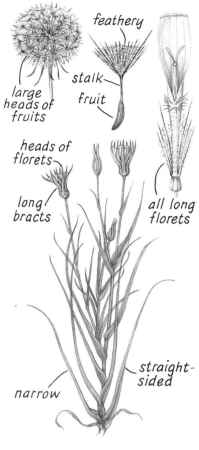

feathery
large heads of fruits
stalk
fruit
heads of florets
long bracts
all long florets
narrow
straight-sided

GOAT'S-BEARD		Bracts	1 row around head, 25–30mm, thin; none between florets
Type	annual to perennial		
Height	30–70cm	Type	florets ♂♀, 20–25mm
Habitat	grassland, roadsides, waste ground, dunes; dry soils	Size	heads 15–22mm
		Colour	yellow
Flowering	June–July	Stalk	absent; long under heads
STEMS AND LEAVES		Sepals	a ring of hairs
Stem	upright, scarcely branched; sap milky	Petals	5, joined, flattened above, 5-toothed
Root	long tap-root	Stamens	5, joined into tube
Hairs	more or less absent	Stigma	1, 2-lobed; style long
Stipules	absent	Ovary	1, below petals, 1-celled
Leaves	basal or spirally arranged on stem, narrow, veins whitish, long-pointed, edge unbroken, base sheaths stem	**FRUIT**	
		Type	nut-like, ribbed, long, thin tip, parachute 12–23mm, hairs feathery, interwoven
Leaf-stalk	absent	Size	10–22mm
FLOWERS		Seeds	1, not released
Position	solitary, dandelion-like head of florets surrounded by bracts		

Bristly Oxtongue *Picris echioides*

A relative of the Dandelion with prickly
leaves and broad, heart-shaped outer
bracts to the flower-heads. The prickly
hairs have a swollen, whitish base and a
tip with three microscopic hooks, like a
miniature grappling-iron. *Status:*
introduced; scattered through area,
most common in south. *Similar species:*
Hawkweed Oxtongue has narrow bracts
and lacks the stalk-like part of the fruit
beneath the parachute. Two further
species have fruits with straight bristles
in the parachute. Smooth Hawk's-beard
is almost hairless and lacks the stalk-
like part to the fruit, although it is
present in the fine-haired Beaked
Hawk's-beard.

1 Hawkweed Oxtongue
(*P. hieracioides*); 2 Smooth Hawk's-
beard (*Crepis capillaris*); 3 Beaked
Hawk's-beard (*C. vesicaria* subsp.
haenseleri)

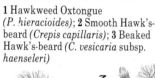
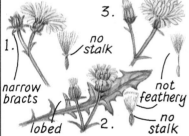

narrow bracts • no stalk • 3. • lobed • 2. • not feathery • no stalk

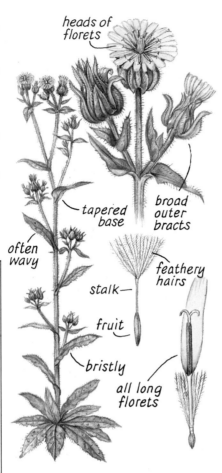

heads of florets • tapered base • broad outer bracts • often wavy • stalk • feathery hairs • fruit • bristly • all long florets

	BRISTLY OXTONGUE		Bracts	3–5 heart-shaped around head, inner longer; none between florets
Type	annual or biennial		**Type**	florets ☿, 8–12mm, flattened
Height	30–90cm		**Size**	heads 20–25mm
Habitat	roadsides, hedges, waste ground; often lime-rich soils		**Colour**	yellow or purple beneath
Flowering	June–October		**Stalk**	absent; short under heads
			Sepals	a ring of hairs
	STEMS AND LEAVES		**Petals**	5, joined, flattened above, 5-toothed
Stem	stout, upright; sap milky		**Stamens**	5, joined into tube
Root	tap-root		**Stigma**	1, 2-lobed; style long
Hairs	broad-based, stiff		**Ovary**	1, below petals, 1-celled
Stipules	absent			
Leaves	basal or spirally on stem, 35–250mm, spear-shaped or oblong, toothed or wavy			**FRUIT**
Leaf-stalk	lower short, upper absent		**Type**	nut-like, ribbed, with stalk-like tip, parachute of hairs 4–6mm, feathery
	FLOWERS		**Size**	5–7mm
Position	loosely clustered dandelion-like heads of florets surrounded by bracts		**Seeds**	1, not released

Prickly Sow-thistle *Sonchus asper*

An abundant plant on waste land
around towns or along roadsides, it has
fleshy, hollow stems bearing weakly
spiny leaves and dandelion-like flowers.
At each leaf-base are two ear-like lobes,
the shape being used to distinguish the
species. Rather crisp leaves of Sow-
thistles are edible, like the related
Dandelion and Lettuce, or were fed to
livestock. *Status:* native; common,
throughout area. *Similar species:*
Smooth Sow-thistle has pointed lobes at
the leaf-base and wrinkled fruits.
Perennial Sow-thistle has rounded lobes
at the leaf-base and flower-heads about
twice as large, the bracts usually
covered with gland-tipped hairs.

1 Smooth Sow-thistle (*S. oleraceus*);
2 Perennial Sow-thistle (*S. arvensis*)

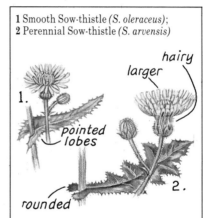

1. • pointed lobes • rounded • larger • hairy • 2. • rounded lobes

hairless • all long florets • heads of florets • hairs not feathery • weak spines • stalkle... • flesh... • uprig... holl...

	PRICKLY SOW-THISTLE			FLOWERS
Type	annual, some overwintering		**Position**	dandelion-like heads of florets enclosed by bracts
Height	2–150cm, rarely 200cm		**Bracts**	long, smooth around head; none between florets
Habitat	cultivated and waste ground		**Type**	florets ☿, 10–15mm, flattened
Flowering	June–August		**Size**	heads 20–25mm
			Colour	yellow, some purple beneath
	STEMS AND LEAVES		**Stalk**	absent; longish under heads
Stem	stout, upright, 5-angled, hollow; sap milky		**Sepals**	a ring of hairs
Root	slender tap-root		**Petals**	5, joined, flattened above, 5-toothed
Hairs	absent		**Stamens**	5, joined into tube
Stipules	absent		**Stigma**	1, 2-lobed; style long
Leaves	basal or spirally around stem, often lobed, wavy, weakly spiny, base of upper leaves with ear-like lobes clasping stem		**Ovary**	1, below petals, 1-celled
Leaf-stalk	mostly absent			**FRUIT**
			Type	nut-like, flattened, smooth ribs, parachute 6–9mm
			Size	2–3mm
			Seeds	1, not released

Hypochaeris radicata Cat's-ear

One of the most common of many yellow-flowered, dandelion-like plants, brightening the Summer meadow and roadside alike with its large, golden flower-heads. Often a problem on lawns, it is one of the best plants to try and establish if a lawn is being turned deliberately into an informal wild-flower meadow. The common name refers to small bracts on the stems, which in shape resemble cat's ears. *Status:* native; most of area except north-east. *Similar species:* Smooth Cat's-ear is an annual that has almost hairless leaves and flower-heads which only open in sunny weather. The florets are little longer than the bracts.

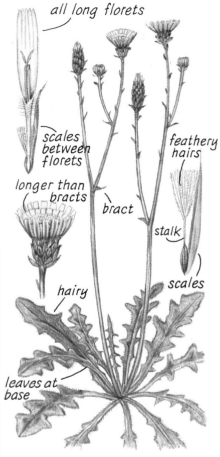

all long florets

scales between florets

longer than bracts

bract

feathery hairs

stalk

scales

hairy

leaves at base

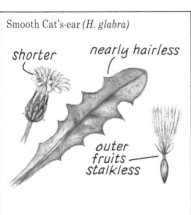

Smooth Cat's-ear (*H. glabra*)

shorter

nearly hairless

outer fruits stalkless

CAT'S-EAR		Bracts	many around head, spear-shaped, bristly; long scales between florets
Type	perennial		
Height	20–60cm, rarely 100cm	Type	florets ♀, 12–18mm, flattened
Habitat	grassland, roadsides, dunes	Size	heads 25–40mm
Flowering	June–September	Colour	bright yellow, outer florets greenish beneath
		Stalk	absent; under heads
STEMS AND LEAVES		Sepals	a ring of hairs
Stem	upright, usually no leaves, few branches; sap milky	Petals	5, joined, flattened above, 5-toothed
Root	tap-root	Stamens	5, joined into tube
Hairs	rather stiff, on leaves	Stigma	1, 2-lobed; style long
Stipules	absent	Ovary	1, below petals, 1-celled
Leaves	basal rosette, 70–250mm, oblong or spear-shaped with wavy lobes or teeth		
		FRUIT	
Leaf-stalk	shorter than blade	Type	nut-like, ribbed, rough, top stalk-like, parachute of feathery hairs 9–12mm
FLOWERS			
Position	few dandelion-like heads of florets enclosed by bracts	Size	4–8mm
		Seeds	1, not released

Taraxacum officinale Common Dandelion

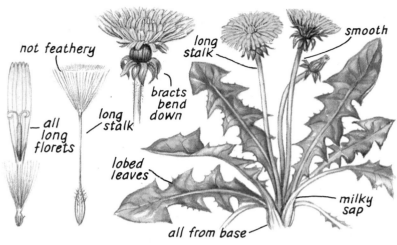

not feathery

all long florets

long stalk

long stalk

bracts bend down

lobed leaves

smooth

milky sap

all from base

A weed, flavouring for a wine, food for pets or a salad vegetable; the lobed leaves and hollow-stalked flowers of Dandelions are familiar to most people. But their biology is complex and more than a thousand species have been described from Europe alone. *Status:* native; throughout area, very common. *Similar species:* Narrow-leaved Marsh-dandelion has upright pale-edged bracts and narrow sparsely-lobed leaves. Two related plants have small bracts on the stems and feathery hairs making up the parachute. Autumn Hawkbit is nearly hairless, often with branched stems, and Rough Hawkbit is hairy.

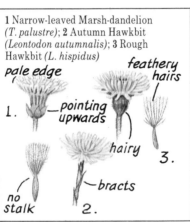

1 Narrow-leaved Marsh-dandelion (*T. palustre*); 2 Autumn Hawkbit (*Leontodon autumnalis*); 3 Rough Hawkbit (*L. hispidus*)

pale edge

feathery hairs

1.

pointing upwards

hairy

3.

no stalk

bracts

2.

COMMON DANDELION		Bracts	2 rows around head, inner upright, outer curved back; none between florets
Type	perennial		
Height	5–40cm	Type	florets ♀, 15–20mm, flattened
Habitat	grassland, roadsides, lawns, waste ground	Size	heads 30–60mm
Flowering	March–October	Colour	yellow, outer brownish under
		Stalk	absent; long under heads
STEMS AND LEAVES		Sepals	a ring of hairs
Stem	upright, unbranched, hollow, leafless; sap milky	Petals	5, joined, flattened above, 5-toothed
Root	tap-root	Stamens	5, joined into tube
Hairs	near top of flower-stalks	Stigma	1, 2-lobed; style long
Stipules	absent	Ovary	1, below petals, 1-celled
Leaves	basal, 50–400mm, oblong or spear-shaped, variably lobed and toothed		
		FRUIT	
Leaf-stalk	short, edges often wing-like	Type	dry, cylindrical, rough above, top stalk-like, parachute of hairs 5–6mm
FLOWERS			
Position	head of florets enclosed by bracts, solitary	Size	3.5–4mm
		Seeds	1, not released

Nipplewort *Lapsana communis*

One of the dandelion relatives with small flowers, common by roadsides or as a garden weed. Lemon-yellow flowers open only in bright weather. Like the related Lettuce, the leaves are edible. The common name derives from a vague similarity in the shape of the buds and milky sap. *Status:* native; common, throughout area. *Similar species:* two other small-flowered species have fruits with a parachute. Great Lettuce has prickly stem-leaves with rounded ear-like lobes at the base, and fruits with a stalk beneath the parachute. Wall Lettuce has smaller flower-heads, usually with five florets, and fruits without a stalk beneath the parachute.

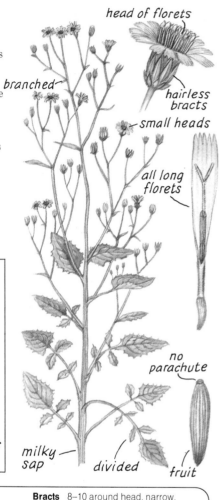

head of florets

branched

hairless bracts

small heads

all long florets

no parachute

milky sap

divided

fruit

1 Great Lettuce *(Lactuca virosa)*;
2 Wall Lettuce *(Mycelis muralis)*

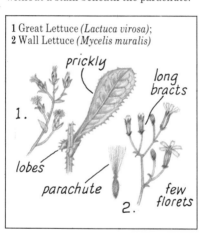

prickly

long bracts

1.

lobes

parachute

few florets

2.

	NIPPLEWORT		Bracts	8–10 around head, narrow, upright; none between florets
Type	annual		Type	florets ☿, 8–15, 7–11mm, all strap-shaped
Height	20–125cm			
Habitat	woods, hedges, roadsides, waste ground		Size	heads 15–20mm
			Colour	pale yellow
Flowering	July–September		Stalk	absent; slender under heads
	STEMS AND LEAVES		Sepals	a ring of hairs
Stem	upright, leafy, widely branched above; sap milky		Petals	5, joined, flattened above, 5-toothed
Root	tap-root		Stamens	5, joined into tube
Hairs	absent except at base		Stigma	1, 2-lobed; style long
Stipules	absent		Ovary	1, below petals, 1-celled
Leaves	basal or spirally arranged on stem, 10–150mm, with wavy teeth, lower lobed		**FRUIT**	
			Type	1, nut-like, flattened, smoothly ribbed, without parachute, outer curved
Leaf-stalk	lower shorter than blade, upper absent			
	FLOWERS		Size	2.5–9mm
Position	dandelion-like heads of florets enclosed by bracts		Seeds	1, not released

Hawkweed *Hieracium umbellatum*

A tall plant with branched heads of dandelion-like flowers. Also like the Dandelion, its unusual reproductive biology has resulted in hundreds of very similar species. *Status:* native; most of area, most common in south. *Similar species:* probably the most common species in the northern half of the area, Common Hawkweed has nearly all of its broader leaves in a basal rosette and has hairy bracts. Fox-and-cubs is often grown in gardens for its orange or red flowers. Mouse-ear Hawkweed has creeping stems that produce rosettes of leaves, whitish with dense hairs beneath, and short stems ending with a single, lemon-yellow flower-head.

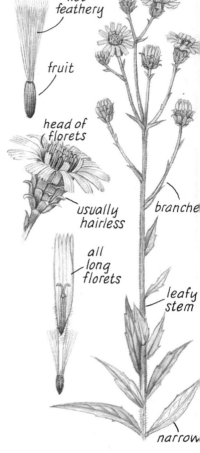

not feathery

fruit

head of florets

usually hairless

branched

all long florets

leafy stem

narrow

1 Common Hawkweed *(H. vulgatum)*;
2 Fox-and-cubs *(H. aurantiacum)*;
3 Mouse-ear Hawkweed *(H. pilosella)*

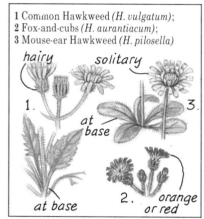

hairy

solitary

1.

3.

at base

at base

2.

orange or red

	HAWKWEED		Bracts	many around head, 9–11mm, usually hairless, blackish-green; none between florets
Type	perennial			
Height	30–100cm, rarely 150cm		Type	florets ☿, 10–15mm
Habitat	grassland, hedges, waste ground		Size	heads 20–30mm
			Colour	bright yellow
Flowering	June–October		Stalk	absent; long under heads, with small bracts
	STEMS AND LEAVES			
Stem	upright, slender; sap milky		Sepals	a ring of hairs
Root	fibrous with slender stock		Petals	5, joined, flattened above, 5-toothed
Hairs	rather sparse			
Stipules	absent		Stamens	5, joined into tube
Leaves	many, spirally arranged on stem, 15–150mm, narrow, with few teeth, pointed		Stigma	1, 2-lobed; style long
			Ovary	1, below petals, 1-celled
Leaf-stalk	lower short, upper absent		**FRUIT**	
	FLOWERS		Type	nut-like, smoothly ridged, parachute 5–6mm, hairs unequal
Position	dandelion-like heads of florets surrounded by bracts, in branched clusters			
			Size	3–4mm
			Seeds	1, not released

Arrowhead, Frogbit, Flowering-rush and Pondweeds

These four groups of aquatic plants begin the collection of families known as the Monocotyledons. These are so-called because the seedlings have one seedling leaf (cotyledon) rather than the two of other flowering plants. While this characteristic is not visible in mature plants, several other features can distinguish the Monocotyledons. The veins on the leaves of the grasses are commonly parallel, while species with broader leaves usually have veins which initially diverge, then converge towards the tip of the leaf.

Pondweeds have tiny flowers that are held in crowded spikes above the water's surface. Pondweeds are eaten by fish, but lack commercial value.

Species of Arrowhead, like the Pondweeds, commonly have two types of leaves, the submerged leaves generally being much narrower than the floating leaves. Arrowhead also has spear-shaped leaves above the water's surface.

Flowering-rush is the only species in an unusual family, the plants having long, sedge-like, three-angled leaves, with tall stems each bearing a single cluster of pink flowers. The Flowering-rush is widely cultivated for ornament.

On a river islet, a lone plant of Flowering-rush stands sentinel. This odd plant combines sedge-like leaves with almost buttercup-like flowers and is the sole member of its family.

Arrowhead *Sagittaria sagittifolia*

A water-plant with attractive white, blackish-centred flowers. Its leaves are remarkably variable. The plant lasts the Winter as a bright blue and yellow bud, sunken in the mud. Submerged leaves are at first ribbon-like, the tips expanded when later leaves reach the surface and float. Only leaves above water have arrow-shaped blades that give the plant its name. *Status:* native; most of area, rarer in north. *Similar species:* Water-plantain has small, pinkish flowers in branched heads, and the leaf-blades are broadly oval. Lesser Water-plantain has much narrower blades, and all flower-stalks usually arise at the same point.

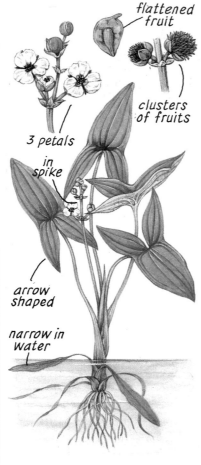

flattened fruit

3 petals

clusters of fruits

in spike

arrow shaped

narrow in water

1 Water-plantain (*Alisma plantago-aquatica*); **2** Lesser Water-plantain (*Baldellia ranunculoides*)

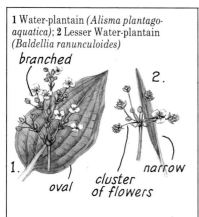

branched

oval

cluster of flowers

narrow

1.

2.

	ARROWHEAD			
Type	perennial			
Height	30–90cm			
Habitat	ponds, slow rivers, canals; in shallow water on mud			
Flowering	July–August			
	STEMS AND LEAVES			
Stem	flowering stems upright; creeping stems at base			
Root	thick, white			
Hairs	absent			
Stipules	absent			
Leaves	submerged ribbon-like, translucent; floating with broad tip; above water with blade 50–200mm, arrow-shaped			
Leaf-stalk	much longer than blade			

	FLOWERS			
Position	rings of 3–5 around stem, ♂ and ♀ on same plant			
Bracts	triangular, short			
Type 1	♂, in upper part of head			
Type 2	♀, at base of head, short-stalked			
Size	18–25mm			
Colour	white, centre dark violet			
Stalk	about equalling flower			
Sepals	3, 6–8mm, oval, edge whitish			
Petals	3, 9–11mm, nearly circular			
Stamens	many, shorter than petals			
Stigmas	1 per ovary			
Ovaries	numerous, 1-celled			
	FRUIT			
Type	many, in globular clusters, dry, flattened edges			
Size	4–5mm			
Seeds	1 per fruit, not released			

Frogbit *Hydrocharis morsus-ranae*

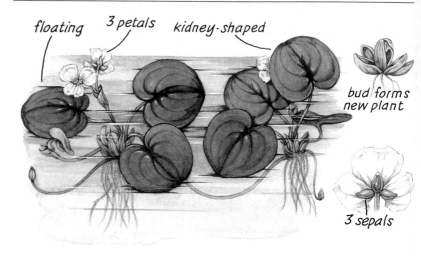

floating

3 petals

kidney-shaped

bud forms new plant

3 sepals

A water-plant with floating leaves like small Water-lilies, but white, three-petalled flowers carried above the water. It spends the Winter as a bud with scale-like leaves, protected from frost and ice in the mud at the bottom of the pond. Although rooted when growth commences, bubbles produced within the tissues soon cause it to float. *Status:* native; scattered through area, sometimes common, rarer in north. *Similar species:* Water-soldier is a floating aquatic plant that has similar flowers but very different foliage. Its tuft of long, pointed, spiny leaves floats in the Summer but sinks in the Winter.

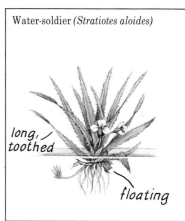

Water-soldier (*Stratiotes aloides*)

long, toothed

floating

	FROGBIT			
Type	perennial			
Height	floating			
Habitat	ponds, ditches; usually lime-rich water			
Flowering	July–August			
	STEMS AND LEAVES			
Stem	long, rooting; over-wintering as bud			
Root	fibrous			
Hairs	absent			
Stipules	large, translucent			
Leaves	tufts along stem, blade 25–40mm, kidney-shaped to nearly circular, floating			
Leaf-stalk	longer than blade			
	FLOWERS			
Position	♂ and ♀ flowers usually on different plants, above water			

Bracts	broad, translucent			
Type 1	2–3 ♂ from pairs of bracts			
Type 2	♀ solitary from bract			
Size	18–25mm			
Colour	white, base yellow			
Stalk	longer than flower			
Sepals	3, 4–5mm, oval			
Petals	3, 9–12mm, nearly circular, crumpled			
Stamens	12, shorter than petals			
Stigma	1, 2-lobed on each of 6 styles			
Ovary	1, below petals, 6-celled			
	FRUIT			
Type	1, berry-like, not opening, almost globular, rarely produced			
Size	c12mm			
Seeds	many, c2mm, sticky-coated			

Butomus umbellatus **Flowering-rush**

A beautiful plant, brightening banks of ponds and rivers with its heads of pink and purple. The attractive, three-petalled flowers seem quite out of context with the sedge-like (rather than rush-like) foliage that is usually associated with inconspicuous, blackish or brown flowers. Flowering-rush is often cultivated in ornamental ponds and is readily available commercially. The swollen stems at the base of the leaves are edible, but it would be a criminal act to take them from the scarce wild plants. However, if surplus garden plants are thinned out then culinary experiments could be attempted. Introduced as a garden plant to North America, Flowering-rush has escaped into the wild and has conquered the Great Lakes. *Status:* native; scattered through area, most common in south. (There are no similar species.)

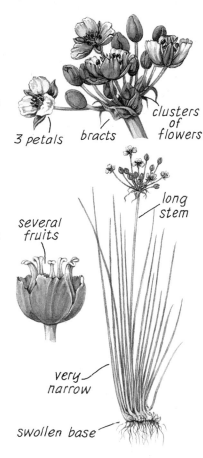

3 petals
bracts
clusters of flowers
several fruits
long stem
very narrow
swollen base

Potamogeton natans **Broad-leaved Pondweed**

An aquatic plant with broad, floating leaves and spikes of tiny flowers above the water. In slow rivers and canals the leaves align with the gentle current, and fish (especially young Pike) lie alongside, beautifully camouflaged until they move. *Status:* native; throughout area, common. *Similar species:* of many other species, most have only submerged leaves. Curled Pondweed has attractively curled and twisted, fine-toothed, translucent leaves. Fennel Pondweed has grass-like leaves and stipules joined into a sheath. Perfoliate Pondweed has broad leaves with the base clasping the stem.

1 Curled Pondweed (*P. crispus*);
2 Fennel Pondweed (*P. pectinatus*);
3 Perfoliate Pondweed (*P. perfoliatus*)

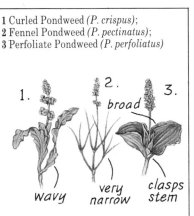

1. wavy
2. very narrow
broad
3. clasps stem

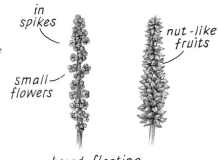

in spikes
nut-like fruits
small flowers

broad floating leaves

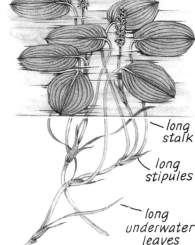

long stalk
long stipules
long underwater leaves

FLOWERING-RUSH		
Type	perennial	
Height	50–150cm	
Habitat	ditches, ponds, rivers, canals; edges of fresh-water	
Flowering	July–September	
STEMS AND LEAVES		
Stem	upright, leafless flowering stem	
Root	thick, fleshy, underground stem	
Hairs	absent	
Stipules	absent	
Leaves	all from base, 50–150mm, long and narrow, 3-angled, upright, pointed, edge unbroken, base sheaths stem	
Leaf-stalk	absent	

FLOWERS	
Position	many, in head at stem-tip
Bracts	narrowly triangular, papery
Type	☿
Size	25–30mm
Colour	pink with darker veins
Stalk	longer than flower, unequal, to 100mm
Sepals	3, 8–10mm, oblong, purplish
Petals	3, 10–15mm, oval
Stamens	6–9
Stigmas	1 per ovary
Ovaries	6–9, 2-celled
FRUIT	
Type	6–9, capsule, almost egg-shaped, tip beak-like
Size	9–12mm
Seeds	many, 1.5–2mm, narrowly oblong

BROAD-LEAVED PONDWEED		
Type	perennial	
Height	up to 100cm, rarely 500cm	
Habitat	rivers, lakes, ponds; mostly on mud in fresh-water	
Flowering	May–September	
STEMS AND LEAVES		
Stem	long, submerged, rarely branched	
Root	creeping, underground stem	
Hairs	absent	
Stipules	50–120mm, conspicuous	
Leaves	on alternate sides of stem, blade 25–125mm, floating, elliptical to broadly spear-shaped; submerged leaves ribbon-like, grooved	
Leaf-stalk	up to 500mm, jointed and wing-like near top	

FLOWERS	
Position	many in crowded, stalked spike, from leaf-base or stem-tip, above water
Bracts	absent
Type	☿
Size	3–4mm
Colour	green
Stalk	absent
Perianth	4 lobes, 1.5–2mm, rounded with stalk-like base
Stamens	4, very short
Stigmas	1 per ovary; style absent
Ovaries	4, 1-celled
FRUIT	
Type	in cylindrical spike, almost egg-shaped, pointed, olive-green, not opening
Size	4–5mm
Seeds	1, not released

Lilies, Daffodils and Irises

These three similar families can be difficult to separate. For example, Crocus belongs to the Iris family, but the superficially similar Meadow Saffron belongs to the Lily family. Nevertheless, there are two major differences between the families: the Lily and Daffodil families have six stamens, while the Iris family has only three; and the Daffodil and Iris families have the ovary positioned beneath the base of the petals, rather than above as in the Lilies.

All three families include familiar and horticulturally important plants. Lilies are in the same family as *Agapanthus*, Fritillaries, *Hosta*, Hyacinths, Lily-of-the-valley, Red-hot-pokers (*Kniphofia*), Tulips and *Yucca*. The Lily family also yields several vegetables such as asparagus, chives, garlic, leek and onion. *Nerine*, Snowdrops and Snowflakes belong to the family that includes Daffodils and the winter-flowering Amaryllis (*Hippeastrum*). The Iris family also has Crocuses, Freesias, *Gladiolus* and Montbretia.

The leaves of these plants are commonly narrow with parallel veins, and there is often a food-storage structure at the base of the plant. The sepals and petals are both petal-like and often more or less indistinguishable (the perianth). Inside the base of the tube of the Daffodil is an extra structure, which forms the characteristic "trumpet" of this flower.

In the dappled shade of coppiced woodland, Bluebells grow luxuriantly and form a thick, blue carpet.

Narthecium ossifragum **Bog Asphodel**

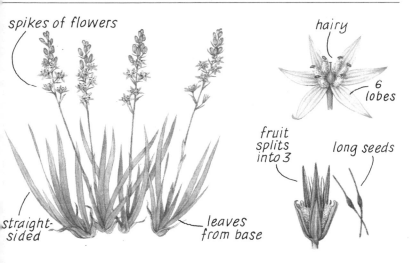

spikes of flowers

hairy

6 lobes

fruit splits into 3

long seeds

straight-sided

leaves from base

A pretty little plant of boggy places on moor and heath, flowering among the Sphagnum mosses and the Sundews. The leaves resemble a diminutive Iris and the yellow, six-petalled flowers deepen in hue to a reddish orange. The base of each of the six stamens has a fuzzy mass of hairs and the pollen-bearing anthers are usually a bright crimson. The flower-spikes were used to make a deep yellow dye. *Status:* native; throughout area, most common in north. *Similar species:* Scottish Asphodel differs in the small, white flowers and narrower leaves.

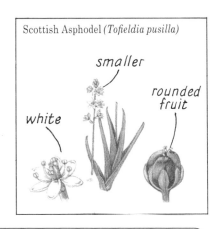

Scottish Asphodel (*Tofieldia pusilla*)

smaller

white

rounded fruit

BOG ASPHODEL

Type	perennial
Height	5–40cm
Habitat	bogs, heaths, moors; wet places, acid soil
Flowering	July–September

STEMS AND LEAVES

Stem	flowering stems upright
Root	creeping, fleshy stem; roots thick, fibrous
Hairs	absent
Stipules	absent
Leaves	mostly basal, 50–300mm, slender, usually curved, with 5 parallel veins, pointed, edge unbroken
Leaf-stalk	absent

FLOWERS

Position	many in stalked spike, 20–100mm long, at stem-tip, stalk with sheath-like leaves at base
Bracts	spear-shaped, equal to flower-stalk
Type	☿
Size	12–16mm
Colour	yellow, turning orange
Stalk	about equal to flower
Perianth	6 lobes, 6–8mm, narrowly spear-shaped, spread apart
Stamens	6, anthers red, base woolly
Stigma	1, tip swollen; style short
Ovary	1, 3-celled

FRUIT

Type	1, capsule, tapered, grooved, splits into 3
Size	10–14mm
Seeds	many, 8–10mm, middle swollen, ends thin, tail-like

Hyacinthoides non-scripta **Bluebell**

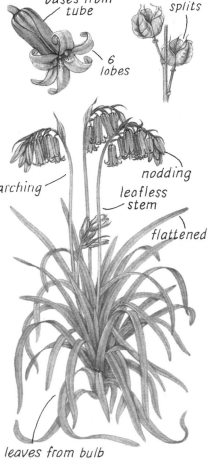

bases from tube

fruit splits

6 lobes

nodding

arching

leafless stem

flattened

leaves from bulb

Few botanical sights equal the beauty of the thick carpet of Bluebells that cover the floor of Spring woodland. Nowhere else in the world is this spectacle repeated, for Bluebells are native only to north-western Europe. Spikes of nodding bells are eagerly sought as cut flowers, although broken leaves may cause irreparable harm to the plant. *Status:* native; western part of region. *Similar species:* flowers of Squills are not nodding and have separate petals. Spring Squill has a single bract under each flower and is leafy when in flower. Autumn Squill lacks bracts and flowers before leaves appear. Grape Hyacinth has petals joined into a swollen tube.

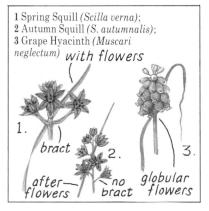

1 Spring Squill (*Scilla verna*);
2 Autumn Squill (*S. autumnalis*);
3 Grape Hyacinth (*Muscari neglectum*)

with flowers

1. bract after flowers

2. no bract

3. globular flowers

BLUEBELL

Type	perennial
Height	20–50cm
Habitat	woods, hedges, sea-cliffs; light, usually acid soils
Flowering	April–June

STEMS AND LEAVES

Stem	flowering stem upright, leafless, tip arching
Root	bulb 20–30mm, egg-shaped
Hairs	absent
Stipules	absent
Leaves	all basal, 20–450mm, narrow, straight-sided
Leaf-stalk	absent

FLOWERS

Position	4–16, in stalked spike, 1-sided, drooping
Bracts	2 under each flower, bluish
Type	☿, nodding
Size	15–20mm
Colour	violet-blue, rarely pink or white
Stalk	shorter than flower, lengthening and turning upright in fruit
Perianth	6 lobes, 15–20mm, bases joined, almost bell-shaped, lobes curved back
Stamens	6, unequal
Stigma	1; style fairly long
Ovary	1, 3-celled

FRUIT

Type	1, capsule, almost globular, splits into 3
Size	10–15mm
Seeds	several, 3–4mm, blackish

Meadow Saffron *Colchicum autumnale*

Pinkish-purple crocus-like flowers of Meadow Saffron appear in Autumn, long before any foliage. Leaves and fruits follow in the Spring and are hard to reconcile with the flower of the previous year. Although potentially lethal, this plant yields a drug used to treat gout and arthritis. *Status:* native or sometimes introduced; scattered through area, mainly in south. *Similar species:* Spring Crocus has only three stamens and the grass-like leaves are present when the flowers open. Sand Crocus has a distinct stalk bearing the small flower, its petals joined only at the base and spreading widely apart.

fruit splits open

leaves with fruit

1 Spring Crocus *(Crocus vernus)*;
2 Sand Crocus *(Romulea columnae)*

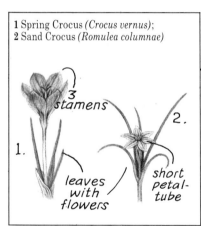
3 stamens
1.
2.
leaves with flowers
short petal-tube

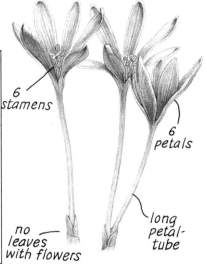
6 stamens
6 petals
no leaves with flowers
long petal-tube

	MEADOW SAFFRON		FLOWERS	
Type	perennial	Position	1–3, from corm
Height	80–300cm	Bracts	absent
Habitat	meadows, woods; damp, often lime-rich soils	Type	♀, crocus-like
		Size	lobes 30–45mm
Flowering	August–October	Colour	pale purple
		Stalk	only stalk-like base of petals visible
	STEMS AND LEAVES	Perianth	6 petal-like lobes, 30–45mm, bases joined forming apparent stalk, 50–200mm long
Stem	absent in flower, short in fruit, sheathed by leaf-bases		
Root	corm 30–50mm, with brown scales	Stamens	6, anthers orange
		Stigmas	3; styles long
Hairs	absent	Ovary	1, underground, 3-celled
Stipules	absent		
Leaves	absent in flower, all basal, 120–300mm, oblong, straight-sided, glossy, blunt	FRUIT	
		Type	1, capsule, oblong to egg-shaped, splits into 3
Leaf-stalk	absent	Size	30–50mm
		Seeds	numerous, 3–4mm, almost globular

Fritillary *Fritillaria meleagris*

Attractive and unique in form, Fritillaries are found in wet meadows almost only where they are protected from flower-pickers and farmers seeking to 'improve' the land. The curious pattern of squarish markings is also visible within the translucent petals. *Status:* native or escaped from gardens; scattered through area, common in some southern localities. *Similar species:* two Lilies with nodding, spotted flowers are found in the south of the area. Martagon Lily has rings of leaves and purplish flowers; Pyrenean Lily has spirally-arranged leaves and yellow flowers. Also native in the south, Wild Tulip has yellow, upright flowers.

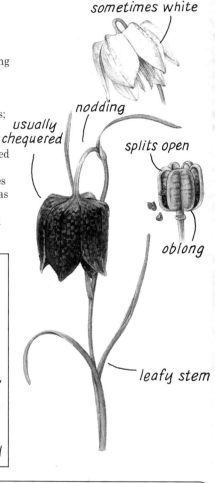
sometimes white
nodding
usually chequered
splits open
oblong
leafy stem

1 Martagon Lily *(Lilium martagon)* ;
2 Pyrenean Lily *(L. pyrenaicum)*;
3 Wild Tulip *(Tulipa sylvestris)*

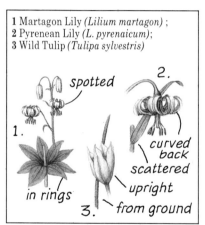
spotted
2.
1.
curved back
scattered
upright
in rings
3.
from ground

	FRITILLARY		Bracts	absent
Type	perennial		Type	♀, nodding
Height	20–50cm		Size	30–50mm
Habitat	grassy places; damp soil		Colour	purplish, usually chequered with light and dark markings, rarely white
Flowering	April–May		
	STEMS AND LEAVES		Stalk	almost equal to flower
Stem	upright		Perianth	6 lobes, 30–50mm, all petal-like, equal, oblong, thickened at tip
Root	small bulb with white scales		
Hairs	absent		Stamens	3, shorter than petals
Stipules	absent		Stigma	1, 3-lobed; style long
Leaves	on alternate sides of stem, 3–6, 80–200mm, narrow, straight-sided, tip pointed		Ovary	1, 3-celled
			FRUIT	
Leaf-stalk	absent		Type	1, capsule, oblong, upright, splits into 3
	FLOWERS		Size	15–20mm
Position	solitary, rarely paired, at stem-tip		Seeds	many, 5–7mm, almost circular, flattened, brown

A bulbous plant with starry, white flowers, each petal backed by a broad, green stripe. This makes the flowers hard to find when they close early in the day or in dull weather. Although the flowers arise at different heights on the stem, the lower stalks are much longer and turn upwards so that the flowers finish at nearly the same level. *Status:* native or escaped from gardens; scattered through most of region, most common in south-east. *Similar species:* Spiked Star-of-Bethlehem has long spikes, its numerous greenish flowers having almost equal stalks. Yellow Star-of-Bethlehem has few greenish-yellow flowers on leafy stems.

1 Spiked Star-of-Bethlehem (*O. pyrenaicum*); **2** Yellow Star-of-Bethlehem (*Gagea lutea*)

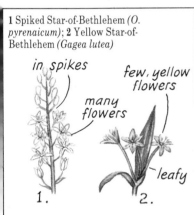

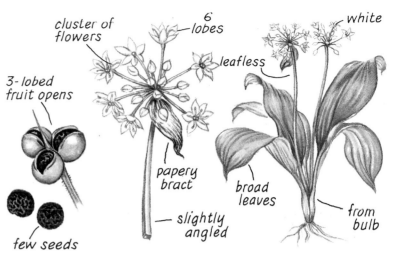

Often in such quantity that it carpets the woodland floor with white, Ramsons advertises itself by an overpowering smell of garlic. Cooking diminishes the aroma. *Status:* native; most of area, often common. *Similar species:* other species have narrower leaves. Cut across, the leaves of Three-cornered Leek are V-shaped and the flowers are larger. Two species of grassy places have similar cylindrical leaves and tiny bulbs between the small, pinkish flowers. Wild Onion has one large sheath-like bract below the flower-head; Field Garlic has a two-lobed sheath, each half with a long, leaf-like tip.

1 Three-cornered Leek (*A. triquetrum*); **2** Wild Onion (*A. vineale*); **3** Field Garlic (*A. oleraceum*)

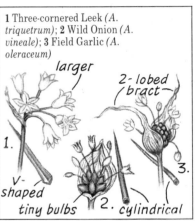

STAR-OF-BETHLEHEM			
Type	perennial	**Bracts**	narrow, whitish, equal to or less than flower-stalk
Height	10–30cm	**Type**	♂, mostly upright
Habitat	grassy places	**Size**	30–40mm
Flowering	April–June	**Colour**	white, green striped beneath
		Stalk	upper about equal to petals, lower longer, to 100mm
STEMS AND LEAVES		**Perianth**	6, 15–20mm, all petal-like, equal, spear-shaped or oblong
Stem	flowering stem leafless, upright	**Stamens**	6, about half length of petals
Root	bulb, 15–30mm, usually many small bulbs at base	**Stigma**	1; style long
Hairs	absent	**Ovary**	1, 3-celled
Stipules	absent		
Leaves	all from base, 150–300mm, narrow, straight-sided, grooved with white stripe	**FRUIT**	
		Type	1, capsule, roughly egg-shaped, 6-angled
Leaf-stalk	absent	**Size**	10–15mm
		Seeds	many, 2.5–3mm, almost globular
FLOWERS			
Position	5–15, in short head		

RAMSONS			
Type	perennial, smells of garlic	**Bracts**	broad, oval, papery, below head, shorter than flower-stalks
Height	10–45cm	**Type**	♂
Habitat	woods, hedges; damp soil	**Size**	16–20mm
Flowering	April–June	**Colour**	white
		Stalk	longer than flowers
STEMS AND LEAVES		**Perianth**	6 parts, 8–10mm, equal, all petal-like, spear-shaped, pointed
Stem	flowering stem upright, slightly 3-angled, leafless	**Stamens**	6, shorter than petals
Root	narrow bulb	**Stigma**	1; style long
Hairs	absent	**Ovary**	1, 3-celled
Stipules	absent		
Leaves	2–3 at base, 100–250mm, elliptical, pointed, edge unbroken	**FRUIT**	
		Type	1, capsule, deeply 3-lobed, each lobe splits open
Leaf-stalk	shorter than blade, twisted	**Size**	8–12mm
		Seeds	few, 3–4mm, angular, black
FLOWERS			
Position	6–20, in rounded cluster at stem-tip		

Herb-Paris *Paris quadrifolia*

A curious plant with a collar of broad leaves beneath the solitary green flower. Four green sepals spread sideways making a cross, separating the very slender, insignificant petals. Although fairly uncommon in the region as a whole, the plants abound in some deciduous woodlands on chalk or limestone. Herb-Paris was believed to have powerful magical properties and was associated with witchcraft. Despite being used medicinally to treat a variety of ailments, the plant is toxic and should be treated with caution. *Status:* native; scattered through area, more common in east. Although no native species are similar, Herb-Paris is related to the Wake-Robin of North America, and several related species are grown in gardens. Most have larger, white or red flowers and some were used in folk-medicine by the North American Indians. (There are no similar species.)

sepal

petal

fleshy fruit

solitary

usually 4

upright, unbranched

Butcher's-broom *Ruscus aculeatus*

Spiny, dark green 'leaves' of Butcher's-broom are in fact modified stems, as indicated by the flowers borne directly on the surface. The species is widely planted for ornament or as cover for game in woodland. *Status:* native, sometimes escaped from gardens; scattered through south of area. *Similar species:* no native plants look quite like Butcher's-broom, but Wild Asparagus is related and has similar true leaves and fruits. The needle-like foliage is similarly formed from specialized branches. Wild Asparagus has larger, stalked flowers with equal, petal-like lobes. Cultivated Asparagus belongs to the same species.

berry

flower on leaf-like stem

spine-tipped

leaf-like stem

short

long

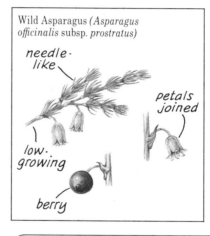

Wild Asparagus (*Asparagus officinalis* subsp. *prostratus*)

needle-like

petals joined

low-growing

berry

tiny leaves

	HERB-PARIS		**Bracts**	absent
Type	perennial		**Type**	♂, upright
Height	15–40cm		**Size**	40–70mm
Habitat	woods; damp, lime-rich soils		**Colour**	green
Flowering	May–August		**Stalk**	20–80mm, usually longer than flower
	STEMS AND LEAVES		**Sepals**	4, rarely to 6, 25–35mm, spear-shaped, spread apart
Stem	upright, unbranched, leafy		**Petals**	4, rarely to 6, 20–30mm, very slender
Root	creeping underground stem		**Stamens**	4–6, elongated
Hairs	absent		**Stigmas**	4–5 on separate styles
Stipules	absent		**Ovary**	1, 4–5-celled
Leaves	usually 4, in ring around stem, 60–120mm, oval, broadest towards tip, 3–5 main veins, pointed, edge unbroken, base wedge-shaped			**FRUIT**
Leaf-stalk	almost absent		**Type**	1, berry-like, globular, black, eventually opens
	FLOWERS		**Size**	14–18mm
Position	solitary, at stem-tip		**Seeds**	many, 2.5–3mm, angular, flattened

---

	BUTCHER'S-BROOM		**FLOWERS**
Type	perennial, evergreen	**Position**	1–2, on upper surface of leaf-like branch; ♂ and ♀ flowers on different plants
Height	25–100cm		
Habitat	woods, rocks; dry soils	**Bracts**	small, triangular, papery
Flowering	January–April	**Type 1**	♂ with stamens
	STEMS AND LEAVES	**Type 2**	♀ with ovary
Stem	upright; side branches leaf-like, 10–60mm, oval, thick, dark green, spine-tipped	**Size**	4–6mm
		Colour	greenish, violet-spotted
Root	creeping, thick, underground stem	**Stalk**	absent
		Perianth	6 lobes, 2.5–3mm, inner smaller than outer
Hairs	absent		
Stipules	absent	**Stamens**	3, bases joined, violet
Leaves	on alternate sides of stem, to 5mm, narrowly triangular, papery, brownish; apparent leaves are special branches	**Stigma**	1; style short
		Ovary	1, 1-celled
			FRUIT
Leaf-stalk	absent	**Type**	1, berry, globular, red
		Size	9–15mm
		Seeds	up to 4, 8–10mm, rounded, smooth

Graceful, arching stems of Solomon's-seal bear small clusters of nodding flowers at the base of broad, parallel-veined leaves. The plant propagates itself by thick, white stems, which run underground along the woodland floor. Round blackish berries contain several seeds. *Status:* native; scattered through most of area except Ireland. *Similar species:* Angular Solomon's-seal has angled stems and the scented, usually solitary flowers are broader at the middle. Lily-of-the-valley, a familiar garden plant, usually has two leaves at the base. The flowering stem bears short, nodding, sweetly-scented flowers, and the berries are red.

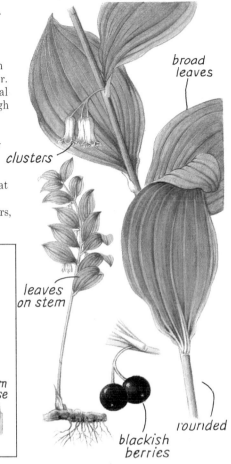

broad leaves

clusters

leaves on stem

rounded

blackish berries

1 Angular Solomon's-seal (*P. odoratum*); **2** Lily-of-the-valley (*Convallaria majalis*)

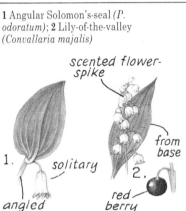

scented flower-spike

from base

1.

solitary

2.

red berry

angled

One of the first heralds of Spring, pushing its clean, white flowers up through the snow, Snowdrop can flower so early because it stores food in a bulb, enabling it to grow without the need to extract materials from the still-frozen ground. It is often grown in gardens, and has many named variants; most populations in the countryside originate from cultivated plants. *Status:* introduced or native in extreme south; most of area. *Similar species:* Summer Snowflake is a much larger plant of wet meadows and has broader, equal petals. Spring Snowflake differs in the shorter stems, usually bearing a solitary flower.

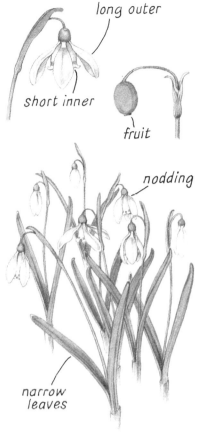

long outer

short inner

fruit

nodding

narrow leaves

1 Summer Snowflake (*Leucojum aestivum*); **2** Spring Snowflake (*L. vernum*)

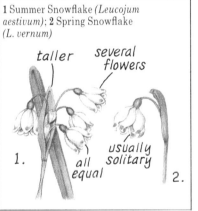

taller

several flowers

1.

all equal

usually solitary

2.

SOLOMON'S-SEAL			
Type	perennial	**FLOWERS**	
Height	30–80cm	**Position**	2–5, in branched cluster at leaf-base
Habitat	woods	**Bracts**	absent
Flowering	May–June	**Type**	☿, nodding
		Size	9–15mm
STEMS AND LEAVES		**Colour**	greenish white
Stem	upright, arching above, smoothly rounded sides	**Stalk**	shorter than flower
Root	thick, creeping, underground stem	**Perianth**	6, equal, petal-like parts, bases form tube, narrowed in middle; lobes oval
Hairs	more or less absent	**Stamens**	6, inside petal-tube
Stipules	absent	**Stigma**	1, 3-lobed; style long
Leaves	on alternate side of stem, 50–150mm, oval or broadly elliptical, tip pointed, edge unbroken	**Ovary**	1, 3-celled
		FRUIT	
Leaf-stalk	absent	**Type**	1, berry, globular, bluish black
		Size	8–10mm
		Seeds	up to 6, nearly globular

SNOWDROP			
Type	perennial	**Bracts**	leaf-like, papery-edged, tip forked
Height	15–25cm	**Type**	☿, nodding
Habitat	woods, grassy places; damp soil, often by streams	**Size**	22–30mm
Flowering	January–March	**Colour**	pure white; inner lobes with green mark near tip
		Stalk	about equal to flower
STEMS AND LEAVES		**Perianth**	6 parts, petal-like, unequal; outer 3 14–17mm, elliptical, blunt; inner 3 6–11mm, oblong or oval, tip notched
Stem	flowering stem upright, curved at tip, base with tubular, papery sheath		
Root	egg-shaped bulb, 10–20mm	**Stamens**	6, inside flower
Hairs	absent	**Stigma**	1; style long
Stipules	absent	**Ovary**	1, below petals, 3-celled
Leaves	all at base, 50–250mm, narrow, straight-sided, tip blunt		
		FRUIT	
Leaf-stalk	absent	**Type**	1, capsule, egg-shaped
		Size	12–15mm
FLOWERS		**Seeds**	many, 5–6mm, elongated, swollen in middle
Position	solitary, at stem-tip		

Wild Daffodil *Narcissus pseudonarcissus*

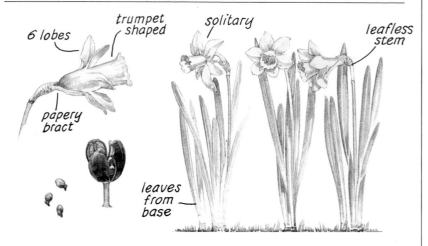

6 lobes
trumpet shaped
solitary
leafless stem
papery bract
leaves from base

Familiar as a garden plant, the Daffodil was formerly much more common in the wild although its numbers were greatly depleted as people uprooted the bulbs. There are still a few places where great drifts of the nodding, yellow flowers flourish in deciduous woodland. *Status:* native or often introduced; southern half of area, fairly abundant in some localities. *Similar species:* Primrose-peerless is one of the long-established garden hybrids and is often naturalized. The central trumpet is much shorter than the whitish petal-lobes and the flowers are usually carried in pairs.

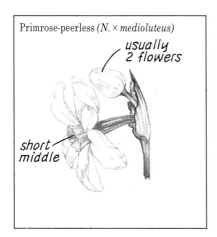

Primrose-peerless (*N. × medioluteus*)

usually 2 flowers
short middle

WILD DAFFODIL				
Type	perennial		**Bracts**	20–60mm, broad, papery
Height	20–50cm		**Type**	♀, often nodding
Habitat	woods, grassland; damp soils		**Size**	35–60mm
Flowering	February–April		**Colour**	pale yellow, centre darker
			Stalk	short beneath flower; long stem bears bract and flower
STEMS AND LEAVES			**Perianth**	6, 35–60mm, equal, petal-like, bases form tube with trumpet-like extra tube on inner face; lobes oval, spread apart
Stem	flowering stem upright, slightly flattened, with 2 angles			
Root	bulb, 20–50mm		**Stamens**	6, inside petal-tube
Hairs	absent		**Stigma**	1, tip swollen; style long
Stipules	absent		**Ovary**	1, below petals, 3-celled
Leaves	all at base, 120–500mm, narrow, straight-sided, bluish green, tip blunt			
Leaf-stalk	absent		**FRUIT**	
			Type	capsule, oval or globular
FLOWERS			**Size**	12–25mm
Position	solitary, at stem-tip		**Seeds**	many, 4–5mm, egg-shaped, slightly roughened

Yellow Iris *Iris pseudacorus*

An imposing plant forming large clumps near water, with stiff, bluish, sword-shaped leaves. The yellow flowers are formed as in the various garden species of Iris, with three broad outer petals and three upright inner petals. Each lower petal is covered by a curious petal-like stigma, forming a tube between the two. *Status:* native; most of area, common. *Similar species:* Stinking Iris has thinner, evergreen leaves that flop over to one side. Its flowers are a mixture of yellow or dull violet and capsules split to reveal bright orange seeds. Blue Iris has violet or lilac flowers and the brown seeds have a loose, papery covering.

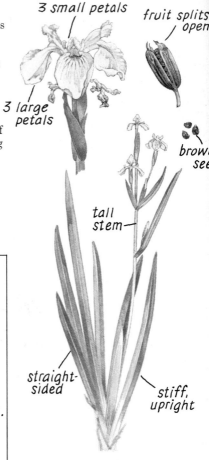

3 small petals
fruit splits open
3 large petals
brown seed
tall stem
straight-sided
stiff, upright

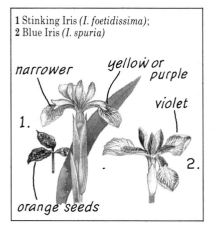

1 Stinking Iris (*I. foetidissima*);
2 Blue Iris (*I. spuria*)

narrower
yellow or purple
violet
1.
2.
orange seeds

YELLOW IRIS				
Type	perennial		**FLOWERS**	
Height	40–150cm		**Position**	2–3 clustered at stem-tip
Habitat	rivers, streams, ditches, marshes, woods; wet ground or shallow water		**Bracts**	40–100mm, edges papery
			Type	♀, upright
			Size	80–100mm
Flowering	May–July		**Colour**	yellow, orange-blotched and purple-spotted at base
STEMS AND LEAVES			**Stalk**	shorter than flower
Stem	upright, often branched, leafy		**Perianth**	6 petal-like parts, unequal, bases joined; outer 3 50–75mm, broad, turned downwards; inner 3 20–30mm, upright
Root	thick, creeping, underground stem; roots fleshy			
Hairs	absent		**Stamens**	3, at base of outer petals
Stipules	absent		**Stigmas**	3, broad, petal-like
Leaves	basal or on flowering stem, 120–900mm, narrow, straight-sided, bluish green, veins parallel, pointed, base sheaths stem		**Ovary**	1, below petals, 3-celled
			FRUIT	
			Type	oblong capsule, 3-angled
Leaf-stalk	absent		**Size**	40–80mm
			Seeds	many, 7–9mm, brown, smooth

Orchids, Lords-and-Ladies and Duckweeds

None of the native species of orchid are as flamboyant as the commercially grown varieties, save perhaps for the beautiful but very rare Lady's-Slipper orchid. But many are attractive, with smaller flowers massed in spikes, and the plants may grow together in large numbers. Even those with dull coloration may be very unusual in form, such as the Lizard Orchid with its tail-like, twisted lower petal. The native species commonly have swollen roots (known as tubers).

In the centre of the orchid flower, the stigma and stamens unite to form a single structure that is important for its specialized pollination mechanism. Positioned below the base of the sepals, the ovary develops into a capsule which can contain a million or more tiny seeds. These require the presence of a fungus before they will germinate.

Lords-and-ladies are curious plants. The tiny flowers are hidden by a broad, leaf-like or petal-like spathe at the base of the purple or yellow spike. In many species, the spike generates heat and a rather putrid odour that attracts flies.

Rootless Duckweed, at around one millimetre across, is the smallest known flowering plant. Though they look like algae, Duckweeds are flowering plants with male flowers reduced to just one or two stamens, and a female flower reduced to a solitary ovary.

In northern Europe most Bee Orchids self-pollinate, but elsewhere they attract bees to pollinate the flowers.

Lords-and-Ladies *Arum maculatum*

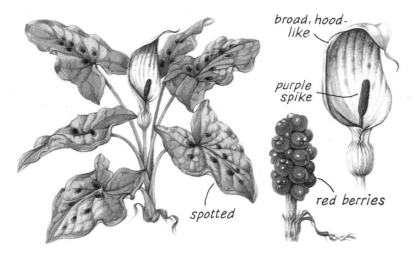

broad, hood-like

purple spike

red berries

spotted

These peculiar flowers are actually complex flower-heads. A central spike-like part gives off a smell and heat which attracts small flies. The hood-like upper part funnels the flies into the base, to be trapped by backward-pointing hairs until they have pollinated the tiny flowers. *Status:* native; most of area except north, often common. *Similar species:* Italian Lords-and-Ladies produces its pale-veined leaves earlier and has a yellow spike-like part to the flower-head. Bog Arum has a smaller, white flower-head; Sweet-flag has iris-like foliage and a leaf-like upper part to the flower-head.

1 Italian Lords-and-Ladies (*A. italicum*); **2** Bog Arum (*Calla palustris*); **3** Sweet-flag (*Acorus calamus*)

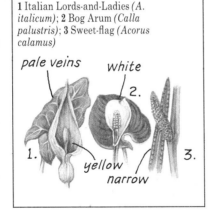

pale veins

white

yellow

narrow

	LORDS-AND-LADIES		Bracts	150–250mm, upright, hooded
Type	perennial		Type 1	♂ above ♀ flowers on spike
Height	30–50cm		Type 2	♀ at base of spike
Habitat	woods, hedges; often lime-rich soils		Size	1–2.5mm
			Colour	yellowish green, sometimes marked with purple
Flowering	April–May		Stalk	absent; head long-stalked
	STEMS AND LEAVES		Sepals	absent
Stem	upright		Petals	absent
Root	fleshy underground stem		Stamens	3–4
Hairs	absent		Stigma	1; style absent
Stipules	absent		Ovary	1, 1-celled
Leaves	basal, blade 70–200mm, with backward-pointing lobes, usually spotted			**FRUIT**
			Type	berries, in cluster 30–50mm long at stem-tip, scarlet
Leaf-stalk	15–25mm, base sheaths stem		Size	4–6mm
			Seeds	1–3, 3–5mm, globular, pitted
	FLOWERS			
Position	at stem-tip, petal-like bract encloses flower-head with purplish, spike-like upper part, ♂ and ♀ flowers on same plant			

Greater Duckweed *Spirodela polyrrhiza*

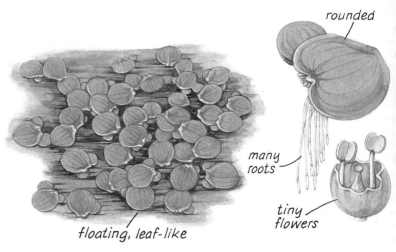

rounded

many roots

tiny flowers

floating, leaf-like

More like an alga than a flowering plant, the diminutive Duckweed forms a floating carpet of green on still water. Although tiny, Duckweeds are distantly related to Lords-and-Ladies. *Status:* native; most of area, fairly common. *Similar species:* two species have only a single root beneath. Fat Duckweed is swollen below, whereas Common Duckweed is smaller and flat below. Ivy-leaved Duckweed forms interconnected masses, usually floating just beneath the surface. The smallest native flowering plant, Rootless Duckweed makes a round blob up to one millimetre across.

1 Fat Duckweed (*Lemna gibba*); **2** Common Duckweed (*L. minor*); **3** Ivy-leaved Duckweed (*L. trisulca*); **4** Rootless Duckweed (*Wolffia arrhiza*)

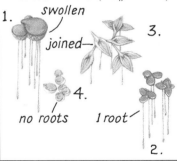

1. swollen

joined

3.

4.

no roots

1 root

2.

	GREATER DUCKWEED			FLOWERS
Type	perennial, floating		Position	♂ and ♀ flowers on same plant, few, rarely produced, 1 ♀ with 2 ♂ flowers in pocket
Height	0.1–0.2cm, width 0.5–1cm			
Habitat	ponds, ditches; fresh-water			
Flowering	June–July		Bracts	tiny, cup-like, papery
			Type 1	♂ with stamen
	STEMS AND LEAVES		Type 2	♀ with ovary
Stem	solitary or 2–5 connected, flattened, oval or circular, leaf-like, often purple below, floating; smaller purplish buds sink and over-winter		Size	1–1.5mm
			Colour	green
			Stalk	absent
			Sepals	absent
			Petals	absent
Root	5–15 per plant, up to 30mm, straight		Stamens	1 per flower
			Stigma	1; style short
Hairs	absent		Ovary	1, 1-celled
Stipules	absent			
Leaves	absent; stems leaf-like			**FRUIT**
			Type	1, more or less globular, not opening
			Size	c1mm
			Seeds	1–4, ridged or smooth

Epipactis helleborine Broad-leaved Helleborine

tall, rather uncommon Orchid, usually found in the shade of deciduous rees or beneath hedges. Slightly odding, green and purple flowers are orne towards the same side of the stem. *tatus:* native; scattered through area. *imilar species:* Marsh Helleborine has hort hairs on the base of the flowers nd the frilled lower lip turns up at the dges. Two white-flowered species have he ovary and centre of the flower ngled upwards, rather than horizontal r nodding. Narrow-leaved Helleborine as slender leaves, short bracts and ointed sepals. White Helleborine has val leaves, bracts mostly longer than he flower, and blunt sepals.

1 Marsh Helleborine (*E. palustris*); **2** Narrow-leaved Helleborine (*Cephalanthera longifolia*); **3** White Helleborine (*C. damasonium*)

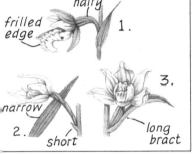

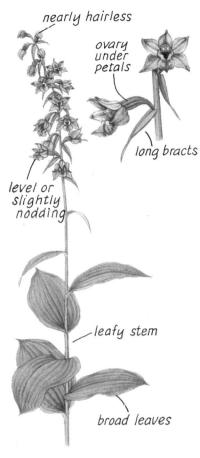
nearly hairless
ovary under petals
long bracts
level or slightly nodding
leafy stem
broad leaves

hairy, *frilled edge*, *1.*, *narrow*, *2.*, *short*, *3.*, *long bract*

	BROAD-LEAVED HELLEBORINE
Type	perennial
Height	25–80cm
Habitat	woods, hedges
Flowering	July–October
	STEMS AND LEAVES
Stem	1–3, upright, often purple-tinged, leafy
Root	short underground stem, many roots
Hairs	few, short, near top of stem
Stipules	absent
Leaves	spirally arranged, to 170mm, lowest scale-like, middle broadly oval or elliptical
Leaf-stalk	absent
	FLOWERS
Position	15–50, in one-sided, spike-like head, 70–300mm long

Bracts	spear-shaped, lower equal flower, upper shorter
Type	♀, nodding
Size	10–16mm wide
Colour	yellowish green and purple
Stalk	very short
Sepals	3, 9–11mm, petal-like, oval
Petals	3, 2 side petals oval, lower petal 6–8mm, hollow, end lobe bent back; spur absent
Stamen	1, stalkless
Stigmas	2; style absent
Ovary	1, below petals, 1-celled
	FRUIT
Type	1, capsule, oblong, angular, points downwards, splits lengthwise
Size	minute
Seeds	numerous, dust-like

Ophrys apifera Bee Orchid

Relatives of Bee Orchid have a remarkable method of pollination. The lower petal resembles an insect and the flower is pollinated as the male insect tries to mate with it. Plants of the Bee Orchid in northern Europe have largely abandoned the method and are self-pollinated. *Status:* native; scattered, southern half of area. *Similar species:* two species have greenish sepals, the lower petal marked with blue. Fly Orchid has a narrow, forked lower petal and thread-like side petals. The broad lower petal of Early Spider-orchid has an almost H-shaped mark. Late Spider-orchid has pink sepals, the broad lower petal with an upturned tip.

1 Fly Orchid (*O. insectifera*); **2** Early Spider-orchid (*O. sphegodes*); **3** Late Spider-orchid (*O. fuciflora*)

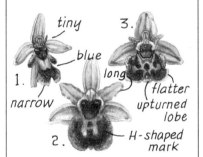

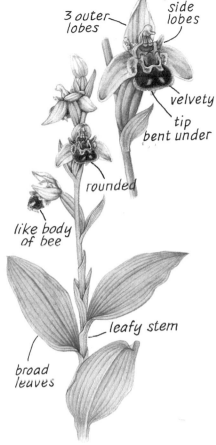
small side lobes
3 outer lobes
velvety
tip bent under
rounded
like body of bee
leafy stem
broad leaves

tiny, *blue*, *3.*, *1.*, *long*, *narrow*, *flatter upturned lobe*, *2.*, *H-shaped mark*

	BEE ORCHID
Type	perennial
Height	15–45cm, rarely 60cm
Habitat	grassy places, wood edges, hedges; lime-rich soil
Flowering	June–July
	STEMS AND LEAVES
Stem	upright, leafy
Root	egg-shaped or globular tubers; few, fleshy roots
Hairs	absent
Stipules	absent
Leaves	spirally arranged, 30–80mm, elliptical to oblong
Leaf-stalk	absent
	FLOWERS
Position	2–5, rarely 10, in spike-like head, 30–120mm long
Bracts	often longer than flower

Type	♀
Size	23–30mm wide
Colour	pink, back green; brown lower petal with yellow mark
Stalk	very short
Sepals	3, 12–15mm, petal-like, elliptical or oblong
Petals	3; side petals spear-shaped; lower 12–15mm, almost globular, velvety, 3-lobed, the lowest bent under; spur absent
Stamen	1, stalkless
Stigmas	2; style absent
Ovary	1, below petals, 1-celled
	FRUIT
Type	oblong capsule, angular, splits lengthwise
Size	15–25mm
Seeds	many, minute, dust-like

Pyramidal Orchid *Anacamptis pyramidalis*

One of the most common Orchids on chalk grassland, often forming large colonies marked by their conical heads of magenta-pink flowers. The long, very slender, curved spur at the base of the flower is an adaptation to pollination by butterflies. *Status:* native; scattered through area, common in some localities. *Similar species:* Fragrant Orchid has more cylindrical heads of sweetly scented flowers. Another Orchid with a short, dense head of flowers, though short-spurred, is Burnt Orchid. The upper buds are purplish brown, as though burnt, and fade as the flowers age.

1 Fragrant Orchid (*Gymnadenia conopsea*); **2** Burnt Orchid (*Orchis ustulata*)

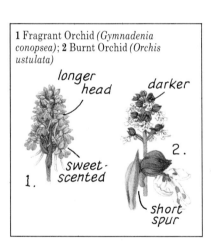

longer head

darker

sweet-scented

1.

2.

short spur

3-lobed petal

long spur

not branched

narrow

leafy stem

	PYRAMIDAL ORCHID		
Type	perennial	**Bracts**	narrowly spear-shaped, about equalling flower
Height	20–75cm	**Type**	♀, strong-smelling
Habitat	grassy places, dunes; lime-rich soils	**Size**	12–15mm
		Colour	purplish pink
Flowering	June–August	**Stalk**	very short
		Sepals	3, 5–6mm, petal-like, spear-shaped
	STEMS AND LEAVES	**Petals**	3; side petals form hood with upper sepal; lower 6–7mm, wedge-shaped, 3-lobed; spur 9–12mm, thin, curved
Stem	upright, slightly angled		
Root	egg-shaped or globular tubers; few, fleshy roots		
Hairs	absent		
Stipules	absent	**Stamen**	1, stalkless
Leaves	spirally arranged, to 150mm, lower scale-like, upper narrowly spear-shaped, pointed, base sheaths stem	**Stigmas**	2; style absent
		Ovary	1, below petals, 1-celled
		FRUIT	
Leaf-stalk	absent	**Type**	1, capsule, oblong, angular, splits lengthwise
	FLOWERS	**Size**	10–15mm
Position	many, in crowded, conical head, 20–50mm long	**Seeds**	numerous, minute, dust-like

Early-purple Orchid *Orchis mascula*

Although most native Orchids are rare, Early-purple Orchid can be more common than some of the meadow plants with which it grows. Its leaves are usually spotted and the thick spur of the purple flowers is tilted upwards. *Status:* native; scattered throughout area, sometimes common. *Similar species:* Green-winged Orchid lacks leaf-spots and has distinctive green veins on the hood-like sepals. Two Orchids have leafy stems, leaf-like bracts and the spur angled downwards. Common Spotted-orchid has broad leaves and a large middle lobe to the lower petal; Heath Spotted-orchid has narrow leaves and a small middle petal-lobe.

1 Green-winged Orchid (*O. morio*); **2** Common Spotted-orchid (*Dactylorhiza fuchsii*); **3** Heath Spotted-orchid (*D. maculata*)

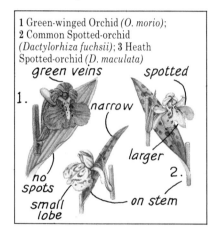

green veins

spotted

1.

narrow

larger

2.

no spots

small lobe

on stem

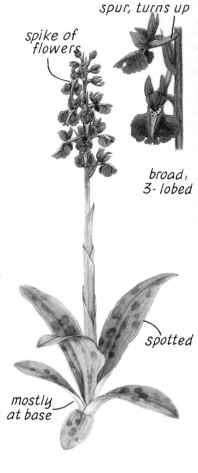

spur, turns up

spike of flowers

broad, 3-lobed

spotted

mostly at base

	EARLY-PURPLE ORCHID		
Type	perennial	**Bracts**	purple, shorter than flower
Height	15–60cm	**Type**	♀
Habitat	grassland, woods, hedges; mostly lime-rich soils	**Size**	18–26mm
		Colour	reddish purple, lower petal with darker spots
Flowering	April–June	**Stalk**	very short
		Sepals	3, 6–8mm, petal-like, oval
	STEMS AND LEAVES	**Petals**	3; 2 side petals oval; lower 8–12mm, broad, 3-lobed; spur 8–11mm, blunt, level or angled upwards
Stem	upright, rather stout		
Root	egg-shaped or globular tubers; few, fleshy roots		
Hairs	absent	**Stamen**	1, stalkless
Stipules	absent	**Stigmas**	2; style absent
Leaves	3–5, basal, oblong or spear-shaped, mostly with purple spots, blunt, base sheaths stem; upper scale-like	**Ovary**	1, below petals, 1-celled
		FRUIT	
Leaf-stalk	absent	**Type**	1, capsule, oblong, angular, splits lengthwise
	FLOWERS	**Size**	c20mm
Position	many in spike-like head, 40–150mm long	**Seeds**	numerous, minute, dust-like

Platanthera chlorantha Greater Butterfly-orchid

A delicate woodland Orchid, with greenish-white flowers. At the base of each flower is a slender, curved spur which holds the nectar. Few insects other than butterflies and moths have tongues that are long enough to reach the nectar, the latter being drawn by a scent which is strongest at night. The long lower petal acts as a landing platform where the insect can alight. *Status:* native; scattered throughout area, most common in south. *Similar species:* Lesser Butterfly-orchid is smaller in all its parts and is more common in the north. Also more common in the north, Small-white Orchid has tiny flowers lacking a spur.

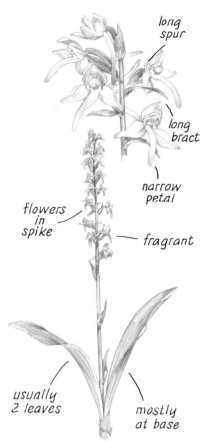

long spur

long bract

narrow petal

flowers in spike

fragrant

usually 2 leaves

mostly at base

1 Lesser Butterfly-orchid (*P. bifolia*); 2 Small-white Orchid (*Pseudorchis albida*)

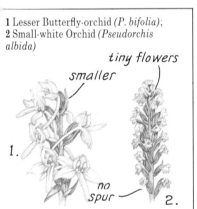

smaller

tiny flowers

no spur

1.

2.

Spiranthes spiralis Autumn Lady's-tresses

A small-flowered Orchid with distinctively twisted flower-spikes. The almost tubular flowers have a frilled lower petal. When a bee seeks nectar which collects at the base of the flower, waxy masses of pollen grains from the stamen become cemented to its tongue and are carried to other flowers. Once the pollen is removed, the stigma becomes exposed for pollination. *Status:* native; scattered through area except for much of north. *Similar species:* mainly a plant of pine-woods, Creeping Lady's-tresses spreads by means of creeping stems. The smaller flowers have a concave lower petal with a tip like the lip of a jug.

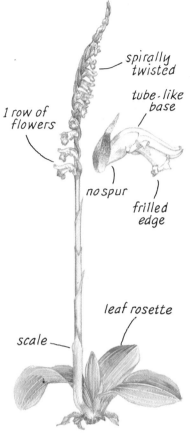

spirally twisted

tube-like base

1 row of flowers

no spur

frilled edge

scale

leaf rosette

Creeping Lady's-tresses (*Goodyera repens*)

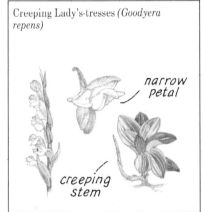

narrow petal

creeping stem

	GREATER BUTTERFLY-ORCHID		**Bracts**	nearly equal to flower
Type	perennial		**Type**	☿, strongly scented
Height	20–40cm, rarely 60cm		**Size**	23–35mm
Habitat	woods, grassy places; mostly lime-rich soils		**Colour**	greenish white
			Stalk	very short
Flowering	May–July		**Sepals**	3, 10–11mm, petal-like, oval to nearly triangular
	STEMS AND LEAVES		**Petals**	3; side petals spear-shaped; lower 10–16mm, narrow, tapered, blunt; spur 19–28mm, slender, usually curved
Stem	upright, leafy			
Root	swollen, tapering tubers; few, fleshy roots			
Hairs	absent		**Stamen**	1, stalkless
Stipules	absent		**Stigmas**	2; style absent
Leaves	spirally arranged, to 200mm, usually 2, elliptical, blunt, 1–5 small leaves above		**Ovary**	1, below petals, 1 celled
				FRUIT
Leaf-stalk	absent		**Type**	cylindrical capsule, angular, splits lengthwise
			Size	c25mm
	FLOWERS		**Seeds**	numerous, minute, dust-like
Position	many, in spike-like head, 50–200mm long			

	AUTUMN LADY'S-TRESSES		**Bracts**	shorter than flower
Type	perennial		**Type**	☿, scented
Height	7–20cm		**Size**	4–5mm
Habitat	grassy places, dunes; usually lime-rich soils		**Colour**	white
			Stalk	very short
Flowering	August–September		**Sepals**	3, 6–7mm, petal-like, oblong, blunt
	STEMS AND LEAVES		**Petals**	3; side petals oblong; lower 6–7mm, oblong, tip rounded, frilled; spur absent
Stem	upright, slender, not leafy			
Root	swollen, tapered tubers; few, fleshy roots			
Hairs	gland-tipped, on upper part of plant		**Stamen**	1, stalkless
			Stigmas	2; style absent
Stipules	absent		**Ovary**	1, below petals, 1-celled
Leaves	4–5 in rosette at base, 20–35mm, oval, bluish green; 3–7 scale-like above			**FRUIT**
			Type	1, capsule, egg-shaped, angular, splits lengthwise
Leaf-stalk	absent		**Size**	5–6mm
	FLOWERS		**Seeds**	numerous, minute, dust-like
Position	7–20 in spirally twisted row, 30–120mm long			

Common Twayblade *Listera ovata*

Contrary to the popular image, many Orchids have greenish, insignificant flowers. Common Twayblade's most obvious feature, giving rise to its common name, is a pair of broad stem-leaves. Nectar secreted on to the lower petal attracts beetles and flies. As the insect's head touches the centre of the flower, a drop of cement squirts out and sets rapidly, anchoring the masses of pollen. *Status:* native; throughout area, sometimes common. *Similar species:* Lesser Twayblade is smaller, the lower petal with pointed lobes. Two species have basal leaves. The large petal of Musk Orchid is three-lobed; that of Fen Orchid is frilled and points upwards.

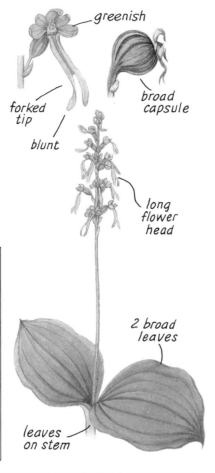
greenish
forked tip
blunt
broad capsule
long flower head
2 broad leaves
leaves on stem

1 Lesser Twayblade (*L. cordata*);
2 Musk Orchid (*Herminium monorchis*); 3 Fen Orchid (*Liparis loeselii*)

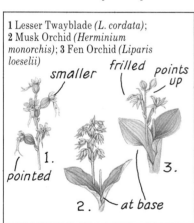
smaller
frilled
points up
pointed
1.
2.
3.
at base

COMMON TWAYBLADE		
Type	perennial	
Height	20–60cm	
Habitat	woods, hedges, pastures; damp, usually lime-rich soil	
Flowering	June–July	
STEMS AND LEAVES		
Stem	upright, leafy, scale-like below	
Root	horizontal underground stem; many roots	
Hairs	gland-tipped on upper part of stem	
Stipules	absent	
Leaves	2 almost paired on stem, 50–200mm, broadly elliptical, 3–5 main veins, blunt	
Leaf-stalk	absent	
FLOWERS		
Position	many, in spike-like head, 70–250mm long	
Bracts	much shorter than flowers	
Type	♀, scented	
Size	14–20mm	
Colour	yellowish green, with reddish edges	
Stalk	much shorter than flower	
Sepals	3, 4–5mm, oval	
Petals	3; side petals oblong; lower 10–15mm, oblong, bent down, tip forked; spur absent	
Stamen	1, stalkless	
Stigmas	2; style absent	
Ovary	1, below petals, 1-celled	
FRUIT		
Type	1, capsule, globular, splits lengthwise	
Size	c10mm	
Seeds	numerous, minute, dust-like	

Lizard Orchid *Himantoglossum hircinum*

An unusual Orchid, its long, twisted, ribbon-like lower petal has two slender lobes near the base. Although generally very rare in the region, it is fairly abundant on stabilized sand-dunes in the extreme south-west. Here, its tall, pale flower-heads rise above surrounding plants and are easily visible at a distance. *Status:* native; south of area, scattered, mostly rare. *Similar species:* although no other native species is quite like the Lizard Orchid, several others have slender, greenish flowers. Frog Orchid has an elongated, much shorter, lower petal with a pair of narrow lobes near the tip. It is fairly common on chalk grassland.

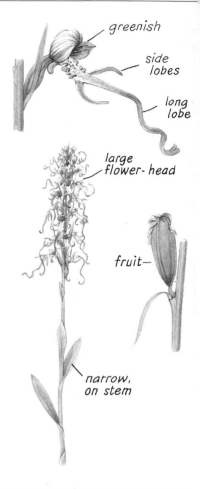
greenish
side lobes
long lobe
large flower-head
fruit
narrow, on stem

Frog Orchid (*Coeloglossum viride*)

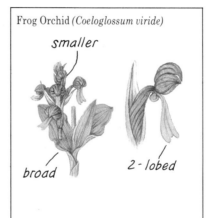
smaller
broad
2-lobed

LIZARD ORCHID		
Type	perennial	
Height	20–40cm, rarely 90cm	
Habitat	woods, grassy places, dunes; lime-rich soils	
Flowering	May–July	
STEMS AND LEAVES		
Stem	upright, stout, leafy	
Root	egg-shaped or globular tubers; few, fleshy roots	
Hairs	absent	
Stipules	absent	
Leaves	4–6 spirally arranged, to 150mm, narrowly elliptical or oblong, base sheaths stem; lowest scale-like	
Leaf-stalk	absent	
FLOWERS		
Position	many in spike-like head, 100–250mm, rarely 500mm long	
Bracts	narrow, shorter than flower	
Type	♀, strong-smelling	
Size	35–55mm	
Colour	greenish, purple markings	
Stalk	very short	
Sepals	3, 7–10mm, oval, blunt	
Petals	3; side petals narrow; lower 30–50mm, ribbon-like, twisted, furry at base, 2 long side lobes, tip forked; spur 3–4mm, conical	
Stamen	1, stalkless	
Stigmas	2; style absent	
Ovary	1, below petals, 1-celled	
FRUIT		
Type	cylindrical capsule, angular, splits lengthwise	
Size	c30mm	
Seeds	numerous, minute, dust-like	

Neottia nidus-avis Bird's-nest Orchid

This curious, pallid Orchid with parchment-coloured flowers is usually found growing in the thick layers of leaf-litter of deciduous woodland, especially beneath Beech trees. Lacking green pigment, it looks like a parasite but is a saprophyte, for the plant obtains its nourishment from dead and decaying plant material. The short, fleshy roots form a thick, tangled mass, which give rise to the common name. *Status:* native; scattered through area. *Similar species:* Coralroot Orchid has few smaller, greenish-yellow and white flowers. The very rare Ghost Orchid has the large petal and blunt spur pointing upwards.

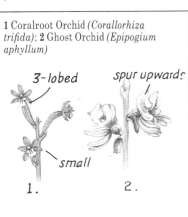

1 Coralroot Orchid (*Corallorhiza trifida*); **2** Ghost Orchid (*Epipogium aphyllum*)

3-lobed
spur upwards
small
1.　2.

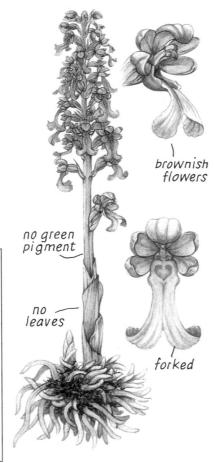

brownish flowers

no green pigment

no leaves

forked

BIRD'S-NEST ORCHID		Bracts	shorter than flower
Type	perennial, saprophyte	**Type**	♂, scented
Height	20–45cm	**Size**	12–16mm
Habitat	shady woods; lime-rich soils, often on leaf mould	**Colour**	pale brown, darker on lower petal
Flowering	June–July	**Stalk**	much shorter than flower
		Sepals	3, 4–6mm, petal-like, oval
STEMS AND LEAVES		**Petals**	3; side petals oval; lower 9–12mm, 2-lobed, angled downwards; spur absent
Stem	upright, with dense scales		
Root	short underground stem, hidden by many short, fleshy roots	**Stamen**	1, stalkless
		Stigmas	2; style absent
Hairs	gland-tipped, in flower-head	**Ovary**	1, below petals, 1-celled
Stipules	absent		
Leaves	spirally arranged, scale-like, papery, brownish	**FRUIT**	
		Type	swollen, angular capsule, splits lengthwise
Leaf-stalk	absent		
		Size	10–12mm
FLOWERS		**Seeds**	numerous, minute, dust-like
Position	many, in spike-like head, 50–200mm long		

Cypripedium calceolus Lady's-slipper

A large, pouch-like petal, of lemon yellow spotted with crimson, surrounded by slender, chocolate-brown side petals and sepals, could not be identified as any native flower other than the Lady's-slipper Orchid. The beauty of this exotic-looking flower is matched by its scarcity. Its numbers have been greatly reduced by people picking flowers and uprooting plants for cultivation. In most of its former range, it is extremely rare or extinct. It survives today only through strict laws preventing removal of material from the wild, and international controls on import and export. Although it is possible to obtain legitimate material for your garden, cultivation is extremely difficult for, like other Orchids, the Lady's-slipper needs a fungus present in its roots to survive. Unless conditions are exactly right for both Orchid and fungus, the Orchid soon perishes. *Status:* native; very rare, scattered through area. (There are no similar native species.)

usually solitary
large flower
pouch-like
broad leaves
twisted

LADY'S-SLIPPER		Size	60–90mm
Type	perennial	**Colour**	reddish brown, lower petal yellow, red-spotted within
Height	15–45cm		
Habitat	woods; lime-rich soils	**Stalk**	very short
Flowering	May–June	**Sepals**	3, 35–50mm, petal-like, spear-shaped, lower 2 often joined except at tips, pointing downwards
STEMS AND LEAVES			
Stem	upright, leafy		
Root	creeping underground stem	**Petals**	3; side petals 40–60mm, slender, twisted; lower 25–35mm, rounded, hollow, pouch-like; spur absent
Hairs	short, denser above		
Stipules	absent		
Leaves	3–4, spirally arranged, 70–170mm, lower scale-like, upper broadly elliptical to oval, base sheaths stem		
		Stamens	2, stalkless
		Stigmas	3, style absent
		Ovary	1, below petals, 1-celled
Leaf-stalk	absent		
		FRUIT	
FLOWERS		**Type**	oblong capsule, angular, splits lengthwise
Position	1–2, at stem-tip		
Bracts	large, leaf-like	**Size**	c40mm
Type	♂	**Seeds**	numerous, minute, dust-like

Index